New York Law School
Legal Practice I
Introduction to Legal Practice

Aspen Custom Publishing Series

New York Law School
Legal Practice I
Introduction to Legal Practice

New York Law School Legal Practice Program

Compiled by Anne Goldstein

Selected pages from

Legal Writing and Analysis, 3rd Edition
© 2011 Linda H. Edwards

Essential Lawyering Skills, 4th Edition
© 2011 Stefan H. Krieger and Richard K.Neumann, Jr.

Basic Legal Research, 5th Edition
© 2012 Amy E. Sloan

Legal Reasoning and Legal Writing, 6th Edition
© 2009 Richard K. Neumann, Jr.

Legal Method and Writing, 6th Edition
© 2011 Charles R. Calleros

Legal Writing, 2nd Edition
© 2011 Richard K. Neumann, Jr. and Sheila Simon

Clear and Effective Legal Writing, 4th Edition
© 2007 Veda R. Charrow, Ph.D., Myra K. Erhardt, Esq. and Robert P. Charrow, Esq.

Legal Writing, 1st Edition
© 2011 Terrill Pollman, Judith M. Stinson, Richard K. Neumann, Jr. and Elizabeth Pollman

. Wolters Kluwer
Law & Business

CONTENTS

PART B

INTRODUCTION TO THE LEGAL SYSTEM   29

7 THE LITIGATION PROCESS 65

21   DEVELOPING A RESEARCH PLAN   187

PART F

CLIENT-CENTERED LAWYERING: INTRODUCTION TO INTERVIEWING AND COUNSELING   197

22   LAWYERING FOR AND WITH THE CLIENT   199

ACKNOWLEDGEMENTS

We thank the authors and copyright holders of the following works for permitting their inclusion in this custom book:

Linda H. Edwards, *Legal Writing and Analysis*, 3rd Ed., (2011).

Stefan H. Krieger and Richard K. Neumann, Jr., *Essential Lawyering Skills*, 4th Ed., (2011).

Amy E. Sloan, *Basic Legal Research*, 5th Ed., (2012).

Richard K. Neumann, Jr., *Legal Reasoning and Legal Writing*, 6th Ed., (2009).

Charles R. Calleros, *Legal Method and Writing*, 6th Ed., (2011).

Richard K. Neumann, Jr. and Sheila Simon, *Legal Writing*, 2nd Ed., (2011).

Veda R. Charrow, Ph.D., Myra K. Erhardt, Esq. and Robert P. Charrow, Esq., *Clear and Effective Legal Writing*, 4th Ed., (2007).

Terrill Pollman, Judith M. Stinson, Richard K. Neumann, Jr. and Elizabeth Pollman, *Legal Writing*, 1st ed., (2011).

We have organized this custom book into nine parts. Chapters 1, 2 and 22–26 of this custom book are comprised of materials from *Essential Lawyering Skills*, 4th Ed., (2011), by Stefan H. Krieger and Richard K. Neumann, Jr. Chapters 3, 10–12, 27–29, 31–35, 39 and 46 of this custom book are comprised of materials from *Legal Writing and Analysis*, 3rd Ed., (2011), by Linda H. Edwards. Chapters 14–21 of this custom book are comprised of materials from *Basic Legal Research*, 5th Ed., (2012), by Amy E. Sloan. Chapters 30 and 37 and Appendix B of this custom book are comprised of materials from *Legal Reasoning and Legal Writing*, 6th Ed., (2009), by Richard K. Neumann, Jr.

Chapter 7 of this custom book is comprised of materials from *Clear and Effective Legal Writing*, 4th Ed., (2007), by Veda R. Charrow, Ph.D., Myra K. Erhardt, Esq. and Robert P. Charrow, Esq. Chapters 8, 9, 40–43, 45, 47, and Appendix A of this custom book are comprised of materials from *Legal Writing*, 2nd Ed., (2011), by Richard K. Neumann, Jr. and Sheila Simon. Chapter 38 of this custom book is is comprised of materials from *Legal Writing*, (2011), by Terrill Pollman, Judith M. Stinson, Richard K. Neumann, Jr. and Elizabeth Pollman. Chapters 4–6 of this custom book are comprised of materials from *Legal Method and Writing*, 6th Ed., (2011), by Charles R. Calleros.

Chapter 13 of this custom book is derived from multiple sources: *Basic Legal Research*, 5th Ed., (2012), by Amy E. Sloan; *Legal Writing and Analysis*, 3rd Ed.,

(2011), by Linda H. Edwards; and *Legal Reasoning and Legal Writing*, 6th Ed., (2009), by Richard K. Neumann, Jr.

Chapter 36 of this custom book is derived from multiple sources: *Legal Writing and Analysis*, 3rd Ed., (2011), by Linda H. Edwards; and *Legal Reasoning and Legal Writing*, 6th Ed., (2009), by Richard K. Neumann, Jr.

Chapter 44 of this custom book is derived from multiple sources: *Legal Writing*, 2nd Ed., (2011), by Richard K. Neumann, Jr. and Sheila Simon; and *Legal Writing and Analysis*, 3rd Ed., (2011), by Linda H. Edwards.

Chapter 45 of this custom text is derived from multiple sources: *Legal Reasoning and Legal Writing*, 6th Ed., (2009), by Richard K. Neumann, Jr.; and *Legal Writing*, 2nd Ed., (2011), by Richard K. Neumann, Jr. and Sheila Simon.

INTRODUCTION TO THE PRACTICE OF LAW

CHAPTER 1

Professionalism

§1.1 The Reflective Practitioner of Law

You go to a doctor and describe the symptoms that bother you. After examining you and perhaps detecting a few symptoms that you had not noticed before, the doctor names a disease, writes a prescription, tells you how many days it should take for the prescription to work, and asks you to telephone by then if it has not. Does the doctor know for certain that you in fact have this disease? Probably not.

The late Donald Schön did the leading research on how professionals in general think. Among many things, he asked doctors to estimate the proportion of their patients who present problems that "are not in the book" in the sense that the doctor needs to "invent and experiment on the spot" to figure out what treatment will work.[1] The estimates he received ranged from 30% to 80%, and he said that the 80% estimate came from "someone whom I regard as a very good doctor."[2]

This is typical of the problems faced by a professional in any field, whether it is medicine or architecture or law. To a layperson, it seems that the distinguishing mark of a professional is knowledge that other people do not have — almost like a sorcerer's secret book of magical formulas. Certainly, professionals do have specialized knowledge. But in professional work there are very few, if any, cookbook answers. Instead, what really distinguishes a professional is *a way of thinking* that enables the professional to solve problems even when a situation is wrapped in a fog of "uncertainty, uniqueness, and conflict."[3]

People who have never practiced law — which means both law students and the laypeople who become clients — easily underestimate the amount of uncertainty inherent in nearly every situation presented to a lawyer for solution. The

---

[1] Donald A. Schön, *Educating the Reflective Legal Practitioner*, 2 Clinical L. Rev. 231, 239 (1995).
[2] *Id.*
[3] Donald A. Schön, *Educating the Reflective Practitioner* xi (1987).

law may be unclear. The facts may be difficult to ascertain. And most often, it is hard to make precise predictions about how judges, juries, administrative officials, adversaries, and opposing parties will react to evidence and arguments. None of that is an excuse for the lawyer to say, "We'll try the first thing that looks good and hope for the best." Professionalism means, among other things, finding a solution that is hidden inside all that uncertainty and conflict.

Schön used the term "reflection-in-action"[4] to describe the process through which professionals unravel problems and solve them. This is not the kind of abstract and academic reflection that you went through when you wrote a term paper in college. Instead, it is a silent dialogue between the professional and the problem to be solved. In that dialogue, the professional uses what is already known in order to learn what is not yet known, through experimentation or some other form of investigation, until a solution is found. (Remember the doctor who does not really know what is making you feel sick. If the medication prescribed works, the doctor has solved the problem. If not, the doctor will experiment with something else.)

The reflective practitioner is one who can reflect *while acting*. To do that well we need "the ability to think about what we are doing while we are doing it, to turn our thought back on itself in the surprising situation."[5] We need to examine our own conduct, self-critically. Effective professionals never stop doing that, no matter how experienced they become.

As Paul Brest has written, "good lawyers bring more to bear on a problem than legal knowledge and lawyering skills. They bring creativity, common sense, practical wisdom, and that most precious of attributes, good judgment."[6]

§1.2 The Most Important Thing That a Lawyer Can Bring to Any Situation is Good Judgment

Good judgment is "the [legal] profession's principal stock in trade."[7] It is "the most valuable thing a lawyer has to offer clients — more valuable than legal learning or skillful analysis of doctrine."[8]

Good judgment causes us to do "precisely the right thing at precisely the right moment."[9] Good judgment is the ability to know what actions are most likely to solve problems. It operates on several levels at once — the practical, the ethical, and the moral — and it includes "appreciating the hidden complexity in questions that seem easy when they are posed in the abstract."[10]

---

[4] *Id.* at 22.

[5] Schön, *supra* note 1, at 244.

[6] Paul Brest, *The Responsibility of Law Schools: Educating Lawyers as Counselors and Problem Solvers*, 58 Law & Contemp. Probs. (Issues 3 & 4) 5, 8 (Summer/Autumn 1995).

[7] David Luban & Michael Millemann, *Good Judgment: Ethics Teaching in Dark Times*, 9 Geo. J. Leg. Ethics 31, 34 (1995).

[8] *Id.* at 31.

[9] Thucydides, *History of the Peloponnesian War* *I.138 (R. Warner trans. 1954).

[10] Luban & Millemann, *supra* note 7, at 71.

Good judgment is also the ability to recognize the wrong things to do, no matter how tempting they might seem. The phrase *a prudent lawyer* is a term of art used to describe an attorney whose judgment is reliably good in this respect. A prudent lawyer makes sure that mistakes do not happen.

If you are a novice hiker with a dozen other novice hikers high in the mountains when a sudden and unpredicted blizzard traps all of you in snowdrifts so deep that you can barely walk, good judgment is what you most hope to find in the guide your group hired to lead you through the mountains. As you glance at this guide and feel cold and hunger, you do not want the guide to make foolish decisions that would make a bad situation much worse, such as by taking you through places where your own movements can set off an avalanche. Instead, you want a guide who is calm; thinks carefully before acting but does act decisively; sees, several steps ahead, the consequences of actions; and can quickly understand all the forces and factors, including human nature, that can influence events. You want this person to get you out, and that requires more than knowledge of the geography of the mountains and the rescue policies of the Forest Service. It requires the ability to make decisions for which there is no script and no formula. Should you try to hike out, for example, or wait where you are on the theory that movement expends energy you need to survive in the cold? How much food should you eat each day? You need to eat enough to keep from succumbing to the cold but not so much that you run out of food before help arrives — and no one can predict how long it will take for rescuers to find you. Judgment is the ability to make these decisions well.

Judgment is the ability to figure out what to *do and say*. Because "it is possible to have knowledge but lack judgment,"[11] knowing the law (or the geography of the mountains) is not enough.

§1.3 Thorough Preparation is Essential

"Winging it" is sloppy and dangerous lawyering. Many lawyering tasks are like icebergs: What the bystander sees (the tip of the iceberg or the visible part of the lawyer's performance) is a tiny fraction of what supports it (the undersea part of the iceberg or the preparation for the performance). In lawyering, the ratio of preparation to performance can easily reach 15 or 20 to 1. It might take 10 hours to prepare for a half-hour counseling session with a client, and it might take 15 hours to prepare for a negotiating meeting that lasts 2 hours. (That is why this book devotes entire chapters to preparing to counsel and preparing to negotiate.)

In preparation, resourcefulness counts more than brilliance does. Few legal problems are solved by astute insights that no one has thought of before. Most legal problems are solved by diligently learning the details that matter and putting them together into a package that gets results.

---

[11] Mark Neal Aaronson, *We Ask You to Consider Learning about Practical Judgment in Lawyering*, 4 Clinical L. Rev. 247, 262 (1998).

§1.4 Everything Revolves Around Facts

Law school can mislead you. You will be spending so much time learning law and how to analyze law that you might get the impression that factual issues are easy. They are not easy, and they are not marginal, either. The analysis of facts permeates the practice of law.

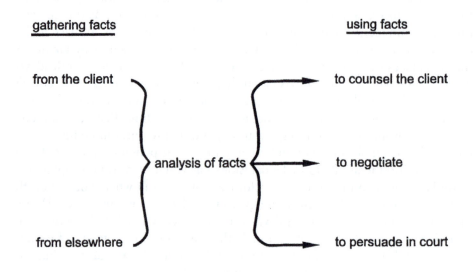

§1.5 Assumptions Can Sabotage Good Lawyering

You realize that you need to make a decision soon. You also realize that you need to know six things to make this decision. You already know five of them. You have made a guess about the sixth thing, and you are confident that your guess is accurate. You could rely on your guess (make an assumption), or you could devote some effort to finding out what the truth is.

When lawyers make assumptions, they and their clients can get hurt. That is because our guesses turn out to be wrong surprisingly often. It is also because clients hire lawyers for important matters, where mistakes cause real suffering.

Not all assumptions are bad. Sometimes, a lawyer will properly make a *temporary* assumption because the truth cannot yet be ascertained and work must proceed in the meantime. Sometimes a lawyer will balance risks and make an assumption because the decision involved is small and the cost of learning the truth is too large. And sometimes a lawyer will have to make an assumption because the truth cannot be learned.

But most of the assumptions you will be tempted to make should not be made. As a general rule, if you do not know whether something is true, find out. And if you must make an assumption, do it explicitly so that you and the people who rely on you know what is happening.

The most dangerous assumptions are the *unconscious* ones — the ones you do not even realize you are making. Suppose that you are chatting with someone in a social situation. Some of the things the other person says are derived from matters that you do not fully know. You might ask a few questions, but for the most part you assume underlying facts without even realizing that you are doing it. You make these assumptions for three reasons. You do not want to appear dumb. You do not want to be a pest, constantly interrupting with questions. And most of the subjects of social conversations are not important enough to merit the kind of thorough exploration that would have to be undertaken if we made no assumptions.

In lawyering, an unconscious assumption is especially dangerous because you do not realize you are making it and therefore cannot control it. You cannot gauge the risk posed by an unconscious assumption, for example, and you cannot commit yourself to learning the truth as soon as possible.

The only way to overcome this problem is to learn to recognize what you do not know and consciously decide what to do about what you do not know.

§1.6 Representing Clients in Disputes is Only Part of What Lawyers Do — The Rest is Transactional

Movies and television almost invariably portray lawyers as cross-examining witnesses and making arguments to judges and juries — in other words, litigating. And law school law is taught through cases, or more precisely through judicial opinions that resolve litigation. But many lawyers almost never go near a courtroom. The practice of law is divided into two parts. One is the resolution of disputes, often through litigation. The other is transactional: advising and representing clients in situations where there is no dispute. Sometimes the situation is contractual: two companies have agreed to do business with each other, for example, and the lawyer will turn the agreement into a contract. Sometimes, it involves noncontractual transfers, such as will-drafting and other forms of estate planning. And sometimes it involves advising the client on how to behave to avoid liability of some kind. Some lawyers do only dispute work. Some do only transactional work. And some do both.

CHAPTER 2

COMMUNICATION SKILLS

§2.1 Why Communication Through the Spoken Word is a Core Lawyerly Skill

You might think that oral communication will not present any particular challenges. After all, you and everyone you know have been talking for as long as you can remember. But that is exactly why learning to communicate orally at a professional level is deceptively difficult: it looks familiar, but habits that have worked before often do not work in a law office. At the same time, you might be afraid to do some things you know how to do conversationally because you think they do not belong in a law office.

For example, you might be in the habit of saying "O.K." when you mean "I've heard what you just said," like this:

You:	How can I get to Magnolia Street?
Friend:	Walk two blocks in that direction. The first street is Jena but keep going. The second street is Cadiz. Turn right there. Then walk four blocks to Magnolia. If you get to Clara Street, you've gone too far.
You:	O.K.

You've heard something complicated, but you think you understand it, so you say O.K. Now, in a client interview:

Client:	I worked for Intercontinental Airlines. When the company went under, I lost my job. And I lost my pension. It was invested entirely in company stock, which is now worthless. I don't have any money to live on. I've applied for hundreds of other jobs and haven't gotten so much as an interview. I think it's because nobody wants to hire a pilot who's 54

	years old. My car has been repossessed, and my landlord has threatened to evict me because I haven't been able to pay the rent.
You:	O.K.

Here, your client will think that you think that the tragedy that has befallen her is O.K., even though all you meant to communicate was "I hear you." (About half of all law students make this mistake in their initial client interviews.) What your client needs from you is something that you already know how to do but might think inappropriate in a law office: empathy, as you would give a friend who tells you something tragic:

Client:	[*same as above*]
You:	Oh, my. That's terrible.

You might think that lawyers are not allowed to talk like that on the job. But they are (although some lawyers do not know that).

How you say something has an enormous effect on the way people respond. In part, it's the words you use. Two words that seem to convey approximately the same idea may actually have two separate meanings with a precise difference between them ("curious" and "nosy," for example). Or they might mean the same thing, but with different connotations (such as "dirty" and "filthy"). Senior lawyers greatly value the ability to communicate orally. When law firm hiring partners were surveyed about the skills they expected new law school graduates to have mastered before they start work, 91% of them mentioned oral communication.[1]

§2.2 Eight Oral Communication Skills

§2.2.1 *Listening*

"Listening," says playwright and actor Anna Deavere Smith, "is not just hearing what someone tells you word for word. You have to listen with a heart.... It is very hard work."[2] "Listening," adds Nance Guilmartin, "isn't just about being quiet. It's about listening to what people say, what they don't say, and what they mean.... Listening is about hearing with our eyes, our ears, and our heart...."[3] Listening includes figuring out the person who is speaking. What matters to her

---

[1] Bryant Garth & Joanne Martin, *Law Schools and the Construction of Competence*, 43 J. Legal Educ. 469, 490 (1993).

[2] Karen W. Arenson, *The Fine Art of Listening: Anna Deavere Smith Helps N.Y.U. Law Students Look Beyond the Legal Questions*, N.Y. Times, Jan. 13, 2002, Educ. Life at 34, 35.

[3] Nance Guilmartin, *Healing Conversations* xx (2002).

as a person? How does she see the world? If you do not ask yourself these questions, you will not understand the full meaning behind the words.

Some lawyers talk too much and listen too little. Here is an example. The client has been in the lawyer's office for less than five minutes and is now beginning to explain why he is there:

Client:	I was walking down the street and found a big envelope.
Lawyer:	What did it look like?
Client:	Tan colored, eight-and-a-half by eleven inches. It was lying right there on the pavement. It looked full of something, so I picked it up.
Lawyer:	Have you ever done this before?
Client:	No.
Lawyer:	What did you do after you picked it up?
Client:	I looked inside and saw money. I looked around for somebody who might have dropped it.
Lawyer:	You want to know whether you can keep the money?
Client:	Oh, no.

The following is better. The lawyer learns much more just by listening.

Client:	I was walking down the street and found a big envelope. It was lying right there on the pavement. It looked full of something, so I picked it up. There was a lot of money in it but no name or address on it. I looked around for somebody who might have dropped it, but nobody seemed to be looking for something. I waited about 15 minutes, but nothing happened. I was late for a dentist appointment, so I left. At home that night, I counted the money. It was $10,000 exactly. I read the newspapers carefully for a week to see if anybody was reported to have lost the money, and nobody was. I'd like to donate it to the West Side Home for Orphans. Can I legally do that?

The ability to listen well is as important in the practice of law as the ability to talk well. The popular image of a lawyer is of a person talking — to juries, to judges, to adversaries, to reporters. But in the end, the lawyer who knows how to listen has a tremendous advantage. Knowledge can be power, and in the practice of law one of the most important means of gaining knowledge is to listen carefully and precisely.

Some lawyers find it hard to listen because they cannot stop talking for very long. Some people talk out of nervousness, to prevent the possibility of uncomfortable silences, no matter how brief. Some people like to hold forth and be the center of attention. And some lawyers talk when they should be listening because they feel that talking helps them control whatever situation they happen to be in.

But listening is not passivity. It is hard work and a skill that can be learned. It includes "active listening": encouraging the other person to talk and occasionally asking the other person to clarify something that is confusing or to add details to something that would otherwise be sketchy. In a sense, it even includes listening with your eyes: what is the other person telling you through attire, facial expression, or body position, for example? (Active listening is more fully explained in §25.1.2.)

You can listen more effectively if you ask yourself these questions while the other person is talking:

What words — exactly — am I hearing, and what do those words mean?
What do the speaker's words imply (hint at)?
What do the speaker's tone of voice and body language (facial expression, posture, etc.) imply?
Why is the speaker saying or implying these things?
What is the speaker *not* saying or implying that other people in her situation might often communicate? Why?

§2.2.2 *Empathizing*

Empathy is feeling what another person feels. Sympathy is more common and less valuable than empathy. "If you are sympathetic to others, your heart goes out to them, and you feel compassion, but these are *your* feelings. You don't know what *they're* feeling. . . . If you are empathetic to others, you are not merely feeling sorry for them but are projecting yourself into their hearts, as though you are sensing what it's like to be in their shoes."[4]

A struggling rock musician recalled two conversations about his difficulties. The first was with a successful performer named Timmy, the brother of a friend.

> My band had played only fifteen shows in the previous year, and even those had been sparsely attended. Regardless of how much we practiced and promoted our shows, we couldn't generate a dedicated following.
>
> When I told this to Timmy, he simply shrugged his shoulders and said, "Let me tell you about my experience. If you rock, the crowds will double every week and someone will offer you a deal. No way I'd do fifteen gigs without having a big crowd. You're in a real bad place there."
>
> To this day I still remember how terrible I felt after that conversation.
>
> In contrast, a week later I met a musician named Joe, the bass player in a successful local reggae band. I shared my problems with Joe, too. Although he was also successful, Joe, trying hard to understand how I felt, blurted out *how uncomfortable he knew it must be to stand in front of those small crowds*. . . . Was there anything he could do to help?
>
> For years I basked in the glow of his kindness. . . . [5]

---

[4] Tim Sanders, *The Likeability Factor* 117 (2005).
[5] *Id.* at 121 (emphasis added).

Empathy is invaluable in interviewing, counseling, and negotiating. Empathy helps you find out who your clients really are and what they are really feeling, and once they sense true empathy from you, they will tell you more and trust you. At the same time, empathy from a lawyer often helps a client feel stronger and more capable of dealing with the problems the client has brought to the lawyer. Even in negotiation, empathy can be helpful, although only in carefully chosen spots. Empathy at the right moment can sometimes break the stalemate of confrontation and move the discussion toward mutual understanding.

But the empathy has to be authentic. If you try to pretend to be empathetic, people will sense that it is not genuine and feel uncomfortable.

§2.2.3 Asking Questions

One of the marks of an effective person — in law and in almost any part of life — is the ability to ask the right question in the most productive way. A good question is artistic. It cuts through a mountain of debris to find hidden treasure. An effective lawyer asks good questions constantly. The questions are put to clients, witnesses (in and out of court), colleagues, opposing lawyers, and government employees.

What can you do to ask questions well? Later, when we cover interviewing, we examine question-asking skills in more detail. Here, however, are some basic concepts:

Ask for all the important information.   Good questions seek things of value, things that really do need to be known. Some people can fill an hour with marginal questions, but others can learn everything in five minutes.

When asking questions, use the words that are most likely to produce valuable information.   Some words help find information and encourage answers, while other words confuse, cloud memory, or provoke resistance.

Ask at the right time and in the right context.   Sometimes other questions have to be asked first, and often the person being asked has to be put into a mood to be helpful.

Know when to ask narrow questions and when to ask broad questions.   A narrow question asks for specific information ("What time did your plane arrive?"). A broad question asks for general information and often invites the person answering the question to decide what to emphasize ("How was your flight?").

If you need to know something specific, a narrow question is the fastest way to find out. If you're not sure what's important, a broad question can produce a lot of information, which you can then begin to sort out. Often (but not always), it is more effective to start with broad questions and then work toward narrow ones. §25.3.2 explains why.

Know when to ask leading questions and when to ask nonleading questions. A leading question not only suggests the answer; it also creates pressure to provide that answer.

"You've just returned from Bermuda, haven't you?" is a leading question. You can expect the questioner to be surprised — and maybe unhappy — if you answer no.

"Have you been to Bermuda lately?" is a narrow nonleading question. It's narrow because it asks for specific information (see above). It's nonleading because the wording implies that the questioner would be satisfied with either yes or no, as long as it is truthful.

"Tell me about any trips you might have taken recently" is a broad nonleading question. It's broad because it asks about traveling in general and not just Bermuda (see above). It's nonleading because, again, the wording implies that the questioner would be happy with any truthful answer.

Leading questions are useful in only two situations. The first is where you think you know the answer and are using the question only to raise a topic so you can then ask other questions to learn things you do not already know:

"You've just returned from Bermuda, haven't you?" [*a leading question*]
"Yes."
"What is it like to visit Bermuda at this time of year?" [*a broad nonleading question*]

The second situation is where you are trying to pin something down or extract a factual concession:

"You've just returned from Bermuda, haven't you?" [*a leading question*]
"Yes."
"And while you were in Bermuda, you explored the possibility of avoiding U.S. taxes by incorporating off-shore, didn't you?" [*another leading question*]

Be patient.   Patience, as Henry Aaron said, is "the art of waiting."[6] Some lawyers do not know how to wait. If they do not get an instantaneous answer to a question, they ask another one immediately. The other person might have been thinking about the first question and about to give an interesting and useful answer, but the second question cut that off. Because of impatience, the lawyer might never learn the answer to the first question.

Let silence help you. You ask a question and hear nothing in response. Actually, you do hear something. You hear the silence of the other person deciding how to answer. Listen to the silence, and wait. If you dislike silence, the other person might, too. And the other person's dislike of silence might cause her to produce lots of information. Be patient.

Listen carefully to answers and ask thorough lines of questions.   You ask a question on Topic A and get some of the information you asked for. If you imitate

---

[6] Henry Aaron with Lonnie Wheeler, *If I Had a Hammer: The Hank Aaron Story* 236 (paperback ed. 1992). (Aaron hit 755 home runs in part by waiting for the right pitch.) See also Stefan H. Krieger, *A Time to Keep Silent and a Time to Speak: The Functions of Silence in the Lawyering Process*, 80 Or. L. Rev. 199, 240–242 (2001) (on "using silences to promote gathering of information").

the interviewers you see on television, you will ignore the missing information and ask an unrelated question on Topic B. But if you act like a good lawyer, you will *not* go on to Topic B without asking all the follow-up questions necessary to get all the information you need on Topic A. Find out everything. Not just a lot of things. *Everything.*

§2.2.4 *Finding and Telling Stories*

A story has characters and a plot, like a novel or a movie. Through their actions, the characters reveal what kind of people they are. We, the audience, decide to like them or dislike them. If we like them, we get upset when they suffer, and we want things to get better. (If we are judges or jurors, we might hope to be able to decide in their favor.) We like characters who are honest, caring, careful, hard-working, not selfish, and so on. We dislike characters who have the opposite qualities, especially if they have harmed characters we like (and if we are judges or jurors, we might enjoy making the bad characters pay).

A story also reveals *why* events happened, especially how harm was caused. For example, one character is suffering, but is it because her own carelessness put her in a dangerous situation or because some other character's carelessness did that? In one kind of compelling story, we can see that the bad characters caused the good characters to suffer — and we want to do something about it. In another kind of compelling story, the bad characters are pretending that the good characters hurt them — and we want to make sure the bad characters don't get away with it. This seems like an oversimplification, but trials are contests between competing stories. And the party with the most compelling story often wins.

In addition to characters and a plot that reveals the characters' nature, an effective story *makes the audience want to act.* And lawyers tell stories to audiences that have the *power* to act. In the courtroom, the audience includes judges and juries. Inside and outside the courtroom, the audience includes, among others, the lawyer who is your adversary — the lawyer who represents the opposing party. In negotiation, you tell the story to that lawyer in hopes that she will foresee that the courtroom audience will be persuaded by your story and therefore offer you concessions to prevent the courtroom audience from deciding in your favor.

Effective lawyers have two clusters of story skills. The first are *story-finding* skills. You interview the client and witnesses and have located a number of documents and other pieces of evidence. Out of this, you have identified exactly 1000 facts. Now in this forest of facts, you have to *find* the story. Which facts reveal what kind of person your client is? Which facts reveal what kind of people the other characters are? Which facts show how harm was caused? Do these few facts coalesce into a plot? You do not invent the story. That would be lying. You find it in the facts.

The second cluster of skills involves *telling* the story. If you are telling the story yourself (as in negotiation), what words will express it in a way that makes it most persuasive? If you are telling it through evidence in the courtroom, what questions put to witnesses, for example, will cause them to bring out the story in the most compelling way?

§2.2.5 *Painting a Picture*

A skill related to storytelling is painting a picture. Here, there is a static situation without a plot. When you paint a picture, you use words to create a scene in the listener's mind. The listener will have to use a little imagination to see the scene, but the more details you provide and the more vivid your words, the easier it will be for the listener to see the scene. Story finding and storytelling are usually thought of as a litigator's skills. But painting a picture is useful both in conflict resolution (such as litigation) and in transactional work (such as contract negotiation).

In counseling, to help a client understand the consequences of a particular option, you might paint this picture, which should be frightening to the client:

> The second option is to refuse the prosecution's offer of a plea bargain and go to trial. The government has videotape, from a hidden camera, of what looks like you accepting a bribe. On the tape, you can be heard saying that in exchange for the $20,000 in the briefcase you are being given, you will prevent enforcement of the air pollution statutes at the factory owned by the person giving you the money. The factory is the only source of industrial air pollution in the city. The prosecution will not be able to get into evidence the fact that the city has one of the highest lung cancer rates in the country. But the jurors all live here, and they will all know about the cancer rate because it's been reported in the newspapers often. Our motion for a change in venue has been denied. . . .

As you read this, do you imagine a picture of the jurors in the courtroom watching the videotape? In your mind, are you already seeing their frowns and grim faces?

In negotiation (here, transactional), you might paint this picture, which the other side, a manufacturer of electronics gadgets, might find intriguing:

> As you know, my client has developed a patent-protected device that silences automobile security alarms within a range of 400 feet.
>
> Although people install these things in their cars, studies show that car thieves are not deterred by them. Nearly every time you hear a car alarm, it has been set off accidentally by electrical malfunction, by a thunderclap, by another car tapping the alarmed car while parking, or even by somebody leaning against the alarmed car. Everybody knows that. So when a car alarm goes off, nobody thinks a car is being stolen. The only thing the alarm accomplishes is to annoy neighbors.
>
> If we can agree on a price, my client would license this device to you exclusively. You would be the only manufacturer in the world selling a product that could be used to stop this ear-shattering racket.
>
> Suppose you live near a parking lot or a street with a lot of parked cars. Every once in a while, one of these alarms goes off in the middle of the night. You were asleep but suddenly you sit bolt upright in bed. If the alarm doesn't turn itself off in

a minute or two, you will listen to it for a long time and won't be able to go back to sleep. Even if it does turn itself off quickly, you will not be rested the next day because rest is accomplished only with uninterrupted sleep.

   This doesn't have to happen. Before you get into bed in the first place, you turn on my client's device. Then you go to sleep confident that you will sleep through the night. Our market surveys suggest that to get this benefit people are willing to pay . . .

From this, are you able to imagine a television commercial for the product?

§2.2.6 *Giving Information*

   Sometimes lawyers give complete information precisely, and sometimes they don't. For example, your client has over ten years built a business from something that operated out of his garage into an enterprise that employs 1000 people and earns $200 million a year. He is now selling the business, and you are involved in negotiating the sale. The buyer's representatives ask what your client plans to do after the sale. If you want to provide a lot of information, you could say:

> He enjoys building up a company from nothing. That's his thrill. And the only business he knows is manufacturing the product he's making now. He's had a few ideas in the last two years for revolutionary changes in the product that would make everything now on the market obsolete. But he hasn't developed them through this company because he knew he was going to sell it and start over. He has already talked informally with investment bankers to get a new company up and running. He's written a business plan already, and the bankers are eager to lend the money, although nothing will be agreed to until after he has taken six months off to travel around the world.

This is very informative. In some situations, it would be exactly the right thing to say. But here, it tells the other side so much that they might walk away from this deal because they will not want to compete with your client's new company. If you want to give the *smallest* amount of information possible, you could answer by speaking incompletely or ambiguously or both:

> He's explored some business ideas, but nothing is certain yet except that he and his family will take a trip around the world for the next six months. They'll go to Paris, Prague, Kenya — the sort of places where you can relax and get away from an exhausting business life. He was telling me the other day about plans to visit the Studio Ghibli museum in Japan. He's an entrepreneur by nature. He'll get into something when he gets back.

Here, the details about the trip are a smokescreen. In negotiation there are ethical rules governing an answer like this one. The buyer asked generally what the seller's post-sale plans are without saying why he wants to know, and the ambiguous answer above contains no untruthful statements. If the buyer wants to know whether the seller will compete in the same market, he has to ask that question directly and listen carefully to the answer.

Two kinds of skills are involved here. The first is knowing *when* to speak completely and precisely and when to speak incompletely or ambiguously. The second is knowing *how* to speak in those ways.

§2.2.7 *Implying Through Tone of Voice and Body Language*

Some things are not communicated very clearly or naturally in words. Suppose that a client is a charming and witty person whose presence you enjoy. If you say that to the client, both of you might feel uncomfortable. But if you smile and speak in a friendly tone whenever you see the client, the message gets across much more naturally. (This should not stop you from using words to compliment the client on qualities that are more directly related to your collaboration with the client. If the client is realistic, reasonable, creative, or perceptive when you work together, it is not inappropriate to mention those things.)

Suppose that in negotiation your adversary has just made a proposal that seems to ignore everything you have said about your client's needs. You will make things worse if you say, "You blockhead! Didn't you understand anything I've told you about my client?" That would introduce pointless interpersonal conflict. And you have concluded that words alone are not getting through to this adversary. You might say, "For the reasons I've explained before, that will not satisfy any of my client's needs," while using a tone of voice and perhaps a facial expression to suggest that the negotiation will fail unless the adversary becomes more responsive.

When are tone of voice and body language better than words? Sometimes, words will make one or both people uncomfortable (as with the charming and witty client). And sometimes, words that convey all you feel will make it hard for the other person to change behavior (as with the negotiating adversary who has not been listening to you). Tone of voice and body language can be used to imply where explicitly saying something would cause additional problems.

§2.2.8 *Making Arguments*

A lawyer's argument is not bickering. An argument is a group of ideas expressed logically to convince a listener to do a particular thing or to adopt a particular belief.

For good reasons, we list making arguments last among oral communication skills. One of the signs of *in*effectiveness in a lawyer is a tendency to make arguments in situations where it would be more productive to do the things we've listed above: listen, empathize, ask questions, find or tell a story, paint a picture, give information, or imply through tone of voice or body language.

Nobody really knows why ineffective lawyers do this. It might be because argument is one of the first communication tools, oral or written, taught in law school, which might leave students with the impression that arguing is the essence of lawyering. Or it might be because the stereotype of lawyers as arguers attracts to the profession people who like to argue.

Certainly, every lawyer needs to know how to make good arguments. There are plenty of times when the only way, or the most effective way, to get what the client wants is through argument. But a threshold skill is knowing when to argue and when to do something else instead.

CHAPTER 3

OVERVIEW OF THE LAWYER'S ROLE

Most students entering law school would not call themselves writers; nor would they expect that in three years they will be professional writers, earning a significant part of their income by writing for publication. Yet that is precisely what lawyers do. Most lawyers write and publish more pages than do novelists, and with greater consequences hanging in the balance.

This book introduces the critical skill of legal writing. In this chapter, we begin with an exploration of the kinds of writing lawyers do, both in litigation and in other kinds of law practice. Understanding this legal landscape will help you understand the legal issues of the cases you read and the various research and writing tasks you will be asked to perform.

§3.1 Writing and the Practice of Law

Lawyers write many kinds of documents — court papers, letters, legal instruments, and internal working documents for the law firm. As different as these documents are from each other, they all fall into one of three categories defined by the lawyer's primary role when writing them: (1) planning and preventive writing, (2) predictive writing, and (3) persuasive writing. A lawyer's writing differs significantly depending on which of these three roles the lawyer is performing.

A Lawyer's Writing Roles

- Planning and Preventive Writing
- Predictive Writing
- Persuasive Writing

Planning and Preventive Writing. Lawyers engage in planning and preventive writing when they draft transactional documents such as wills, trusts, leases, mortgages, partnership agreements, and contracts. Planning documents define the rights of the parties and the limits of their conduct, much as case law and statutes do for society at large. Thus, planning documents create what is, in effect, the "law" of the transaction. In some ways, planning and preventive writing is the most satisfying of the lawyering roles. Through planning and preventive writing, the lawyer creates and structures some of the most important transactions and relationships in an individual client's life or in the commercial world. Also, with careful planning, the lawyer can forestall future disputes, and most lawyers would rather help clients prevent injury than recover for injury.

Predictive Writing. Predictive writing is part of another satisfying task — client counseling. Clients often seek a lawyer's advice when they must make an important decision. When that decision has legal implications, the lawyer must research the law and predict the legal result of the contemplated action.

Lawyers engage in predictive writing in both transactional and litigation settings. In transactional settings, the lawyer must predict legal outcomes in order to analyze and prevent possible problems. In litigation, the client and the lawyer must decide many questions, ranging from relatively routine matters of litigation management (such as which motions to file) to such fundamental matters as whether to settle the case. To resolve any of these questions, the lawyer must predict the legal outcomes of the possible courses of action and must communicate those predictions to the client or to another lawyer working on the case.

In predictive writing, the lawyer must analyze the relevant law *objectively*, as a judge would do. The most common documents for communicating predictive analysis are the *office memo* (addressed to another lawyer who has requested the analysis) or the *opinion letter* (addressed to the client). The lawyer's role is to predict a legal result as accurately as possible, objectively weighing the strengths and weaknesses of the possible arguments. The answer might not be the answer the client or the requesting lawyer wants to hear, but it is the answer they need in order to make a good decision.

Persuasive Writing. Legal problems cannot always be prevented, and some of them inevitably result in litigation or a proceeding before some other decision-maker. When that happens, the lawyer takes on a persuasive role. No matter what result the lawyer might have *predicted*, the lawyer now must try to persuade the decision-maker to reach the result most favorable to the client. The lawyer must marshal the strongest arguments in her client's favor and refute opposing arguments. The most common persuasive document is the *brief* (also called a *memorandum of law*).

Although the goals of prediction and persuasion differ, on a fundamental level predictive (objective) analysis and persuasive analysis cannot be separated. To predict a result, a writer must understand the arguments each side would present. To persuade, a writer must understand how the argument will strike a neutral reader. Thus, as you improve your predictive analysis, you will be improving your persuasive analysis as well, and vice versa.

§3.2 Overview of a Civil Case

Because most of your first-year courses focus on reading appellate opinions, your understanding of those cases will be improved if you have an overview of how a civil case proceeds through the litigation process. This section summarizes the course of a fairly simple personal injury lawsuit with only one legal claim against only one defendant and raising no ancillary issues. As you read it, notice how many litigation stages require legal research and the writing of a legal document (identified by italics), even in a relatively simple case. A more detailed description of the litigation process is provided in Chapter 7.

Initial Research. A civil case begins when a client consults a lawyer about a legal problem. Usually the client has been injured and believes that his injury was caused by the wrongful conduct of someone else. The client wants to know whether he has any legal recourse and, if so, whether he should pursue it.

To decide these questions, the lawyer must gather all the relevant facts and research the relevant legal issues. Rarely will the lawyer already know all the law that will be required to answer these initial questions, and the lawyer might not have time to research all of them herself. She might ask an associate to research some of them for her. The requesting lawyer will write *file memos* to the associate, providing the necessary information and setting out exactly what she needs to know. After finishing the requested research, the associate will write an *office memo* to the requesting lawyer, communicating the results of the research.

The first lawyer will review the research, analyze the client's possible claims, and provide that analysis to the client. The lawyer and client are likely to discuss the analysis face to face, but often the lawyer also writes an *opinion letter* memorializing the results of the research and her advice to the client. Together the client and the lawyer decide whether to proceed with the claim.

Initial Negotiation Process. The next step is writing a *demand letter* to the party whose conduct appears to have caused the injury (the defendant). Typically, the demand letter will explain the legal basis for believing that the defendant's conduct was wrongful; the legal and factual basis for believing that the conduct caused the plaintiff's injury; and the kinds of damages the law permits in such a case. The lawyer for the defendant will write a *response to the demand letter* explaining the legal and factual bases for the defendant's defenses. The negotiation process may continue for some time, with settlement offers and counteroffers communicated by additional *settlement letters* between the lawyers and *client letters* conveying settlement offers.

Filing a Lawsuit and Resolving Initial Defenses. If the case does not settle, the plaintiff's lawyer chooses the appropriate court and files a *complaint*, a document that sets out the facts of the case and the legal basis for the claim. Once the defendant's lawyer receives the complaint, he has only a few weeks to draft and file a response. His research might have shown that the defendant has one or more defenses that can be raised immediately. If so, the lawyer will raise these defenses in documents called *motions*, which state the defense and ask the court for some kind of action, such as dismissal of the case. Each motion will be supported by a *brief* (also called a *memorandum of law*), explaining the legal and factual basis for the defense. The motions may also be accompanied by other supporting documents, such as *affidavits* from witnesses and copies of evidentiary documents bearing on the defense.

Each time one party files a motion asking the court to take some action, the other party must file a *responsive brief,* usually explaining the legal and factual basis for the argument that the court should deny the motion. The responsive brief may be accompanied by other supporting documents such as *affidavits.* The party who filed the motion (the moving party) will file a *reply brief* addressing the arguments raised in the responsive brief, and there might be a hearing on the motion, after which the court will decide the issue.

Assuming that the court declines to dismiss the case, the defendant's lawyer must file an *answer,* a document that admits or denies all the facts alleged in the complaint and may raise additional defenses as well. The defendant's lawyer also may file a *counterclaim,* a document that alleges some wrongful and injurious conduct on the part of the plaintiff. The plaintiff will then file an *answer* to the defendant's counterclaim. The answer admits or denies all the facts alleged in the counterclaim and raises all possible remaining defenses against the counterclaim.

Factual Discovery. Now the case is ready for the discovery phase. In this phase, the parties gather all the available evidence in an effort to prepare for trial. During discovery, both parties draft and file *interrogatories* (questions directed to each other) and *responses to interrogatories* (answers to the questions). They draft and file *requests for production of documents, requests for admissions,* and *notices of depositions* (occasions for oral questioning of witnesses under oath). Parties can file *requests for entry on land* (to inspect the premises) or *requests for medical examination* (to subject a person to a physical or psychiatric examination). During the discovery phase, disputes might arise over how much or what kind of information can be sought. These disputes can become the subject of *motions to compel* (filed by the party seeking discovery) or *motions for a protective order* (filed by the party seeking to prevent discovery). Like other motions, discovery motions and *responses* to them are accompanied by supporting *briefs* and *affidavits.*

Motions for Summary Judgment. After the discovery phase, the parties often draft and file *motions for summary judgment.* A party seeking summary judgment is asking the court to rule on some or all of the claims or defenses without the necessity of a trial. Summary judgment motions are supported by *briefs,* by *statements of uncontested facts,* and by *affidavits,* excerpts from depositions, evidentiary documents, and excerpts from written discovery. The opposing party files a *responsive brief, affidavits,* and other supporting documents resisting the motion, to which the moving party files a *reply brief.* Oral argument is often held. The court might resolve the entire case at the summary judgment stage, or it might resolve some of the claims or defenses, thus narrowing the issues remaining for trial.

Trial. If the parties do not reach a settlement, they continue with trial preparations. If the case will be tried to a jury, both parties draft and file a set of proposed *jury instructions*. Jury instructions are statements to be read to the jury to help them understand the law governing the case and their role in the process. Each party also drafts and files a *trial brief*, a document that summarizes the evidence expected to be introduced, raises and argues any evidentiary issues the party anticipates, and argues for the adoption of that party's version of the jury instructions.

Trial begins with jury selection (if the case will be tried to a jury) and opening statements by each party's lawyer. Then the parties call their witnesses and offer their evidence. The trial concludes with closing statements from each lawyer, the reading of the jury instructions (if the case is tried to a jury), and a decision by the judge or the jury. Some *post-trial motions* may be decided, and then a final *judgment* will be entered.

Appeal(s). A party who is dissatisfied with the result of the trial court proceedings usually can file a *notice of appeal* to a higher court. This party is called the appellant. The other party (the appellee) may file a *notice of appeal* as well, raising other objections to the trial court result. A series of documents identify the issues to be argued in the appeal and designate the record of the trial court proceedings that will be sent to the appellate court.

After the record has been prepared and filed, the parties each file *briefs*, *responsive briefs*, and *reply briefs* arguing the issues raised in the appeal. Oral argument is often held, after which the appellate court issues an opinion. In some circumstances, either or both parties may seek to appeal the appellate court's decision to an even higher court. If so, the procedure described in this paragraph is repeated there. When all appeals are completed, the losing party either complies with the judgment (if applicable) or enforcement proceedings begin. After the judgment has been paid, a *satisfaction of judgment* is filed, and the case is closed.

§3.3 Ethical Duties

Your legal practice, including your legal writing, will be governed by the ethical standards your jurisdiction has adopted for lawyers. Most jurisdictions have adopted a version of either the American Bar Association's Model Rules of Professional Conduct or the earlier Model Code of Professional Responsibility. Sanctions for violation of these rules range from private censure to disbarment. No matter what your jurisdiction's ethical rules or your lawyering role, your legal writing must meet at least the following professional obligations:

1. *Competency.* A lawyer must provide competent representation, including legal knowledge, skill, thoroughness, and preparation.[1]

---

[1] Model R. Prof. Conduct 1.1 (2007).

2. *Diligence.* A lawyer's representation must be diligent.[2]
3. *Promptness.* A lawyer must do the client's work promptly.[3]
4. *Confidentiality.* Generally, a lawyer must not reveal a client's confidences except with the client's permission.[4]
5. *All lawyers are bound by the rules of ethics.* Every lawyer is bound by the rules of professional conduct, no matter whether that lawyer is in charge of the case or working under the direction of another lawyer.[5]
6. *Loyalty.* A lawyer's advice must be candid and unbiased. The advice must not be adversely influenced by conflicting loyalties to another client, to a third party, or to the lawyer's own interests.[6]

In addition to these general standards, your predictive legal writing must meet at least the following ethical standards dealing with giving advice:

7. *Moral, economic, and political factors.* While a lawyer's advice must provide an accurate assessment of the law, it may refer also to moral, economic, social, and political factors relevant to the client's situation.[7] However, the lawyer's representation of a client does not constitute a personal endorsement of the client's activities or views.[8]
8. *Criminal or fraudulent activity.* A lawyer must not advise or assist a client to commit a crime or a fraud.[9] When the client expects unethical assistance, the lawyer must explain to the client the ethical limitations on the lawyer's conduct.[10]

Finally, your persuasive legal writing must meet at least the following ethical standards:

9. A brief-writer must not knowingly make a false statement of law.[11]
10. A brief-writer must not knowingly fail to disclose to the court directly adverse legal authority in the controlling jurisdiction.[12]
11. A brief-writer must not knowingly make a false statement of fact or fail to disclose a material fact when disclosure is necessary to avoid assisting a criminal or fraudulent act by the client.[13]
12. A brief-writer must not assert a legal argument unless there is a non-frivolous basis for doing so.[14]

---

[2] Model R. Prof. Conduct 1.3 (2007).
[3] Model R. Prof. Conduct 1.3 (2007).
[4] Model R. Prof. Conduct 1.6 (2007).
[5] Model R. Prof. Conduct 5.2 (2007).
[6] Model R. Prof. Conduct 1.7 and 2.1 (2007).
[7] Model R. Prof. Conduct 2.1 (2007).
[8] Model R. Prof. Conduct 1.2(b) (2007).
[9] Model R. Prof. Conduct 1.2(d) (2007).
[10] Model R. Prof. Conduct 1.4(a)(5) (2007).
[11] ABA Model R. Prof. Conduct 3.3(a)(1) (2007).
[12] Model R. Prof. Conduct 3.3(a)(3) (2007).
[13] Model R. Prof. Conduct 3.3(a)(1) and (2) (2007).
[14] Model R. Prof. Conduct 3.1 (2007).

13. A brief-writer must not communicate ex parte[15] with a judge about the merits of a pending case, unless the particular ex parte communication is specifically permitted by law.[16]
14. A brief-writer must not intentionally disregard filing requirements or other obligations imposed by court rules.[17]

These ethical standards will apply to your legal writing after you are a lawyer. They will also apply, directly or indirectly, to the legal writing you do as a law clerk before you are admitted to the bar. They will be among the standards by which your legal writing teacher evaluates your law school writing. Be sure that every document you write meets these standards of professional responsibility.

---

[15] *Ex parte*, in this context, means without notice to other parties in the litigation.
[16] Model R. Prof. Conduct 3.5(b) (2007).
[17] Model R. Prof. Conduct 3.4(c) and 3.2 (2007).

INTRODUCTION TO THE LEGAL SYSTEM

CHAPTER 4

COMMON LAW

§4.1 Overview — Sources of Lawmaking Powers

The United States Constitution allocates powers between the state and national governments and thus establishes the framework for our federal system of government. In turn, each state's constitution establishes the framework for that state's government. A fundamental tenet of these state and federal constitutions is the separation of powers between the legislative, judicial, and executive branches of government. Although lawmaking functions rest primarily with the legislative branch, all three branches exercise some form of lawmaking power.

§4.1.1 Legislative and Executive Branches

The state and federal legislatures create law by enacting statutes within the authority granted to them by the state and federal constitutions. Although the primary function of the executive branch is enforcement of laws, the executive branch may lead in policy development by proposing legislation to a legislature. Moreover, a legislature may delegate some of its lawmaking power to the executive branch by statutorily authorizing an executive agency to issue rules and regulations designed to help implement a statutory scheme.

For example, in the exercise of its federal constitutional authority to regulate commerce, the United States Congress has enacted comprehensive labor relations statutes, such as the National Labor Relations Act.[1] It has also created the National Labor Relations Board (NLRB), an agency of the United States, and has authorized the NLRB to issue administrative rules and regulations necessary to help the NLRB enforce the labor relations statutes.[2]

Legislatures cannot amend a constitution in the same way that they enact statutes. For example, Article V of the United States Constitution authorizes

---

[1] 49 Stat. 449 (1935).
[2] 29 U.S.C. §§153, 156 (2006); Am. Hosp. Ass'n v. NLRB, 499 U.S. 606, 609 (1991).

Congress to propose constitutional amendments, but such proposals do not become effective until ratified by the legislatures or constitutional conventions of three-fourths of the states. For convenience, this book uses the term "enacted law" to refer to both statutes and constitutions.

§4.1.2 Judicial Branch

The judicial branch of government develops law in two ways, both of them in the context of particular disputes. First, state and federal courts contribute to the development of constitutional and statutory law by interpreting the necessarily general terms of such enacted law and applying those terms to the facts of disputes. Second, as offspring of the English judicial system, courts in the United States have adopted and continue to develop a substantial body of common law: judge-made law that applies to issues that constitutional or statutory law does not address. State courts are the primary source of common law, because federal courts no longer create and develop "federal general common law."[3] Nonetheless, the federal courts retain the power in a few restricted fields, such as admiralty law, to develop "specialized federal common law."[4]

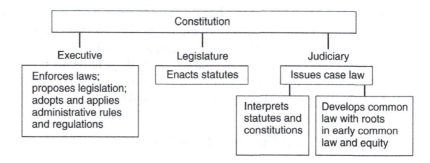

§4.1.3 Common Law as a Backdrop for Legislation

An example of the interplay between statutory law and common law is provided in your first-year contracts course. Many principles of contract law — such as consideration, offer and acceptance, performance and breach, and remedies — find their source in a substantial body of common law, developed by judges, first in England and later in the United States.

The common law of contracts forms a backdrop against which state legislatures have enacted statutes, which supersede some of the common law rules. In the resulting hybrid system, the statutes provide the rule of law on issues to which they apply, while common law applies to gaps within and between statutes, and to whole topics not addressed by statutes.

---

[3] Erie R.R. v. Tompkins, 304 U.S. 64, 78 (1938).
[4] Henry J. Friendly, *In Praise of* Erie — *And of the New Federal Common Law*, 39 N.Y.U. L. Rev. 383, 405 (1964).

§4.1.4 Local and Tribal Governments

These fundamental principles of state and federal lawmaking apply only in limited fashion to two other kinds of governments in the United States: (1) local governments, such as those of cities and counties, and (2) American Indian tribal governments.

Local governments come in a variety of models. Although many of them exercise legislative, executive, and judicial powers, they do not always practice the same degree of separation of these powers as do state and federal governments. A state's constitution and statutes may partially define the legal structure that a local government in the state can adopt and the powers that it can exercise. Typically, a municipality further defines its structure with a city or county charter that operates within limits set by state law.

More nearly autonomous are American Indian tribes. Although their powers may be limited by federal law, they are otherwise sovereign governments with inherent powers to exercise tribal authority. Not all of the tribes have chosen to adopt every fundamental tenet of the state and federal governments. For example, the Navajo Nation of the southwestern United States has no constitution, and it has not always recognized complete separation of legislative, judicial, and executive powers. Nonetheless, its legal system is similar to the Anglo-American system in several important respects. Constituents elect the members of the Navajo Tribal Council, which enacts statutory law in the form of codes. The executive power rests primarily in the president, an elected official. Finally, the Navajo trial courts and the Navajo Supreme Court apply federal law and tribal codes, and they develop and apply a common law based on Navajo custom and cultural values or compatible state laws.

§4.2 Common Law

§4.2.1 Historical Roots

The common law that courts in the United States develop and apply has its roots in the English common law, which was dispensed in the courts of the English king or queen. This English law came to be known as the "common law" because it applied generally throughout medieval England. For many kinds of claims, the common law thus replaced a less uniform system of customary law dispensed in local courts and in the private courts of feudal lords. The English Court of Chancery supplemented the remedies of the early common law courts by developing and applying a form of "equity" that provided relief when common law remedies were inadequate.

Distinctions between common law and equitable claims, defenses, and remedies continue to have significance for some purposes, such as determining the right to a jury trial in some circumstances.[5] Most United States jurisdictions,

---

[5] *See, e.g.,* City of Monterey v. Del Monte Dunes at Monterey, 526 U.S. 687, 708-09 (1999) (discussing whether federal statutory claim was "legal" rather than "equitable," for purposes of

however, have eliminated the dual court system and have largely merged law and equity procedure.[6] Accordingly, this book uses the term "common law" to refer generally to laws created and developed by the courts, regardless of whether the principles have their roots in early common law or equity law.

Oliver Wendell Holmes traced the origins of some English and United States common law to early Germanic and Roman law.[7] Other common law principles simply reflect judicial recognition of community needs, habits, or customs, and are "accounted for by their manifest good sense."[8] More generally, common law is "the embodiment of broad and comprehensive unwritten principles... inspired by natural reason and an innate sense of justice."[9]

The term "common" may be misleading when applied to common law in the United States: The courts in each state are free to develop the common law of that state in a manner that reflects local policies; therefore, variations in common law among the states are inevitable. Nonetheless, to a surprising degree, courts in different states share common views on general principles of law. For example, a federal appellate court has noted that "the principles of contract law do not differ greatly from one jurisdiction to another."[10] Perhaps more important for law students and practitioners, the method employed by courts in deciding disputes and developing common law does not vary substantially among the states.

§4.2.2 Examples: Common Law Burglary and Murder

Although criminal law is now comprehensively addressed by statutes, it was once primarily within the domain of the common law. The early common law crime of burglary, which was punishable by death, illustrates the judicial development of common law rules to serve particular needs of the community. In imposing capital punishment for this crime, the common law courts sought to deter a serious invasion of the home during hours of darkness, when the inhabitants were

---

applying the Seventh Amendment's guarantee of a jury trial to common law actions); Hutchinson v. Spanierman, 190 F.3d 815, 823 (7th Cir. 1999) (applying Indiana law and finding that stale claim was barred by the equitable doctrine of laches even though the legal statute of limitations had not expired); 1 Dan B. Dobbs, Dobbs Law of Remedies §2.6(1), at 150-53 (2d ed. 1993) (discussing continuing limitations on equitable remedies, such as injunctive relief, that do not apply to legal remedy of money damages).

[6] See, e.g., Fed. R. Civ. P. 2 ("There is one form of action — the civil action."); Ross v. Bernhard, 396 U.S. 531, 539-40 (1970) (discussing the procedural joinder of legal and equitable claims and remedies under rules of procedure for federal courts); Dobbs, supra note 5, at 149 ("In most states and in the federal system, there are no longer separate equity rules of procedure.").

[7] Oliver Wendell Holmes, Jr., The Common Law 2, 18, 34, 340-44, 360 (Dover Publ. 1991) (1881).

[8] Id. at 2, 337-39.

[9] Stanley Mosk, The Common Law and the Judicial Decision-Making Process, 11 Harv. J.L. & Pub. Pol'y 35 (1988) (citing Rodriguez v. Bethlehem Steel Co., 525 P.2d 669, 682-83 (Cal. 1974)). Indeed, some scholars believe that humans have a biological predisposition to prefer some forms of legal order. See generally, e.g., Richard D. Alexander, The Biology of Moral Systems (1987); cf. John R. Alford, Carolyn L. Funk, & John R. Hibbing, Are Political Orientations Genetically Transmitted?, Am. Pol. Sci. Rev., May 2005, at 153-67 (study supports conclusion that political attitudes and ideologies are partly shaped by genetics).

[10] E.g., In re Cochise College Park, Inc., 703 F.2d 1339, 1348 n.4 (9th Cir. 1983).

most vulnerable to attack and the invader most likely to escape recognition. Efforts by the common law courts to narrowly address that evil are reflected in the general definition of common law burglary, which separates the crime into distinct elements: (1) the breaking and (2) entering (3) of the dwelling house (4) of another (5) in the night (6) with the intent to commit a felony.

In defining and applying these elements of common law burglary in the context of successive cases, the courts were reluctant to extend the crime beyond the minimum reach necessary to achieve the underlying purposes of the crime, probably because of the severity of punishment. For example, the courts viewed an intruder as less culpable if the occupant of a dwelling encouraged the intrusion by failing to properly secure the dwelling. Accordingly, many courts held that a trespasser who gained entry by further opening a partially open door or window had not committed the "breaking" necessary for a burglary.[11]

The history of another common law crime, murder, illustrates the manner in which courts gradually developed common law doctrine "over several centuries of time as a parade of cases, involving different fact situations, came before the judges for decision."[12] The common law decisions generally defined murder as the unlawful killing of another human being with malice aforethought. Early decisions defined "malice aforethought" narrowly by requiring proof of a premeditated intent to kill. Subsequent cases, however, presented unpremeditated or even unintentional killings that reflected sufficient culpability to warrant classification as murder. In those cases, courts effectively expanded the definition of "malice aforethought" by recognizing other circumstances that would justify conviction for murder: intentional but unpremeditated killing without sufficient provocation; unintentional killing during the commission of another felony; unintentional killing through conduct that reflects a reckless disregard for the lives of others; and killing while engaged in conduct with the intent to do serious bodily harm short of death.[13]

§4.2.3 Common Law in Constant Change

This process of incremental development of the common law does not always proceed in an unbroken line. Courts sometimes abandon previously adopted lines of authority to chart new courses that better reflect current social, economic, and technological realities:

> The inherent capacity of the common law for growth and change is its most significant feature. It is constantly expanding and developing to keep up with the advancement of civilization and the new conditions and progress of society, and adapting itself to the gradual changes in trade, commerce, arts, inventions, and the needs of the country.... The vitality of the common law can flourish if the courts remain alert to their obligation and have the opportunity to change it when reason and equity so demand. The common law requires that each time a rule of law is

---

[11] Wayne R. LaFave, Criminal Law §21.1, at 1017-18 (4th ed. 2003).
[12] Id. §14.1, at 725.
[13] Id. at 725-26.

applied, it must be carefully scrutinized to make sure that the conditions and needs of the times have not so changed as to make further application of the rule an instrument of injustice. Although the legislature may speak to the subject, in the common law system the primary instruments of legal evolution are the courts.[14]

A change in conditions is not the only possible inspiration for abandoning existing common law. A court will occasionally conclude that a previous decision was flawed from its inception. Hindsight may show that the previous court premised its decision on erroneous factual assumptions about conditions existing at that time. Alternatively, the current court, which itself may have changed in intellectual composition, may find intolerable flaws in the reasoning of the previous decision.[15] This process of evolution, however, is restricted by the doctrine of stare decisis, explored in Chapter 6.

§4.3 Summary

Legislatures enact statutes within the authority granted to them by state and federal constitutions. Courts create case law in the context of individual disputes by (1) interpreting and applying the provisions of constitutions and statutes and (2) developing and applying a separate body of judge-made common law. The common law continually grows as new cases present the courts with opportunities to keep the common law current with social, economic, and technological developments.

---

[14] Mosk, *supra* note 9, at 36.
[15] *See generally* Geoffrey R. Stone, *Precedent, the Amendment Process, and Evolution in Constitutional Doctrine*, 11 HARV. J.L. & PUB. POL'Y 67, 71 (1988).

CHAPTER 5

LEGISLATION

§5.1 Roles of Constitutional and Statutory Law

"The Constitution states the framework for all our law. Legislation is one great tool of legal change and readaptation."[1] As noted by a state supreme court, constitutional and statutory law reflect collective expressions of public policy: "As the expressions of our founders and those we have elected to our legislature, our state's constitution and statutes embody the public conscience of the people of this state."[2]

Of the three branches of government, the legislature is the paramount policy-making body. Consistent with that role, a legislature often enacts statutes to address problems that it concludes are not adequately addressed by the common law.

§5.1.1 Example: Embezzlement

The early common law crime of theft was defined as a trespassory taking and carrying away of personal property of another with intent to steal.[3] The requirement of a trespassory taking was not satisfied by one who took possession of another's property lawfully, but who subsequently converted the property to his own use with the intent to permanently deprive the owner of it.

Legislators in England and the United States were aware that the common law did not impose criminal liability for the latter misappropriation, and they were determined to criminalize such conduct. Consequently, they created the statutory crime of embezzlement, generally defined as the fraudulent conversion of another's property by one who is already in lawful possession of it.[4] Had the legislatures not acted, the courts might have eventually achieved the same result

---

[1] Karl N. Llewellyn, THE BRAMBLE BUSH 10 (10th prtg. 1996).
[2] Wagenseller v. Scottsdale Mem'l Hosp., 710 P.2d 1025, 1033 (Ariz. 1985).
[3] Wayne R. LaFave, CRIMINAL LAW §19.2, at 923 (4th ed. 2003).
[4] Id. §8.6.

through further development of the common law, but legislative action sometimes provides a quicker and more certain change of course.

§5.1.2 Example: Consumer-Protection Legislation

A more contemporary example deals with the process of reaching a legally
binding agreement through the process of offer and acceptance. Under the common law of contracts, a department store's newspaper advertisement typically
amounts to an invitation to negotiate rather than an offer to enter into a binding
contract; in most cases, a customer makes the first offer by entering the store and
requesting to purchase the advertised goods. Under common law, the storeowner
is free to reject the customer's offer without incurring any contractual liability.[5]

Unfortunately, this allocation of legal rights and obligations has encouraged some
sellers to use bait-and-switch tactics: They lure customers into their stores with the
"bait" of goods advertised at spectacularly reduced prices; then they "switch" goods by
resisting the customer's desire to purchase the advertised goods and by persuading the
customer to purchase a more expensive item. In response, state legislatures have pro-
moted public policy favoring consumer protection by enacting legislation that
restricts or prohibits such bait-and-switch tactics.[6] These statutes have altered rights
and obligations as they were defined under the common law of contracts.

Common Law of Contracts: If store's ad is not an offer, Customer makes first offer. Store can reject that offer and can "switch" Customer to more expensive item.	**Consumer-Protection Legislation:** Legislature concludes that common law is deficient and enacts protective legislation to address the "bait-and-switch" problem.

§5.1.3 Increasing Significance of Legislation

Prior to the twentieth century, legislatures in England and the United States
tended not to replace common law wholesale with a comprehensive system of
statutes. Instead, they typically enacted statutes to correct specific defects or fill
gaps in a well-developed body of common law. Statutory law thus assumed a role
of secondary importance in the United States, inspiring one scholar to characterize them as "warts on the body of the common law."[7]

State and federal legislation, however, has so proliferated in recent history
that most American jurisdictions now are Code states.[8] Codes are collections of
legislative enactments, organized by subject matter.

---

[5] *See* 1 Arthur L. Corbin, Corbin on Contracts §25 (1963); John D. Calamari & Joseph M.
Perillo, Contracts §2.6(d), at 32 (6th ed. 2009).

[6] *See, e.g.*, Note, *State Control of Bait Advertising*, 69 Yale L.J. 830 (1960).

[7] Llewellyn, *supra* note 1, at 89; *see also* Roscoe Pound, *Common Law and Legislation*, 21
Harv. L. Rev. 383 (1908).

[8] Stanley Mosk, *The Common Law and the Judicial Decision-Making Process*, 11 Harv. J.L. &
Pub. Pol'y 35 (1988).

§5.1.4 Vagueness and Ambiguity

Statutory language sometimes is vague or ambiguous. A vague term is uncertain in its meaning and indefinite in its scope, making it difficult to identify the meaning or meanings that it encompasses.[9] An ambiguous term has multiple meanings, although each of the meanings may be precise and all of the meanings may be easily identified.

Some statutes are necessarily vague because the legislature deliberately used general language, and some statutes are ambiguous because the legislature unintentionally used less precise language than it should have. Consequently, parties to a dispute frequently may reasonably disagree about the way in which statutory language applies to the facts of their dispute. Courts give greater specificity and precision to the vague or ambiguous statutory language by interpreting and applying the statute in the context of specific disputes.

According to one judge, legislatures should not be faulted for keeping judges so busy with cases requiring statutory interpretation,

> because however careful, wise and farseeing the Legislature, the abstract words of a statute often require fitting and tailoring when applied to real-life cases, which may be more bizarre than anyone could possibly have imagined. Fitting and tailoring are what judges do, and what they are supposed to do — they make judgments.[10]

On the other hand, a court does not engage in a wholly creative process when it interprets a vague or ambiguous statute. Rather, it seeks to determine and to give effect to the intent of the enacting legislature by analyzing the statutory language, the stated or apparent purpose of the statute, and the legislative activities related to enactment of the bill.[11]

This search for the intended meaning of a statute is governed by a separate layer of judicially developed rules of interpretation and construction. See Chapter 12 for an overview of statutory interpretation and construction."

§5.2 Interplay Between Legislation and Common Law

§5.2.1 Relationship Between Legislation and Common Law

§5.2.1.1 Legislative Primacy

Although the legislature and the judiciary both exercise lawmaking powers, the legislature is the paramount lawmaking authority, and legislative enactments supersede inconsistent common law. The following United States Supreme Court statement about the federal system applies as well to the state governments:

---

[9] See generally William Van Orman Quine, WORD AND OBJECT 85, 129 (1960).

[10] Judith S. Kaye, Things Judges Do: State Statutory Interpretation, 13 TOURO L. REV. 595, 608 (1997).

[11] See, e.g., Jackson Transit Auth. v. Local Div. 1285, Amalgamated Transit Union, 457 U.S. 15, 22-29 (1982); Mohasco Corp. v. Silver, 447 U.S. 807, 815 (1980).

[W]e consistently have emphasized that the federal lawmaking power is vested in the legislative, not the judicial, branch of government; therefore, federal common law is "subject to the paramount authority of Congress."[12]

Accordingly, the legislature may enact statutes that modify, overrule, or codify existing common law.

§5.2.1.2 Legislation as Guidance for Common Law

Even if no statute currently applies to a dispute, a court may decline to extend common law principles to the area if it concludes that the matter is better left to legislative action.[13] Moreover, if the court decides to develop and apply the common law, it nonetheless may look to statutory law for expressions of public policy that help the court formulate the common law rule. In one case, for example, a court drew guidance from an enacted, but not yet effective, commercial code to develop a common law doctrine of unconscionability in sales contracts.[14]

§5.2.1.3 Common Law as Background for Legislation

Although statutory law supersedes common law, the common law at the time of a statute's enactment may provide a helpful context for analyzing legislative intent.[15] If a statute overrules a common law rule or seeks to address a problem left untouched by the common law, a court can better understand the statute's intended scope if it appreciates the deficiencies of the common law to which the legislature responded.[16] Conversely, if a statute codifies existing common law, cases that developed the common law rule obviously will provide guidance in interpreting the statute.

Moreover, a statute often addresses only selected issues within the general subject matter touched by the statute, thereby creating gaps that common law may fill. In some cases, the statute itself provides for reference to common law, as in the Uniform Commercial Code:

Unless displaced by the particular provisions of [the Uniform Commercial Code], the principles of law and equity, including the law merchant and the law relative to capacity to contract, principal and agent, estoppel, fraud, misrepresentation, duress,

---

[12] Northwest Airlines, Inc. v. Transport Workers Union, 451 U.S. 77, 95 (1981) (quoting New Jersey v. New York, 283 U.S. 336, 348 (1931)).

[13] See, e.g., City & County of S. Fr. v. United Ass'n of Journeymen etc. of U.S. & Can., 726 P.2d 538 (Cal. 1986); see also Heard v. Stamford, 3 P. Wms. 409, 411 (1735) (in explaining why an English court of equity should not intervene, stating that "[i]f the law as it now stands be thought inconvenient, it will be good reason for the legislature to alter it, but till that is done, what is law at present, must take place") (as quoted in Gary Watt, EQUITY STIRRING: THE STORY OF JUSTICE BEYOND LAW 20 (2009)).

[14] Williams v. Walker-Thomas Furniture Co., 350 F.2d 445 (D.C. Cir. 1965).

[15] 2B Norman J. Singer, SUTHERLAND STATUTORY CONSTRUCTION §50.01 (6th ed. 2000); see Wayne R. LaFave, CRIMINAL LAW §2.2, at 90-91 (4th ed. 2003) (discussing interpretation of criminal statutes in light of common law); City of Okla. City v. Tuttle, 471 U.S. 808, 835-38 (1985) (Stevens, J., dissenting).

[16] See, e.g., Heydon's Case, 76 Eng. Rep. 637, 638 (1584), quoted in Singer, supra note 60, §45.05, at 25-26.

coercion, mistake, . . . and other validating or invalidating cause supplement its provisions.[17]

In other cases, statutes only implicitly incorporate common law principles. For example, a federal civil rights statute imposes liability for certain conduct without any express qualifications or limitations. Yet, courts have assumed that Congress intended the statute to implicitly incorporate common law defenses of immunity from liability for money damages:

> It is by now well settled that the tort liability created by [42 U.S.C.] §1983 cannot be understood in a historical vacuum. In the Civil Rights Act of 1871, Congress created a federal remedy against a person who, acting under color of state law, deprives another of constitutional rights. . . . One important assumption underlying the Court's decisions in this area is that members of the 42d Congress were familiar with common-law principles, including defenses previously recognized in ordinary tort litigation, and that they likely intended these common-law principles to obtain, absent specific provisions to the contrary.[18]

§5.2.2 *Judicial Power and Limitations Regarding Legislation*

Although legislatures can modify or overrule common law principles developed by courts, the courts retain an important role in the development of statutory law. Courts may review statutes for consistency with constitutional requirements and will refuse to enforce unconstitutional legislation.[19] Additionally, courts determine the scope and effect of legislation by interpreting statutes and applying them to particular disputes.

Nonetheless, courts have less flexibility in interpreting statutory law than in developing common law. True, if a court finds good reason to abandon its previous analysis of legislative intent, it may overrule its earlier interpretation of a statute, just as it sometimes overrules its previous statement or application of a principle of common law.[20] However, the court may not ignore a statute or modify its terms to reflect judicial views that are inconsistent with legislative intent. In contrast, a court may directly reject the substance and reasoning of a common law principle that it had announced and applied in a prior decision: "[W]e have not hesitated to change the common law . . . where . . . such course was justified."[21]

---

[17] U.C.C. §1-103(b) (rev. 2001).

[18] City of Newport v. Fact Concerts, Inc., 453 U.S. 247, 258 (1981).

[19] *See* Marbury v. Madison, 5 U.S. (1 Cranch) 137 (1803) (setting forth seminal dictum regarding judicial authority in the federal system); Dickerson v. United States, 530 U.S. 428 (2000) (striking down congressional attempt to legislatively overrule the celebrated *Miranda* decision, which protected constitutional rights).

[20] *See, e.g.*, Monell v. Dep't of Soc. Servs. of N.Y., 436 U.S. 658 (1978) (overruling the Court's previous decision that the term "person" in 42 U.S.C. §1983 does not include municipalities); Wayne R. LaFave, CRIMINAL LAW §2.2, at 101-02 (4th ed. 2003).

[21] Kelley v. R.G. Indus., 497 A.2d 1143, 1150-51 (Md. 1985).

§5.3 Summary

A state or federal legislature is the primary policymaking body within a jurisdiction, and it can modify or overrule common law by enacting a superseding statute. Nonetheless, courts review statutes for constitutionality, and they interpret and apply statutes in the context of particular disputes. In interpreting statutes, a court begins with the statutory language in question, viewed in the context of the statute as a whole. If that language is ambiguous, the court may look to other evidence of legislative intent, including legislative purpose and legislative history. If evidence of legislative intent is inconclusive, the court may apply a rule of construction, which gives the statute a meaning that is consistent with general legislative and public policies.

CHAPTER 6

THE ROLE OF PRECEDENT: THE COURT SYSTEM AND STARE DECISIS

§6.1 Introduction to Stare Decisis

In the United States, previous court decisions may influence, or even dictate, the result in a dispute currently before a court. The legal effect of the previous decisions is governed by a complex set of conventions for which the Latin phrase "stare decisis" is often used as convenient shorthand.

"Stare decisis" means standing by what has been decided. Under the doctrine of stare decisis, a court endeavors to decide each case consistently with its own previous decisions, which are called its "precedent." Moreover, the deciding court ordinarily is strictly bound by the precedent of a higher court that reviews the decisions of the deciding court, if the precedent addressed essentially the same question currently before the deciding court.

Judicial adherence to the doctrine of stare decisis serves several significant goals:

- it promotes efficiency in judicial administration by relieving judges of the burden of revisiting settled legal questions in each case;
- it facilitates private and commercial transactions by ensuring a degree of certainty and predictability in the law that regulates such transactions; and
- it satisfies the common moral belief that persons in like circumstances should be treated alike.[1]

The strength of an authority as precedent depends in part on the relationship between the court that created the precedent and the court that may subsequently apply it. Therefore, our exploration should begin with an introduction to the court system.

The structure of the court system and the hierarchy of authority is also discussed in the context of legal research in Part D of this text.

---

[1] *See* Edgar Bodenheimer, Jurisprudence: The Philosophy and Method of the Law 425-28 (rev. ed. 1974); Frederick Schauer, *Precedent*, 39 Stan. L. Rev. 571, 595-602 (1987); *see also* Payne v. Tennessee, 501 U.S. 808, 827 (1991) (stare decisis "promotes the evenhanded, predictable, and consistent development of legal principles, fosters reliance on judicial decisions, and contributes to the actual and perceived integrity of the judicial process").

§6.2 The Court System

§6.2.1 *Structure of State and Federal Courts*

Most state court systems include courts of limited jurisdiction, which hear disputes on limited matters such as domestic relations, traffic violations, and civil suits with small amounts in controversy. All other disputes are tried in branches of a trial court of general jurisdiction, typically named "Superior Court," "Circuit Court," or "District Court."

In most states, final decisions of this trial court may be reviewed in appellate courts at two different levels: A disappointed litigant may appeal a trial court judgment to an intermediate court of appeals; further appeals are taken to a court of last resort, known as the "Supreme Court" in nearly all states. Some court systems, however, have no intermediate appellate court. Instead, a single state court of last resort hears appeals directly from judgments of the trial courts of general jurisdiction.[2] Under either model, a disappointed litigant in state court may seek further review on questions of federal law in the United States Supreme Court.[3]

The state court system in California is representative of those systems with two levels of appellate review:

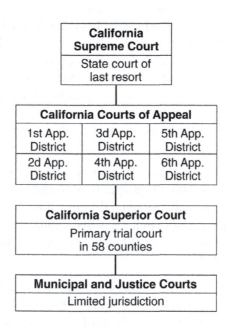

In California, two courts of limited jurisdiction, Justice Courts and Municipal Courts, hear restricted classes of cases. The trial court of general jurisdiction

---

[2] In 2010, those court systems included those of the District of Columbia and the following states: Delaware, Maine, Montana, Nevada, New Hampshire, Rhode Island, South Dakota, Vermont, West Virginia, and Wyoming. BNA'S DIRECTORY OF STATE AND FEDERAL COURTS, JUDGES, AND CLERKS xi-xiv (2010) [hereinafter, BNA'S DIRECTORY OF COURTS].

[3] 28 U.S.C. §1257 (2006).

is the Superior Court, which serves each of 58 counties throughout the state. The Superior Court hears appeals from the courts of limited jurisdiction, and it entertains original actions in a wide variety of civil and criminal cases. Disappointed litigants in a criminal or civil case may appeal from a judgment of the Superior Court to the California Court of Appeal. This intermediate appellate court is divided into six districts, each of which hears civil and criminal appeals from departments of the Superior Court in counties assigned to that district. A disappointed litigant in the Court of Appeal may appeal to the California Supreme Court in certain kinds of cases and may petition for discretionary review in others.[4]

For example, California's Second Appellate District includes the counties of Los Angeles, San Luis Obispo, Santa Barbara, and Ventura. The California Court of Appeal for the Second Appellate District would hear appeals from the decisions of the California Superior Court in those counties. A litigant disappointed by a decision of the Court of Appeal for the Second Appellate District could appeal to the California Supreme Court or petition it for discretionary review.

The structure of the federal court system is similar to that of the California court system:

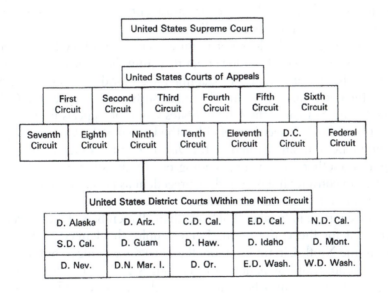

The primary federal trial courts are the United States District Courts. With few exceptions, disappointed litigants appeal from a judgment of a district court to the appropriate one of 13 "circuits" of the United States Courts of Appeals. Petitions for further review are taken to the United States Supreme Court. The chart above shows the line of review from judgments of the United States District Courts that serve the geographical area within the jurisdiction of the United States Court of Appeals for the Ninth Circuit.

---

[4] BNA'S DIRECTORY OF COURTS, *supra* note 2, at 87.

The Ninth Circuit encompasses a large portion of the United States. Although Congress has repeatedly considered proposals to split this circuit into two circuits, the Ninth Circuit still includes the states and territories of Alaska, Arizona, California, Guam, Hawaii, Idaho, Montana, Nevada, the Northern Mariana Islands, Oregon, and Washington. Each of those states and territories has at least one district court; California and Washington have more. For example, California is divided into four district courts: the United States District Courts for the Central, Eastern, Northern, and Southern Districts of California.

§6.2.2 Court Structure and Stare Decisis

Precedent has only limited stare decisis effect on the decision-making of the court that created the precedent: Although a court will do so only in unusual circumstances, it can depart from its own prior rulings. For lower courts within the same court system, stare decisis is less flexible: With very limited exceptions, precedent on the same issue is binding on the lower courts for which the precedent-creating court acts as a court of review.[5] The California Court of Appeal, for example, is bound by decisions of the California Supreme Court. As discussed further in §6.3 below, the lower court must either distinguish the reviewing court's precedent or apply it as controlling authority.

Stare decisis generally does not require a court to follow the precedent of coequal, autonomous courts, of lower courts within the same court system, or of any courts outside that system. For example, the Florida Supreme Court is not bound by the decisions of the other Florida courts or by those of the California Supreme Court. Similarly, the United States Court of Appeals for the First Circuit is not bound by the decisions of either the United States Court of Appeals for the Second Circuit or any United States District Court. Nonetheless, even if the precedent of another court is not binding on the deciding court, the deciding court is free to consider the nonbinding precedent as persuasive authority and to follow its reasoning as a matter of choice.

In some courts, a judicial unit of fewer than all members of the court may create precedent for the entire court. For example, the United States Court of Appeals for the Ninth Circuit has more than two dozen judges, but most appeals in the circuit are heard by panels of three judges each. Each three-judge panel creates precedent that must be followed by all other three-judge panels in the

---

[5] *See* State Oil Co. v. Khan, 522 U.S. 3, 20 (1997) ("The Court of Appeals was correct in applying [Supreme Court precedent] despite its disagreement with [it], for it is this Court's prerogative alone to overrule one of its precedents."). In limited circumstances, a trial court may be compelled to depart from precedent of the intermediate court of appeals in its system. *E.g.*, Miller v. Gammie, 335 F.3d 889, 899-900 (9th Cir. 2003) (en banc) (federal district court could disregard precedent of court of appeals that reviews its decisions, if a decision of a yet higher authority, the United States Supreme Court, even though not precisely on point, has undermined the theory or reasoning underlying the court of appeals precedent); Auto Equity Sales, Inc. v. Super. Ct. of Santa Clara County, 369 P.2d 937, 940 (Cal. 1962) (if trial court is faced with conflicting decisions of two coequal panels or divisions of its reviewing court, it cannot follow them both but must choose between the two).

circuit. Within the circuit, a decision of a three-judge panel can be overruled only by an "en banc" panel of 11 members of the court.[6]

§6.3 Scope and Application of Stare Decisis

§6.3.1 *Building a Wall of Case Law, Brick by Brick*

Courts add to existing common law or statutory interpretations incrementally, as they decide individual disputes on specific facts. Each resolution of a dispute, when published as a written opinion, adds one more "brick" of precedent to a wall of case law. When courts adhere to precedent under stare decisis, they build on the foundation created by the precedent of judicial "bricks" laid in previous decisions.

Some form of stare decisis is justified in any society that values efficiency, certainty, and at least those notions of fairness predicated on equal treatment for similarly situated parties. On the other hand, unquestioning adherence to precedent may inappropriately extend the rule of previous decisions beyond the rationale and policy of the original decision, or it may retain outdated or otherwise unsound precedent. A wall that rises ever higher on a flawed or outdated foundation will eventually fall.

Two limits to stare decisis help to avoid rigidity in the law while maintaining consistency:

(1) A court may *distinguish* a prior decision if it concludes that the prior decision addressed a significantly different dispute from the one now before the court. If so, even if the prior decision was issued by the same court or by a higher court within the jurisdiction, the prior decision does not control the result in the case now before the court. Of course, if the prior decision was issued by a lower court or by a court from another jurisdiction, it would never be *binding* on the current court. Moreover, if such a prior decision is distinguishable from the current case, the prior decision may lose even the persuasive value that it might otherwise have had.

(2) Alternatively, a court's own precedent may be indistinguishable from the dispute currently before the court. If so, the court normally would be bound under the doctrine of stare decisis to follow its precedent. Nonetheless, the doctrine of stare decisis is grounded in policy rather than inexorable mandate. In special circumstances, the court may depart from the normal dictates of stare decisis and reject its own precedent as authority for the present dispute.

The following sections thoroughly examine each of these limits on stare decisis. §6.3.2 explores means of determining whether a prior decision is sufficiently analogous that it creates precedent on the issue now before the court, or whether the prior decision instead is distinguishable. §6.3.3 assumes that a court's own prior decision is not distinguishable and therefore creates precedent that normally

---

[6] *See, e.g.,* United States v. McLennan, 563 F.2d 943, 948 (9th Cir. 1977); 9th Cir. R. 35-3.

would be controlling in the current dispute. It then discusses the special circumstances in which a court may depart from such precedent.

§6.3.2 Analogizing and Distinguishing Precedent

§6.3.2.1 An Inexact Science with Ample Room for Argument

Few disputes are so similar in their facts and legal issues that resolution of the first dispute provides a clear basis for resolving the second. In those relatively rare cases, the prior decision is clearly "controlling" precedent in the same court or a lower court within the jurisdiction. Such controlling precedent normally dictates the result of the subsequent case under stare decisis.[7]

More often, differences between two cases in the facts or in the nature of the legal claims and defenses raised by the litigants are sufficiently substantial that the prior decision does not clearly dictate the resolution of the second. Whether the differences meet this standard often is a question of degree on which reasonable lawyers may disagree.[8]

Assuming that the precedent is not nearly identical to the current dispute and thus is not strictly controlling, it may still be sufficiently analogous to provide a strong basis for deciding the current dispute. Whether the prior decision is analogous or distinguishable is a matter of judgment and analysis, which provides opposing attorneys with plenty of room for argument.

In analyzing the precedential value of arguably distinguishable authority, you should pay attention to the rationale underlying the prior decision. Differences between the cases may be such that the reasons for the result in the prior decision do not apply to the current case. If so, the distinctions between the two cases justify a different result in the current case, or at least an analysis free of deference to the prior decision. Conversely, even though a prior decision does not provide a clear resolution of the current case because of differences between the two cases, many of the reasons for the legal result in the prior decision may apply equally to the current case. If so, the prior case — although not clearly controlling — is *analogous* to the current case in a way that may justify the same legal result in both.

Of course, this process of either restricting or extending the application of precedent in relation to a new dispute is far from an exact science. The determination whether a prior decision supports a proposed outcome in a new case may implicate the most deeply held values of those who must interpret and apply the precedent:

> Like the antebellum judges who denied relief to fugitive slaves . . . the Court today claims that its decision, however harsh, is compelled by existing legal doctrine. On the contrary, the question presented by this case is an open one, and our Fourteenth Amendment precedents may be read more broadly or narrowly depending upon how one chooses to read them. Faced with the choice, I would

---

[7] *See generally* Hutto v. Davis, 454 U.S. 370 (1982).

[8] *Compare id.* at 372-75 (majority opinion), *and id.* at 375-81 (Powell, J., concurring), *with id.* at 381-88 (Brennan, J., dissenting).

adopt a "sympathetic" reading, one which comports with dictates of fundamental justice and recognizes that compassion need not be exiled from the province of judging.[9]

Although uncertainty about the reasons for a prior decision often complicates the analysis, courts regularly engage in the processes of distinction and analogy to limit, extend, refine, and clarify the rules of prior decisions. Indeed, the precise parameters of the rule of a decision typically do not become clear until courts analyze the decision in subsequent decisions in the context of other disputes. This inquiry is largely one of defining, limiting, and extending the holdings of prior decisions.

§6.3.2.2 *Gaining Comfort with Legal Uncertainty*

This "ample room for argument" retained in a flexible doctrine of stare decisis is illustrative of a more general characteristic of uncertainty or indeterminacy in our legal system. New law students are often eager to write down the "answer" to every legal question posed by their professors. But, the most interesting legal questions — the ones that are fully litigated and appealed — are ones to which the answer is uncertain prior to the final judicial determination. If the resolution of the legal dispute were perfectly certain, the parties likely would have settled the dispute well short of full litigation. And if the answer were certain during litigation, why would parties and attorneys wait with great anticipation for the jury's verdict on the evidence, and why would so many appellate decisions be decided on a split vote of learned judges or justices, who frequently disagree on the merits of the appeal?

British Professor Gary Watt describes the uncertainty in the outcome of legal disputes in a particularly colorful manner:

> There is never only one answer to a legal dispute; indeed it is a rare case that has only one *right* answer. As Lord Macmillan admitted: "in almost every case except the very plainest, it would be possible to decide the issue either way with reasonable legal justification." Ronald Dworkin fantasizes that there is always one right answer to every case and that a hypothetical Herculean judge could find it. Perhaps Hercules might, but then perhaps Zeus would find another answer on appeal. . . . [T]he outcome often turns in large part on the purely practical contingency of running out of courts. The nature of the law in such a system is less like a scientific experiment and more like a wheel of fortune: the nature of the legal outcome is determined at the point the wheel stops spinning, and would have [been] determined earlier if the litigants had been at any stage unwilling, or financially unable, to give it an extra push. From the judges' perspective it is a living conversation across a range of reasonable alternative possibilities, and it just happens that the conversation must stop sometime.[10]

---

[9] DeShaney v. Winnebago County Dep't of Soc. Serv., 489 U.S. 189, 212-13 (1989) (Blackmun, J., dissenting).

[10] Gary Watt, EQUITY STIRRING: THE STORY OF JUSTICE BEYOND LAW 12-13 (2009) (footnotes with citations are omitted from the quoted text).

The example in the next subsection illustrates Professor Watt's metaphor of a roulette wheel signifying the outcome of a dispute by stopping its spinning and "running out of courts." It reminds us that the main task of law students and attorneys alike is not to know or discover the "right answer" to a novel legal question. Your main task instead is to identify issues — matters that are reasonably in dispute on the facts and the existing law — and to recognize or develop the arguments that can be persuasively advanced on either side of the dispute.

§6.3.2.3 Example: Warrantless Searches of Cars, Houses, and Mobile Homes

Supreme Court decisions interpreting and applying the Fourth Amendment to the United States Constitution[11] illustrate the techniques of analogy and distinction as well as the difficulty of predicting legal outcomes. In *Carroll v. United States*,[12] the Supreme Court held that the Fourth Amendment permitted federal officers to search an automobile without first obtaining a warrant. The Court reasoned that, although a suspect may have privacy interests in the contents of an automobile, the ready mobility of the automobile makes it impracticable for officers to obtain a warrant before searching.[13] Seven months later, in *Agnello v. United States*,[14] the Supreme Court held that the Fourth Amendment prohibited the warrantless search of the home of a suspect who had been arrested in another location.[15] In disapproving the warrantless search, the *Agnello* Court distinguished *Carroll* on the bases of the immobility of the house and the particularly great privacy interests the owner has in the contents of a house.[16]

Sixty years after *Carroll* and *Agnello*, in *California v. Carney*,[17] the Court considered whether the Fourth Amendment prohibited law enforcement officers from engaging in a warrantless search of a fully mobile motor home. Neither *Carroll* nor *Agnello* clearly controlled, because a motor home arguably combines the mobility of an automobile and the privacy interests associated with a house.[18] Consequently, the result in *Carney* under the doctrine of stare decisis depended

---

[11] The Fourth Amendment to the United States Constitution prohibits unreasonable searches and seizures by government officials:

> The right of the people to be secure in their persons, houses, papers, and effects, against unreasonable searches and seizures, shall not be violated, and no Warrants shall issue, but upon probable cause, supported by Oath or affirmation, and particularly describing the place to be searched, and the persons or things to be seized.

[12] 267 U.S. 132 (1925).

[13] *Id.* at 153; California v. Carney, 471 U.S. 386, 390 (1985) (quoting and interpreting *Carroll*). Under *Carroll*, even if a warrant is not required, the searching officers must have probable cause to believe that the car contains contraband before they can search it. *Carroll*, 267 U.S. at 153-62. Discussion of the issue of probable cause, however, is not necessary to the analysis in the text above.

[14] 269 U.S. 20 (1925), *overruled in part*, United States v. Havens, 446 U.S. 620 (1980).

[15] Long before Carroll v. United States, the Supreme Court had assumed that police generally could not search a house without a warrant, unless the search was incidental to a lawful arrest in the house. *Agnello*, 269 U.S. at 32 (interpreting Boyd v. United States, 116 U.S. 616 (1886)). The Court did not directly decide that question, however, until *Agnello*, a few months after *Carroll*. *Agnello*, 269 U.S. at 32.

[16] *Agnello*, 269 U.S. at 31-33; *see also* Payton v. New York, 445 U.S. 573, 585-90 (1980).

[17] 471 U.S. 386 (1985).

[18] *See id.* at 395 (Stevens, J., dissenting).

on whether the Court found the facts of the case to be more nearly analogous to those of *Carroll* or to those of *Agnello,* as the next step in the Court's continuing interpretation of the Fourth Amendment.

On a vote of eight to one, the California Supreme Court had disapproved the search on two grounds. First, it had analogized *Carney* to cases like *Agnello,* reasoning that the nature of the contents of the motor home, in which the defendant was residing, created similarly high expectations of privacy in those contents as the privacy expectations that one has in the contents of a house. Second, it had distinguished *Carroll* on the basis of the comparatively low expectation of privacy that an owner has in the contents of an automobile.[19]

On review, the United States Supreme Court voted six to three to reverse the decision of the California Supreme Court and to approve the warrantless search. It analogized the case to *Carroll,* reasoning that an automobile and a motor home are not only similarly mobile but are similar in the reduced expectations of privacy in their contents. The expectations of privacy in a motor home are low partly because of the pervasive governmental regulation applicable to all licensed motor vehicles.[20]

The majorities in the state and federal Supreme Courts applied the precedent differently because they differed in their analyses, primarily factual, of the expectations of privacy that one has in the contents of a motor home. The United States Supreme Court's decision to approve the warrantless search was not unanimous and it was not the only "correct" or reasonable decision open to it. Indeed, if you count up the combined votes of the justices in both the California and United States Supreme Courts, you will find that a total of eleven state and federal justices voted to require a warrant in the case, while only seven voted to approve the warrantless search. Because the United States Supreme Court is the highest court in the land, however, so that no further appeals are possible, our society accepts as final the decision of a majority of its justices.

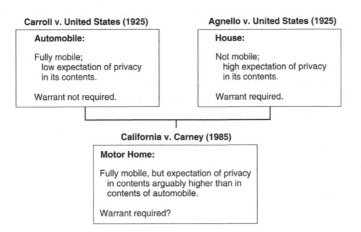

Carroll v. United States (1925)

Automobile:

Fully mobile; low expectation of privacy in its contents.

Warrant not required.

Agnello v. United States (1925)

House:

Not mobile; high expectation of privacy in its contents.

Warrant required.

California v. Carney (1985)

Motor Home:

Fully mobile, but expectation of privacy in contents arguably higher than in contents of automobile.

Warrant required?

---

[19] People v. Carney, 668 P.2d 807, 810-14 (Cal. 1983).

[20] California v. Carney, 471 U.S. 386, 390-94 (1985); *see also* New York v. Class, 475 U.S. 106 (1986).

§6.3.3 Overruling Precedent

§6.3.3.1 Standards for Departing from Normal Application of Stare Decisis

A court's own precedent, or that of a higher court within the same jurisdiction, normally is controlling if it is materially indistinguishable from the dispute now before the court. Ordinarily, a lower court is absolutely bound by the controlling precedent of the appellate courts that review its decisions.[21] However, the doctrine of stare decisis is more flexible in the courts that created the precedent.[22] In exceptional circumstances, a court may depart from a strict application of stare decisis and refuse to follow its own, otherwise controlling precedent. In so doing, it overrules the prior decision and substitutes new precedent in its place.

To return to our metaphor of a wall of precedents, a court may change the direction of its own brickwork, if it has a very good reason to do so.

An early decision of the United States Supreme Court was surprisingly liberal in its approval of such departures from stare decisis:

> The rule of *stare decisis*, though one tending to consistency and uniformity of decision, is not inflexible. Whether it shall be followed or departed from is a question entirely within the discretion of the court, which is again called upon to consider a question once decided.[23]

A statement of the Supreme Court in 2010 is more cautious: "Our precedent is to be respected unless the most convincing of reasons demonstrates that adherence to it puts us on a course that is sure error."[24] More specifically, "informed by a series of prudential and pragmatic considerations," the Supreme Court may feel justified in overruling its prior decision if that decision is outdated in light of intervening changes in law and society or if the prior decision has otherwise come to be viewed as hopelessly flawed, such as in any of the following four special circumstances:

1. "related principles of law have so far developed as to have left the old rule no more than a remnant of abandoned doctrine"; or
2. "facts have so changed or come to be seen so differently, as to have robbed the old rule of significant application or justification"; or
3. "a prior judicial ruling should come to be seen so clearly as error that its enforcement was for that very reason doomed"; or
4. "the rule has proved to be intolerable simply in defying practical workability."[25]

---

[21] See, e.g., Hutto v. Davis, 454 U.S. 370, 375 (1982); see also supra note 5 (identifying rare exceptions).

[22] See, e.g., Jaffree v. Wallace, 705 F.2d 1526, 1532 (11th Cir. 1983), aff'd, 472 U.S. 38 (1985).

[23] Hertz v. Woodman, 218 U.S. 205, 212 (1910).

[24] Citizens United v. Federal Elections Comm'n, 130 S. Ct. 876, 911-12 (2010); see also Arizona v. Rumsey, 467 U.S. 203, 212 (1984) (departure from precedent requires "special justification").

[25] Planned Parenthood of S.E. Pa. v. Casey, 505 U.S. 833, 854-55 (1992); see also Montejo v. Louisiana, 129 S. Ct. 2079, 2088-89 (2009) ("Beyond workability, the relevant factors in deciding

§6.3.3.2 *Changes in Social and Legal Context*

In accordance with the first two justifications, a court may overrule a previous decision that was sensible in light of its original social, economic, technological, and legal context but that fails to serve important policies in current conditions. In one case, for example, a court overruled its own precedent when it recognized a legal right on behalf of a deceased fetus under wrongful death and survival statutes.[26] The court justified its departure from precedent partly on the basis of intervening advances in medical knowledge and on changes in the laws of other states.[27] Although some precedents retain their force for centuries, "it must be true that most cases will eventually become obsolete because society as a whole does not stand still."[28]

§6.3.3.3 *Abandonment of Erroneous or Unworkable Precedent*

Even absent an intervening change in conditions, a court may overrule a prior decision simply because it thinks that the prior decision was poorly reasoned at the outset or has proved to be unworkable in light of experience.[29] In 1985, for example, the United States Supreme Court overruled a decision it had issued in 1976 on a question of state sovereignty under the Tenth Amendment,[30] even though that precedent had itself overruled another decision that the Supreme Court had issued in 1968.[31] In the last of these three decisions the Court explained:

> We do not lightly overrule recent precedent. We have not hesitated, however, when it has become apparent that a prior decision has departed from a proper understanding of congressional power under the Commerce Clause.[32]

§6.3.3.4 *Flexible Application of Stare Decisis to Constitutional Issues*

The Supreme Court's double reverse on the proper interpretation of the Tenth Amendment in the space of 17 years may simply exemplify a more general relationship between the Supreme Court and the United States Constitution. Stare decisis can safely apply with full force in cases of federal statutory

---

whether to adhere to the principle of *stare decisis* include the antiquity of the precedent, the reliance interests at stake, and of course whether the decision was well reasoned.").

[26] Amadio v. Levin, 501 A.2d 1085 (Pa. 1985).

[27] *Id.* at 1094-97.

[28] Gary Watt, EQUITY STIRRING: THE STORY OF JUSTICE BEYOND LAW 77 (2009).

[29] *See* Geoffrey R. Stone, *Precedent, the Amendment Process, and Evolution in Constitutional Doctrine*, 11 HARV. J.L. & PUB. POL'Y 67, 71 (1988).

[30] The Tenth Amendment to the United States Constitution reserves power to the states:

The powers not delegated to the United States by the Constitution, nor prohibited by it to the States, are reserved to the States respectively, or to the people.

[31] Garcia v. San Antonio Metro. Transit Auth., 469 U.S. 528 (1985), *overruling* Nat'l League of Cities v. Usery, 426 U.S. 833, 854-55 (1976) (which itself had overruled Maryland v. Wirtz, 392 U.S. 183, 198 (1968), on the ground that *Wirtz* had relied on "simply wrong" dicta in United States v. California, 297 U.S. 175, 184-85 (1936)).

[32] *Garcia*, 469 U.S. at 557.

interpretation, because Congress can correct judicial mistakes in statutory analysis simply by passing new legislation.[33] In contrast, Article V of the Constitution provides that an amendment to the Constitution is not effective unless approved by two-thirds of each house of Congress and ratified by three-fourths of the states. Thus, Congress cannot easily amend the Constitution to reflect changing social or economic conditions or to overrule judicial interpretations of the Constitution with which Congress disagrees.[34] Consequently, some scholars and judges believe that the Supreme Court should "keep [constitutional] law in accord with the dynamic flow of the social order," with less than the normal restraints of stare decisis.[35]

Nonetheless, countervailing considerations may justify adherence to stare decisis in some cases, even when they address challenges to previous interpretations of the Constitution. First, people may have so substantially relied on an established proposition of law that overruling the prior decision would result in "special hardship" and "inequity."[36] Second, an extraordinarily divisive issue may call for a ruling that is sufficiently durable to erase all doubts about its vulnerability to continuing political pressures. This second consideration is present

> whenever the Court's interpretation of the Constitution calls the contending sides of a national controversy to end their national division by accepting a common mandate rooted in the Constitution.
>
> The Court is not asked to do this very often. . . . But when the Court does act in this way, its decision requires an equally rare precedential force to counter the inevitable efforts to overturn it and to thwart its implementation. . . . [O]nly the most convincing justification under accepted standards of precedent could suffice to demonstrate that a later decision overruling the first was anything but a surrender to political pressure and an unjustified repudiation of the principle on which the Court staked its authority in the first instance.[37]

In *Planned Parenthood of Southeastern Pennsylvania v. Casey*,[38] the Supreme Court invoked both of these considerations in declining to abandon the central rule of *Roe v. Wade*,[39] which established a woman's limited constitutional right to terminate a pregnancy.

---

[33] *See* Pearson v. Callahan, 129 S. Ct. 808, 816-17 (2009); Edelman v. Jordan, 415 U.S. 651, 671 & n.14 (1974).

[34] In an exceptional reaction to a particular ruling of the Supreme Court, Congress proposed, and the states ratified, the Eleventh Amendment as a way of overruling Chisholm v. Georgia, 2 U.S. (2 Dall.) 419 (1793).

[35] Edgar Bodenheimer, JURISPRUDENCE: THE PHILOSOPHY AND METHOD OF THE LAW 430 (rev. ed. 1974); *see also* Seminole Tribe of Fla. v. Florida, 517 U.S. 44, 63 (1996) (adopting flexible approach to stare decisis in abandoning Supreme Court precedent interpreting the Eleventh Amendment). *But cf.* Arizona v. Rumsey, 467 U.S. 203, 212 (1984) (even though stare decisis may be relaxed in constitutional cases, departure from precedent still "demands special justification").

[36] Planned Parenthood of S.E. Pa. v. Casey, 505 U.S. 833, 854 (1992); *see also* Dickerson v. United States, 530 U.S. 428 (2000) (invoking stare decisis in declining to overrule Miranda v. Arizona, 384 U.S. 436 (1966), which spawned the *Miranda* warnings and which in turn "have become part of our national culture").

[37] *Casey*, 505 U.S. at 867.

[38] 505 U.S. 833 (1992).

[39] 410 U.S. 113 (1973).

The Court conceded that the reliance factor weighs most heavily in commercial contexts, "where advance planning of great precision is most obviously a necessity."[40] However, even in the noncommercial contexts of reproduction and sexual equality, reliance could not be discounted:

> [F]or two decades of economic and social developments, people have organized intimate relationships and made choices that define their views of themselves and their places in society, in reliance on the availability of abortion in the event that contraception should fail. The ability of women to participate equally in the economic and social life of the Nation has been facilitated by their ability to control their reproductive lives. . . . The Constitution serves human values, and while the effect of reliance on *Roe* cannot be exactly measured, neither can the certain cost of overruling *Roe* for people who have ordered their thinking and living around that case be dismissed.[41]

Indeed, in the context of extraordinary national division over abortion rights, a dramatic change in the course of constitutional law might fan the flames of controversy by suggesting that continued strife could inspire further changes in course:

> The Court's duty in the present case is clear. In 1973, it confronted the already-divisive issue of governmental power to limit personal choice to undergo abortion, for which it provided a new resolution based on the due process guaranteed by the Fourteenth Amendment. Whether or not a new social consensus is developing on that issue, its divisiveness is no less today than in 1973, and pressure to overrule the decision, like pressure to retain it, has grown only more intense. A decision to overrule *Roe*'s essential holding under the existing circumstances would address error, if error there was, at the cost of both profound and unnecessary damage to the Court's legitimacy, and to the Nation's commitment to the rule of law.[42]

Moreover, the central rule of *Roe* had not proved unworkable and had not been eroded by changes in facts or in related principles of law. Accordingly, although the Court departed from *Roe* in other respects, it reaffirmed *Roe*'s "essential holding,"[43] staying substantially within the boundaries dictated by stare decisis.

§6.4 Summary

Under the doctrine of stare decisis, a court endeavors to decide each case consistently with its prior decisions. Even so, a court may depart from its prior decisions, or precedent, if those decisions are distinguishable from the current

---

[40] *Casey*, 505 U.S. at 855-56.
[41] *Id.* at 856.
[42] *Id.* at 868-69.
[43] *Id.* at 846.

dispute. Even if a prior decision is not distinguishable, a court may overrule its own precedent in special circumstances.

Stare decisis is less flexible with respect to the precedent of a higher court in the same jurisdiction: A trial court or intermediate court of appeals must distinguish or apply the precedent of a court that reviews its decisions. A court is never bound to apply the precedent of a lower court or any court in another jurisdiction, although it may treat such decisions as persuasive authority.

§6.5 Closer Reading: *Citizens United*

In his State of the Union address in January 2010, President Obama criticized a Supreme Court decision issued less than a week earlier, prompting one of the Justices attending the address to react momentarily in apparent disagreement. The decision was *Citizens United v. Federal Election Commission*, 130 S. Ct. 876 (2010), in which a nonprofit corporation challenged the constitutionality of federal legislation that arguably prohibited it from using its general treasury funds to broadcast a movie critical of Hillary Clinton within 30 days of the 2008 Democratic presidential primary election. The Supreme Court held in a 5 to 4 decision that the federal statute could not be enforced because it violated the corporation's free speech rights guaranteed by the First Amendment. Because the *Citizens United* decision required rejection of principles embraced by previous Supreme Court decisions, the lengthy combination of majority, concurring, and dissenting opinions includes a remarkable debate among the justices about the application of stare decisis to the case.

For an advanced exploration of stare decisis, read the excerpts of the *Citizens United* opinions below, and ponder the following questions:

1. **The Debate.** In what way do the dissenting Justices differ in their views about application of stare decisis from the Justices who joined the majority and concurring opinions?
2. **Is the Test Changing?** Is the majority signaling that it is embracing a newly relaxed test for stare decisis, such as one that permits the Supreme Court to accord less deference to a precedent if the precedent has remained controversial within a divided Court since it was decided, or if the party seeking to retain a precedent relies on a supporting rationale other than the one originally adopted in the precedent? Or one that minimizes the significance of legislative reliance on precedent, as contrasted with citizen reliance? Or does the Court's analysis of stare decisis fit comfortably within standards previously announced?
3. **Opinions as Advocacy.** How do you rate each opinion as persuasive writing? Do the majority and concurring opinions persuade you that the Court can overrule precedent in this case without offending or relaxing the doctrine of stare decisis? If so, does the dissenting opinion then cause you to reconsider?
4. **Judging Stare Decisis.** After considering this debate about the application of stare decisis in a particular case, what is your view of stare decisis generally?

Does it perform an important function of facilitating orderly development of the law, yet leaving ample opportunity to correct serious mistakes? Or does it unwisely encourage retention of outdated or ill-advised judicial decisions? Alternatively, do you view stare decisis as an overly flexible doctrine that is easily manipulated so that it allows a majority of the Court to accept or reject a precedent at its will depending on how it views the merits of the precedent?

Citizens United v. Federal Election Commission

Supreme Court of the United States 130 S. Ct. 876 (2010)

[*Footnotes and parallel citations omitted.*]

Justice KENNEDY delivered the opinion of the Court [joined by Justices ROBERTS, SCALIA, and ALITO, and by Justice THOMAS except with respect to Section IV].

Federal law prohibits corporations and unions from using their general treasury funds to make independent expenditures for speech defined as an "electioneering communication" or for speech expressly advocating the election or defeat of a candidate. 2 U.S.C. §441b. Limits on electioneering communications were upheld in *McConnell v. Federal Election Comm'n*, 540 U.S. 93, 203-209 (2003). The holding of *McConnell* rested to a large extent on an earlier case, *Austin v. Michigan Chamber of Commerce*, 494 U.S. 652 (1990). *Austin* had held that political speech may be banned based on the speaker's corporate identity.

In this case we are asked to reconsider *Austin* and, in effect, *McConnell*. We . . . hold that *stare decisis* does not compel the continued acceptance of *Austin*. The Government may regulate corporate political speech through disclaimer and disclosure requirements, but it may not suppress that speech altogether. We turn to the case now before us.

. . . .

III

. . . .

C

Our precedent is to be respected unless the most convincing of reasons demonstrates that adherence to it puts us on a course that is sure error. "Beyond workability, the relevant factors in deciding whether to adhere to the principle of *stare decisis* include the antiquity of the precedent, the reliance interests at stake, and of course whether the decision was well reasoned." *Montejo v. Louisiana*, [129 S. Ct. 2079, 2088-89 (2009)] (overruling *Michigan v. Jackson*, 475 U.S. 625 (1986)). We have also examined whether "experience has pointed up the precedent's shortcomings." *Pearson v. Callahan*, [129 S. Ct. 808, 816 (2009)] (overruling *Saucier v. Katz*, 533 U.S. 194 (2001)).

These considerations counsel in favor of rejecting *Austin*, which itself contravened this Court's earlier precedents in *Buckley* and *Bellotti*. "This Court has not hesitated to overrule decisions offensive to the First Amendment." *WRTL*, 551 U.S., at 500 (opinion of SCALIA, J.). "[S]tare decisis is a principle of policy and not a mechanical formula of adherence to the latest decision." *Helvering v. Hallock*, 309 U.S. 106, 119 (1940).

. . . [I]t must be concluded that *Austin* was not well reasoned. The Government defends *Austin*, relying almost entirely on "the quid pro quo interest, the corruption interest or the shareholder interest," and not *Austin's* expressed antidistortion rationale. . . . When neither party defends the reasoning of a precedent, the principle of adhering to that precedent through *stare decisis* is diminished. . . .

Austin is undermined by experience since its announcement. Political speech is so ingrained in our culture that speakers find ways to circumvent campaign finance laws. . . . Our Nation's speech dynamic is changing, and informative voices should not have to circumvent onerous restrictions to exercise their First Amendment rights. Speakers have become adept at presenting citizens with sound bites, talking points, and scripted messages that dominate the 24-hour news cycle. Corporations, like individuals, do not have monolithic views. On certain topics corporations may possess valuable expertise, leaving them the best equipped to point out errors or fallacies in speech of all sorts, including the speech of candidates and elected officials.

. . . .

No serious reliance interests are at stake. As the Court stated in *Payne v. Tennessee*, 501 U.S. 808, 828 (1991), reliance interests are important considerations in property and contract cases, where parties may have acted in conformance with existing legal rules in order to conduct transactions. Here, though, parties have been prevented from acting — corporations have been banned from making independent expenditures. Legislatures may have enacted bans on corporate expenditures believing that those bans were constitutional. This is not a compelling interest for *stare decisis*. If it were, legislative acts could prevent us from overruling our own precedents, thereby interfering with our duty "to say what the law is." *Marbury v. Madison*, 1 Cranch 137, 177 (1803).

Due consideration leads to this conclusion: *Austin*, 494 50 U.S. 652, should be and now is overruled. We return to the principle established in *Buckley* and *Bellotti* that the Government may not suppress political speech on the basis of the speaker's corporate identity. No sufficient governmental interest justifies limits on the political speech of nonprofit or for-profit corporations.

D

Austin is overruled, so it provides no basis for allowing the Government to limit corporate independent expenditures. . . .

. . . The *McConnell* Court relied on the antidistortion interest recognized in *Austin* to uphold a greater restriction on speech than the restriction upheld in *Austin*, . . . and we have found this interest unconvincing and insufficient. This part of *McConnell* is now overruled.

. . . .

Chief Justice ROBERTS, with whom Justice ALITO joins, concurring.

. . . .

II

. . . .

A

Fidelity to precedent — the policy of *stare decisis* — is vital to the proper exercise of the judicial function. "*Stare decisis* is the preferred course because it promotes the evenhanded, predictable, and consistent development of legal principles, fosters reliance on judicial decisions, and contributes to the actual and perceived integrity of the judicial process." *Payne v. Tennessee*, 501 U.S. 808, 827 (1991). For these reasons, we have long recognized that departures from precedent are inappropriate in the absence of a "special justification." *Arizona v. Rumsey*, 467 U.S. 203, 212 (1984).

At the same time, *stare decisis* is neither an "inexorable command," *Lawrence v. Texas*, 539 U.S. 558, 577 (2003), nor "a mechanical formula of adherence to the latest decision," *Helvering v. Hallock*, 309 U.S. 106, 119 (1940), especially in constitutional cases, *see United States v. Scott*, 437 U.S. 82, 101 (1978). If it were, segregation would be legal, minimum wage laws would be unconstitutional, and the Government could wiretap ordinary criminal suspects without first obtaining warrants. . . .

Stare decisis is instead a "principle of policy." *Helvering, supra,* at 119. . . .

. . . [W]e must keep in mind that *stare decisis* is not an end in itself. It is instead "the means by which we ensure that the law will not merely change erratically, but will develop in a principled and intelligible fashion." *Vasquez v. Hillery*, 474 U.S. 254, 265 (1986). Its greatest purpose is to serve a constitutional ideal — the rule of law. It follows that in the unusual circumstance when fidelity to any particular precedent does more to damage this constitutional ideal than to advance it, we must be more willing to depart from that precedent.

Thus, for example, if the precedent under consideration itself departed from the Court's jurisprudence, returning to the " 'intrinsically sounder' doctrine established in prior cases" may "better serv[e] the values of *stare decisis* than would following [the] more recently decided case inconsistent with the decisions that came before it." *Adarand Constructors, Inc. v. Peña*, 515 U.S. 200, 231 (1995). . . . Abrogating the errant precedent, rather than reaffirming or extending it, might better preserve the law's coherence and curtail the precedent's disruptive effects.

Likewise, if adherence to a precedent actually impedes the stable and orderly adjudication of future cases, its *stare decisis* effect is also diminished. This can happen in a number of circumstances, such as when the precedent's validity is so hotly contested that it cannot reliably function as a basis for decision in future cases, when its rationale threatens to upend our settled jurisprudence in related areas of law, and when the precedent's underlying reasoning has become so discredited that the Court cannot keep the precedent alive without jury-rigging new and different justifications to shore up the original mistake. *See, e.g., Pearson v. Callahan*, [129 S. Ct. 808, 817 (2009)]; *Montejo v. Louisiana*, [129 S. Ct. 2079, 2088-89 (2009)] (stare decisis does not control when adherence to the prior decision requires "fundamentally revising its theoretical basis").

B

These considerations weigh against retaining our decision in *Austin*. . . . *Austin*'s reasoning was — and remains — inconsistent with *Buckley*'s explicit repudiation of any government interest in "equalizing the relative ability of individuals and groups to influence the outcome of elections." 424 U.S., at 48-49. *Austin* was also inconsistent with *Bellotti*'s clear rejection of the idea that "speech that otherwise would be within the protection of the First Amendment loses that protection simply because its source is a corporation." 435 U.S., at 784. . . .

Second, the validity of *Austin*'s rationale . . . has proved to be the consistent subject of dispute among Members of this Court ever since. . . . The simple fact that one of our decisions remains controversial is, of course, insufficient to justify overruling it. But it does undermine the precedent's ability to contribute to the stable and orderly development of the law. In such circumstances, it is entirely appropriate for the Court — which in this case is squarely asked to reconsider *Austin*'s validity for the first time — to address the matter with a greater willingness to consider new approaches capable of restoring our doctrine to sounder footing.

Third, the *Austin* decision is uniquely destabilizing because it threatens to subvert our Court's decisions even outside the particular context of corporate express advocacy. The First Amendment theory underlying *Austin*'s holding is extraordinarily broad. *Austin*'s logic would authorize government prohibition of political speech by a category of speakers in the name of equality — a point that most scholars acknowledge (and many celebrate), but that the dissent denies. . . .

. . . .

These readings of *Austin* do no more than carry that decision's reasoning to its logical endpoint. In doing so, they highlight the threat Austin poses to First Amendment rights generally, even outside its specific factual context of corporate express advocacy. Because *Austin* is so difficult to confine to its facts — and because its logic threatens to undermine our First Amendment jurisprudence and the nature of public discourse more broadly — the costs of giving it *stare decisis* effect are unusually high.

Finally and most importantly, the Government's own effort to defend *Austin* — or, more accurately, to defend something that is not quite *Austin* — underscores its weakness as a precedent of the Court. . . .

Instead of endorsing *Austin* on its own terms, the Government urges us to reaffirm *Austin's* specific holding on the basis of two new and potentially expansive interests — the need to prevent actual or apparent quid pro quo corruption, and the need to protect corporate shareholders. *See* Supp. Brief for Appellee 8-10, 12-13. Those interests may or may not support the result in *Austin*, but they were plainly not part of the reasoning on which *Austin* relied.

. . . .

To the extent that the Government's case for reaffirming *Austin* depends on radically reconceptualizing its reasoning, that argument is at odds with itself. *Stare decisis* is a doctrine of preservation, not transformation. It counsels deference to past mistakes, but provides no justification for making new ones. There is therefore no basis for the Court to give precedential sway to reasoning that it has never accepted, simply because that reasoning happens to support a conclusion reached on different grounds that have since been abandoned or discredited.

Doing so would undermine the rule-of-law values that justify *stare decisis* in the first place. It would effectively license the Court to invent and adopt new principles of constitutional law solely for the purpose of rationalizing its past errors, without a proper analysis of whether those principles have merit on their own. This approach would allow the Court's past missteps to spawn future mistakes, undercutting the very rule-of-law values that *stare decisis* is designed to protect.

[T]he Government's new arguments must stand or fall on their own; they are not entitled to receive the special deference we accord to precedent. . . .

Because continued adherence to *Austin* threatens to subvert the "principled and intelligible" development of our First Amendment jurisprudence, *Vasquez*, 474 U.S., at 265, I support the Court's determination to overrule that decision.

* * *

. . . Congress violates the First Amendment when it decrees that some speakers may not engage in political speech at election time, when it matters most.

Justice STEVENS, with whom Justice GINSBURG, Justice BREYER, and Justice SOTO-MAYOR join, concurring in part and dissenting in part.

The real issue in this case concerns how, not if, the appellant may finance its electioneering. Citizens United is a wealthy nonprofit corporation that runs a political action committee (PAC) with millions of dollars in assets. Under the Bipartisan Campaign Reform Act of 2002 (BCRA), it could have used those assets to televise and promote *Hillary: The Movie* wherever and whenever it wanted to. It also could have spent unrestricted sums to broadcast *Hillary* at any time other than the 30 days before the last primary election. Neither Citizens United's nor any other corporation's speech has been "banned," *ante*, at 886. All that the parties dispute is whether Citizens United had a right to use the funds in its general treasury to pay for broadcasts during the 30-day period. The notion that the First Amendment dictates an affirmative answer to that question is, in my judgment, profoundly misguided. Even more misguided is the notion that the Court must rewrite the law relating to campaign expenditures by for-profit corporations and unions to decide this case.

. . . .

The majority's approach to corporate electioneering marks a dramatic break from our past. Congress has placed special limitations on campaign spending by corporations ever since the passage of the Tillman Act in 1907, ch. 420, 34 Stat. 864. We have unanimously concluded that this "reflects a permissible assessment of the dangers posed by those entities to the electoral process," *FEC v. National Right to Work Comm.*, 459 U.S. 197, 209 (1982) (NRWC), and have accepted the "legislative judgment that the special characteristics of the corporate structure require particularly careful regulation," *id.*, at 209-210. The Court today rejects a century of history when it treats the distinction between corporate and individual campaign spending as an invidious novelty born of *Austin v. Michigan Chamber of Commerce*, 494 U.S. 652 (1990).

. . . .

II

The final principle of judicial process that the majority violates is the most transparent: *stare decisis.* I am not an absolutist when it comes to *stare decisis,* in the campaign finance area or in any other. No one is. But if this principle is to do any meaningful work in supporting the rule of law, it must at least demand a significant justification, beyond the preferences of five Justices, for overturning settled doctrine. "[A] decision to overrule should rest on some special reason over and above the belief that a prior case was wrongly decided." *Planned Parenthood of Southeastern Pa. v. Casey*, 505 U.S. 833, 864 (1992). No such justification exists in this case, and to the contrary there are powerful prudential reasons to keep faith with our precedents. The Court's central argument for why *stare decisis* ought to be trumped is that it does not like *Austin.* The opinion "was not well reasoned," our colleagues assert, and it conflicts with First Amendment principles. *Ante,* at 47-48. This, of course, is the Court's merits argument, the many defects in which we will soon consider. I am perfectly willing to concede that if one of our precedents were dead wrong in its reasoning or irreconcilable with the rest of our doctrine, there would be a compelling basis for revisiting it. But neither is true of *Austin,* as I explain at length in Parts III and IV, *infra,* at 23-89, and restating a merits argument with additional vigor does not give it extra weight in the *stare decisis* calculus.

. . . .

The majority also contends that the Government's hesitation to rely on *Austin*'s antidistortion rationale "diminishe[s]" "the principle of adhering to that precedent." *Ante,* at 48;. . . . Why it diminishes the value of *stare decisis* is left unexplained. We have never thought fit to overrule a precedent because a litigant has taken any particular tack. Nor should we. Our decisions can often be defended on multiple grounds, and a litigant may have strategic or case-specific reasons for emphasizing only a subset of them. Members of the public, moreover, often rely on our bottom-line holdings far more than our precise legal arguments; surely this is true for the legislatures that have been regulating corporate electioneering since *Austin.* The task of evaluating the continued viability of precedents falls to this Court, not to the parties.

Although the majority opinion spends several pages making these surprising arguments, it says almost nothing about the standard considerations we have used to determine *stare decisis* value, such as the antiquity of the precedent, the workability of its legal rule, and the reliance interests at stake. It is also conspicuously silent about *McConnell*, even though the *McConnell* Court's decision to uphold BCRA §203 relied not only on the antidistortion logic of *Austin* but also on the statute's historical pedigree, *see, e.g.,* 540 U. S., at 115-132, 223-224, and the need to preserve the integrity of federal campaigns, *see id.,* at 126-129, 205-208, and n. 88.

We have recognized that "[s]*tare decisis* has special force when legislators or citizens 'have acted in reliance on a previous decision, for in this instance overruling the decision would dislodge settled rights and expectations or require an extensive legislative response.'" *Hubbard v. United States,* 514 U.S. 695, 714 (1995) (quoting *Hilton v. South Carolina Public Railways Comm'n,* 502 U.S. 197, 202 (1991)). *Stare decisis* protects not only personal rights involving property or contract but also the ability of the elected branches to shape their laws in an effective and coherent fashion. Today's decision takes away a power that we have long permitted these branches to exercise. State legislatures have relied on their authority to regulate corporate electioneering, confirmed in *Austin,* for more than a century. The Federal Congress has relied on this authority for a comparable stretch of time, and it specifically relied on *Austin* throughout the years it spent developing and debating BCRA. The total record it compiled was 100,000 pages long. Pulling out the rug beneath Congress after affirming the constitutionality of §203 six years ago shows great disrespect for a coequal branch.

By removing one of its central components, today's ruling makes a hash out of BCRA's "delicate and interconnected regulatory scheme." *McConnell,* 540 U.S., at 172. . . .

Beyond the reliance interests at stake, the other *stare decisis* factors also cut against the Court. Considerations of antiquity are significant for similar reasons. *McConnell* is only six years old, but *Austin* has been on the books for two decades, and many of the statutes called into question by today's opinion have been on the books for a half century or more. The Court points to no intervening change in circumstances that warrants revisiting *Austin.* Certainly nothing relevant has changed since we decided *WRTL* two Terms ago. And the Court gives no reason to think that *Austin* and *McConnell* are unworkable.

In fact, no one has argued to us that *Austin*'s rule has proved impracticable. . . . In the end, the Court's rejection of *Austin* and *McConnell* comes down to nothing more than its disagreement with their results. Virtually every one of its arguments was made and rejected in those cases, and the majority opinion is essentially an amalgamation of resuscitated dissents. The only relevant thing that has changed since *Austin* and *McConnell* is the composition of this Court. Today's ruling thus strikes at the vitals of *stare decisis,* "the means by which we ensure that the law will not merely change erratically, but will develop in a principled and intelligible fashion" that "permits society to presume that bedrock principles are founded in the law rather than in the proclivities of individuals." *Vasquez v. Hillery*, 474 U.S. 254, 265 (1986).

. . . .

V

. . . .

. . . At bottom, the Court's opinion is thus a rejection of the common sense of the American people, who have recognized a need to prevent corporations from undermining self-government since the founding, and who have fought against the distinctive corrupting potential of corporate electioneering since the days of Theodore Roosevelt. It is a strange time to repudiate that common sense. While American democracy is imperfect, few outside the majority of this Court would have thought its flaws included a dearth of corporate money in politics.

I would affirm the judgment of the District Court.

CHAPTER 7

THE LITIGATION PROCESS

§7.1 Preparing and Serving the Complaint

Litigation is a formal method for resolving a dispute in a socially acceptable manner. When we think of litigation, we are likely to think of a courtroom trial, usually followed by some sort of appeal to a higher court. A lawsuit commences when a plaintiff files a complaint with a court. A *complaint* is a legal document that, among other things, names the parties to the controversy, sets out the facts giving rise to the controversy, identifies the legal bases of the plaintiff's claims (for example, breach of contract, negligence, violations of a civil rights act), and specifies the types of remedies he or she wants the court to grant (for example, payment for lost wages, for medical expenses, or for pain and suffering). In essence, a well-drafted complaint tells a story and links that story to some recognized *cause of action*. Below is a sample complaint that might be used in a case in which the plaintiff is attempting to recover money for personal injuries.[1]

After filing the complaint with the court, the plaintiff must then serve the defendant with a copy of that complaint together with a *summons* (a document that requires the defendant to answer the complaint within a specified number of days). Sometimes it is difficult to complete service, especially if defendants go out of their way to avoid being served. In one case, for example, a North Carolina company instituted suit against a woman who owed the company over $300,000. For months, the plaintiff unsuccessfully tried to locate the woman so that she could be served with the complaint. Finally, the plaintiff hired a private detective. He discovered that the woman lived with a man who had been named as a defendant in other

---

[1] It would be a mistake to view litigation as synonymous with courtroom trials. Most litigation does not take place in a courtroom. A growing percentage of litigation is now being conducted privately through binding arbitration. The Federal Arbitration Act permits parties to contract away their normal right to sue in court and to replace that right with private arbitration. The Supreme Court, in a series of recent cases, has affirmed that an arbitration clause in a contract can oust a trial court of jurisdiction to hear the case. See Circuit City Stores, Inc. v. Adams, 532 U.S. 105 (2001). Also, a significant percentage of litigation is before state and federal administrative agencies. See, e.g., 5 U.S.C. §554 et seq. Depending on the agency, administrative adjudication can involve relatively simple disputes, such as whether an individual is entitled to receive Social Security Disability, or complex disputes such as determining the rates that interstate pipelines can charge their commercial customers. Arbitrations and administrative adjudications, although tending to be less formal than traditional courtroom litigation, can be every bit as intense and acrimonious as traditional litigation.

unrelated lawsuits and that he too was evading being served. The investigator also learned that neither the man nor the woman ever answered their door. Instead, their child would answer and find out whom the caller wanted to see. If the caller was looking for the man, the woman would then come to the door and tell the caller that he did not live there and that she had never heard of him. Similarly, if someone came around looking for the woman, the man would come to the door and state that the woman did not live there. After discovering this, the investigator knocked at the door and told the child that he was looking for the man. When the woman came to the door, she was served with the summons and complaint.

SAMPLE COMPLAINT

IN THE UNITED STATES DISTRICT COURT FOR THE CENTRAL DISTRICT OF CALIFORNIA

Alan Booth,	)	Civil Action No. 92-1456
	)	
Plaintiff,	)	Complaint
v.	)	
LifeAir, Inc., an Illinois Corporation	)	
Defendant.	)	

DISCUSSION

CAPTION — This is called the "caption" of the lawsuit and indicates the court, the parties, the Docket Number (Civil Action No.), and the type of pleading (e.g., Complaint). When the complaint is filed with the court, the clerk gives it a civil action number. All subsequent papers filed with the court will contain the identical caption and civil action number, except of course for the name of the document.

This is a diversity action to recover money damages for serious bodily injury caused when the defendant's oxygen system exploded in a hospital room where plaintiff was a patient. Plaintiff demands a trial by jury.

INTRODUCTION — Short statement summarizing the case. The plaintiff also indicates that he wants the case tried by a jury as opposed to a judge.

Jurisdiction

1. This court has jurisdiction on the basis of diversity of citizenship pursuant to 28 U.S.C. §1332. Venue is appropriate in this court under 28 U.S.C. §1391.

JURISDICTIONAL STATEMENT — Informs the court that it has jurisdiction to hear this case because it is one between citizens of different states (i.e., diversity jurisdiction).

Parties

2. The defendant LifeAir, Inc., is a corporation organized under the laws of Illinois with its principal place of business in that state.

3. The plaintiff Alan Booth is a citizen of the State of California. Plaintiff resides at 8230 Aorta Street, Los Angeles, California.

Background

4. At all times relevant to this case, defendant LifeAir, Inc. manufactured and distributed oxygen systems to hospitals and other health care providers in at least 25 states, including California. An oxygen system of the type manufactured by defendant consists of a metal tank which contains gaseous oxygen under extreme pressure. The pressure in the tank is regulated by a series of valves and gauges.

5. On or about June 26, 1990, defendant entered into a two-year contract with Mercy Hospital, Los Angeles, California. Under the terms of that contract, defendant agreed to supply Mercy with 100 tanks of oxygen each month. At the end of each month, defendant would pick up the empty tanks and replace them with full tanks of oxygen.

6. The oxygen tanks supplied to Mercy by defendant were manufactured by defendant at its Illinois manufacturing facility. The tanks were refilled by defendant at its Los Angeles facility and were to be used by Mercy without further inspection.

7. On or about May 15, 1991, defendant sent a letter to all of its customers, including Mercy, advising them that it was introducing a new, highly innovative oxygen tank, known as the OX-A100. According to the announcement, the new tank was extraordinarily light and furthermore, incorporated a "state-of-

PARTIES — Identifies the parties to the lawsuit. Notice how the plaintiff indicates that each party is a citizen of a different state. This is necessary because this is a "diversity" action in federal court.

BACKGROUND — Lays out the facts that give rise to the complaint by telling the court and the defendant how the plaintiff was injured. Notice that the section is organized chronologically, like a story. This complaint contains details that could only have been gathered with a fair amount of investigation or significant help from the hospital. Indeed, the detail should alert defense counsel to the likelihood that the hospital and plaintiff may be working together.

The facts contained in this section will be used to support recognized "causes of action" or "claims."

the-art" computerized valve system. On or about June 1, 1991, defendant supplied to Mercy 100 OX-A100 tanks.

8. On June 2, 1991, Alan Booth underwent delicate surgery at Mercy Hospital. Following surgery, an OX-A100 oxygen tank was placed in Booth's hospital room and the oxygen from the tank was supposed to assist him in breathing following the surgery. The tank was located no more than 5 feet from Booth.

9. Shortly thereafter, on June 2, 1991, defendant's OX-A100 oxygen tank exploded, seriously injuring Booth.

Claim I
Strict Liability

10. Plaintiff incorporates by reference the allegations set forth in ¶¶1-9, above.

11. Defendant's OX-A100 oxygen tank contained a defect in design or manufacture, or both, which made the tank unreasonably dangerous.

12. As a proximate cause of the defect noted above, the tank exploded, seriously and permanently injuring the plaintiff.

13. As a result, the plaintiff has incurred and will continue to incur medical expenses, lost wages, and pain and suffering, all in excess of $75,000.

Claim II
Negligence

14. Plaintiff incorporates by reference the allegations set forth in ¶¶1-9, above.

15. Defendant negligently designed or manufactured, or both, the OX-A100 oxygen tank.

16. As a proximate cause of the defendant's negligence, the tank exploded, seriously and permanently injuring the plaintiff.

CLAIM I—Strict Liability: Plaintiff uses the facts in the background section to satisfy each element of a strict liability claim.

To support a strict liability claim, plaintiff must allege that the product was defective and that as a result of the defect the plaintiff was injured and incurred damages. This causal link is called "proximate causation." Notice that the plaintiff alleges that the amount of his damages exceeds $75,000. This allegation is presented to satisfy the minimum amount of damages necessary for diversity jurisdiction.

CLAIM II—Negligence: Plaintiff uses the facts in the background section to satisfy each element of a negligence claim.

To support a negligence claim, plaintiff must allege that the product was negligently designed or manufactured or both and that as a result of the negligence the plaintiff was injured and incurred damages.

17. As a result, the plaintiff has incurred and will continue to incur medical expenses, lost wages, and pain and suffering, all in excess of $50,000.

THEREFORE, plaintiff requests that the court enter judgment in his favor and against the defendant

a. For damages in such amounts as to compensate the plaintiff for injuries sustained as a result of the defendant's conduct as described above;
b. For court costs and post-judgment interest; and
c. For such other relief as the court deems appropriate.

RELIEF—Plaintiff sets forth the remedies that he is asking the court to grant.

Ames, Fisher & Chun
Albert Ames (Bar #4350045)
113 Main Street
Smallville, California 91607
(818) 555-1234
Attorney for Plaintiff

SIGNATURE—Complaint must be signed by an attorney or by the plaintiff. Many jurisdictions require the attorney to note his or her bar number.

§7.2 Pretrial Proceedings and Procedures

Drafting and filing the complaint and perfecting service on the defendant represent only the initial phase of litigation. The subsequent steps are designed to ready the case for trial by narrowing down the factual differences, resolving legal issues, and providing the parties with opportunities to settle the matter short of trial. For purposes of simplicity, it may be helpful to view the pretrial happenings as falling into three categories: (1) responsive pleadings; (2) discovery; and (3) pretrial statements.

§7.2.1 Responsive Pleadings: Responding to the Complaint

§7.2.1.1 The Answer

Once a defendant has been served with the complaint, he or she is required to file some sort of response. In the federal system, the response usually must be filed within 20 days of the date that service is perfected.[2] The initial response can

---

[2] The federal government is normally given 60 days in which to file an answer to a complaint. This time period may vary, though, depending on the type of action involved. For instance, in suits

take a variety of forms. One common response is called an answer. One purpose of an answer is to flesh out those factual aspects of the case where the plaintiff and defendant agree and to highlight those where they disagree. A typical answer consists of two parts. In the first part, the defendant responds to each of the factual allegations in the complaint by either admitting that a given allegation is true or denying that allegation. In the second part of the answer, the defendant can set forth certain affirmative defenses. For example, a defendant might allege as an affirmative defense that the statute of limitations has run (that is, the plaintiff waited too long to file suit). Below is a sample answer that defendant might use to respond to the sample complaint in *Booth v. LifeAir*.

<u>SAMPLE ANSWER</u>

IN THE UNITED STATES DISTRICT COURT FOR THE CENTRAL DISTRICT OF CALIFORNIA

Alan Booth,	)	Civil Action No. 92-1456
	)	
	)	
Plaintiff,	)	Answer
	)	
	)	
v.	)	
	)	
LifeAir, Inc., an Illinois	)	
Corporation	)	
	)	
Defendant.	)	

The defendant, LifeAir, Inc., answers the plaintiff's Complaint in the above-captioned matter as follows:

1. Defendant lacks sufficient information to respond to the allegations contained in ¶1 of the Complaint and, therefore, denies each allegation in that paragraph.
2. Defendant admits the allegations set forth in ¶2 of the Complaint.

---

arising under the Freedom of Information Act, the federal government must respond within 20 days, and in suits arising under the National Childhood Vaccine Compensation Act, the government is required to respond within 45 days.

3. Defendant lacks sufficient information to respond to the allegations contained in ¶3 of the Complaint and, therefore, denies each allegation in that paragraph.
4. Defendant admits the allegations contained in the first sentence of ¶4, and denies the allegations set forth in the remainder of that paragraph.
5. Defendant admits the allegations contained in the first sentence of ¶5, and denies the allegations set forth in the remainder of that paragraph.
6. Defendant denies the allegations in ¶6 to the extent that those allegations imply that all of the oxygen tanks supplied to Mercy by the defendant were manufactured at its Illinois facility and refilled at its Los Angeles facility. Defendant further denies the allegation that the oxygen systems supplied to Mercy by defendant were to be used by Mercy without further inspection.
7. Defendant admits the allegations contained in ¶7 of the Complaint.
8. Defendant lacks sufficient information to respond to the allegations contained in ¶¶8 and 9 of the Complaint and, therefore, denies each allegation in those paragraphs.
9. Defendant responds to the allegations in ¶10 by incorporating ¶¶1-8 of its Answer.
10. Defendant denies the allegations in ¶¶11-13.
11. Defendant responds to the allegations in ¶14 by incorporating ¶¶1-8 of its Answer.
12. Defendant denies the allegations in ¶¶14-17.
13. Defendant further denies that it is liable to the plaintiff in any sum and asks that judgment be entered in favor of the defendant and against the plaintiff.

Affirmative Defenses

FIRST DEFENSE

The Complaint fails to state a claim upon which relief may be granted, because plaintiff's action is preempted by the provisions of the Federal Food, Drug, and Cosmetic Act.

SECOND DEFENSE

Plaintiff's injuries, if any, were caused by a third party and not by the defendant.

THIRD DEFENSE

The product in question was used by a third party not in accordance with the manufacturer's instructions and that use was the sole cause of the injuries the plaintiff allegedly sustained.

Claire Winston, Esq. (Bar 44603)
Johnson & Winston
16144 Gold Coast Avenue
Los Angeles, CA 96387
(213) 555-1212
Attorneys for defendant LifeAir, Inc.

§7.2.1.2 *Motion to Dismiss*

Rather than immediately filing an answer, a defendant may choose to file a motion to dismiss, which if granted by the trial court would terminate the suit immediately. A *motion to dismiss* is a direct challenge to the legal sufficiency of the complaint. For example, suppose that the suit in *Booth v. LifeAir* was filed on July 2, 1992, 13 months after the oxygen tank exploded. In California, suits to recover for personal injury must be filed within one year of the date of the injury — that is, the statute of limitations is one year. Thus, LifeAir could move to dismiss because the statute of limitations had run before the suit was filed. As you will learn in your civil procedure class, there are a variety of grounds on which a defendant can move to dismiss a complaint. A motion to dismiss, though, has one important limitation: When a court passes on the validity of the motion, it can only consider what has been presented in the complaint and, furthermore, the court must assume that all of the allegations in that complaint are true. For instance, if Booth did not state in the complaint the date on which the oxygen tank exploded, LifeAir could not file a motion to dismiss because it would not be apparent from the face of the complaint that the statute of limitations had run.

§7.2.1.3 *Motion for Summary Judgment*

A motion to dismiss does not provide a terribly efficient means of disposing of meritless lawsuits because a court must assume, when ruling on that motion, that all the allegations in the complaint are true. As long as the plaintiff's allegations are legally sufficient, a court is duty bound to deny a motion to dismiss even though the court may know that the plaintiff will never be able to prove the allegations in his or her complaint. A motion for summary judgment (*see* Fed. R. Civ. P. 56(b)) is designed to fill this gap; it provides the courts with a way of "weeding out" meritless cases. It is designed to permit an early resolution to a case.

Summary judgment means a judgment without a trial; it can be entered in favor of either party. Summary judgment, however, is only appropriate if the evidence before the court indicates that there are no disputed issues of material fact and that the party making the motion is entitled to prevail on the undisputed facts. If there is a dispute over a material fact, then the court must deny the motion for summary judgment and permit the case to go to trial. The party against whom a summary judgment motion is filed does not have to prove his or her case in order to defeat the motion. All that party has to do is present *some* evidence that a material fact is in dispute. It is then up to the jury (if the case is tried before a jury) to figure out whose version is correct.

For example, in the sample complaint, *Booth v. LifeAir*, the plaintiff alleged that the oxygen tank that exploded in his hospital room had been manufactured and distributed to the hospital by the defendant, LifeAir. LifeAir, in its answer, denied that the tank that exploded was one of its products. Suppose that during the course of discovery LifeAir learns that Mercy Hospital also purchased some of its oxygen tanks from another company, one of LifeAir's competitors. LifeAir, after reviewing Mercy's inventory records, discovers that after the explosion there were still 100 LifeAir tanks in the hospital. If the explosion had involved a LifeAir tank, there should only have been 99 tanks. LifeAir also learns that the hospital is unable to account for one of its competitor's tanks. To get to the bottom of the matter, LifeAir is provided with a piece of metal from the exploded tank. A metallurgical analysis reveals that the metal is not the type used by LifeAir but rather is identical to the metal used by its competitor.

Given all of this information, LifeAir is now in a position to file a motion for summary judgment. It attaches to its motion the hospital's inventory records and an affidavit from its expert metallurgist. In its motion, LifeAir argues that the plaintiff named the wrong defendant because the tank that exploded was not a LifeAir product. If the plaintiff, Booth, cannot produce some evidence rebutting LifeAir's evidence, then there is no genuine dispute over a material fact — that the tank that exploded was not a LifeAir product — and the court should enter a summary judgment.

However, suppose that Booth also has the metal tested by an expert retained by his attorney. That expert disagrees with LifeAir's expert and she concludes that the metal came from a LifeAir tank and not from a tank manufactured by Life-Air's competitor. Even though LifeAir's evidence is stronger (metallurgist plus inventory records) than Booth's evidence (metallurgist only), the court should deny LifeAir's summary judgment motion because there is now a genuine dispute over which company manufactured the tank. The jury will be left to decide which party is correct.

§7.2.2 Discovery: Discovering What Happened

In the federal system and in all of the state systems, there are elaborate rules that permit the parties in civil actions to get a better idea of what really happened and what evidence the other side plans to introduce at trial. The discovery process, as it is known, is designed to minimize unpleasant surprises during the trial. As a result of discovery, each party should know, well before the trial ever starts, the identities of the witnesses whom the other party will call to testify, the nature of their testimony, and the documents that the other side will attempt to introduce into evidence. Aside from helping to shape trial strategy, discovery serves other critical purposes. First, it provides each party with sufficient information to objectively judge the merits of its case. Consequently, discovery ought to help the parties settle their dispute, thereby eliminating the need for an expensive and time-consuming trial. Second, discovery, if conducted in good faith, should also help the parties narrow the questions of fact that need to be resolved at trial, thereby shortening the trial.

All too frequently, though, discovery itself is extraordinarily expensive and time-consuming. In many cases, the parties spend more time fighting over the scope of discovery than actually trying the case.

There are a variety of different types of discovery, each with its own set of rules and procedures. Since this section is intended to provide you with an overview of the litigation process, we will describe only briefly some of the more common types of discovery. You will learn the limitations, intricacies, and nuances of the various discovery techniques in your civil procedure course.

§7.2.2.1 Interrogatories

Interrogatories are written questions drafted by one party and intended to be answered by the other party. Normally, only parties to a lawsuit can be compelled to answer written interrogatories. While a party has wide latitude in developing interrogatories, some courts restrict the number of questions that can be asked.

Another type of discovery that is closely related to interrogatories is known as *requests for admissions*. Requests for admissions consist of a set of factual statements prepared by one party and sent to an opposing party. The party that receives the document is required to either admit or deny the validity of each assertion.

§7.2.2.2 Document Production

Each side in a dispute normally asks the other to produce documents in its possession that meet certain critieria. In federal courts, document production is governed by Fed. R. Civ. P. 34, and most states have comparable rules. Under Rule 34, "[a]ny party may serve on any other party a request . . . to produce and permit the party making the request . . . to inspect and copy, any designated documents." Fed. R. Civ. P. 34(a). "The request shall set forth, either by individual item or by category, the items to be inspected and describe each with reasonable particularity." In practice, each side usually copies or scans its own documents and forwards them to the other side either in hard copy or on a CD or DVD.

Before a party produces its documents, it normally goes through each page of each document to make certain that the document does not contain material protected either by the attorney-client privilege or the attorney work-product privilege. *See Hickman v. Taylor*, 329 U.S. 495 (1947) (establishing the attorney work-product privilege). Materials protected by either privilege and that consequently will not be provided to the other side must be listed on a "privilege log," which is provided to the opposing side along with the documents produced. *See* Fed. R. Civ. P. 26(b)(5). The privilege log allows the receiving party to see which documents the other side has declined to produce and the reason why. The log must be detailed enough to allow the other side to evaluate the merit of the claimed privilege.

Because so much of discovery is now done using computers (for example, through the production of CDs and DVDs) and because more and more communication is being done through electronic mail, the Federal Rules of Civil Procedure have recently been modified to take into account electronic communications, both for filing documents and providing notices and for purposes of discovery. *See* Letter from Chief Justice Roberts to the Speaker of the House of Representatives and Vice President of the United States transmitting amendments to the Federal Rules of Civil Procedure (April 12, 2006).

§7.2.2.3 *Depositions*

A *deposition* is an oral examination of a person under oath conducted by an attorney representing one of the parties. A party can depose any person who has evidence relevant to the case. The person being deposed does not have to be a party to the case. After the party that has initiated the deposition has completed his or her questioning, the other parties are permitted to question the witness.

Depositions are normally conducted in the office of one of the attorneys. The questions and answers are transcribed by a court reporter and can be used not only for certain purposes during the trial but to flesh out the facts in the event that a party wishes to file a motion for summary judgment.

§7.3 The Trial Brief

Once discovery has been completed, most courts require the parties in civil cases to submit trial briefs. A *trial brief* is a detailed outline of a party's case. The typical trial brief includes, among other things, a listing of each element of each claim that the party intends to prove at trial, along with the names of the witnesses and the documentary evidence that will be used to prove that element. The court may also require the parties to review the documentary evidence and other tangible exhibits that will be offered into evidence at trial and to stipulate beforehand, wherever possible, to the authenticity of a given piece of evidence. These stipulations are designed to streamline the actual trial by eliminating the need for a witness to authenticate a given exhibit.

Frequently, well before trial, a party may become aware of certain types of evidence which the opposing party may seek to introduce, but which the party believes to be legally objectionable. As part of the trial brief, a party may seek an advance ruling from the court concerning the admissibility of such evidence. This is often done through a "motion *in limine.*"

In cases that will be tried before a jury, the trial brief will contain a party's proposed jury instructions. *Jury instructions* are the rules of law that the court will read to the jury immediately before the jury begins its deliberations. Each party is responsible for assembling a complete packet of proposed jury instructions, together with the relevant statutory and case law supporting each proposed instruction. The instructions that the judge actually reads to the jury will usually be drawn from the proposed instructions submitted by the parties.

§7.4 The Trial

Finally, after conducting innumerable depositions, drafting and arguing countless motions, reviewing and summarizing hundreds of documents, interviewing scores of witnesses, and engaging in many agonizing settlement conferences, your case is called for trial. All of your thorough pretrial preparation will give way to intense pretrial anxiety: Your stomach may knot up, you may wonder whether you are really prepared, and you may even conjure up the specter of your star witness being demolished during cross-examination. These are natural emotions and ones that you are likely to experience no matter how many cases you have tried. Indeed, some experienced trial attorneys have likened the opening morning of a trial to the opening night of a Broadway play — only without a script.

If you are about to start your first trial, these anxieties are likely to be amplified by fear of the unknown. You will be surprised by the number of seemingly trivial questions that will race through your mind when you enter the courtroom. Where should I sit? Should I look at the jury? How much latitude will the judge give me in questioning prospective jurors? These are a few of the questions that are not addressed in most law schools because the answers are best learned through experience.

In the following pages, we will outline the various stages of the typical civil trial and will emphasize those phases that normally receive scant attention in law school. However, we are doing so only to provide you with a context in which to better understand and appreciate the case materials that you will be reading in your other courses. This section is not intended to be a primer on trial practice.

§7.4.1 Selecting the Jury

If a case is being tried before a jury, the first phase involves the selection of that jury. In civil actions, the size of the jury will vary from jurisdiction to jurisdiction. Typically, civil juries range in size from six to twelve jurors. Since the rules governing jury selection vary greatly from court to court and even from judge to judge, we will present only one of a number of possible methods.

Before the trial begins, court personnel will escort a large number of prospective jurors into the courtroom. Counsel for both parties will be provided with a list of the names, addresses, and perhaps professions of these individuals. The judge will then introduce the parties and their attorneys and will briefly tell the prospective jurors the type of case that will be tried. The judge will then ask the prospective jurors, usually en masse, a number of basic questions designed to determine if any members of the panel would be unable to judge the case without bias. For example, the judge might ask whether any prospective juror knows the parties, their attorneys, or any of the witnesses. Thereafter, the clerk of the court will randomly draw the names of a number of prospective jurors equal to the size of the jury. Thus, if the jury is to consist of six jurors, the clerk will draw six names. Those individuals will then be seated in the jury box, and the judge might then ask each of those individuals a series of more detailed questions. Many of these questions will have been submitted by the attorneys in advance in the trial briefs. In some courts, the attorneys may be given an opportunity to question each of these individuals. After the questioning has been completed, the court will ask each attorney if he or she wishes to challenge any juror for cause — that is, to ask the court to remove a prospective juror because the attorney believes that that juror will be unable to discharge his or her responsibilities in an unbiased manner. If a juror is removed for cause, the clerk will draw another name and that juror will be seated in place of the one who was stricken for cause. This new juror will then be asked a series of questions by the judge and perhaps by the attorneys. This process will continue until all parties have "passed for cause." Thereafter, each side will be given the opportunity to exercise a limited number of peremptory challenges, which means they may ask to strike any juror as a matter of right and without reason. Jurors who have been peremptorily challenged are replaced, and the process continues until both parties pass or exhaust their peremptory challenges, whichever occurs first.

§7.4.2 Opening Statements

After the jury has been empaneled, counsel for each party is given the opportunity to make an opening statement to the jury, with plaintiff's counsel going first. In the opening statement, the attorney will outline her case and detail what she intends to prove at trial. An opening statement, unlike a closing argument, should not be argumentative.

§7.4.3 The Cases-in-Chief

Following the opening statements, each party will be given an opportunity to present its case-in-chief, with the plaintiff again going first. The plaintiff will then call her first witness. Each witness who is called will be subjected to a direct examination by the party that called him or her, followed by cross-examination. After the cross-examination, the witness may be subjected to a redirect examination and a recross-examination. After the plaintiff has presented all of her witnesses, the plaintiff's case-in-chief is concluded and the plaintiff will "rest."

After the plaintiff has rested, the defendant presents his case-in-chief. The evidence introduced by the defendant should not only undercut the plaintiff's case, it should also support whatever affirmative defenses the defendant may have raised (for example, contributory negligence). Normally, a defendant will have both the burden of producing evidence (that is, introducing the first evidence) and the burden of proof (that is, proving the point by a preponderance of the evidence) with respect to each affirmative defense.

§7.4.4 Motions after the Cases-in-Chief

At the conclusion of each party's case-in-chief, the opposing party, out of the jury's presence, may move for a directed verdict. For example, a defendant's motion for a directed verdict is a challenge to the sufficiency of the plaintiff's case-in-chief. The defendant is asking the court to take the case away from the jury and end the trial immediately because either the plaintiff has failed to present evidence supporting an essential element of the claim or the evidence presented was so weak that no rational jury could find for the plaintiff. In short, a motion for a directed verdict tests whether the party against whom the motion has been filed has discharged its burden of producing evidence.

§7.4.5 Rebuttal

After the parties have presented their cases-in-chief — and assuming that the court denies the various motions for a directed verdict — the plaintiff will be given a limited opportunity to introduce evidence rebutting the evidence presented during the defendant's case-in-chief. The defendant is then given an opportunity to present evidence rebutting evidence presented during the plaintiff's rebuttal. It is important to recognize, though, that the scope of a rebuttal is limited to challenging evidence presented by the opposing party. Thus, a plaintiff may not use the rebuttal to cure defects in his or her case-in-chief.

§7.4.6 Closing the Trial

After the evidentiary phase of the trial has ended, the parties make their closing arguments to the jury. A closing argument should be designed to convince the jury of the merits of a party's case. An effective closing argument will link the evidence presented to the law that the judge will read to the jury. Thus, if a given claim has four elements, the plaintiff's closing argument should highlight the evidence that has been presented to support each of these four elements and should aim to convince the jury that such evidence is more reliable and credible than the contrary evidence presented by the defendant.

Following closing arguments, the judge will *charge* the jury; that is to say, the judge will read to the jury the instructions of law that the jury must use in resolving the case. The jury will then retire to deliberate its verdict.

§7.4.7 Motions Following the Verdict

The case does not end with a jury verdict. Rather, following the jury verdict, the parties may make a number of motions designed to overturn or modify that verdict.

§7.4.7.1 Motion for a Judgment Notwithstanding the Verdict

One common post-trial motion filed by the party against whom the jury verdict was rendered is called a *motion for a judgment notwithstanding the verdict* or, simply, a motion for a judgment n.o.v. In federal courts, a judgment n.o.v. is now called a "judgment as a matter of law." Fed. R. Civ. P. 50. As its name implies, this motion is designed to nullify and take the place of the jury verdict. A motion for a judgment n.o.v. is similar to a motion for a directed verdict and the same criteria apply.

§7.4.7.2 *Motion for a New Trial*

Another device designed to overturn a jury verdict is a *motion for a new trial*. In a motion for a new trial, a party seeks only to abrogate the jury verdict and not to have the court substitute its verdict for that of the jury. If a court were to grant a motion for a judgment n.o.v., it would enter a judgment in favor of the moving party. In contrast, if a court were to grant a motion for a new trial, it would set aside the jury verdict and order the case tried for a second time.

ANALYZING CASES AND STATUTES

CHAPTER 8

INSIDE A JUDICIAL OPINION ("A CASE")

§8.1 What's in a Judicial Opinion

When law teachers refer to "a case," they mean a judicial opinion through which a court makes a decision. A judicial opinion can include up to ten ingredients:

1. the case name and citation
2. the factual story (what happened *before* the lawsuit began)
3. the procedural story (what happened *during* the lawsuit)
4. the issue or issues to be decided by the court
5. the arguments made by each side
6. the court's holding on each issue
7. the rule or rules of law the court enforces through each holding
8. the court's reasoning
9. dicta
10. the remedy the court granted or denied

Most opinions don't include *all* these things, although a typical opinion probably has most of them.

When you first look at an opinion, it can seem mysterious. Reading the opinion is a lot easier if you label each passage as one or another of these ingredients. That breaks the opinion down into smaller chunks so that you can more easily understand its parts. It also helps you see how the parts are related to each other and produce the court's decision.

The *case name* is made up of the names of the plaintiff and defendant separated by "v." (That's how lawyers abbreviate "versus.") The *citation* is the volume, publication, and page where opinion can be found, together with the date.

Opinions often begin with the *factual story*. What did the parties and other people do before the lawsuit began? The court can know this story from what the parties allege in their pleadings or from what the witnesses testify to or what other evidence shows. For that reason, sometimes it's hard to separate this part of the opinion from the next part (the procedural story).

Often the court will next describe the *procedural story*, which lawyers and teachers more often call the *procedural history*. What did the lawyers and judges do? Examples are motions, trial, judgment, and appeal. Although a court might ascribe a procedural action to a party ("The defendant moved to dismiss . . ."), that's really a lawyer's work. As you will learn later in this book, and in your course in Civil Procedure, the manner in which an issue is raised determines the method a court will use to decide it.

A court might also set out — or at least imply — the *issue or issues* to be decided and *the arguments* made by each side. A court will further state, or at least imply, the *holding* on each of the issues and the *rule or rules of law* the court enforces in making each holding, together with the *reasoning* — often called the *rationale* — for its decision. The reasoning often discusses or hints at the *policy* behind the rules the court enforces. A rule's policy is its purpose, what the law tries to accomplish generally through the rule. Somewhere in the opinion, the court might place some *dicta*, which is discussion unnecessary to support a holding and therefore not part of binding precedent.

An opinion usually ends with *the relief granted or denied*. If the opinion is the decision of an appellate court, the relief may be an affirmance or a reversal of the lower court's decision. If the opinion is from a trial court, the relief is most commonly the granting or denial of a motion.

In an appellate court, several judges will decide together. An appellate court's decision is announced in *the court's opinion* or *the majority opinion*. If one of the judges does not agree with some aspect of the decision, that judge may write a *concurrence* or *dissent*. A dissenting judge thinks the court reached the wrong result. A concurring judge agrees with the result the majority reached but would have used different reasoning to get there. Concurrences and dissents are not binding precedent. Only the court's opinion has that authority.

§8.2 Why Reading in Law School is Different — and What to do about it

In college, most assigned reading is in textbooks. Textbook authors try to write in a way that communicates efficiently to their audience, which is primarily students.

Law school is different. Law students read mostly judicial opinions and statutes. A judge writing a judicial opinion does not wonder, "How should I write this so that any first-year law student can understand it?" A judge instead writes for an audience of lawyers and judges — who quickly understand wording and concepts that may baffle students.

Several studies have shown that an important part of success in the first year of law school is learning to read the way that experienced lawyers do.[1]

---

[1] See Ruth Ann McKinney's book, *Reading Like a Lawyer: Time-Saving Strategies for Reading Law Like an Expert* (2005), as well as the following law review articles: Leah M. Christensen, *Legal Reading and Success in Law School: An Empirical Study*, 30 Seattle U. L. Rev. 603 (2007); Laurel

Experienced lawyers don't move from sentence to sentence waiting for meaning to appear. Instead, they read *aggressively*, dissecting the opinion as they go through it.

You can start to develop this skill by carving up judicial opinions, looking for the ingredients listed at the beginning of this chapter and marking each ingredient with handwritten notes in the margin. Experienced lawyers identify the ingredients quickly and almost unconsciously. Because of their experience, they no longer need to write notes in the margin, but they instantly recognize, for example, the end of the factual story and the beginning of the procedural story. They also interpret to find meaning at every step along the way, asking themselves questions like, "Now that I know the factual story, what does that tell me about what's going on here?"

Learning how to read like a professional takes time. Most law students are challenged by this task at the beginning, but within a few months they will begin to become more efficient. You will see much more meaning in what you read and take less time to read it. But it will take time and work to get there.

Currie Oates, *Beating the Odds: Reading Strategies of Law Students Admitted through Alternative Admissions Programs*, 83 Iowa L. Rev. 139 (1997).

CHAPTER 9

READING A CASE FOR ISSUES, RULES, AND DETERMINATIVE FACTS

§9.1 How to Identify Issues, Rules, and Determinative Facts

Many facts are mentioned in an opinion just to provide background, continuity, or what journalists call "human interest." Of the remaining facts, some are related to the court's thinking but are not crucial. Still others *caused* the court to come to its decision.

This last group could be called the *determinative facts* or the *essential facts.* They're essential to the court's decision because they determined the outcome: if they had been different, the decision would have been different. The determinative facts lead to the *rule of the case* — the rule of law for which the case stands as precedent — and discovering that rule is the most important goal of reading cases. Of course, when several issues are raised together in a case, the court must make several rulings and an opinion may thus stand for several different rules.

The determinative facts can be identified by asking the following question: *If a particular fact had not happened, or if it had happened differently, would the court have made a different decision?* If so, it's one of the determinative facts. This can be illustrated through an example of a decision that has nothing to do with law.

Suppose you're trying to find a place where you can live while attending school. A rental agent has just shown you an apartment. The following are also true:

A. The apartment is located half a mile from the law school.
B. It is a studio apartment (one room plus a kitchenette and bathroom).
C. The building appears to be well maintained and safe.
D. The apartment is at the corner of the building, and windows on two sides provide ample light and ventilation.
E. It is on the third floor, away from the street, and the neighbors do not appear to be disagreeable.
F. The rent is $500 per month, furnished.

G. You have a widowed aunt, with whom you get along well and who lives alone in a house 45 minutes by bus from the law school, and she has offered to let you use the second floor of her house during the school year. The house and neighborhood are safe and quiet, and the living arrangements would be satisfactory to you.

H. You have taken out substantial loans to go to law school.

I. You neither own nor have access to a car.

J. Reliable local people have told you that you're not likely to find an apartment that is better, cheaper, or more convenient than the one you have just inspected.

Which facts are *essential* to your decision? For example, if the apartment had been two miles from the law school (rather than a half-mile), would your decision have been different? If the answer is no, fact A could not be determinative. It might be part of the factual mosaic and might explain why you looked at the apartment in the first place, but you would not base your decision on it.

The determinative facts, the issue, the holding, and the rule all depend on each other. In the apartment hypothetical, for example, if the issue were different — say, "How should I respond to an offer to join the American Automobile Association?" — the selection of determinative facts would also change. (In fact, the only determinative one would be fact I: "You neither own nor have access to a car.") You will often find yourself using what the court tells you about the issue or the holding to fill in what the court has not told you about the determinative facts, and vice versa.

Often, courts do not explicitly state the issue, the holding, or the rule for which the case stands as precedent, and courts do not usually label the determinative facts as such. Whenever a court gives less than a full explanation, we have to use what's explicitly stated to pin down what's only implied.

If the court states the issue but doesn't identify the rule or specify which facts are determinative, you might discover the rule and the determinative facts by answering the following questions:

Who is suing whom over what series of events and to get what relief?
What issue does the court say it intends to decide?
How does the court decide that issue?
On what facts does the court rely in making that decision?
What rule does the court enforce?

Facts from a case can often be reformulated to be more general than the court described them. In the hypothetical above, for example, a generalized reformulation of fact G might be the following: "You have a rent-free alternative to the apartment, but the alternative would require 45 minutes of travel each way plus the expense of public transportation." Why would you generalize the facts in this way? The generalized version of the facts can supply a guide to deciding later cases where the factual details are not identical. For example, suppose a later case involves a person who is a member of the clergy in a religious organization that has granted a leave of absence to attend law school and who may continue to live rent-free in the satisfactory quarters the religious organization has provided, but getting to the law school would require walking for 15 minutes and then riding a subway for 30 minutes, at the same cost as a bus ride. Isn't this really the same situation, but with different details? The generalized reformulation covers both sets of facts.

§9.2 Formulating a Narrow, Middling, or Broad Rule

When a court does not state a rule of the case, you might be able to formulate the rule by converting the determinative facts into elements of a rule. Often, you can interpret the determinative facts narrowly (specifically) or broadly (generically). Notice how different formulations of a rule can be extracted from the apartment example. If the student decides to stay with the aunt, a narrow rule formulation might be the following:

> A law student who has a choice between renting an apartment and living in the second floor of an aunt's house should choose the latter when the student has had to borrow money to go to law school and when the apartment's rent is $500 per month but the aunt's second floor is free except for bus fares.

Because this formulation is limited to the specific facts given in the hypothetical, it could directly govern only a tiny number of future decision-makers. But it could be stated more broadly to govern a wider range of situations:

> A student on a tight budget should not pay rent when a nearly free alternative is available.

An even more general formulation would govern an even wider circle of applications:

> A person with limited funds should not lease property when there is a satisfactory and nearly free alternative.

The following, however, is so broad as to be meaningless:

> A person should not spend money unnecessarily.

CHAPTER 10

BRIEFING CASES

To understand case law, a lawyer must read and interpret the written decisions of judges. The lawyer looks for cues from the language of the opinion, evaluating the meaning and significance of each cue and synthesizing the results. Thus, the lawyer creates an interpretation that synthesizes the facts, the result, and the judge's explanation of that result. One can even say that a lawyer "constructs" the law through this interpretive process. The starting point for learning this interpretive process is the case brief.[1]

§10.1 Introduction to Case Briefing

A case brief is a method for reading, analyzing, and making notes about a case. Formats and preferred methods for case briefing vary widely, partly because case briefs are personal study tools. People process information differently, so they develop personalized study methods that best accommodate their own learning styles.

Briefing formats differ also according to the legal task to be performed. When you brief a case for your torts class, your most immediate goal is to be ready to answer classroom questions about the case. Your torts professor might have given you a format to use, or you might be able to devise your own format based on your observations of the kinds of questions your professor tends to ask.

When you brief cases for a legal writing assignment, however, your purpose is different in several ways. First, you have a hypothetical client with a set of facts and a specific legal question to answer. Having a discrete task means you can focus your case brief on the aspects of the case most applicable to your client's facts. Second, you will be reading many cases on a particular legal point, not just

---

[1] The term "brief" is also used to refer to a formal court document a lawyer submits to a judge to advocate for a favorable ruling in a case. A case brief often is called simply a "brief," so some confusion of terminology is possible. Usually, though, the context will clarify the meaning.

one or two. Your assignment will require you not only to understand the case you are reading, but also to understand how it relates to a number of other cases on the same point. This broader task requires you to notice additional features about the case. Third, you will be writing a document (perhaps an office memo or a memorandum of law) describing the case and referring to its language. Therefore, you will need to be able to find the case again, and you will need to take more careful notes about the parts you anticipate describing in your office memo or memorandum of law. These notes will save you time when you are writing, and they will save you from committing plagiarism.

The following section sets out a suggested format for briefing the cases you read as part of your legal writing assignment. You might find that much of this format also works well in your other courses. The key is to remember that case briefing is a personal study tool, so adapt the format freely to fit your own learning style and your particular analytical task.

§10.2 A Format for Case Briefing

Read the case through once before you start to write, perhaps underlining or highlighting a bit. Then read the case again, this time making the following notations:

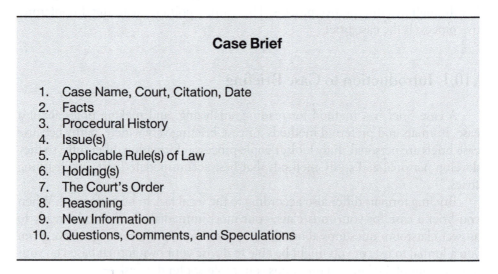

Case Brief

1. Case Name, Court, Citation, Date
2. Facts
3. Procedural History
4. Issue(s)
5. Applicable Rule(s) of Law
6. Holding(s)
7. The Court's Order
8. Reasoning
9. New Information
10. Questions, Comments, and Speculations

Case Name, Court, Citation, Date. You will need to know the name of the court and the date so you can examine how this case fits with other cases and gauge its precedential value for your assignment. Also, correctly recording these pieces of information during your research stage will save you time and frustration when you start to write.

Facts. Describe in your own words the facts of the case. You need include only the facts that pertain to the legal issues relevant to your assignment. For example, if the case concerns a dispute over whether a person revoked her will before she died, normally you will not need to include facts about what property she owned or about the cause of her death. You would include those facts only if they should pertain to the question of whether she had revoked her will.

Procedural History. The procedural history is the story of the case's progress through the litigation process. If the case is on appeal, include the procedural posture of the trial court decision being appealed, such as a decision on a motion to dismiss, a motion for summary judgment, some other kind of motion, a jury verdict, or a judgment after a bench trial.

Issue(s). The issue is the legal question the opinion resolves. Usually, the opinion tells you how the court thought the governing rule of law applied to the facts of that case, so you can state the issue in those terms. You can use either a question or a phrase beginning with "whether." Here is an example of an issue statement:

> Can a testator effectively revoke a will by marking a large "X" across only the first page of a five-page will and not signing or initialing the "X"?

Focus on the part of the governing rule that actually was at issue in the case. For instance, assume the case concerns a dispute over whether a testator had revoked her will before she died, as in the issue statement above. The parties were before the court to find out whether there is a valid will, but an issue statement that broad would not help you isolate the precise point on which this larger question turned: whether the existing will had been revoked.

Some opinions decide only pure questions of law and do not apply law to facts. In such a case, the issue statement simply poses the legal question the court answered, for example:

> Whether Illinois law allows recovery for the wrongful death of a fetus.

If the issue relates to how a term in a statute will be defined or applied, your brief should identify the statutory language at issue. A good place to do that is here in the issue statement, for example:

> Whether the "nighttime" element of the burglary statute is satisfied if the entry occurred 20 minutes before sunrise.

Applicable Rule(s) of Law. This section will help you begin to understand the legal principles (rules of law) governing your issue. A rule of law is a statement of the legal test the court will apply to resolve a legal issue. Here is an example of a governing rule of law for deciding the will revocation issue:

> To revoke a will, a testator must have the intention to revoke and must take some action that demonstrates that intent.

The court may state some other legal rules to provide context for the issue it actually will decide. Feel free to note these also. That legal context will help you understand the law governing your assignment, and when you begin to write your memo or brief, you might need to provide the same kind of context for your reader. If so, that information will be readily available in your case briefs.

Holding(s). The holding is the court's decision on the particular legal issue plus the important facts — the facts that seem to make the most difference for the result. If your issue statement included a sufficient description of the key facts, you need not repeat those facts in the holding statement. If not, include facts in the statement of the holding. The combination of your issue statement and your holding statement should include the key facts and the court's decision on the legal issue. For example:

> A testator can effectively revoke a will by marking a large "X" across only the first page of a five-page will and not signing or initialing the "X" if the other evidence of the testator's intent is sufficiently strong.

Notice the difference between a holding and the governing rule of law. The rule sets out the legal test the court will use to decide the case. The holding states the court's conclusion about whether the facts of the case meet that legal test.

If the issue is a pure question of law, you need not include the facts unless the answer to the question depends on a certain set of facts. For instance, if the issue is "Does State *X* allow recovery for the wrongful death of a fetus?" (a pure question of law), the answer (holding) might include facts: "Recovery for the wrongful death of a fetus is permitted if the fetus was medically viable at the time of the injury."

The Court's Order. After deciding the legal issue, the court either will take some action itself or will order that a person or another court take some action. For instance, a trial court might grant or deny a motion or might order the clerk to enter a judgment. An appellate court might affirm or reverse the lower court's ruling and might remand the case to the lower court for further proceedings. Note the legal result of the court's decision under this category of your brief.

Reasoning. Usually, a court uses its written opinion to explain the reasons for its decision. These reasons will be important to you as you work on your assignment. They will give you important clues about how the court might decide future cases, and they can provide you with effective arguments for your client. Chapter 27 identifies the major forms of legal reasoning, but whether you use those names or not, note in your case brief the court's reasons for its decision.

Pay particular attention to the court's *policy* rationales. Policy rationales justify a decision based on what result will be best for society at large. Courts realize that their rulings will affect the way people act in the future. They want to apply the law in ways that will encourage desirable societal results or discourage undesirable results. For instance, a court might adopt a particular legal rule because that rule will reduce the number of disputes resulting in litigation or because it will encourage people to think more carefully before entering into a contract. Including policy statements in your brief will help you understand whether and how the court's decision might apply to future cases. The opinion is likely to apply to future cases that raise these same policy concerns.

New Information. This category is optional, but it can be especially helpful when you are working on a legal writing assignment. It provides a place to record what you learned about the rule or its application that you did not know before you read this case. Notice especially anything about this case that could apply in some way to your assignment. Perhaps this opinion modified or expanded the rule. Perhaps the court discussed a part of the rule you have not seen discussed so thoroughly before. Perhaps the court phrased the governing rule in a way particularly helpful to your client's facts. Perhaps the opinion explains the historical developments in this area of the law. You will notice more information in the opinion if you consciously look for new information, and you will be better able to use that information in your assignment if you have made note of it in your case brief. Here are some tools that will help you find new information about a rule:

1. *Notice what the court said about the rule.* In most opinions, the author gives the reader some explanation of the rule before applying it to the facts of that particular case. Here, the author's primary goal is to tell the reader about the rule. Begin with this part of the opinion. The *court's* explicit explanation of the rule gives you the most basic new information from the case.

2. *Notice how the court applied the rule.* After you have examined carefully what the court *said* about the rule, look at how the court *applied* the rule to the facts before it. You might expect an opinion to state and explain a rule of law and then to apply that rule of law exactly as the opinion just explained it. Often, that is exactly what happens. But sometimes the court's *application* of the rule differs from the court's explanation of it. One of the best ways to understand the rule is to observe how the court applied it. A court "holds" what it *does*, not what it *says*.

3. *Notice how the court did* not *apply the rule.* After you have observed how the court applied the rule, ask yourself how the court did *not* apply it. A court's unexplained silence rarely can be characterized as a binding rule of law.

However, judicial silence can have persuasive value if the most likely reason for the silence is that the ignored topic is not a part of the relevant legal analysis. For instance, in a child custody case, if the facts state that one spouse is Christian and one spouse is Moslem but the opinion does not mention religious differences, you might be able to infer that religious differences will not be relevant to custody decisions.

After all, your goal here is to figure out what rule was governing the judge when deciding the case and how that rule would apply to your client's facts. If you are wondering whether a certain fact true of your client's situation would affect the outcome, ask yourself whether that kind of fact seemed to affect the judge's ruling in the earlier case.

4. *Notice any facts the court emphasized.* When a court sets out the facts or applies the law, it sometimes will emphasize a particular fact. Usually, the court's explanation of the law will tell you why the court found that fact important. However, sometimes a court will emphasize a fact without explicitly explaining the fact's significance. Even if the court did not directly explain whether or why that fact was important, the opinion's emphasis on it implies that the judge found it legally significant.

5. *Find out what leading commentators have said about the case.* Case opinions actually make law, but a wealth of secondary authorities exist. Secondary authorities are explanations of the law written by legal commentators. Secondary authorities have persuasive value, depending on factors such as the reputation of the author, the level of detail of the discussion, and the recency of the writing. If you are working with a well-known and influential case, commentators might have discussed it. Finding secondary authority can help you understand the case and its significance for your assignment.

Questions, Comments, and Speculations. Finally, note any questions, speculations, or thoughts of your own about the case and how it might apply to your assignment. It is common to have passing thoughts and questions as you read a case. These thoughts, speculations, and questions are the first steps toward a clearer understanding of the applicable law and how it might apply to your client. If you do not record them, you are likely to forget them.

CHAPTER 11

SYNTHESIZING CASES

Case briefing will help you understand a single case, but a lawyer faced with multiple authorities must do more than analyze each authority separately. Such a discussion would be little more than reading a series of case briefs. Instead, she must explain how the cases fit together to create the law governing her client's issue. She must compare the authorities to find and reconcile any seeming inconsistencies and to combine the content of the authorities so she can present a unified statement of the governing rule of law. Therefore, after you have identified the cases that will be important to your analysis, you must consider how they fit together. This process is called "synthesizing" cases.

§11.1 Using Consistent Cases

Sometimes the cases will use similar language to state the governing rule and will apply that rule consistently. Or perhaps some jurisdictions follow one rule and others follow a different rule. However, the cases within each jurisdiction are consistent with each other. In either of these situations, it will not be difficult to combine the language of the cases into one explanation of the law with a consistent explanation of how the courts have applied it. Simply identify the points you want to make about the law and its application, and select and discuss the cases that best illustrate each point. Usually those points will include each element or factor and may include other observations about how the rule is usually applied. For example, recall our rule on whether a person had effectively revoked her will:

> To revoke a will, a testator must have the intention to revoke and must take some action that demonstrates that intent.

Your written analysis would discuss each element (intention and action) separately. For each element you would identify several cases that best explain that element and discuss them in your description of that element.

Similarly, if jurisdictions are split between two different approaches, your written analysis would discuss each approach separately. For each approach, you would identify several cases that best explain that approach and discuss them in your description of that element. For instance, assume you are writing an office memo on the question of whether parents can recover for the wrongful death of a fetus. You might find that some jurisdictions do not permit recovery at all, whereas others permit recovery if the fetus was medically viable at the time of the injury. You would explain to your reader that jurisdictions disagree and then discuss separately each of the two approaches. For each approach, you would select and discuss the several cases that best illustrate that approach.

§11.2 Reconciling Seemingly Inconsistent Cases

Cases in the same jurisdiction are not always consistent, however. If you find seemingly inconsistent cases in the same jurisdiction, and if these cases will be important for your analysis, you must try to reconcile them. Reread carefully all of the language in both opinions, and also look for later cases that might resolve the inconsistency. Even if the later cases do not mention the inconsistency, these later cases will probably articulate and apply a rule. As you study the way these later cases articulate and apply the law, you will probably find clues about how to reconcile the cases.

One possibility is that the later case implicitly overruled the earlier case. As we saw in Chapter 2 [Linda H. Edwards, Legal Writing and Analysis, 3rd ed., (2011)], a court can overrule an earlier opinion implicitly, however, by ignoring the earlier opinion and reaching a result inconsistent with the earlier opinion. Another possibility is that the seemingly inconsistent legal rules are meant to apply to different situations. Perhaps one rule is meant to be an exception to the other. In either case, the rule in one of the cases will apply to your client's situation and the other will not. This explanation handily resolves the inconsistency. Analysis that leads to a conclusion that the two opinions apply to different situations is called "distinguishing" cases.

Finally, you might be able to study the language of each opinion and find meanings in the text that will allow you to read the two cases consistently. Identify the seemingly inconsistent aspects of the opinions. Then reread the opinions carefully, exploring whether you can imagine a possible explanation that would reconcile the statements.

Inconsistencies in Rule Statements. Cases can seem inconsistent because they appear to state two different legal rules. For instance, assume that a lawyer is representing Sharon Watson, a sales employee of Carrolton Company, headquartered in Atlanta, Georgia. Watson had sold Carrolton to its present owners. She remained employed by Carrolton and signed a covenant not to compete, an agreement promising not to compete with Carrolton in certain ways for a certain period of time after the termination of her employment. Watson is considering leaving Carrolton to form a new business that would compete with Carrolton. She needs to know whether Carrolton would be able to enforce the covenant against her.

The lawyer researches the issue and finds *Coffee System of Atlanta v. Fox*[1] and *Clein v. Kapiloff*[2], two Georgia cases dealing with enforcement of covenants not to compete. In *Fox*, the court uses the following language to articulate the rule governing when a covenant is enforceable:

> A covenant not to compete is enforceable if all of the following elements are reasonable: the kind of activity restrained; the geographical area in which it is restrained; and the time period of the restraint.

If *Fox* were the only authority, the lawyer would use this rule to analyze Watson's question. He would analyze the reasonableness of each of the identified characteristics of the Watson covenant. But *Fox* is not the only authority. The lawyer also found *Clein*, and there the court seems to articulate the governing rule differently. In *Clein*, the court stated:

> A covenant not to compete is enforceable if it is reasonable. The test for determining reasonableness is whether the covenant is reasonably necessary to protect the interests of the party who benefits by it; whether it unduly prejudices the interests of the public; and whether it imposes greater restrictions than are necessary.

Fox and *Clein* seem to lay out different rules. There seem to be two different legal standards governing the enforceability of covenants not to compete. Novice legal writers might be tempted to analyze the Watson issue by describing and applying, one at a time, the "rules" set out in *Fox* and in *Clein*. The discussion would first give a sort of "case brief" of *Fox*, describing the facts, the "rule" language that court used, and the result. The discussion would then apply the "rule" from *Fox* to the Watson facts. Then the discussion would do the same thing with

---

[1] 176 S.E.2d 71 (Ga. 1970).
[2] 98 S.E.2d 897 (Ga. 1957).

Clein, setting out the "rule" language from that case and applying that "rule" to the Watson facts. The organizational structure would look something like this:

Is the Watson covenant not to compete enforceable?

1. The rule in the *Fox* case: The covenant is enforceable if
   a. the kind of activity restrained is reasonable;
   b. the geographical area of restraint is reasonable;
   c. the duration of the restraint is reasonable.
2. The rule in the *Clein* case: The covenant is enforceable if
   a. it is reasonably necessary to protect the employer's interests;
   b. it does not unduly prejudice the interests of the public; and
   c. it does not impose greater restrictions than are necessary.

This approach is problematic, however. The lawyer needs to know *Georgia's* rule of law on enforcing covenants not to compete. Determining Georgia's rule is the most important analytical task. Organizing by the separate cases here would give the client two possible rules and two possible outcomes. Yet our legal system contemplates that a jurisdiction ordinarily will have only one rule of law on a particular issue so people can know what the law is and how it will apply to their conduct.

The lawyer must try to reconcile these seemingly inconsistent statements in *Fox* and *Clein.* After rereading the cases several times and carefully considering the court's possible meanings, the lawyer might conclude that the language in *Fox* identifies the particular terms that must be reasonable while the language in *Clein* identifies the criteria the court will use to judge whether those terms are reasonable. In other words, each contract term (kind of restraint, area of restraint, and duration of restraint) must meet the three criteria identified in *Clein.* This reconciliation salvages precedential value for each case and combines them into one unified statement of the jurisdiction's legal rule. Here is a rule statement that reconciles *Fox* and *Clein:*

A covenant not to compete is enforceable if the kind of activity restrained, the geographical area of the restraint, and the duration of the restraint are reasonable. Reasonableness is judged according to whether the restraint is necessary to protect the employer's interests, does not unduly prejudice the interests of the public, and does not impose greater restrictions than are necessary.

This reconciled rule statement might produce an analysis organized like this:

Is the Watson covenant not to compete enforceable?

The covenant is enforceable if its terms are reasonable according to the following criteria:

A. Are its terms necessary to protect the employer's interests?

    1. The kind of activity;
    2. the geographical area;
    3. the duration.

B. Do its terms unduly prejudice the interests of the public?

    1. The kind of activity;
    2. the geographical area;
    3. the duration.

C. Do its terms impose greater restrictions than necessary?

    1. The kind of activity;
    2. the geographical area;
    3. the duration.

Inconsistencies in Results. You might find cases that seem to apply the same governing rule to seemingly similar sets of facts but reach puzzlingly different results. To reconcile them, search for differences in the facts that might adequately explain these results.

Consider this example: To establish adverse possession of land, a claimant must prove several things, one of which is "possession." The kind of possession that will ripen into title is gauged by the kind and degree of the claimant's use of the land. Here are summaries of two hypothetical cases dealing with the issue of whether the kind and degree of use was sufficient. Do they seem inconsistent? If so, can you reconcile them?

Allen v. Baxter: Fifteen years ago, Anne Allen bought Lot A in a suburban neighborhood. Lot B, the vacant and overgrown lot next door, was owned by Jacob Baxter. Allen built a house on lot A and moved in. In 1981, Allen began gardening on Lot B. During the eight-month growing season, she worked in the garden nearly every day, growing vegetables for herself and her neighbors. During the four remaining months, she seldom went on the lot. The court held that this use did not establish a sufficient degree of "possession" for the purposes of adverse possession.

Clay v. Davidson: Fifteen years ago, Charles Clay bought a lakeside lot in a resort area. The lot already contained a cabin, and Clay built a dock. Every year since then, he has spent about six weekends a year and two weeks during the summer at the cabin. He has now discovered that the legal description of the lot was incorrect in that it actually describes the lot next door. Darlene Davidson is the actual record title-holder of the lot Clay thought to be his. The court held that Clay's facts established a sufficient degree of "possession" for the purposes of adverse possession.

The results in these two cases seem inconsistent. The degree of possession in *Allen* seems much greater than the degree of possession in *Clay*. Allen was physically present on the land for many more days of the year than was Clay, and Allen did more to the land than did Clay. Yet the court held that Clay possessed the land to a sufficient degree, and Allen did not. Reconciling these cases requires you to search for differences that could explain this seeming inconsistency. Perhaps the court will be satisfied with a lesser degree of possession in the case of vacation property, where an owner would not be expected to be in possession year round. Perhaps the court counted the continuous presence of Clay's improvements as part of Clay's possession. Or perhaps the court will require a greater degree of possession in the case of a possessor who knows she does not have record title. Any of these explanations could reconcile *Allen* and *Clay*.[3]

---

[3] If you study adverse possession in your property class, you might learn more about how to reconcile these two cases. The purpose of this exercise is simply to give you some practice in *imagining possible reconciliations*.

CHAPTER 12

INTERPRETING STATUTES

While the roots of the American legal system remain in the common law, the 1930s saw the beginning of "an orgy of statute-making".[1] Today, most legal issues are controlled or significantly affected by statutes. Thus, your skills of statutory analysis will be crucial to your success as a lawyer. The skills basic to statutory analysis are (1) reading the statute, (2) identifying the issues, and (3) interpreting the statute's language.

§12.1 Reading Statutes

The starting point for reading a statute is understanding the legislature's relationship to the courts. An applicable statute binds the courts of that jurisdiction, but a court has the authority to interpret the statute's language. Once a court has interpreted the statute, the doctrine of stare decisis applies, and the court's interpretation binds all other courts for whom the opinion is mandatory authority. If the legislature disagrees with the court's interpretation, the legislature is free to amend the statute to clarify its intended meaning. The court is then bound once again, this time by the newly amended statute.

Also, a court has the authority to rule on the constitutionality of the statute. On the question of constitutionality, the court has the last word. The legislature can amend the statute to cure the constitutional infirmity the court identified, but the legislature cannot enact another statute declaring the original statute constitutional. A statute that has been held unconstitutional will not be enforced within the jurisdiction of the court that issued the opinion.

Within the boundaries set by these interlocking roles, courts must read statutory language and tell litigants whether the statute applies to their situation, and if so, what that language means. To advise clients and represent litigants, therefore, lawyers must read statutes precisely, accurately, and sometimes creatively. You

---

[1] Grant Gilmore, *The Ages of American Law* 95 (Yale U. Press 1977).

can think of the questions critical to this inquiry as similar to the famous five Ws that guide a journalist:[2]

The Five Ws of Reading a Statute

Who?	Whose actions are covered?
What?	What kinds of actions are required, prohibited, or permitted?
When?	When was the statute effective?
Where?	Where must the actions have taken place to be covered?
What then?	What consequences follow?

Often, the scope of the material you must read closely is larger than the specific statutory provision you first identify. If you are dealing with an act containing individual separately numbered provisions, you must read carefully at least the following parts of the act:

Read These Parts of a Statute

1. The language of the individual provisions that appear to deal directly with the legal issue;
2. The language of any other individual provisions expressly cross-referenced by the directly applicable provisions;
3. The titles of these individual provisions and of the entire act;
4. Any set of definitions applying to the individual provisions or to the act as a whole;
5. Any statement of purpose and any preamble to the individual provisions or the act as a whole;
6. If length is not prohibitive, read the entire act;
7. If the entire act is too long to read, at least read carefully the titles of all other individual provisions to identify any that might relate to the issue at hand;
8. The dates on which the act as a whole and the individual provisions were enacted and on which they became effective;
9. All of the same information for any amendments to important provisions;

---

[2] A journalist asks "five Ws and an H": who, what, when, where, why, and how.

10. If available, read the same information for any prior versions of impor-
     tant provisions (to understand what changes the legislature intended
     to make when it enacted the current version).

Read each of these parts of the statute word by word and phrase by phrase,
paying attention to every detail. Reading a statute is more like reading an alge-
braic formula than it is like reading standard prose. Each word and punctuation mark is important. Even the internal tabulation (numbering or lettering)
can be significant. Pay particular attention to words that signal structural
information.

Some Words that Signal Structural Information

and	include	unless	other
or	limited to	outweighs	shall
either	except	all	May

Also, notice whether any list set out in the statute is meant to be exclusive.
The statute might tell you expressly that the list is not exclusive, using such language as the phrase "and any other factors relevant to the child's best interests."
Or the statute might merely imply whether the list is exclusive, for instance, by
introducing the list with a word like "including."

§12.2 Identifying Issues

Recall that when you brief cases, you should read the whole case through
once before you begin to prepare your brief. Similarly, when you are ready to
identify statutory issues, read through all the material identified on pages 104-105
to establish the context for your analysis and to identify the key provisions of the
statute. When you have identified the provisions that will govern your issue,
return to those provisions for another and even more careful reading. Read with a
pen or pencil in your hand. Read the text of the statute word for word, looking for
key terms that tell you what conduct the statute covers.

One way to find the key terms is to focus on the answers to the 5 Ws set out
on page 104. Another way is to ask yourself what someone would have to prove to
show that the requirements of the statute were or were not met. If you can mark
on the actual text of the statute, underline each word that tells you something
about the answers to those questions. Then circle all the terms that tell you something about the relationships among the key terms (words like "and," or "or"). If

you are working from hard copy library materials, write these words on a sheet of paper instead of underlining them. Here is an example:

The statute:

No cemetery shall be hereafter established within the corporate limits of any city or town; nor shall any cemetery be established within two hundred and fifty yards of any residence without the consent of the owner of the legal and equitable title of such residence.[3]

Key terms:

Cemetery	hereafter	established	corporate limits
city	town	250 yards	residence
consent	owner	legal title	equitable title

Relational terms:

Or	nor	and

Notice that each of the key terms raises an issue. Something other than a cemetery would not be covered by this statute, so to know whether this statute would apply to your client's facts, you must find out what the term "cemetery" means in this context. There might be a definition section in this same act, or there might be cases in which prior courts have defined the term. Either way, the term "cemetery" raises an issue you must resolve.

The same is true with the word "hereafter." The statute does not prohibit all cemeteries; it prohibits only those established "hereafter." After what? The date of the statute's passage? Or the date on which the statute became effective? What are those dates? Another issue to resolve. And what does the term "established" mean? Is a cemetery "established" when construction begins? Ends? When the cemetery first opens for business? Each key term identified above raises an issue the lawyer must resolve before the lawyer can know whether and how the statute might apply to her client's facts.

Are you surprised to find so many issues raised in one statutory sentence? Statutes are packed tightly with key terms, each of which sets out an important component of the statute and each of which raises an issue. If you were analyzing whether and how this statute applies to your client's facts, you would have at least twelve issues to consider.

---

[3] Va. Code, §56 (Michie 1942), construed in *Temple v. Petersburg*, 29 S.E.2d 357 (Sup. Ct. Apps. Va. 1944).

One word of caution about identifying key terms: You might be tempted to treat a phrase as a single key term. For example, consider a statute providing that a donor must transfer possession of the gifted item with "a manifested intent" to part with ownership. You might first think of the words "manifested intent" as a single key term. However, that phrase would require the party seeking to establish the gift to prove two things, not one: (1) that the donor actually intended to part with ownership and (2) that this intent was sufficiently "manifested" to others. This phrase raises two issues, not one. Your list of key terms should treat these words separately.

One more strategy is helpful for reading statutes and identifying issues: rewriting the statute in your own words. Restating the rule in your own words is an effective tool of analysis, and you often can state the rule more simply and clearly than its original writer did. Do not, however, rephrase the *key terms* of the statute. Those terms will be defined and explained by the authorities; thus, they will have developed their own meaning, and as we saw above, that meaning is the critical question of the analysis.

§12.3 Interpreting the Statute's Language

Statutes are interpreted by case opinions. If case authority has already told you what the statute means, you can rely on that case law to the extent of its precedential value. But if no binding case law has answered your particular question, you must use other tools of interpretation. The most important of these tools are (1) the text itself, (2) the intent of the legislature, (3) the policies implicated by the possible interpretations, (4) the interpretation of any governmental agencies charged with enforcement of the statute, and (5) the opinions of other courts and of respected commentators.

The Text Itself. The most important inquiry is the "plain meaning" of the text itself. When the plain meaning is unambiguous, a court generally will give effect to the plain meaning unless the result would be absurd. Look first at the plain meaning of the statute's text. Also look for other parts of the statute or act that might tell you more about the language you are concerned with, such as the section explaining the act's purpose. Many acts contain separate definition sections. Even when your term is not defined, other parts of the statute could give you clues about what the term means.

The Legislature's Intent. Often, the text of the statute will be unclear. In such a case, many courts will try to decide what the legislature intended by the text's language. This search for the legislature's intent is problematic at best. The statute was probably enacted by a large group of elected officials who were serving in that office some years ago. The particular language you are concerned with could have been the result of political compromise, and various factions of the legislature might have had vastly different intentions surrounding that language. Quite possibly, your question never occurred to them at all. How can one decide the intent of the legislature as if the legislature were an entity with one mind? Yet, when a statute's language is unclear, a court applying the statute will have to have some basis for a decision. In such a circumstance, the court often will try to discern the legislature's intent.

Many courts are willing to consider the legislative history of the statute as evidence of legislative intent. Legislative history consists primarily of the documents or other records generated by the legislative body during its deliberations about the bill that ultimately became the statute. Legislative history comes in many forms, such as committee reports, speeches, witness testimony, or studies introduced into the record. Your research text will tell you more about legislative history and how to find it.

Policy. The fourth tool for statutory interpretation is analysis of the policy concerns implicated by a particular construction of the statute. Some implicated policies probably were part of the legislature's intent, but the legislature might not have foreseen all the policy concerns. Issues of interpretation implicating these other policies may arise. If the legislature has not spoken on the issue, the court is free to consider its own view of which possible interpretation of the statute would produce the best overall results for society.

In addition to the policies specifically applicable to a statute, some *kinds* of statutes carry a general policy leaning applicable to all statutes of that particular kind. These policies call for either a strict or a liberal construction of that kind of statute. The most common of these policies are:

- Statutes that change long-standing case law (statutes "in derogation of the common law") should be strictly construed. (A statute is strictly construed when it is read narrowly, so that it changes the legal environment as little as possible.)
- Statutes intended to remedy a problem ("remedial statutes") should be liberally construed to accomplish their remedial purpose. (A statute is liberally construed when it is read broadly to include more kinds of situations than a narrow reading would allow.)
- Statutes making certain conduct a crime ("penal statutes") should be narrowly construed, out of concern for the rights of the citizen-accused.

Finally, courts are guided by the general policy that, if possible, the meaning of a statute should be construed in a way that will render the statute constitutional.

Agency Interpretation. When enforcement of a statute is assigned to a particular agency, that agency must decide what the statute means to enforce it. Courts often look to this agency as the entity with the most expertise in the relevant issues and thus might give deference to the agency's interpretation. The court also may consider the interpretation of an agency that has no authority to enforce the statute but nonetheless works with the statute routinely. Look for agency interpretations in the agency's regulations, in the agency's decisions, and in case law.

Commentators and Other Courts. Finally, courts may recognize persuasive value attaching to the opinions of other courts and of respected commentators.

The persuasive value of another court's opinion depends on the factors identified in Chapter 13. The persuasive value of a commentator's opinion depends on the reputation of the commentator and on the commentator's well-reasoned reliance on the other tools of construction.

§12.4 Canons of Construction

To decide how to construe a statute, a court also may consider commonly accepted maxims of interpretation known as "canons of construction." Here are some of the most generally applicable:

- Read the statute as a whole.
- Give effect to rules of grammar and punctuation.
- Construe technical terms technically and ordinary terms in their ordinary sense.
- When the same language is used in various parts of an act, the language is presumed to have the same meaning throughout.
- Where general words (such as "and any other") follow a list, the general words should be construed to refer to things similar to the items in the list. This principle is sometimes called the principle of "ejusdem generis," meaning literally "of the same genus."
- Modifying words or phrases refer to the possible referent immediately prior to the modifier.
- Where a statute from state X is adopted in state Y, the construction given the statute by the courts of state X should be followed in state Y.
- If the statute does not contain an exception for a particular situation, the courts should apply the statute to that situation.
- Absent clear indication, the court should presume that the legislature did not intend to enact a statute that impairs fundamental and commonly held societal values.
- Specific description of one or more situations in the text of a statute implies the exclusion of other kinds of situations not mentioned.
- Different statutes on the same legal issue (statutes "in pari materia") should be read consistently, especially where the legislature intended to create a consistent statutory scheme.
- Sometimes the courts of state X will have interpreted a particular word or phrase in a certain way. If, subsequently, the legislature of state X enacts a different statute using that word or phrase, the language in the new statute should be interpreted as having the meaning previously given it by the courts.
- Although not technically part of the statute's text, such items as titles, preambles, and section headings are persuasive evidence of legislative intent.
- Sometimes courts will have construed the language of a statute in a particular way. Subsequently the legislature may amend the statute in ways that change or clarify other issues but do not address the issue the courts have

interpreted. A later court might conclude that the legislature's lack of action to change the judicial construction is evidence of the legislature's approval of the court's construction.

Where courts have relied on these maxims, they are treated as legal principles in and of themselves. Therefore, when you rely on one of them as part of the analysis of a rule, cite to a persuasive case opinion that adopts that maxim if you can. Even if you cannot find case authority adopting the maxim, however, a court still will be willing to consider the maxim's logic.

None of these guidelines for interpreting statutes will provide a certain answer. As a matter of fact, when you apply several, they might support contradictory results.[4] However, courts generally will consider these guidelines, so they will help you to predict what a court might decide or to persuade a court to interpret a statute favorably for your client.

---

[4] Karl N. Llewellyn, *Remarks on the Theory of Appellate Decision and Rules or Canons About How Statutes Are to Be Construed*, 3 Vand. L. Rev. 395 (1950).

INTRODUCTION TO LEGAL RESEARCH

CHAPTER 13

INTRODUCTION TO LEGAL RESEARCH

What is legal research and why do you need to learn about it? Researching the law means finding the rules that govern conduct in our society. To be a successful lawyer, you need to know how to research the law. Lawyers are often called upon to solve problems and give advice, and to do that accurately, you must know the rules applicable to the different situations you and your clients will face. Clients may come to you after an event has occurred and ask you to pursue a remedy for a bad outcome, or perhaps defend them against charges that they have acted wrongfully. You may be asked to help a client accomplish a goal like starting a business or buying a piece of property. In these situations and many others, you will need to know your clients' rights and responsibilities, as defined by legal rules. Consequently, being proficient in legal research is essential to your success in legal practice.

As a starting point for learning about how to research the law, it is important to understand some of the different sources of legal rules. This chapter discusses what these sources are and where they originate within our legal system. It also provides an introduction to the process of legal research, an overview of some of the research tools you will learn to use, and an introduction to legal citation. Later chapters explain how to locate legal rules using a variety of resources.

§13.1 Introduction to the Legal System

§13.1.1 *Sources of Law*

The discussion that follows reiterates some of the material in Part B of this text. We include it here because of its critical importance to virtually all aspects of legal research. There are four main sources of law, which exist at both state and federal levels:

- constitutions;
- statutes;

- court opinions (also called cases);
- administrative regulations.

A constitution establishes a system of government and defines the boundaries of authority granted to the government. The United States Constitution is the pre-eminent source of law in our legal system, and all other rules, whether promulgated by a state or the federal government, must comply with its requirements. Each state also has its own constitution. A state's constitution may grant greater rights than those secured by the federal constitution, but because a state constitution is subordinate to the federal constitution, it cannot provide lesser rights than the federal constitution does. All of a state's legal rules must comport with both the state and federal constitutions.

Since grade school, you have been taught that the U.S. Constitution created three branches of government: the legislative branch, which makes the laws; the judicial branch, which interprets the laws; and the executive branch, which enforces the laws. State governments are also divided into these three branches. Although this is elementary civics, this structure truly does define the way government authority is divided in our system of government.

The legislative branch of government creates statutes, which must be approved by the executive branch (the president, for federal statutes; the governor, for state statutes) to go into effect. The executive branch also makes rules. Administrative agencies, such as the federal Food and Drug Administration or a state's department of motor vehicles, are part of the executive branch. They execute the laws passed by the legislature and create their own regulations to carry out the mandates established by statute.

The judicial branch is the source of court opinions. Courts interpret rules created by the legislative and executive branches of government. If a court determines that a rule does not meet constitutional requirements, it can invalidate the rule. Otherwise, however, the court must apply the rule to the case before it. Court opinions can also be an independent source of legal rules. Legal rules made by courts are called "common-law" rules. Although courts are empowered to make these rules, legislatures can adopt legislation that changes or abolishes a common-law rule, as long as the legislation is constitutional.

Figure 13.1 shows the relationships among the branches of government and the types of legal rules they create.

An example may be useful to illustrate the relationships among the rules created by the three branches of the federal government. As you know, the U.S. Constitution, through the First Amendment, guarantees the right to free expression. Congress could pass legislation requiring television stations to provide educational programming for children. The Federal Communications Commission (FCC) is the administrative agency within the executive branch that would have responsibility for carrying out Congress's will. If the statute were not specific about what constitutes educational programming or how much educational programming must be provided, the FCC would have to create administrative regulations to execute the law. The regulations would provide the information not detailed in the statute, such as the definition of educational programming.

Figure 13.1   Branches of Government and Legal Rules

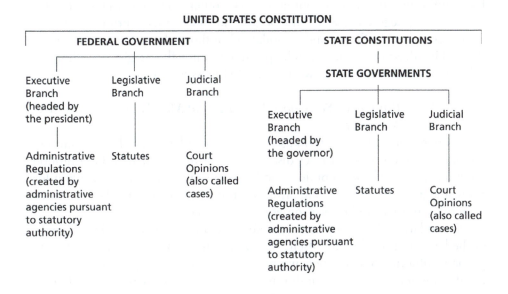

A television station could challenge the statute and regulations by arguing to a court that prescribing the content of material that the station must broadcast violates the First Amendment. The court would then have to interpret the statute and regulations to decide whether they comport with the Constitution.

Another example illustrates the relationship between courts and legislatures in the area of common-law rules. The rules of negligence have largely been created by the courts. Therefore, liability for negligence is usually determined by common-law rules. A state supreme court could decide that a plaintiff who sues a defendant for negligence cannot recover any damages if the plaintiff herself was negligent and contributed to her own injuries. This decision would create a common-law rule governing future cases of negligence within that state. The state legislature could step in and pass a statute that changes the rule. For example, the legislature could enact a statute providing that juries are to determine the percentage of negligence attributable to each party and to apportion damages accordingly, instead of completely denying recovery to the plaintiff. Courts in that state would then be obligated to apply the rule from the statute, not the former common-law rule.

Although these examples are simplified, they demonstrate the basic roles of each of the branches of government in enunciating the legal rules governing the conduct of society. They also demonstrate that researching a legal issue may require you to research several different types of legal authority. The answer to a research question may not be found exclusively in statutes or court opinions or administrative regulations. Often, these sources must be researched together to determine all of the rules applicable to a factual scenario.

§13.1.2 Types and Weight of Authority

One term used to describe the rules that govern conduct in society is "legal authority." Rules, however, are only one type of legal authority, and some types of legal authority are more authoritative than others. To understand how legal authority is categorized, you must be able to differentiate "primary" authority from "secondary" authority and "mandatory" authority from "persuasive" authority. Making these distinctions will help you determine the weight, or authoritative value, a legal authority carries with respect to the issue you are researching.

§13.1.2.1 Primary vs. Secondary Authority and Mandatory vs. Persuasive Authority

Primary authority is the term used to describe rules of law. Primary authority includes all of the types of rules discussed so far in this chapter. Constitutional provisions, statutes, court opinions, and administrative regulations contain legal rules, and as a consequence, are primary authority. Because "the law" consists of legal rules, primary authority is sometimes described as "the law."

Secondary authority, by contrast, refers to commentary on the law or analysis of the law, but not "the law" itself. An opinion from the U.S. Supreme Court is primary authority, but an article written by a private party explaining and analyzing the opinion is secondary authority. Secondary authority is often quite useful in legal research because its analysis can help you understand complex legal issues and refer you to primary authority. Nevertheless, secondary authority is not "the law" and therefore is distinguished from primary authority.

Mandatory and persuasive authority are terms courts use to categorize the different sources of law they use in making their decisions. Mandatory authority, which can also be called binding authority, refers to authority that the court is obligated to follow. Mandatory authority contains rules that you must apply to determine the correct answer to the issue you are researching. Persuasive authority, which can also be called nonbinding authority, refers to authority that the court may follow if it is persuaded to do so, but is not required to follow. Persuasive authority, therefore, will not dictate the answer to an issue, although it may help you figure out the answer. Whether an authority is mandatory or persuasive depends on several factors, as discussed in the next section.

§13.1.2.2 Weight of Authority

The degree to which an authority controls the answer to a legal issue is called the weight of the authority. Not all authorities have the same weight. The weight of a legal authority depends on its status as primary or secondary authority, and as mandatory or persuasive authority. Some primary authorities are mandatory, and others are persuasive. Secondary authority, by contrast, is always persuasive authority. You must be able to distinguish among these categories of authority to determine how much weight a particular legal authority has in the resolution of the issue you are researching.

I. Secondary authority: always persuasive: A legal authority's status as a primary or secondary authority is fixed. An authority is either part of "the law," or it is not. Because secondary authority is always persuasive authority, it is not binding. Once you identify an authority as secondary, you can be certain that it will not control the outcome of the issue you are researching.

Although secondary authority is not binding, some secondary authorities are more persuasive than others. Some are so respected that a court, while not technically bound by them, would need a good reason to depart from or reject their statements of legal rules. Others do not enjoy the same degree of respect, leaving a court free to ignore or reject such authorities if it is not persuaded to follow them. Further discussion of the persuasive value of various secondary authorities appears in Chapter 16, on secondary source research. The important thing to remember for now is that secondary authority is always categorized as persuasive or nonbinding authority.

II. Primary authority: sometimes mandatory, sometimes persuasive: Sometimes primary authority is mandatory, or binding, authority, and sometimes it is not. You must be able to evaluate the authority to determine whether it is binding on the issue you are researching. One factor affecting whether a primary authority is mandatory is jurisdiction. The rules contained in primary authority apply only to conduct occurring within the jurisdiction in which the authority is in force. For example, all laws in the United States must comport with the federal constitution because it is primary authority that is mandatory, or binding, in all United States jurisdictions. The New Jersey constitution is also primary authority because it contains legal rules establishing the scope of state government authority, but it is mandatory authority only in New Jersey. The New Jersey constitution's rules do not apply in Illinois or Michigan.

Determining the weight of court opinions is a little more complex. All court opinions are primary authority. Whether a particular opinion is mandatory or persuasive is a function not only of jurisdiction, but also level of court. To understand how these factors work together, it is easiest to consider level of court first and jurisdiction second.

i. Determining the weight of court opinions: level of court: The judicial branches of government in all states and in the federal system have multiple levels of courts. Trial courts are at the bottom of the judicial hierarchy. In the federal system, the United States District Courts are trial-level courts, and each state has at least one federal district court. Intermediate appellate courts hear appeals of trial court cases. Most, but not all, states have intermediate appellate courts. In the federal system, the intermediate appellate courts are called United States Courts of Appeals, and they are divided into 13 separate circuits: 11 numbered circuits (First through Eleventh), the District of Columbia Circuit, and the Federal Circuit. The highest court or court of last resort is often called the supreme court. It hears appeals of cases from the intermediate appellate courts or directly from trial courts in states that do not have intermediate appellate courts. In the federal system, of course, the court of last resort is the U.S. Supreme Court.

Trial court opinions, including those from federal district courts, are not mandatory authority. These opinions bind the parties to the cases but do not bind other courts considering similar cases. They are persuasive authority.

The opinions of intermediate appellate courts bind the courts below them. In other words, intermediate appellate opinions are mandatory authority for the trial courts subordinate to them in the court structure. The weight of intermediate appellate opinions on the intermediate appellate courts themselves varies. In jurisdictions with multiple appellate divisions, the opinions of one division may or may not be binding on other divisions. In addition, in some circumstances, intermediate appellate courts can overrule their own prior opinions. Intermediate appellate opinions are persuasive authority for the court of last resort.

The court of last resort may, but is not required to, follow the opinions of the courts below it. The opinions of the court of last resort, however, are mandatory authority for both intermediate appellate courts and trial courts subordinate to it in the court structure. The court of last resort is not bound by its own prior opinions, but will be reluctant to change an earlier ruling without a compelling justification.

Figure 13.2 illustrates the structures of federal and state court systems and shows how level of court affects the weight of opinions.

ii. Determining the weight of court opinions: jurisdiction: The second factor affecting the weight of court opinions is jurisdiction. As with other forms of primary authority, rules stated in court opinions are mandatory authority only within the court's jurisdiction. An opinion from the Texas Supreme Court is mandatory only for a court applying Texas law. A California court deciding a question of California law would consider the Texas opinion persuasive authority. If the California court had to decide a new issue not previously addressed by mandatory California authority (a "question of first impression"), it might choose to follow the Texas Supreme Court's opinion if it found the opinion persuasive.

On questions of federal law, opinions of the U.S. Supreme Court are mandatory authority for all other courts because it has nationwide jurisdiction. An opinion from a circuit court of appeals is mandatory only within the circuit that issued the opinion and is persuasive everywhere else. Thus, a decision of the U.S. Court of Appeals for the Eleventh Circuit would be binding within the Eleventh Circuit, but not within the Seventh Circuit. **Figure 13.3** shows the geographic boundaries of the federal circuit courts of appeal.

In considering the weight of a court opinion, it is important to remember that the federal government and each state constitute different jurisdictions. On questions of state law, each state's courts get the last word, and on questions of federal law, the federal courts get the last word. For an issue governed by state law, the opinions of the courts within the relevant state are mandatory authority. For an issue governed by federal law, the opinions of the relevant federal courts are mandatory authority.

Ordinarily, understanding how jurisdiction affects weight of authority is fairly intuitive. When a Massachusetts trial court is resolving a case arising out of conduct that took place in Massachusetts, it will treat the opinions of the Massachusetts Supreme Judicial Court as mandatory authority. Sometimes, however, a court has to resolve a case governed by the law of another jurisdiction. State courts sometimes decide cases governed by the law of another state or by federal law. Federal courts sometimes decide cases governed by state law. When that happens,

Figure 13.2   Structure of the Federal Court System and Most State Court Systems

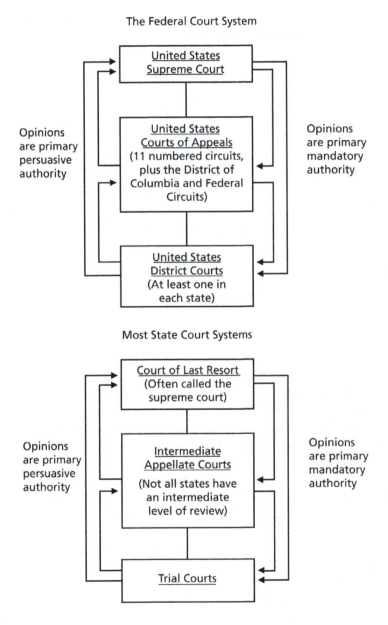

the court deciding the case will treat the law of the controlling jurisdiction as mandatory authority.

For example, assume that the U.S. District Court for the Western District of Texas, a federal trial court, has to decide a case concerning breach of a contract

Figure 13.3   Geographic Boundaries of the Federal Courts of Appeals

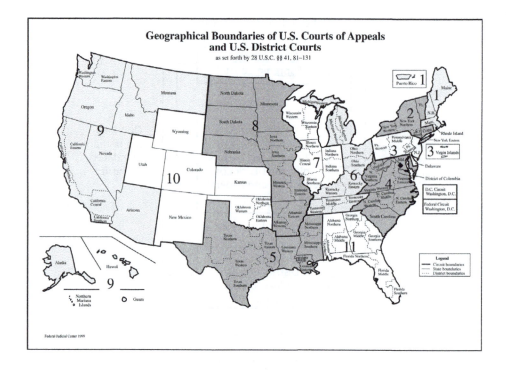

to build a house in El Paso, Texas. Contract law is, for the most part, established by the states. To resolve this case, the federal court will apply the contract law of the state where the dispute arose, in this case, Texas. The Texas Supreme Court's opinions on contract law are mandatory authority for resolving the case. Now assume that the same court has to decide a case concerning immigration law. Immigration law is established by the federal government. To resolve the case, the court will apply federal law. The opinions of the U.S. Supreme Court and the U.S. Court of Appeals for the Fifth Circuit are mandatory authority for resolving the case.

This discussion provides an overview of some common principles governing the weight of authority. These principles are subject to exceptions and nuances not addressed here. Entire fields of study are devoted to resolving questions of jurisdiction, procedure, and conflicts regarding which legal rules apply to various types of disputes. As you begin learning about research, however, these general principles will be sufficient to help you determine the weight of the authority you locate to resolve a research issue.

Figure 13.4 illustrates the relationships among the different types of authority.

Figure 13.4   Types of Authority

TYPE OF AUTHORITY	MANDATORY (BINDING)	PERSUASIVE (NONBINDING)
PRIMARY (legal rules)	Constitutional provisions, statutes, and regulations in force within a jurisdiction are mandatory authority for courts within the same jurisdiction. Decisions from higher courts within a jurisdiction are mandatory authority for lower courts within the same jurisdiction.	Decisions from courts within one jurisdiction are persuasive authority for courts in other jurisdictions. Decisions from lower courts within a jurisdiction are persuasive authority for higher courts within the same jurisdiction.
SECONDARY (anything that is not primary authority; usually commentary on the law)	Secondary authority is *not* mandatory authority.	Secondary authority is persuasive authority.

§13.2 The Hierarchy of Authority

You will be able to follow the hierarchy of authority more easily if you visualize it this way:

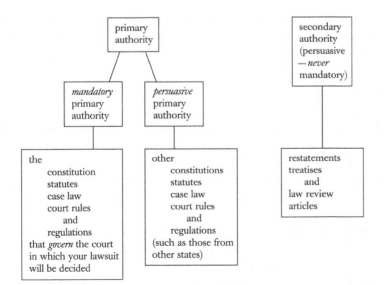

§13.3 Other Characteristics Affecting the Persuasive Value of Cases

The degree of deference a court will give to any particular case will be affected in more subtle ways by additional factors, including the following:

The relative level of the issuing court. The more prestigious the court, the more persuasive its opinions. For instance, a decision of the United States Supreme Court is powerful persuasive authority, even when it is not mandatory.

The date of the opinion. All other things being equal, more recent opinions carry more persuasive value.

The strength of the opinion's reasoning. A well-reasoned opinion is more persuasive than a poorly reasoned one. An opinion that explains the rationale of the decision rather than simply announcing it is more persuasive than an opinion that simply applies existing legal authorities without exploration of the policy rationale for the rule.

The subsequent treatment of the opinion by other authorities. The more the case has been followed by subsequent cases, the greater its precedential value. The more it has been discussed approvingly in treatises or law review articles, the greater its precedential value.

The number of other jurisdictions that follow the same approach. If a majority of jurisdictions follow this court's approach, the opinion's precedential value is increased. We refer to the approach of the majority of jurisdictions as the "majority rule" and to a minority approach as the "minority rule."

Whether the court's statements about the issue are part of the holding or dicta. As Part III in this chapter explained, statements that are dicta are not as persuasive as statements that are part of the holding.

How factually similar the opinion is to the facts of the present situation. The more similar the facts of the precedent case and the pending case, the surer the judge can be that the authority was meant to apply to situations like the pending case.

The number of subscribing judges. Most federal intermediate-level appellate cases are decided by a panel of the court, often three judges. Far less frequently, a case will be decided by all judges of that court (the court sitting en banc). En banc opinions are binding on future panels of the same court. Other courts generally find them more persuasive than panel decisions. Unanimous opinions are more persuasive than split decisions. A majority opinion generally is more persuasive than a concurring opinion, which is in turn more persuasive than a dissenting opinion.

Be careful with concurring or dissenting opinions. If the statement of law you are interested in is part of a disagreement between the concurring or dissenting opinion and the majority opinion, the statement in the concurring or dissenting opinion might actually establish that what it says is *not* the law. After all, the opinion is disagreeing with the majority opinion on that point (or agreeing for different reasons), and it is the majority opinion that establishes the law.

En banc opinion	An opinion issued in a case that was heard by all of the judges of the court.
Majority opinion	An opinion subscribed to by a majority of the judges who heard the case.
Concurring opinion	An opinion that agrees with the result reached by the majority opinion but for reasons different from or in addition to those of the majority opinion.
Dissenting opinion	An opinion that disagrees with the result reached by the majority opinion.

Whether the opinion is published. If the opinion does not appear in an official collection of published opinions (an official case reporter), it is not "published." In some jurisdictions, the precedential value of an unpublished opinion is limited or nonexistent. Be sure to check the court rules on this point.

The reputation of the particular judge writing the case opinion. Some judges have earned significant respect personally, separate from the position they hold. The opinions of those judges might have added persuasive value.

Trends in the law. If you can discern a trend among other courts in the nation or in your state, opinions consistent with that trend could have greater precedential value than inconsistent opinions. For instance, if, over the past several years your state's highest court has been extending the liability of manufacturers in various situations, a case opinion consistent with that trend might have more precedential weight than an opinion that questions that trend.

§13.4 Introduction to the Process of Legal Research

Imagine that you are standing in the parking lot at Disney World. You have a key in your hand, but you have no idea which car it starts. The key is not much use to you unless you have some way of figuring out which car it starts. The more information you can gather about the car, the easier the car will be to find. Knowing the make, model, or color would narrow the options. Knowing the license plate number would allow you to identify the individual vehicle.

Understanding the mechanics of using various legal research tools is like having that key in your hand. You have to know the features of the research tools available to you to conduct research, just as you must have the key to start the car.

But that is not enough to make you an effective researcher. Effective legal research combines mastery of the mechanics of research with legal problem solving skills. The research process is part of the reasoning process. It is not a rote task you complete before you begin to evaluate an issue. Rather, it is an analytical task in which you narrow the field of all legal information available to the subset of information necessary to assess an issue. As you locate and evaluate information, you will learn about the issue you are researching, and that knowledge will help you determine both whether you have located useful information and what else you should be looking for to complete your understanding of the issue.

To understand the process of research, you must first understand how legal information is organized. Most, if not all, of the authorities you will learn to research are available from a variety of sources. They may be published in print, electronically, or in both formats. Electronic research services that provide access to legal publications include commercial databases that charge a fee for access and Internet sources freely available to anyone.

Most legal information is organized by type of authority and jurisdiction. In print, this means individual types of authority from individual jurisdictions are published in separate sets of books. Court opinions from Maryland will be in one set of books (called "reporters"), and those from Massachusetts will be in another set of reporters. The same holds true for print collections of statutes and other types of legal authority.

Electronic research tools are organized similarly. Some are like print sets of books in that they provide access to one type of authority from one jurisdiction. The website for the Texas Supreme Court, for example, contains only Texas Supreme Court opinions. Others provide access to multiple types of authority from many different jurisdictions. Although these services aggregate a wide range of legal authority, they subdivide their contents much like print sources into individual databases organized by jurisdiction and type of authority. There are many commercial and government sources that provide electronic access to legal authority.

Westlaw and Lexis are the best known electronic legal research services. They are commercial databases that allow you to access all of the types of legal authority discussed in this chapter. They charge subscribers for use of their services, although your law school undoubtedly subsidizes the cost of student research while you are in school. Both Lexis and Westlaw offer two versions of their services. Lexis offers Lexis.com and Lexis Advance. Westlaw offers Westlaw.com and WestlawNext. When you see a general reference to one of these services in this text, that general reference includes both versions (e.g., a general reference to Lexis includes both Lexis.com and Lexis Advance). This text refers to the specific version of each service (e.g., Westlaw.com or WestlawNext) when describing functions unique to that version.

The organization of legal information by jurisdiction and type of authority affects the way individual legal authorities are identified. All legal authorities have citations assigned to them. The citation is the identifying information you can use to retrieve a document from a book or database. Thus, if you have the citation to an authority, you can locate it using that identifying information. To return to the key analogy, this is like knowing the license plate number of the car you are trying to locate in the parking lot.

Citations were originally formulated so that researchers could find authorities in print. Although most authorities are now available electronically, they are still primarily identified by their print citations. In print research, the citation generally includes the name of the book in which the source is published, the volume of the book containing the specific item, and the page or section number where the item begins. For example, each court opinion is identified by a citation containing the volume number of the reporter in which it is published, the name of the reporter, and the starting page of the opinion. If you had the citation for a case, you could go to the library or get online and locate it easily. Statutes, secondary sources, and other forms of authority also have citations you can use to retrieve specific documents.

Of course, with most research projects, you will not know the citations to the authorities you need to find. You will have been assigned the project to find out which legal authorities, if any, pertain to the subject of your research issue. Moreover, although occasionally you will need to locate only one specific item, such as a specific case, more often you will need to collect a range of authorities that pertain to the issue, such as a statute and cases that have interpreted the statute. Therefore, you will need to narrow the field of all legal information to that subset of information necessary to analyze your research issue.

The choices for narrowing the field are driven largely by the organization of legal information by jurisdiction and type of authority. To narrow the field, you must determine the jurisdiction whose legal rules will govern the issue you are analyzing, the type or types of legal authority you want to research (e.g., cases, statutes, or secondary sources), and the subject or topic of the information you need.

With most research tools, you must determine jurisdiction and type of authority before you begin to look for content related to your research issue because the information available is organized into separate books or databases according to jurisdiction and type of authority. In other words, you pre-filter, or narrow, the scope of your research by source first and then identify relevant content within each source. This is a source-driven approach to research. With WestlawNext and Lexis Advance you can, but do not have to, pre-filter by jurisdiction or type of authority. You have the option of searching for content related to your research issue first and then filtering the results by jurisdiction, type of authority, or both. This is a content-driven approach to research. With either approach, once you locate information, you must evaluate the results of your research to determine whether the information you have found is useful. The source-driven and content-driven approaches are illustrated in **Figure 13.5**.

One question you may have is whether it is better to use a source- or content-driven approach. The answer depends on the nature of your research project and your level of expertise about the subject matter. With a source-driven approach, you have to think carefully about a research issue to figure out which type(s) of authority are most likely to contain relevant information. Although selecting a type of authority can be challenging, choosing specific types of authority to research can make it easier to analyze the results because they are confined to the

Figure 13.5   Source-Driven and Content-Driven Approaches to Research

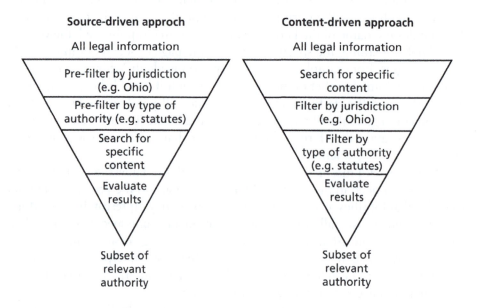

particular type of authority you selected. In addition, a savvy researcher may know exactly what type of authority governs — such as a state statute — and may not want to bother filtering through other types of authority included in the results. Conversely, if you are not sure which type(s) of authority to use, you may miss some relevant material altogether if it is in a source you did not consider using.

Because the content-driven approach allows you to search without first selecting a source, it shifts much of the analytical work involved in research to filtering the search results. This can be an advantage because the search results can include sources you might not have considered using. On the other hand, this approach frequently retrieves a large amount of information that has to be sifted carefully. Retrieving hundreds or thousands of documents can feel overwhelming if you do not understand your research issue well enough to filter the results effectively. Chapter 15 explains source-driven and content-driven searching in greater detail to help you learn how to determine which approach is better for your research project.

§13.5 Introduction to Research Planning

The chapters that follow explain how to use both print and electronic research tools to locate various types of legal authority. As noted above, however, knowing the mechanics of the research tools available to you is only part of learning to be an effective researcher. To research effectively, you must incorporate your technical knowledge into a research plan so that you can find the information you need to analyze your research issue. To do this, you will want to proceed in an organized manner to make sure your research is accurate and complete. Chapter 21, Developing a Research Plan, explores research planning in depth. This introduction to the planning process will help provide context as you learn the features of various research tools.

When you have a research task to complete, you will ordinarily proceed as follows:

- Define the scope of your research project and the issue(s) you need to research.
- Generate a list of search terms specific to your research issue(s).
- Plan your research path for each issue.
- Execute your research plan to search for relevant information.
- Assess the information you find and update your research to ensure that all the information is current.
- Revise your search terms and research plan as necessary and repeat the search process to complete your understanding of your research issue.

It is always a good idea to define the scope of your project before searching for information. Think about what you are being asked to do. Are you being asked to spend three weeks locating all information from every jurisdiction on a particular subject, or do you have a day to find out how courts in one state have ruled on an issue? Will you write an extensive analysis of your research, or will you summarize the results orally to the person who made the assignment? Evaluating the type of work product you are expected to produce, the amount of time you have, and the scope of the project will help you determine the best way to proceed.

You should also think carefully about the issue(s) you are being asked to research. Sometimes you will be asked to research a specific issue. Sometimes you will be presented with a research scenario and asked to determine the issue(s) it presents. It sounds almost silly to say this, but knowing what you are looking for will make it easier to find what you need.

Once you have defined your research task, you will need to generate search terms to use to search for information. Chapter 14 discusses different ways to do this. In general, however, you will need to construct a list of words or concepts to use to search for relevant content.

You will then want to plan your research path. The more you know about your research issue going in, the easier it will be to plan your research process. The less you know, the more flexible you will need to be in your approach. One of the goals of this text is to help you learn to plan your research path and assess the appropriate starting, middle, and ending points for your research.

Your ultimate goal in most research projects will be to locate primary mandatory authority, if it exists, on your research issue. Thus, regardless of whether you use a source- or content-driven approach, at some point you must consider type of authority and jurisdiction because these two factors determine whether the information you have located is primary mandatory authority. If primary mandatory authority is not available or does not directly answer your research question, persuasive authority (either primary or secondary) may help you analyze the issue. Therefore, in planning your research path, it may be helpful for you to think about three categories of authority: primary mandatory authority, primary persuasive authority, and secondary authority.

Because your goal will usually be to locate primary mandatory authority, you might think that that should be the starting point for all your research. In fact, if you know a lot about the issue you are researching, you might begin with primary mandatory authority, but that is not always the case. Secondary authorities that cite, analyze, and explain the law can provide a very efficient way to obtain background information and references to primary authority. Although secondary authorities are not controlling in your analysis, they are invaluable research tools and can be a good starting point for your project. Persuasive primary authority will rarely provide a good starting place because it provides neither the controlling rules nor analysis explaining the law. **Figure 13.6** shows the relationships among these three categories of authority.

Many research sources contain notes that refer to other sources, so once you locate one relevant source, you may be able to use the research notes to find additional useful information. Thus, there may be more than one appropriate starting point for your research. This text explains the features of a wide range of research sources so you can learn to make this assessment for different types of research projects.

Once you have planned your research path, you will execute your plan to search for information. As you locate information, you will need to evaluate its relevance to your research issue. One important aspect of assessing the information you find is making sure it is up-to-date. The law can change at any time. New cases are decided; older cases may be overruled; statutes can be enacted, amended, or repealed. Therefore, keeping your research current is essential. One way to update your research is with a specialized research tool called a citator, which is explained in Chapter 18. In addition, most sources of legal information will indicate how recently they have been updated to help you assess whether the information is current.

Most print research sources consist of hardcover books that can be difficult to update when the law changes. Some print resources are published in chronological order. For those resources, new books are published periodically as new material is compiled. Many, however, are organized by subject. For those resources, publishers cannot print new books every time the law changes. This would be prohibitively expensive, and because the law can change at any time, the new books would likely be out of date as soon as they were printed. To keep the books current, therefore, many print sources are updated with softcover pamphlets containing new information that became available after the hardcover book was published. These supplementary pamphlets are often called "pocket parts" because many of them fit into a "pocket" in the inside back cover of the hardcover book. Both the hardcover book and the pocket part will indicate the period of

Figure 13.6   Where to Begin Your Research Project

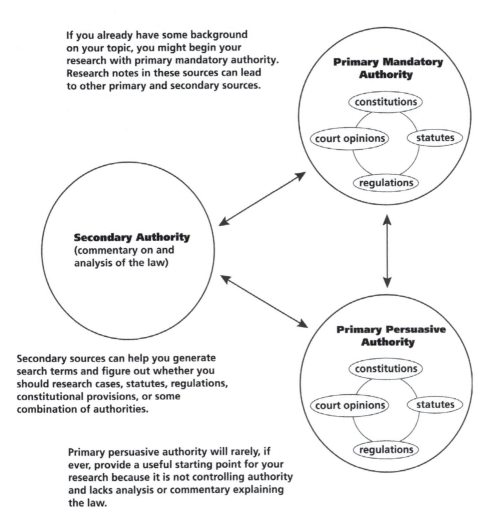

time each covers. You will see pocket parts mentioned throughout this text in reference to print research tools.

Electronic sources also usually contain publication or revision date information that you can use to assess how current it is. Electronic sources can be updated easily in the sense that new information can be added and older information revised at any time and as frequently as necessary. Westlaw and Lexis update at least some of their content on a daily basis. Providers other than major commercial vendors may not update their content as frequently. In addition, updates for some content may only become available when the print version of the source is updated, which means the electronic version may only be as current as the latest print version. Therefore, whether you conduct research in print or electronically, you must pay careful attention to the date of the information you locate.

Because research is not a linear process, you may find that you have to revise your search terms or your research plan to complete your research. If you do not find any information, or find too much information, you may need to backtrack or rethink your approach. Even if you find relevant information from the start, what you learn when you assess that information may take you in new directions. The process of searching, reading, and assessing will continue until you have narrowed the field of all legal information to the subset of information necessary to evaluate your research issue. This text explains a variety of search strategies you can use to tailor your research process to the specific issue you are researching.

CHAPTER 14

GENERATING SEARCH TERMS

As Chapter 13 explains, generating search terms is part of the research planning process. Developing a list of words or concepts that are likely to lead you to useful information is a preliminary step necessary for almost any type of research. Regardless of whether you use a source-driven or content-driven approach, you must generate a list of search terms related to your research issue to find relevant information. This chapter explains techniques you can use to generate search terms for virtually any research project.

§14.1 Generating Search Terms Based on Categories of Information

When presented with a set of facts, you could generate a list of search terms by constructing a random list of words that seem relevant to the issue. But a more structured approach — working from a set of categories, instead of random terms that sound relevant — will help ensure that you are covering all of your bases in conducting your research.

There are a number of ways that you could categorize the information in your research issue to create a list of search terms. Some people prefer to use the six questions journalists ask when covering a story: who, what, when, where, why, and how. Another way to generate search terms is to categorize the information presented by the facts as follows.

■ **THE *PARTIES* INVOLVED IN THE PROBLEM, DESCRIBED ACCORDING TO THEIR RELATIONSHIPS TO EACH OTHER**
Here, you might be concerned not only with parties who are in direct conflict with each other, but also any other individuals, entities, or groups involved. These might include fact witnesses who can testify as to what happened, expert witnesses if appropriate to the situation, other potential plaintiffs (in civil cases), or other potential defendants (in criminal or civil cases).

In describing the parties, proper names will not ordinarily be useful search terms, although if one party is a public entity or corporation, you might be able to locate other cases in which the entity or corporation was a party. Instead, you will usually want to describe the parties in terms of their legal status or relationships to each other, such as landlords and tenants, parents and children, employers and employees, or doctors and patients.

■ THE *PLACES AND THINGS* INVOLVED IN THE PROBLEM

In thinking about place, both geographical locale and type of location can be important. For example, the conduct at issue might have taken place in Pennsylvania, which would help you determine which jurisdiction's law applies. It might also have taken place at a school or in a church, which could be important for determining which legal rules apply to the situation.

"Things" can involve tangible objects or intangible concepts. In a problem involving a car accident, tangible things could include automobiles or stop signs. In other types of situations, intangible "things," such as a vacation or someone's reputation, could be useful search terms.

■ THE *POTENTIAL CLAIMS AND DEFENSES* THAT COULD BE RAISED

As you become more familiar with the law, you may be able to identify claims or defenses that a research problem potentially raises. The facts could indicate to you that the problem potentially involves particular claims (such as breach of contract, defamation, or bribery) or particular defenses (such as consent, assumption of the risk, or self-defense).

Lawyers use their accumulated knowledge, including both specialized knowledge gained in practice and foundational legal principles that all lawyers learn in law school, to identify legal doctrines that may apply to a client's situation. Even as a beginning law student, you are being introduced to a body of information common to all lawyers that you can use to brainstorm potential legal theories. When that is the case, you can often use claims and defenses effectively as search terms to help you identify applicable rules of law.

If you are dealing with an unfamiliar area of law, however, you might not know of any claims or defenses potentially at issue. In that situation, you can generate search terms by thinking about the conduct and mental states of the parties, as well as the injury suffered by the complaining party. Claims and defenses often flow from these considerations, and as a result, these types of terms can appear in a research tool's indexing system. When considering conduct, consider what was not done, as well as what was done. The failure to do an act might also give rise to a claim or defense. For example, you could be asked to research a situation in which one person published an article falsely asserting that another person was guilty of tax evasion, knowing that the accusation was not true. You might recognize this as a potential claim for the tort of defamation, which occurs when one person publishes false information that is damaging to another person's reputation. Even if you were unfamiliar with this tort, however, you could still generate search terms relevant to the claim by considering the defendant's conduct (publication) or mental state (intentional actions), or the plaintiff's injury (to reputation). These search terms would likely lead you to authority on defamation.

■ THE *RELIEF* SOUGHT BY THE COMPLAINING PARTY

The relief a party is seeking is another way to categorize information. Damages, injunction, specific performance, restitution, attorneys' fees, and other terms relating to the relief sought can lead you to pertinent information.

As an example of how you might go about using these categories to generate search terms, assume you have been asked to research the following situation:

> Your client recently ended a long-term relationship with her partner. She and her partner never participated in a formal marriage ceremony, but they had always planned to get married "someday." They lived together for five years and referred to each other as husband and wife. Your client and her former partner orally agreed to provide support for each other, and your client's former partner repeatedly made statements like, "What's mine is yours." Your client wants to know if she is entitled to part of the value of the assets her former partner acquired during their relationship or to any support payments.

- PARTIES: husband, wife, spouse, unmarried couple, unmarried cohabitants.
- PLACES AND THINGS: property, assets, ownership, support, non-marital relationship.
- POTENTIAL CLAIMS AND DEFENSES: common-law marriage, breach of contract, detrimental reliance.

  These terms might not have occurred to you if were not already familiar with the relevant legal principles. Additional terms could be generated according to conduct ("reliance" on "promises" of support) or mental state ("misrepresentation" if the client was misled into believing the parties shared ownership of the assets).
- RELIEF: damages, division or disposition of assets, support.

This is not an exhaustive list of search terms for this problem, but it illustrates how you can use these categories of information to develop useful search terms.

§14.2 Expanding the Initial Search

Once you have developed an initial set of search terms for your issue, the next task is to try to expand that list. The terms you originally generated may not appear in an index or database. Therefore, once you have developed your initial set of search terms, you should try to increase both the breadth and the depth of the list. You can increase the breadth of the list by identifying synonyms and terms related to the initial search terms, and you can increase the depth by expressing the concepts in your search terms both more abstractly and more concretely.

Increasing the breadth of your list with synonyms and related terms is essential to your research strategy. This is especially true for database word searches. As Chapter 15 explains in more detail, some research tools can cross-reference

Figure 14.1   Expanding the Breadth of Search Terms

Increasing breadth with synonyms and related terms:	title
	↕
	ownership
	↕
	possession

Figure 14.2   Increasing the Depth of Search Terms

Increasing depth with varying levels of abstraction:	intimate partners
	↕
	unmarried cohabitants
	↕
	boyfriend, girlfriend

content related to your search terms. A literal word search, however, searches only for the specific terms you identify. Therefore, to make sure you locate all of the pertinent information on your issue, you need to have a number of synonyms for the words and concepts in your search. In the research scenario described above, there are a number of synonyms and related terms for one of the initial search terms: ownership. As **Figure 14.1** illustrates, you might also search for terms such as title or possession.

You are also more likely to find useful research material if you increase the depth of your list by varying the level of abstraction. In the research scenario described above, the client and her former partner were unmarried cohabitants. You might find relevant information if you described the relationship more abstractly as "intimate partners" or more concretely as "boyfriend" or "girlfriend." See **Figure 14.2**.

§14.3 Prioritizing Search Terms

Once you have generated and expanded a list of search terms, you must prioritize them. Recall the key analogy from Chapter 13: If you had the key to a car parked at Disney World, how would you figure out which car it starts? Three relevant criteria would be make, model, and color, and ideally you would narrow the field by all three together. If that were not possible, which criterion would you use first? When you generate an extensive list of search terms for legal research, you will often use some combination of terms together, but you usually will not use all of them simultaneously. You can only look up one term or concept at a time in a print index. You can combine terms together in a word search, but putting too many in one search may limit the search's effectiveness. Consequently, you must decide where to focus your attention first.

You may find it helpful to think about two goals when you prioritize your search terms: identifying the legal rules that apply to your client's situation, and determining how the facts of the situation fit with the requirements of the rules. Of course, this is a bit of a chicken-or-egg problem in that the facts of the situation determine which rules apply and the application of the rules depends on the facts of the situation. Nevertheless, one element of your search strategy will be deciding whether to prioritize terms describing legal doctrines or terms describing the specific facts of your client's situation. This does not mean that you will ignore or discard other terms; it simply means that you must decide which terms to emphasize initially and which to use in fine-tuning the search results.

Prioritizing terms relating to legal doctrines makes sense when you know the theory or theories most likely to apply to your client's situation. To return to the key analogy, using the make and model to narrow the field of options would make sense. Prioritizing search terms related to the legal doctrine that applies to your research issue can similarly be an effective way to narrow the field of legal information.

As you begin learning about legal research, your professor may specify the legal doctrines you are to research. In the research scenario in §14.1, above, regarding the dissolution of a long-term relationship, your professor might direct you to research whether the parties formed a common-law marriage. You would certainly prioritize "common-law marriage" as a search term based on your professor's instructions.

In real life, clients bring the facts of their problems to you, not instructions to research particular legal theories, and as you become a more experienced researcher, the less likely your professor is to identify the legal doctrines or rules that apply to your research scenario. As you gain experience in the law, you will learn to identify the legal issues a situation presents and will be able to prioritize terms related to those issues in your research.

Sometimes, however, you will not begin your research with a sense of the applicable legal doctrines and will need to prioritize the facts of your client's situation instead. You can then use the search results to determine the legal doctrines that govern situations involving those types of facts. To return to the key analogy again, prioritizing facts is like trying to find the parked car by searching by color. This will narrow the field, but the remaining choices will reflect substantial diversity of makes and models. Similarly, prioritizing terms relating to the specific facts of the client's situation can lead to diffuse search results involving many different legal rules. The search results will also be affected by the level of abstraction of your terms. Search terms that are too concrete may yield little information, or little relevant information. More abstract factual terms may better steer you toward authority that describes applicable legal doctrines.

In the example involving dissolution of a client's long-term relationship, prioritizing factual terms relating to the parties' relationship could lead to rules about common-law marriage but would also likely lead to information about a variety of other legal doctrines. This is especially true for concrete terms like "boyfriend" or "girlfriend," which can occur in virtually any legal context. Although prioritizing factual terms may not be a useful approach when you need to locate information about a particular legal doctrine (such as common-law marriage), it can be useful when you need to identify all possible avenues of recovery for a client or do not have a sense of the legal doctrines that may apply to the situation.

Neither the list nor the priority of your search terms should remain static. Reading the information you find early in your research may reveal new search terms you can use to locate better information. The terminology of applicable legal rules that you did not consider at first might appear in the documents you locate in your initial research efforts, and they can then become useful terms for additional research (unless you have been instructed to limit your research to a particular legal doctrine). Facts that did not seem important at first could turn out to be critical to your analysis. As you work through your research path, therefore, you should revise both the content and priority of your search terms.

CHAPTER 15

Evaluating Search Options

§15.1 Introduction to Search Approaches

Recall the research scenario introduced in Chapter 14:

> Your client recently ended a long-term relationship with her partner. She and her partner never participated in a formal marriage ceremony, but they had always planned to get married "someday." They lived together for five years and referred to each other as husband and wife. Your client and her former partner orally agreed to provide support for each other, and your client's former partner repeatedly made statements like, "What's mine is yours." Your client wants to know if she is entitled to part of the value of the assets her former partner acquired during their relationship or to any support payments.

Assume that your supervisor asked you to find out whether the parties' relationship qualified as a common-law or "informal" marriage under the state's family law statutes and to submit a summary of your research by the end of the day. How would you approach the task? Assume instead that your supervisor gave you a week to research the law and submit a memorandum analyzing any legal theories that might apply to your client's situation. How would you approach that task?

Neither of these assignments requires you to explain how you conducted your research. Your supervisor and the client will be focused on the substantive results of your research, not on the process. But each of these research tasks is different in terms of the complexity of the research required, the work product to be produced, and the deadline for completion. Accordingly, you would use a different research process for each one. Knowing how to vary your research process to suit the task you need to accomplish is vital for performing complete, accurate, and efficient research.

Chapter 13 gave you a brief introduction to the source-driven and content-driven approaches to research and summarized the research planning process.

This chapter will explain these search approaches in more detail so you can learn how to assess which approach is best for the specific research tasks you will be asked to do as a student and in legal practice. This assessment is important for effective research planning. As you read this chapter, consider how you might approach the research tasks described above. The last section of this chapter sets out possible approaches to these assignments. You can compare your approaches with those outlined in §15.4.

As a starting point, §15.2 and §15.3, below, contrast source- and content-driven research strategies and are organized around two questions:

- What source(s) will be included in my search?
- What content will my search strategy identify?

§15.2 Source-Driven Search Process

The source-driven approach can be used with virtually any source of information: print, Lexis.com, Lexis Advance, Westlaw.com, WestlawNext, Bloomberg Law, and other providers of legal information. When you use the source-driven approach, you will select a source to search, search for content within the source, and read and evaluate the information you find.

§15.2.1 What Source(s) Will Be Included in My Search?

With the source-driven approach, only the publication(s) you select will be included in the search. In print, each publication is a separate book or set of books, and, as explained in Chapter 13, the publication will often be organized by jurisdiction and type of authority. For example, each set of statutes for each jurisdiction is in a separate set of books. The California state code is in one set of books, and the Illinois state code is in another. Therefore, the source you would select to research California statutes is the California state code.

Electronic services typically divide individual sources of information into separate databases organized by jurisdiction and type of authority, although some databases will combine related information. For example, in Westlaw.com and Lexis.com, you would research California statutes by selecting the California code database and Illinois statutes by selecting the Illinois code database, but a database containing all state codes is also available in both of those services.

To research effectively with the source-driven approach, you need to know two things: the range of publications or databases available to you and the type of source you want to research. You have to know that a publication or database exists to select it as a source. You also have to have at least a general idea about the type of information you need so you can select a source that contains that information. If you do not realize that an issue is likely one of federal law instead of state law or statutory law instead of common law, you may have trouble finding relevant information because you will not be looking in the right source or sources. Conversely, however, when you know the source of the information you need, researching only that source is efficient because all the information you find will be from the appropriate source.

§15.2.2 *What Content Will My Search Strategy Identify?*

Once you have selected a source, you are ready to search for information within that source. In print or electronically, you can search by subject. Electronic providers also allow you to execute word searches. Both of these methods of searching are discussed below.

§15.2.2.1 *Subject Searching*

In print, you can search by subject using the table of contents or index to a publication to find information within that publication. The index will usually contain more detail than the table of contents, and because it is organized by subject, will contain cross-references to related material. Some electronic providers provide access to the tables of contents or indices of selected publications, and you can use those the same way you would in print. Electronic providers also often offer specialized subject-searching tools that provide a directory of subject area topics.

One advantage to subject searching is that if the concept you are searching is described with commonly used words, an index or other subject compilation will reference only significant discussions of the concept, not every occurrence of commonly used words. For example, virtually every civil law suit is initiated by the filing of a document called a complaint. "Complaint," however, is both a technical legal term and a common, everyday word. If you wanted to research "complaints," you would want references to the document used to initiate a civil suit, not to the everyday use of the term. Subject-searching tools like an index prioritize the information within a source to help direct you to the most important information even when the topic you are researching is described with commonly used words.

Another advantage of subject searching is that index cross-references will point you in the right direction if you look up terms that are close to, but perhaps not exactly on point with, the topic you are researching. For example, a concept in contract law called the "mailbox" rule is also known as the "deposit acceptance" rule and the "postal acceptance" rule. If you knew one of those terms but not the others, index cross-references would likely direct you to an alternative entry containing relevant information under a different heading.

On the other hand, if you want to search for terms or topics that the publisher did not include in the index or subject compilation, you have no way to find the information you need. And if the publisher has compiled the material using topic names that are completely unfamiliar to you, you may not be able to find index or subject entries that are helpful.

§15.2.2.2 *Word Searching*

Word searching is a search option when you use electronic services. A word search allows you to search for documents that contain terms you specify. You have probably executed thousands of word searches in search engines like Google. Most electronic services offer two options for word searching: terms and connectors searching, and natural language searching. WestlawNext uses a variation on natural language searching that this text calls descriptive term searching. Terms and connectors, natural language, and descriptive term search techniques are discussed in Chapter 20.

Because word searches look for specific terms, you can establish your own search criteria without regard for whether the publisher included those words in the index. This can be helpful for fact-specific research, such as when you are searching for cases with specific facts similar to the facts of your research issue, or when the applicable legal concepts are expressed with relatively unique phrasing, such as "negligence per se," a well-known tort doctrine.

But because a word search is a literal search for the terms you identify, it can retrieve irrelevant documents or miss important documents. For example, executing a word search for a commonly used term such as "complaint" can retrieve many documents that use the term in an everyday sense instead of as a term of art. Although all concepts must ultimately be expressed in words, a literal search for the individual terms that express a general concept may not be focused enough to be as effective as a subject search. Conversely, a word search for the "mailbox" rule in a source that uses the alternative label "deposit acceptance" rule to characterize the concept may miss important documents because the search term "mailbox" will not appear in that source.

§15.3 Content-Driven Search Process

As this text goes to press, the content-driven process is available only through Lexis Advance and WestlawNext. Other search providers may change their search capabilities over time. The capabilities of Lexis Advance and WestlawNext are continuing to evolve as these products become more established. The discussion here focuses on research techniques that are, at this point in time, unique to these two services.

The content-driven approach uses the same steps as the source-driven approach, but it modifies the order of the steps. With content-driven research, you can search for content before you select a source.

§15.3.1 *What Source(s) Will Be Included in My Search?*

With Lexis Advance and WestlawNext you can do a true general search for information from all jurisdictions and all types of authority, much as you search for content without regard to source in Google. Although this sort of broad search is possible, it is not likely to be a strategy you will use often. What you are more likely to do with Lexis Advance or WestlawNext is pre-filter or narrow the scope of your research before you execute a search for specific content. For example, if you pre-filter by selecting a specific jurisdiction, the search results will be limited to sources from that jurisdiction but will include many types of information, including cases, statutes, secondary sources, court filings, and the like.

When you search this way, you may retrieve hundreds or thousands of documents. Your task then becomes one of narrowing the results to target the information you need. You can narrow or filter the results by type of authority, level of court, or other more specific criteria. You can also search for terms within the results.

The advantage of this approach is that it may prompt you to review sources you would not otherwise have considered. For example, if you thought an issue was governed by common law, but in fact, a statute applied to the issue, the general search may retrieve the relevant statute. The disadvantage is that a search that retrieves a large number of documents may be overwhelming, especially if you do not know enough about the issue to filter the results effectively. Another caution is the need to pay close attention to differences among sources of information. Regulations issued by agencies may look very similar to statutes. Briefs and other court filings may look very similar to a court's opinion, but only the opinion constitutes legal authority. When all sources of information are combined in a single search result, it is easy to lose track of the authoritative value of an individual document.

§15.3.2 *What Content Will My Search Strategy Identify?*

The default option for searching in Lexis Advance is natural language searching. The Lexis Advance search engine uses a more complex natural language algorithm than the Lexis.com search engine. This means you may get different results from the same natural language search executed in both services.

WestlawNext uses a form of natural language searching that this text calls descriptive term searching. It not only looks for your search terms within the text of documents, but also searches background information (meta-data) and evaluates prior search results to identify documents that appear to be relevant to your research issue even if they do not contain your precise search terms.

Both Lexis Advance and WestlawNext offer menu options and search commands that will allow you to execute a terms and connectors search without first selecting a source or database. In addition, terms and connectors searching is very important in filtering your search results. One filtering option in both services allows you to execute a word search within your search results. This search within the search results will be a terms and connectors search. Therefore, even when you execute a natural language search in Lexis Advance or WestlawNext, you must be familiar with terms and connectors searches to filter your search results effectively.

Natural language, descriptive term, and terms and connectors search techniques are discussed in Chapter 20.

§15.4 Evaluating Search Options

Now that you have read about the source-driven and content-driven approaches to research, consider how you might approach the research tasks described at the beginning of this chapter. Compare your approach with the potential research strategies outlined below.

The scenario involved disposition of assets upon dissolution of a non-marital relationship:

> Your client recently ended a long-term relationship with her partner. She and her partner never participated in a formal marriage ceremony, but they had always planned to get married "someday." They lived together for five years and referred to each other as husband and wife. Your client and her former partner orally agreed to provide support for each other, and your client's former partner repeatedly made statements like, "What's mine is yours." Your client wants to know if she is entitled to part of the value of the assets her former partner acquired during their relationship or to any support payments.

The first task was to determine whether the parties' relationship qualified as a common-law or "informal" marriage and summarize your research by the end of the day. For this task, your supervisor has given you some direction about the type of authority you need to locate: family law statutes. The statutes will likely set out the requirements for establishing a common-law marriage. The statutory language alone, however, may not fully answer the question. For example, if the statutory language does not say how long people must hold themselves out as married to establish a common-law marriage, cases interpreting the statute may provide some guidance.

After you generate your search terms, using a source-driven approach would be a good way to accomplish your research task. You know the jurisdiction and type of authority you need, so you can limit your search to the state code. This will reduce the number of documents you locate and make it easier to evaluate what you have found. Your search terms would relate to the legal theory you have been instructed to research. Looking up index entries or executing word searches for terms such as "common-law marriage" or "informal marriage" would likely lead you in the right direction.

Once you locate the relevant provision(s) of the code, you can read the language to determine the requirements for this type of marriage. Research notes accompanying the statute will likely summarize cases interpreting the statute, making it easy for you to locate and read pertinent cases. Given the short deadline for reporting the results of your research, this would be a good approach for making a preliminary assessment of the law so that you and your supervisor can decide whether further research is appropriate.

Now consider the second task: to research any legal theories that might apply to your client's situation. This is a more complex research task because you have not been instructed to research any specific legal theory or type of authority. Your job is to identify the theories that potentially provide a remedy. Unless you are already familiar with applicable legal rules, you will need to begin in a more general way by learning about potential theories of recovery and then evaluating the potential success of those theories under your state's law. This work could be accomplished with either a source-driven or content-driven approach.

Again, you would begin by generating search terms. Terms relating to property rights of unmarried cohabitants or boyfriend and girlfriend living together would likely be relevant. From there, you could use a source-driven approach for your research. You know that your state is the controlling jurisdiction, but you may not know which type(s) of primary mandatory authority will apply to your client's situation. Recall from Chapter 13, however, that secondary authorities can be a good starting point for research when you need background information because they cite, analyze, and explain the law. You could begin your research by selecting a secondary source. Chapter 16, on secondary source research, describes a range of secondary sources you could use to obtain background information. One that might be useful is *American Jurisprudence*, Second Edition, a legal encyclopedia with general information about a wide range of legal issues. You could use *American Jurisprudence* in print or online to search for content related to property rights of unmarried cohabitants. The results of your search would reveal that legal rules relating to detrimental reliance on a promise, common-law marriage, and breach of contract (among other theories) may apply to your client's situation. You could then use this information to search for relevant cases and statutes to determine whether your client might be able to prevail under these or other theories.

Another option would be to use a content-driven approach in Lexis Advance or WestlawNext. You would likely pre-filter the search by selecting your state as the jurisdiction. By searching for content related to property rights of unmarried cohabitants, you could retrieve secondary sources, cases, statutes, and other material that may be germane to your client's situation. After executing a search, you could filter this information according to any number of criteria and read what you found to identify rules that might apply to your client's situation. For example, you might retrieve secondary sources (like *American Jurisprudence*) describing detrimental reliance on a promise, a statute regarding the status of common-law marriage in your state, and a case analyzing a breach of contract claim by an unmarried person against a former partner. The search might also retrieve documents relating to domestic violence, wills and estates, same-sex marriage, or any number of other legal matters that could arise between unmarried partners but that do not apply to your client's situation. With no limitation on the type of authority, the search would likely retrieve several hundred to several thousand documents, making the post-search filtering process critical to identifying relevant information.

The differences between the source- and content-driven approaches can seem abstract when you read a textual description of the research process. When you start doing research, the differences will become readily apparent. You might try searching for information about the property rights of unmarried cohabitants in your state using the source- and content-driven approaches to see how the results differ and which you think is most effective. More detailed information on research planning appears in Chapter 21.

As you begin conducting research independently, you may find yourself gravitating toward the content-driven process that is presently only available through WestlawNext and Lexis Advance. It will likely feel familiar because it strives to replicate the types of Internet searching everyone does on a regular basis, and it has appealing features that make it a good choice for many types of research. It is worthwhile for you to learn effective content-driven searching.

Nevertheless, it is important for you to gain facility with source-driven searching as well. Source-driven searching is often the most effective way to conduct research, which is why it remains an option with Lexis Advance and WestlawNext. Additionally, many employers continue to rely on providers of legal information that offer only source-driven searching. Lexis Advance and WestlawNext can cost more than Westlaw.com, Lexis.com, and other services. Employers may proceed cautiously before subscribing to premium products that are unfamiliar to them. Some employers have invested thousands of dollars in print collections and see more benefit in having their attorneys use those resources than in investing in new electronic services.

Incentives such as reward points that can be redeemed for products may also provide inducements unrelated to your research goals to use particular research services. There is nothing wrong with these incentives as long as you understand that they are marketing efforts by commercial entities directed toward you as a consumer of information products. You do not rely exclusively on sellers' marketing messages when making purchases in your daily life. You should not do so when you select research services, either. As a consumer, you should make your own assessment of the resources available to you so that you can employ search processes most in line with your professional goals and needs.

SELECTED LEGAL RESEARCH SOURCES AND STRATEGIES

CHAPTER 16

SECONDARY SOURCE RESEARCH

§16.1 Introduction to Secondary Sources

Primary authority refers to sources of legal rules, such as cases, statutes, and administrative regulations. Secondary sources, by contrast, provide commentary on the law. Although they are not binding on courts and are not cited as frequently as primary sources, secondary sources are excellent research tools. Because they often summarize or collect authorities from a variety of jurisdictions, they can help you find mandatory or persuasive primary authority on a subject. They also often provide narrative explanations of complex concepts that would be difficult for a beginning researcher to grasp thoroughly simply from reading primary sources. Equipped with a solid understanding of the background of an area of law, you will be better able to locate and evaluate primary authority on your research issue.

§16.1.1 When Secondary Sources Will Be Most Useful

Secondary sources will be most useful to you in the following situations:

(1) **WHEN YOU ARE RESEARCHING AN AREA OF LAW WITH WHICH YOU ARE UNFAMILIAR.** Secondary sources can give you the necessary background to generate search terms. They can also lead you directly to primary authorities.

(2) **WHEN YOU ARE LOOKING FOR PRIMARY PERSUASIVE AUTHORITY BUT DO NOT KNOW HOW TO NARROW THE JURISDICTIONS THAT ARE LIKELY TO HAVE USEFUL INFORMATION.** If you need to find primary persuasive authority on a subject, conducting a nationwide survey of the law on the topic is not likely to be an efficient research strategy. Secondary sources can help you locate persuasive authority relevant to your research issue.

(3) WHEN YOU ARE RESEARCHING AN UNDEVELOPED AREA OF THE LAW.   When you are researching a question of first impression, commentators may have analyzed how courts should rule on the issue.

(4) WHEN AN INITIAL SEARCH OF PRIMARY SOURCES YIELDS EITHER NO AUTHORITY OR TOO MUCH AUTHORITY.   If you are unable to find any authority at all on a topic, you may not be looking in the right places. Secondary sources can educate you on the subject in a way that may allow you to expand or refocus your research efforts. When your search yields an unmanageable amount of information, secondary sources can do two things. First, their citations to primary authority can help you identify the most important authorities pertaining to the research issue. Second, they can provide you with information that may help you narrow your search or weed out irrelevant sources.

§16.1.2 *Limits on the Appropriate Use of Secondary Sources*

Knowing when *not* to use secondary sources is also important. As noted above, secondary sources are not binding on courts. Therefore, you will not ordinarily cite them in briefs or memoranda. This is especially true if you use secondary sources to lead you to primary authority. It is important never to rely exclusively on a discussion of a primary authority that appears in a secondary source. If you are discussing a primary authority in a legal analysis, you must read that authority yourself and update your research to make sure it is current.

This is true for two reasons. First, a summary of a primary authority might not include all of the information necessary to your analysis. It is important to read the primary authority for yourself to make sure you represent it correctly and thoroughly in your analysis.

Second, the information in the secondary source might not be completely current. Although most secondary sources are updated on a regular basis, the law can change at any time. The source may contain incomplete information simply because of the inevitable time lag between changes to the law and the publication of a supplement. One mistake some beginning researchers make is citing a secondary source for the text of a case or statute without checking to make sure that the case has not been overturned or that the statute has not been changed. Another potential error is citing a secondary source for a proposition about the state of the law generally, such as, "Forty-two states now recognize a cause of action for invasion of privacy based on disclosure of private facts." While statements of that nature were probably true when the secondary source was written, other states may have acted, or some of those noted may have changed their law, in the intervening time period. Accordingly, secondary sources should only be used as a starting point for locating primary authority, not an ending point.

§16.1.3 *Commonly Used Secondary Sources*

This section describes the following commonly used secondary sources: legal encyclopedias, treatises, legal periodicals, *American Law Reports*, Restatements of the law, and uniform laws and model acts.

§16.1.3.1 *Legal Encyclopedias*

Legal encyclopedias are just like the general subject encyclopedias you have used in the past, except they are limited in scope to legal subjects. Legal encyclopedias provide a general overview of the law on a variety of topics. They do not provide analysis or suggest solutions to conflicts in the law. Instead, they simply report on the general state of the law. Because encyclopedias cover the law in such a general way, you will usually use them to get background information on your research topic and, to a lesser extent, to locate citations to primary authority. You will rarely, if ever, cite a legal encyclopedia.

There are two general legal encyclopedias, *American Jurisprudence*, Second Edition (Am. Jur. 2d) and *Corpus Juris Secundum* (C.J.S.). In addition, encyclopedias are published for many individual states (e.g., *California Jurisprudence*, *Maryland Law Encyclopedia*, and *Michigan Law and Practice*). When you are researching a question of state law, state encyclopedias are often more helpful than general encyclopedias for two reasons. First, the summary of the law will be tailored to the law of that state, and therefore is likely to be more helpful. Second, the citations to primary authority will be from the controlling jurisdiction. Consequently, state encyclopedias can be more useful for leading you to primary sources.

§16.1.3.2 *Treatises*

Treatises have a narrower focus than legal encyclopedias. Where legal encyclopedias provide a general overview of a broad range of topics, treatises generally provide in-depth treatment of a single subject, such as torts or constitutional law. The goal of a treatise is to address in a systematic fashion all of the major topics within a subject area. Treatises often trace the history of the development of an area of law and explain the relationship of the treatise's subject to other areas of the law. To provide a comprehensive treatment of the subject's major topics, a treatise will explain the legal rules in the subject area, analyze major cases and statutes, and address policy issues underlying the rules. In addition to providing textual explanations, treatises also usually contain citations to many primary and secondary authorities.

Some treatises are widely respected and considered definitive sources in their subject areas. These treatises have often existed for a number of years and may be identified by the names of their original authors, even though other scholars now update and revise them. These well-known treatises may address broad areas of the law (Prosser on torts, Corbin on contracts, Wright & Miller on federal civil procedure) or more specialized subjects (Nimmer on copyright, White & Summers on the Uniform Commercial Code, Sutherland on statutory interpretation). These are not, however, the only treatises. Any book that provides comprehensive treatment of a single subject in a systematic fashion is a treatise, and many treatises exist on both broad areas of the law and narrower subjects. If you use a definitive treatise in your research, you might cite it in a brief or memorandum. Ordinarily, however, you will use treatises for research purposes and will not cite them in your written analysis.

§16.1.3.3 *Legal Periodicals*

Articles in legal periodicals can be very useful research tools. You may hear periodical articles referred to as "law review" or "journal" articles. Many law schools publish periodicals known as law reviews or journals that collect articles on a wide range of topics. Many other types of legal periodicals also exist, however, including commercially published journals, legal newspapers, and magazines.

The commercial legal press includes magazines such as the *ABA Journal* and local bar journals and newspapers such as *The National Law Journal*. These publications are good for keeping abreast of newsworthy developments in the law. Because they are news sources, their articles are generally short and focused more on describing legal developments than on analysis. These types of articles can provide limited background information, but they usually do not focus on the kinds of issues first-year law students research.

Articles published in law reviews or journals, by contrast, are thorough, thoughtful treatments of legal issues by law professors, judges, practitioners, and even students. The articles are usually focused fairly narrowly on specific issues, although they often include background or introductory sections that provide a general overview of the topic. They are generally well researched and contain citations to many primary and secondary authorities. In addition, they often address undeveloped areas in the law and propose solutions for resolving problems in the law. As a result, periodical articles can be useful for obtaining an overview of an area of law, finding references to primary and secondary authority, and developing ideas for analyzing a question of first impression or resolving a conflict in the law.

Law review or journal articles fall into the following general categories:

■ ARTICLES WRITTEN BY LEGAL SCHOLARS

These are articles written by law professors and other scholars. They frequently address problems or conflicts in the law. They may propose solutions to legal problems, advocate for changes to the law, identify new legal theories, or explore the relationship between the law and some other discipline. Articles by leading or established scholars may be helpful in your research, especially if they explain doctrines or developments in a useful way. The weight of an individual article will depend on a number of factors, including the author's expertise, the reputation of the journal in which it is published, the article's age, and the depth of the article's research and analysis.

■ ARTICLES WRITTEN BY JUDGES AND PRACTITIONERS

These are articles written by people who work with the law on a daily basis in very practical ways. Judges often write about their judicial philosophies or to offer advice or insights to practitioners. Practitioners may write about areas of law in which they practice. These articles may help you understand a legal issue and provide an overview of important authorities, but practitioner articles in particular may not have the depth of other types of articles.

■ STUDENT NOTES OR COMMENTS

These are articles written by law students. Often, they describe a significant new case or statute. They may analyze a problem in the law and propose a solution. Because these articles are written by students, they carry less weight than other periodical articles and are useful primarily for background information and citations to primary authorities.

These are, of course, generalizations that may not hold true in every instance. For the most part, however, law review and journal articles will be useful to you as research tools, rather than as support for written analysis. You will not ordinarily cite an article if you can support your analysis with primary authority. If you cannot find primary support, however, you might cite a persuasive article. Additionally, if you incorporate an argument or analysis from an article in your written work, it is important to cite the source to avoid plagiarism.

Periodical articles are unique among legal authorities in that there is no way to update an individual article, short of locating later articles that add to or criticize an earlier article. As a consequence, it is important to note the date of any periodical article you use. If the article is more than a few years old, you may want to supplement your research with more current material. In addition, if you use the article to lead you to primary authority, you will need to update your research using the updating tools available for those primary sources to make sure your research is completely current.

§16.1.3.4 *American Law Reports*

American Law Reports, or A.L.R., contains articles called "Annotations." Annotations collect summaries of cases from a variety of jurisdictions to provide an overview of the law on a topic. A.L.R. combines the breadth of topic coverage found in an encyclopedia with the depth of discussion in a treatise or legal periodical. Nevertheless, A.L.R. is different from these other secondary sources in significant ways. Because A.L.R. Annotations provide summaries of individual cases, they are more detailed than encyclopedias. Unlike treatises or legal periodicals, however, they mostly report the results of the cases without much analysis or commentary. A.L.R. Annotations are especially helpful at the beginning of your research to give you an overview of a topic. Because Annotations collect summaries of cases from many jurisdictions, they can also be helpful in directing you toward mandatory or persuasive primary authority. More recent Annotations also contain references to other research sources, such as other secondary sources and tools for conducting additional case research. Although A.L.R. is a useful research tool, you will rarely, if ever, cite an A.L.R. Annotation.

There are eight series of A.L.R. that address United States law: A.L.R., A.L.R.2d, A.L.R.3d, A.L.R.4th, A.L.R.5th, A.L.R.6th, A.L.R. Fed., and A.L.R. Fed. 2d.[1] Each series contains multiple volumes organized by volume number. A.L.R. Fed. and Fed. 2d cover issues of federal law. The remaining series usually cover issues of state law, although they do bring in federal law as appropriate to the topic.

§16.1.3.5 Restatements

The American Law Institute publishes what are called Restatements of the law in a variety of fields. You may already be familiar with the Restatements for contracts or torts from your other classes. Restatements essentially "restate" the common-law rules on a subject. Restatements have been published in the following fields:

- Agency
- Conflicts of Laws
- Contracts
- Foreign Relations Law of the United States
- Judgments
- Property
- Restitution
- Security
- Suretyship and Guaranty
- The Law Governing Lawyers
- Torts
- Trusts
- Unfair Competition.

In determining what the common-law rules are, the Restatements often look to the rules in the majority of United States jurisdictions. Sometimes, however, the Restatements will also state emerging rules where the rules seem to be changing or proposed rules in areas where the authors believe a change in the law would be appropriate. Although the Restatements are limited to common-law doctrines, the rules in the Restatements are set out almost like statutes, breaking different doctrines down into their component parts. In addition to setting out the common-law rules for a subject, the Restatements also provide commentary on the proper interpretations of the rules, illustrations demonstrating how the rules should apply in certain situations, and summaries of cases applying and interpreting the Restatement.

---

[1] A new A.L.R. series — A.L.R. International — was introduced in 2010 and addresses international law issues. As this text goes to press, it is unclear how many law libraries are adding this series to their print collections. It is not a publication that is typically available with student Lexis and Westlaw passwords.

Although a Restatement is a secondary source, it is one with substantial weight. Courts can adopt a Restatement's view of an issue, which then makes the comments and illustrations especially persuasive in that jurisdiction. If you are researching the law of a jurisdiction that has adopted a Restatement, you can use the Restatement effectively to locate persuasive authority from other Restatement jurisdictions. As a result, a Restatement is an especially valuable secondary source.

§16.1.3.6 Uniform Laws and Model Acts

Uniform laws and model acts are proposed statutes that can be adopted by legislatures. Two examples with which you may already be familiar are the Uniform Commercial Code (U.C.C.) and the Model Penal Code. Uniform laws and model acts are similar to Restatements in that they set out proposed rules, followed by commentary, research notes, and summaries of cases interpreting the rules. Unlike Restatements, which are limited to common-law doctrines, uniform laws and model acts exist in areas governed by statutory law.

Although uniform laws and model acts look like statutes, they are secondary sources. Their provisions do not take on the force of law unless they are adopted by a legislature. When that happens, however, the commentary, research references, and case summaries become very useful research tools. They can help you interpret the law and direct you to persuasive authority from other jurisdictions that have adopted the law.

You are most likely to research uniform laws and model acts when your project involves research into state statutes. If you decide to use this resource, you may also want to review Chapter 19, which discusses statutory research.

§16.1.4 Methods of Locating Secondary Sources

You can locate secondary sources using either a source-driven or content-driven approach. If you use a source-driven approach, the first step will be deciding which type(s) of source(s) to use.

Once you know which types of secondary sources are likely to meet your research needs, you will need to locate relevant information within each source. Three common search techniques are retrieving a document from its citation, searching by subject, and executing a word search. Some secondary sources are only published in print. Few of the ones published electronically are available on the Internet. Therefore, you will use these search techniques most often either in print or in a commercial database such as Westlaw or Lexis.

If you are just beginning your research, searching by subject is often a good strategy. Most secondary sources, other than legal periodicals, have subject indices (in print) and tables of contents (in print and online). To locate legal periodicals, you can use a separate periodical index that organizes periodical citations by subject. Word searching is another search option for locating secondary sources in a full-text database and may be an option in a periodical index as well.

If you choose content-driven searching in Lexis Advance or WestlawNext, your search results will include secondary sources. In Lexis Advance, secondary sources appear under the **Secondary Materials** tab. In WestlawNext, a few secondary sources will appear on an **Overview** page summarizing your search results. You will see more results if you choose the **Secondary Sources** link from the **View** menu; this link typically appears below the links for primary authorities and court filings. When you view the secondary sources your search retrieved, you can filter the results according to a number of criteria to focus on specific publications or types of content.

Many secondary sources cross reference other secondary sources. Therefore, once you have located one secondary source on your research issue, it may refer you to other secondary sources that you can locate by citation.

An overview of how to research secondary sources in print and electronically is provided in the Research Checklist at the end of this chapter.

§16.2 Checklist for Secondary Source Research

1. **LEGAL ENCYCLOPEDIAS**
    - ☐ Use legal encyclopedias for very general background information and limited citations to primary authority, but not for in-depth analysis of a topic.
    - ☐ Use Am. Jur. 2d or C.J.S. for a general overview; look for a state encyclopedia for an overview of the law in an individual state.
    - ☐ Locate material in a print encyclopedia by (1) using the subject index or table of contents; (2) locating relevant sections in the main subject volumes; and (3) updating with the pocket part.
    - ☐ Locate material in legal encyclopedias in Lexis.com, Westlaw.com, and WestlawNext by executing word searches in the databases for individual publications or by viewing the table of contents.
    - ☐ Locate material in legal encyclopedias in WestlawNext and Lexis Advance by executing a content-driven search, reviewing results for secondary sources, and filtering the content by source or other appropriate criteria.

2. **TREATISES**
    - ☐ Use treatises for an in-depth discussion and some analysis of an area of law and for citations to primary authority.
    - ☐ Locate treatises in print through the online catalog or by asking a reference librarian for a recommendation; locate material within a treatise by (1) using the subject index or table of contents; (2) locating relevant sections within the main text; and (3) updating with the pocket part.
    - ☐ Locate material in treatises in Lexis.com, Westlaw.com, and WestlawNext by executing word searches in the databases for individual publications. View the table of contents for individual publications, if available.
    - ☐ Locate material in treatises in WestlawNext and Lexis Advance by executing a content-driven search, reviewing results for secondary sources, and filtering the content by source or other appropriate criteria.

3. **LEGAL PERIODICALS**
   - ☐ Use legal periodicals for background information, citations to primary authority, in-depth analysis of a narrow topic, or information on a conflict in the law or an undeveloped area of the law.
   - ☐ Locate citations to periodical articles with the *Index to Legal Periodicals* (ILP) or LegalTrac periodical indices; execute a search to obtain a list of citations. Full text of some articles is available through these services.
   - ☐ Locate legal periodicals in Lexis.com, Westlaw.com, and WestlawNext by searching in the databases for multiple or individual publications.
   - ☐ Locate legal periodicals in WestlawNext and Lexis Advance by executing a content-driven search, reviewing results for secondary sources, and filtering the content by appropriate criteria.
   - ☐ Locate legal periodicals in .pdf format using HeinOnline or SSRN.
   - ☐ Locate selected legal periodicals using a law-related website or general Internet search engine.

4. *AMERICAN LAW REPORTS*
   - ☐ Use A.L.R. Annotations for an overview of an area of law and citations to primary authority (especially to locate persuasive authority from other jurisdictions), but not for in-depth analysis of a topic.
   - ☐ Locate material within A.L.R. in print by (1) using the A.L.R. Index; (2) locating relevant Annotations in the main volumes; and (3) updating with the pocket part.
   - ☐ Locate A.L.R. Annotations in Lexis.com, Westlaw.com, and WestlawNext by executing word searches in the *American Law Reports* (ALR) database.
   - ☐ Locate A.L.R. Annotations in WestlawNext by executing a content-driven search, reviewing results for secondary sources, and filtering the content by source or other appropriate criteria. The same process should apply to Lexis Advance when its coverage includes A.L.R. Annotations.

5. **RESTATEMENTS**
   - ☐ Use Restatements for research into common-law subjects and to locate mandatory and persuasive authority from jurisdictions that have adopted a Restatement.
   - ☐ Locate Restatements in print through the online catalog.
   - ☐ Locate information within a print Restatement by (1) using the subject index or table of contents to identify relevant sections within the Restatement volumes; (2) using the noncumulative Appendix volumes to find pertinent case summaries; and (3) using the pocket part in the latest Appendix volume to locate the most recent cases.
   - ☐ Locate Restatements in Lexis.com, Westlaw.com, and WestlawNext by executing word searches or viewing the table of contents.
     - In Lexis.com, Restatement rules and case annotations are in separate databases.
     - In Westlaw, Restatement rules and case annotations are combined; case annotations will follow individual Restatement rules.

☐ Locate Restatements in WestlawNext by executing a content-driven search, reviewing results for secondary sources, and filtering the content by source or other appropriate criteria. The same process should apply to Lexis Advance when its coverage includes Restatements.

6. **UNIFORM LAWS AND MODEL ACTS**

☐ Use uniform laws and model acts to interpret a law adopted by a legislature and to locate persuasive authority from other jurisdictions that have adopted the law.

☐ Locate uniform laws and model acts in print using *Uniform Laws Annotated, Master Edition* (ULA).

☐ Locate information in the ULA set by (1) using the *Directory of Uniform Acts and Codes: Tables and Index* to search by subject, by the name of the law, or by adopting jurisdiction; (2) locating relevant provisions in the main volumes; and (3) updating with the pocket part.

☐ Locate selected uniform laws and model acts in Lexis.com, Westlaw.com, and WestlawNext by executing word searches in the appropriate database or viewing the table of contents. Lexis Advance may include uniform laws and model acts as its coverage increases.

CHAPTER 17

CASE RESEARCH

§17.1 Introduction to Cases

§17.1.1 *The Structure of the Court System*

The United States has more than 50 separate court systems, including the federal system, the 50 state systems, and the District of Columbia system. You may recall from Chapter 13 that there are three levels of courts in the federal system: the United States District Courts (the trial courts), the United States Courts of Appeals (the intermediate appellate courts), and the United States Supreme Court (the court of last resort). Most state court systems are structured the same way as the federal court system.

Judges from any of these courts can issue written decisions, and their decisions are one source of legal rules. This chapter focuses on where these decisions are published and how they are indexed.

§17.1.2 *Case Reporters*

Court opinions, or cases, are published in books called reporters. Reporters are sets of books collecting cases in chronological order. Many sets of reporters are limited to opinions from a single jurisdiction or level of court. Thus, for example, federal reporters contain opinions from federal courts, and state reporters contain opinions from state courts. In addition, each set of reporters may be subdivided into different series covering different time periods.

A reporter published under government authority is known as an official reporter.[1] Reporters published by commercial publishers are called unofficial reporters. Because these two types of reporters exist, the same opinion may be published in more than one reporter. The text of the opinion should be exactly the same in an official and an unofficial reporter; the only difference is that the former is published by the government, and the latter is not. When a case appears

---

[1] The government may publish the reporter itself, or it may arrange for the reporter to be published by a commercial publisher. As long as the government arranges for the publication, the reporter is official, even if it is physically produced by a commercial publisher.

in more than one reporter, it is described as having parallel citations. This is because each set of reporters will have its own citation for the case.

The only federal court opinions published by the government are those of the U.S. Supreme Court; these are published in a reporter called *United States Reports*. State governments usually publish the decisions of their highest courts, and most also publish decisions from some of their lower courts.

Perhaps the largest commercial publisher of cases is Thomson Reuters/West, formerly West Publishing Company. West has created a network of unofficial reporters called the *National Reporter System*, which comprises reporters with decisions from almost every U.S. jurisdiction.

West publishes U.S. Supreme Court decisions in the *Supreme Court Reporter*. Decisions from the U.S. Courts of Appeals are published in the *Federal Reporter*, and those from U.S. District Courts are published in the *Federal Supplement*. West also publishes some specialized reporters that contain decisions from the federal courts. For example, *Federal Rules Decisions* (F.R.D.) contains federal district court decisions interpreting the Federal Rules of Civil and Criminal Procedure, and the *Federal Appendix* (Fed. Appx. or F. App'x) contains non-precedential decisions from the federal courts of appeals. (Non-precedential decisions are discussed in more detail below.)

West publishes state court decisions in what are called regional reporters. West has divided the country into seven regions. The reporter for each region collects state court decisions from all of the states within that region.

Because West publishes reporters for almost every jurisdiction in a common format with common indexing features, this chapter focuses on research using West publications. The chart in **Figure 17.1** shows where cases from the various state and federal courts can be found.

Decisions for most states can be found in the state's official reporter, as well as in the reporters listed in **Figure 17.1**.[2]

§17.1.3 *The Anatomy of a Published Case*

A case published in a West reporter has five components:

1. The heading containing the parallel citation (if any) to an official reporter, the case name, the court that rendered the decision, and the date of the decision.
2. A synopsis of the decision written by case editors, not by the court.
3. One or more paragraphs summarizing the key points within the decision. These summary paragraphs are called headnotes, and they are written by case editors, not by the court.

---

[2] West also publishes separate unofficial state reporters for New York, California, and Illinois. Thus, New York, California, and Illinois cases may appear in three places: (1) an official state reporter; (2) a West regional reporter; and (3) a West unofficial state reporter. Some lower court opinions published in West's New York and California reporters are not published in the regional reporters covering those states. By contrast, all of the cases in West's *Illinois Decisions* are included in the regional reporter covering Illinois.

Figure 17.1   Reporters

COURT or JURISDICTION	REPORTER (followed by reporter abbreviation; multiple abbreviations denote multiple series)
United States Supreme Court[*]	*United States Reports* (U.S.) *Supreme Court Reporter* (S. Ct.) *United States Supreme Court Reports, Lawyer's Edition* (L. Ed., L. Ed. 2d)
United States Courts of Appeals	*Federal Reporter* (F., F.2d, F.3d) *Federal Appendix* (Fed. Appx. or F. App'x)
United States District Courts	*Federal Supplement* (F. Supp., F. Supp. 2d) *Federal Rules Decisions* (F.R.D.)
Atlantic Region states (Connecticut, Delaware, District of Columbia, Maine, Maryland, New Hampshire, New Jersey, Pennsylvania, Rhode Island, Vermont)	*Atlantic Reporter* (A., A.2d, A.3d)
North Eastern Region states (Illinois, Indiana, Massachusetts, New York, Ohio)	*North Eastern Reporter* (N.E., N.E.2d) New York: *New York Supplement* (N.Y.S., N.Y.S.2d) Illinois: *Illinois Decisions* (Ill. Dec.)
South Eastern Region states (Georgia, North Carolina, South Carolina, Virginia, West Virginia)	*South Eastern Reporter* (S.E., S.E.2d)
Southern Region states (Alabama, Florida, Louisiana, Mississippi)	*Southern Reporter* (So., So. 2d, So. 3d)
South Western Region States (Arkansas, Kentucky, Missouri, Tennessee, Texas)	*South Western Reporter* (S.W., S.W.2d, S.W.3d)
North Western Region states (Iowa, Michigan, Minnesota, Nebraska, North Dakota, South Dakota, Wisconsin)	*North Western Reporter* (N.W., N.W.2d)
Pacific Region states (Alaska, Arizona, California, Colorado, Hawaii, Idaho, Kansas, Montana, Nevada, New Mexico, Oklahoma, Oregon, Utah, Washington, Wyoming)	*Pacific Reporter* (P., P.2d, P.3d) California: *California Reporter* (Cal. Rptr., Cal. Rptr. 2d, Cal. Rptr. 3d)

---

[*] Official reporter published by the federal government.

4. The names of the attorneys who represented the parties and the judge or judges who decided the case.
5. The opinion of the court. If the decision has any concurring or dissenting opinions, these will follow immediately after the majority or plurality opinion.

Only the fifth item on this list, the opinion of the court, constitutes legal authority. All of the remaining items are editorial enhancements. These editorial enhancements are very useful for locating cases, but they are not part of the court's opinion. Therefore, you should never rely on any part of a case other than the text of the opinion itself.[3]

Figure 17.2 shows an excerpt from a case published in a West reporter.

§17.1.4 Unpublished, or Non-Precedential, Opinions

Not all court decisions are published; only those designated by the courts for publication appear in print reporters. The decisions not designated for publication are called unpublished decisions. In the past, the only ways to obtain copies of unpublished decisions were from the parties to the case or from the clerk's office at the courthouse. This is still true today for some unpublished decisions, especially those issued by state courts. Many unpublished decisions, however, are available through electronic research services and on the Internet. The federal courts of appeals make many of their unpublished decisions available on their websites. In addition, unpublished decisions issued by the federal courts of appeals since 2001 are now available in print in the *Federal Appendix*, a West reporter.

Because these decisions are increasingly available electronically and in print, the term "unpublished" opinion has become a misnomer. A more accurate term is "non-precedential" opinion. Non-precedential decisions are often subject to special court rules. For example, unlike decisions published in the *Federal Reporter*, those appearing in the *Federal Appendix* are not treated as binding precedent by the courts, which is why they are described as "non-precedential" decisions. In the past, the federal courts of appeals often limited the circumstances under which non-precedential decisions could be cited in documents filed with the court, although all non-precedential opinions issued on or after January 1, 2007, may now be cited without restriction. Because of restrictions on citations to earlier non-precedential opinions, many decisions in the *Federal Appendix* contain notations indicating that they are not binding precedent and cautioning readers to check court rules before citing the opinions. Non-precedential decisions by other courts may also be subject to special rules.

---

[3] There are limited exceptions to this rule. For example, in Ohio, the text of the opinion is preceded by a "syllabus," or summary of the opinion, which is written by the court and which contains the holding of the decision. Ordinarily, however, everything other than the opinion itself is an editorial enhancement. Unless you see a notation indicating otherwise, you should assume that only the text of the opinion is authoritative.

Figure 17.2   Excerpt From *Popkin v. New York State*

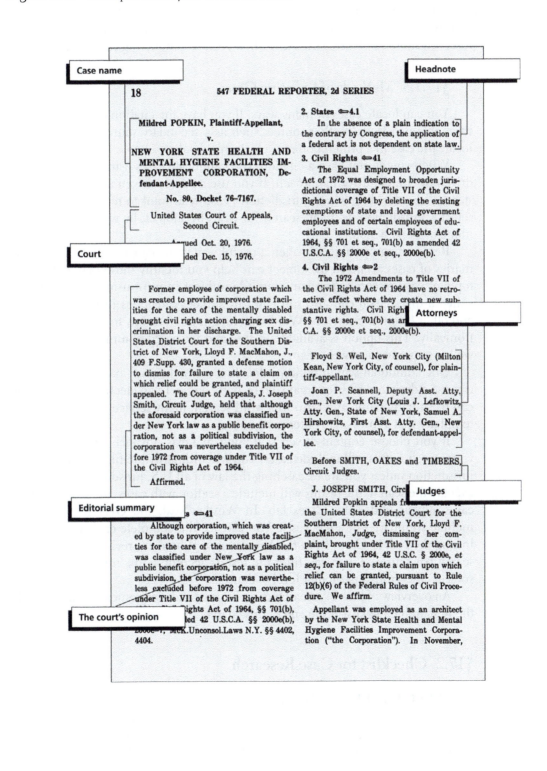

Although courts have issued non-precedential opinions for many years, the practice is not without controversy. The authoritative value of non-precedential decisions is a subject of ongoing debate in the legal community. Regardless of the controversy, non-precedential decisions can be valuable research tools. Therefore, you should not disregard them when you are conducting case research.

§17.1.5 *Methods of Locating Cases*

You can locate cases in many ways. If you have the citation to a case that you have obtained from another source, such as a secondary source, you can easily locate the case in a print reporter or electronic database.

When you do not have a citation, you can locate cases using either a source-driven or content-driven approach. If you use a source-driven approach, the first step will be deciding which jurisdiction's cases you want to research. Once you select a jurisdiction, you can search for cases by subject, by words in the document, or by party name.

Researching by subject is often a useful way to locate cases. Reviewing summaries of cases arranged by subject can help you identify those that address the topic of your research. You can search by subject in print using a research tool called a digest. You can also sort cases by subject categories in Lexis, Westlaw, and other electronic services. Word searching is another way to locate cases electronically. This option is available in free and fee-based commercial services as well as on some court websites.

One additional search option is locating a case by party name. In print, you can use a directory of cases organized by party name. In an electronic service, you can use a party name as a term in a word search; many services also have search templates that allow you to enter party names.

If you choose content-driven searching in Lexis Advance or WestlawNext, your search results will include cases. You will ordinarily pre-filter your search by jurisdiction unless you are researching the law of all U.S. jurisdictions. Once you execute the search, the results will include a section with cases. In Lexis Advance, cases appear under the **Cases** tab. In WestlawNext, the **Overview** page will include summaries of a few cases. You can see the complete case results by following the link to **Cases** from the **View** menu. When you review the cases your search has retrieved, you can filter the results according to a number of criteria, such as cases from a particular level of court.

An overview of how to research cases in print and electronically is provided in the Research Checklist at the end of this chapter.

§17.2 Checklist for Case Research

1. **SELECT A PRINT DIGEST**
    - ☐ Use *West's Federal Practice Digest* to locate all federal cases.
    - ☐ Use a state digest to locate state and federal cases from an individual state.
    - ☐ Use a regional digest to locate state cases only within the region.

☐ Use a combined digest to locate state and federal cases from all U.S. jurisdictions.

2. **LOCATE TOPICS AND KEY NUMBERS IN A PRINT DIGEST**
   ☐ From a case on point, use the headnotes at the beginning of the decision to identify relevant topics and key numbers.
   ☐ From the Descriptive-Word Index, look up relevant subjects, check the pocket part for new index headings, and look up the topics and key numbers in the subject volumes.
   ☐ From a topic entry, review subjects included and excluded and the outline of key numbers.

3. **READ THE CASE SUMMARIES IN THE PRINT DIGEST**
   ☐ Use the court and date abbreviations to target appropriate cases.

4. **UPDATE PRINT DIGEST RESEARCH**
   ☐ Check the pocket part for the subject volume.
   ☐ Check any cumulative or noncumulative interim pamphlets at the end of the digest set.
   ☐ Check the closing table on the inside front cover of the most recent interim pamphlet (if there is no interim pamphlet, check the closing table on the inside front cover of the pocket part).
   ☐ If necessary, check the mini-digests in the back of each reporter volume published after the latest volume listed in the closing table.

5. **ELECTRONIC CASE RESEARCH — SEARCHING BY SUBJECT**
   ☐ In Westlaw, search for cases by subject.
   - Use the **West Key Number** (Custom Digest) function to find summaries of cases organized by topic and key number.
   - From a case on point, search for cases under a particular topic and key number by following the link to the key number in a relevant headnote.
   ☐ In Lexis.com, search for cases by subject.
   - Use the **Topic or Headnote** search function to find citations to cases organized by topic and headnote subject.
   - From a case on point, use the **More Like This Headnote** option to search for cases under the same headnote subject.

6. **ELECTRONIC CASE RESEARCH — WORD SEARCHING**
   ☐ In Westlaw and Lexis, execute word searches.
   - In Westlaw.com, WestlawNext, and Lexis.com, select a database to search for cases from a specific jurisdiction.
   - In WestlawNext, pre-filter by jurisdiction and execute a content-driven search; filter the results to target appropriate cases.
   - In Lexis Advance, pre-filter by content type (cases), jurisdiction, and/or topic and execute a search; filter the results to target appropriate cases.

☐ In Google Scholar, search for published legal opinions; choose **Advanced Scholar Search** to pre-filter by jurisdiction.

☐ Use websites for courts or other tribunals to locate very recent opinions, unpublished (non-precedential) opinions, or opinions unavailable from other sources.

CHAPTER 18

RESEARCH WITH CITATORS

§18.1 Introduction to Citators

§18.1.1 The Purpose of a Citator

Virtually all cases contain citations to legal authorities, including other cases, secondary sources, statutes, and regulations. These decisions can affect the continued validity of the authorities they cite. For example, earlier cases can be reversed or overruled, or statutes can be held unconstitutional. Even if an authority remains valid, the discussion of the authority in later cases can be helpful in your research. As a consequence, when you find an authority that helps you answer a research question, you will often want to know whether the authority has been cited elsewhere, and if so, what has been said about it.

The tool that helps you do this is called a citator. Citators catalog cases, secondary sources, and other authorities, analyzing what they say about the sources they cite. Some citators also track the status of statutes and regulations, indicating, for example, whether a statute has been amended or repealed. Citators will help you determine whether an authority is still "good law," meaning it has not been changed or invalidated since it was published. They will also help you locate additional authorities that pertain to your research question.

The most well-known print citator is Shepard's Citations. Because Shepard's was, for many years, the only citator most lawyers ever used, checking citations came to be known as "Shepardizing." Generations of law students learned how to interpret print Shepard's entries, which are filled with symbols and abbreviations. Today, however, few legal researchers use Shepard's in print. Many libraries no longer carry the print version of Shepard's. Instead, virtually all legal researchers use electronic citators. Shepard's is still a well-respected citator, and it is available in Lexis. Westlaw also has its own citator — called KeyCite — and other electronic service providers offer their own citators.

Because print citators are largely unavailable, this chapter focuses on electronic citators. Citators can be used in researching many types of authority, including cases, statutes, regulations, and some secondary sources. The process of using a citator, however, is the same for almost any type of authority. Accordingly, for purposes of introducing you to this process, this chapter focuses on the use of citators in case research.

§18.1.2 When to Use a Citator in Case Research

You must check every case on which you rely to answer a legal question to make sure it is still good law. In general, you will want to use Shepard's or Key-Cite early in your research, after you have identified what appear to be a few key cases, to make sure you do not build your analysis on authority that is no longer valid. Using a citator at this stage will help direct you to other relevant authorities as well. You should also check every case you cite before handing in your work to make sure each one continues to be authoritative. Citing bad authority is every attorney's nightmare, and failing to check your citations can constitute professional malpractice. As a consequence, now is the time to get in the habit of updating your case research carefully.

§18.1.3 Terms and Procedural Concepts Used in Citator Research

Before you begin learning how to use citators, it is important to understand the terminology and procedural concepts used in the process. A case citator contains entries for decided cases that list the later authorities (cases, secondary sources, and other forms of authority) that have cited the case. This chapter uses the term "original case" to describe the case that is the subject of the citator entry. The terms "citing case" and "citing source" refer to the later authorities that cite the original case. Thus, for example, if you located the case of *Uddin v. Embassy Suites Hotel*, 165 Ohio App. 3d 699 (2005), and wanted to use a citator to verify its continued validity, *Uddin* would be referred to as the original case. The later authorities that cite *Uddin* would be referred to as citing cases (for cases) or citing sources (for all other types of authority).

Two procedural concepts you need to understand are direct and indirect case history. Direct history refers to all of the opinions issued in conjunction with a single piece of litigation. One piece of litigation may generate multiple opinions. A case may be appealed to a higher court, resulting in opinions from both an intermediate appellate court and the court of last resort. A higher court may remand a case — that is, send a case back to a lower court — for reconsideration, again resulting in opinions issued by both courts. Or a court might issue separate opinions to resolve individual matters arising in a case. All of these opinions, whether issued before or after the original case, constitute direct history. Opinions issued before the original case may be called prior history; those issued after the original case may be called subsequent history or subsequent appellate history, as appropriate. Indirect history refers to an opinion generated from a different piece of litigation than the original case. Every unrelated case that cites the original case is part of the indirect history of the original case.

Both direct and indirect case history can be positive, negative, or neutral. Thus, if the original case is affirmed by a higher court, it has positive direct history, but if the original case is reversed, it has negative direct history. A related opinion in the same litigation on a different issue could be neutral; the opinion resolving the second issue could have no effect on the continued validity of the opinion resolving the first issue. Similarly, if the original case is relied upon by a court deciding a later, unrelated case, the original case has positive indirect history, but if the original case is overruled, it has negative indirect history. A citing case could discuss the original case in a way that does not include any positive or negative analysis. In that situation, the indirect history would be considered neutral.

Below are two charts (Figure 18.1 and Figure 18.2) explaining some of the abbreviations used in citators. Following the charts is a Checklist for Research with Citators that will help explain and guide you through the process of case research using citators.

§18.1.4 Abbreviations Used in Citators

Figure 18.1   Shepard's® Signals

SIGNAL	MEANS
Red stop sign	*Warning: Negative treatment is indicated.* This signal indicates that citing references in the Shepard's® Citations Service contain strong negative history or treatment of your case (e.g., overruled by or reversed).
Orange square surrounding the letter Q	*Questioned: Validity questioned by citing references.* This signal indicates that citing references in the Shepard's® Citations Service contain treatment that questions the continuing validity or precedential value of your case because of intervening circumstances, including judicial or legislative overruling.
Yellow triangle	*Caution: Possible negative treatment.* This signal indicates that citing references in the Shepard's® Citations Service contain history or treatment that may have a significant negative impact on your case (e.g., limited or criticized by).
Green diamond surrounding a plus sign	*Positive treatment is indicated.* This signal indicates that citing references in the Shepard's® Citations Service contain history or treatment that has a positive impact on your case (e.g., affirmed or followed by).
Blue circle surrounding the letter A	*Citing references with neutral analysis available.* This signal indicates that citing references in the Shepard's® Citations Service contain treatment of your case that is neither positive nor negative (e.g., explained).
Blue circle surrounding the letter l	*Citation information available.* This signal indicates that citing references are available in the Shepard's® Citations Service for your case, but the references do not have history or treatment analysis (e.g., the references are law review citations).

Figure 18.2   Westlaw Status Flags Indicating Keycite History

NOTATION	MEANS
Red flag	The case is no longer good law for at least one of the points it contains.
Yellow flag	The case has some negative history but has not been reversed or overruled.
Blue H	The case has direct history.
Green C	The case has citing references but no direct history or negative citing references.

§18.2 Checklist for Case Research with Citators

1. **USE SHEPARD'S IN LEXIS**
    - ☐ Access Shepard's and enter a citation or use the **Shepardize** link from a relevant case.
    - ☐ Interpret the entry.
        - Use the Shepard's Signal as a qualified indicator of case status, not a definitive determination.
        - The entry contains direct history, citing decisions (divided by jurisdiction) and other citing sources.
        - Use the descriptions of the history (e.g., affirmed, reversed) and treatment (e.g., followed, distinguished, overruled) to identify citing cases that may affect the validity of the original case.
        - Use headnote references to identify citing cases that discuss propositions most relevant to your research.
        - In Lexis Advance, use the **Map** view for a snapshot of case history in chart form and the **Grid** view for a snapshot of treatment by later citing cases in chart form.
    - ☐ Filter the display in Lexis.com.
        - Use **Shepard's for Validation** to retrieve an abbreviated entry.
        - Use the display options and **All Neg** or **All Pos** restrictions to limit the display.
        - Use **FOCUS™-Restrict By** to limit the display by type of analysis, jurisdiction, headnote, date, or terms you specify.
    - ☐ Filter the display in Lexis Advance with the narrowing options in the left margin.
    - ☐ Create a Shepard's Alert® for automatic updates to the Shepard's entry for the original case.

2. **USE KEYCITE IN WESTLAW**
   - ☐ Access KeyCite from a relevant case (or the **KeyCite** link in Westlaw.com).
   - ☐ Interpret the entry.
     - Use the KeyCite status flag as a qualified indicator of case status, not a definitive determination.
     - In Westlaw.com:
       - View the **Full History** of the original case to see direct history and negative indirect history.
       - View the **Direct History (Graphical View)** to see the history of the original case in chart form.
       - View the **Citing References** to see indirect history and citing sources; negative cases appear first, followed by positive cases (divided by depth of treatment and then by jurisdiction) and citing sources.
     - In WestlawNext:
       - View direct and indirect negative history under the **Negative Treatment** tab.
       - View the direct history in list and chart form under the **History** tab.
       - View citing references under the **Citing References** tab.
     - Use the descriptions of the history (e.g., affirmed, reversed) and treatment (e.g., distinguished, disagreed with, overruled) to identify citing cases that may affect the validity of the original case.
     - Use headnote references to identify citing cases that discuss propositions most relevant to your research.
     - Use quotation marks to identify citing cases that quote the original case.
   - ☐ Filter the results.
     - In Westlaw.com, use the **Limit KeyCite Display** option to show negative treatment only and to limit the display by headnote, specific terms using Locate, jurisdiction, date, document type, or depth of treatment.
     - In WestlawNext, use the narrowing options in the left margin to limit the display by document type, treatment, jurisdiction, and other criteria.
   - ☐ Create a KeyCite Alert for automatic updates to the KeyCite entry for the original case.

CHAPTER 19

STATUTORY RESEARCH

§19.1 Introduction to Statutory Law

§19.1.1 The Publication of Statutory Law

Statutes enacted by a legislature are organized by subject matter into what is called a "code." Codes are published by jurisdiction; each jurisdiction that enacts statutes collects them in its own code. Thus, the federal government publishes the federal code, which contains all federal statutes. Statutes for each state are published in individual state codes. Most codes contain too many statutes to be included in a single volume. Instead, a code usually consists of a multivolume set of books containing all of the statutes passed within a jurisdiction. The federal code also includes the text of the U.S. Constitution. Most state codes contain the text of the state constitution, and many include the text of the U.S. Constitution as well.

When a federal law is enacted, it is published in three steps: (1) it is published as a separate document; (2) it is included in a chronological listing of all statutes passed within a session of Congress; and (3) it is reorganized by subject matter and placed within the code. In the first step of the process, every law passed by Congress is assigned a public law number. The public law number indicates the session of Congress in which the law was passed and the order in which it was passed. Thus, Public Law 103-416 was the 416th law passed during the 103d session of Congress. Each public law is published in a separate booklet or pamphlet containing the full text of the law as it was passed by Congress. This booklet is known as a slip law and is identified by its public law number.

In the second step of the process, slip laws for a session of Congress are compiled together in chronological order. Laws organized within this chronological compilation are called session laws because they are organized according to the session of Congress during which they were enacted. Session laws are compiled in a publication called *United States Statutes at Large*. A citation to *Statutes at Large* will tell you the volume of *Statutes at Large* containing the law and the page number on which the text of the law begins. Thus, a citation to 108 Stat.

4305 tells you that this law can be located in volume 108 of *Statutes at Large*, beginning on page 4305. Both the slip law and session law versions of a statute should be identical. The only difference is the form of publication.

The third step in the process is the codification of the law. When Congress enacts a law, it enacts a block of legislation that may cover a wide range of topics. A single bill can contain provisions applicable to many different parts of the government. For example, a drug abuse prevention law could contain provisions applicable to subject areas such as food and drugs, crimes, and public health. If federal laws remained organized chronologically by the date of passage, it would be virtually impossible to research the law by subject. Laws relating to individual subjects could have been passed at so many different times that it would be extremely difficult to find all of the relevant provisions.

In the third step of the process, therefore, the pieces of the bill are reorganized according to the different subjects they cover, and they are placed by subject, or codified, within the federal code. Once legislation is codified, it is much easier to locate because it can be indexed by subject much the way cases are indexed by subject in a digest.

Figure 19.1 illustrates the publication process.

Figure 19.2 contains an example of a statute that has been codified within the federal code.

Figure 19.1   Publication Process For a Federal Statute

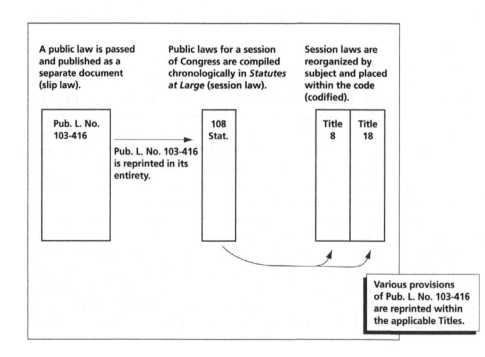

Figure 19.2   18 U.S.C.A. § 2725

Section number	Title of the section

> **18 § 2725**   **CRIMES   Part 1**
>
> **§ 2725. Definitions**
>
> In this chapter—
>
> **(1)** "motor vehicle record" means any record that pertains to a motor vehicle operator's permit, motor vehicle title, motor vehicle registration, or identification card issued by a department of motor vehicles;
>
> **(2)** "person" means an individual, organization or entity, but does not include a State or agency thereof; and
>
> **(3)** "personal information" means information that identifies an individual, including an individual's photograph, social security number, driver identification number, name, address (but not the 5-digit zip code), telephone number, and medical or disability information, but does not include information on vehicular accidents, driving violations, and driver's status.
>
> (Added Pub.L. 103–322, Title XXX, § 300002(a), Sept. 13, 1994, 108 Stat. 2102.)

Text of the statute

Reprinted with permission from Thomson Reuters/West, *United States Code Annotated*, Title 18 (2000), p. 340. © 2000 Thomson Reuters/West.

§19.1.2 Title and Subject-Matter Organization of Codes

Although all codes are organized by subject, not all codes are numbered the same way. The federal code is organized into Titles. For many years, the federal code had 50 Titles. In 2010, however, Congress enacted Title 51, so now the federal code has 51 Titles. Additional Titles may be enacted in the future. Each Title covers a different subject area. Title 18, for instance, contains the laws pertaining to federal crimes, and Title 35 contains the laws pertaining to patents. Each Title is subdivided into chapters, and each chapter is further subdivided into sections. To locate a provision of the federal code from its citation, you would need to know the Title and the section number assigned to it. For example, the provision of the federal code prohibiting bank robbery is located in Title 18, section 2113.

Not all codes are organized this way. Some states organize their codes by subject name, rather than Title number. Within each subject name, the code is then usually subdivided into chapters and sections. To find a provision of the code from its citation, you would need to know the subject area and the section number assigned to that provision. For example, the provision of New York law that prohibits issuing a bad check is located in the subject volume of the New York code containing the Penal Law, section 190.05.

§19.1.3 Official vs. Unofficial Codes and Annotated vs. Unannotated Codes

Although there is only one "code" for each jurisdiction, in the sense that each jurisdiction has only one set of statutes in force, the text of the laws may be published in more than one set of books or electronic databases. Sometimes a government arranges for the publication of its laws; this is known as an "official" code.[1] Sometimes a commercial publisher will publish the laws for a jurisdiction without government authorization; this is known as an "unofficial" code. Some jurisdictions have both official and unofficial codes. If both official and unofficial codes are published for a jurisdiction, they will usually be organized and numbered identically (e.g., all sets will be organized by subject or by Title). For federal laws, the government publishes an official code, *United States Code* or U.S.C. Two other sets of the federal code are also available through commercial publishers, *United States Code Annotated* (U.S.C.A.) and *United States Code Service* (U.S.C.S.).

In addition, a published code can come in one of two formats: annotated or unannotated. An annotated code contains the text of the law, as well as different types of research references. The research references may include summaries of cases or citations to secondary sources discussing a statute. An unannotated code contains only the text of the law. It may have a few references to the statutes' original public law numbers, but other than that, it will not contain research references. Most unofficial codes are annotated codes. Official codes may or may not be annotated. As you might imagine, an annotated code is much more useful as a research tool than an unannotated code.

In the federal code, U.S.C. (the official code) is an unannotated code. The two unofficial codes, U.S.C.A. and U.S.C.S., are annotated codes. See Figure 19.3 for a summary of the characteristics of official and unofficial codes.

§19.1.4 Methods of Locating Statutes

You can locate statutes in many ways. If you have the citation to a statute that you have obtained from another source, such as a secondary source, you can easily locate the statute in a print code or retrieve it from an electronic database.

When you do not have a citation, you can locate statutes using either a source-driven or content-driven approach. If you use a source-driven approach, the first step will be deciding which jurisdiction's statutes you want to research. Once you select a jurisdiction, you can search for statutes by subject, by words in the document, or by the name of an act.

---

[1] The government may publish the code itself, or it may arrange for a commercial publisher to publish the code. As long as the government arranges for the publication, the code is an official code, even if it is physically produced by a commercial publisher.

Figure 19.3   Characteristics of Official and Unofficial Codes

OFFICIAL CODES	UNOFFICIAL CODES
Published under government authority (e.g., U.S.C.).	Published by a commercial publisher without government authorization (e.g., U.S.C.A. and U.S.C.S.).
May or may not contain research references (annotations). U.S.C. is not an annotated code.	Usually contain research references (annotations). Both U.S.C.A. and U.S.C.S. are annotated codes.

Researching by subject is often a useful way to locate statutes. The index to a code will be organized by subject, and using an index is one of the most common subject searching techniques for statutory research. All print codes have subject indices. If you are searching electronically, you may or may not have access to the index. Every code also has a table of contents, which you can view in print or electronically. Reviewing the table of contents can be a difficult way to begin your research unless you know the subject area of the statute you are trying to find. Once you find a relevant provision of the code, however, viewing the table of contents can help you find related code sections, as described more fully below.

Word searching is another way to locate statutes electronically. Because legislatures often use technical terms in statutes, however, word searching can be more difficult than subject searching if you are not already familiar with the statutory terminology.

An additional search option is locating a statute by name. Many statutes are known by their popular names, such as the Americans with Disabilities Act. In print, you can use a directory listing statutes according to their popular names. In an electronic service, you can use a statute's name as a word search; many services also have popular name search options.

If you choose content-driven searching in Lexis Advance or Westlaw-Next, your search results will include statutes. You will ordinarily pre-filter your search by jurisdiction unless you are researching the law of all U.S. jurisdictions. Once you execute the search, the results will include a section with statutes. In WestlawNext, statutes appear under the **Statutes** link from the **View** menu. In Lexis Advance, statutes appear under the **Legislative** tab. When you view the statutes your search retrieved, you can filter the results according to a number of criteria.

Regardless of the search method you use initially to locate a relevant section of a code, you should plan to expand your search to consider the entire statutory scheme. Rarely will an individual code section viewed in isolation resolve your research question. More often you will need to research interrelated code provisions. For example, assume you retrieved a code provision applicable to your research issue but failed to retrieve a nearby section containing definitions of terms used in the applicable provision. If you relied only on the one section your

Figure 19.4   Chapter Outline in Title 18

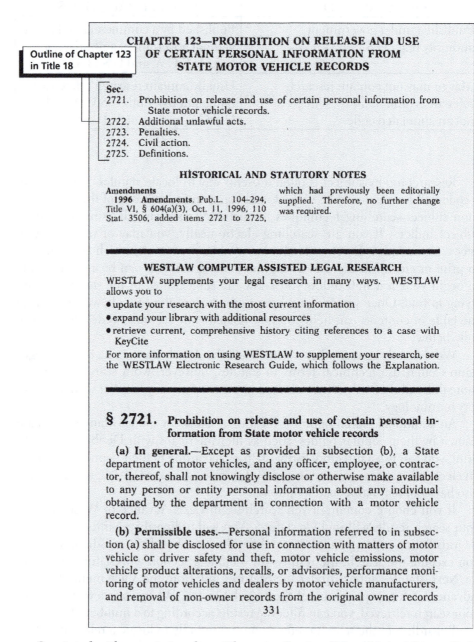

CHAPTER 123—PROHIBITION ON RELEASE AND USE
OF CERTAIN PERSONAL INFORMATION FROM
STATE MOTOR VEHICLE RECORDS

Outline of Chapter 123 in Title 18

Sec.
2721. Prohibition on release and use of certain personal information from State motor vehicle records.
2722. Additional unlawful acts.
2723. Penalties.
2724. Civil action.
2725. Definitions.

HISTORICAL AND STATUTORY NOTES

Amendments
1996 Amendments. Pub.L. 104–294, Title VI, § 604(a)(3), Oct. 11, 1996, 110 Stat. 3506, added items 2721 to 2725, which had previously been editorially supplied. Therefore, no further change was required.

WESTLAW COMPUTER ASSISTED LEGAL RESEARCH

WESTLAW supplements your legal research in many ways. WESTLAW allows you to

- update your research with the most current information
- expand your library with additional resources
- retrieve current, comprehensive history citing references to a case with KeyCite

For more information on using WESTLAW to supplement your research, see the WESTLAW Electronic Research Guide, which follows the Explanation.

§ 2721. Prohibition on release and use of certain personal information from State motor vehicle records

(a) In general.—Except as provided in subsection (b), a State department of motor vehicles, and any officer, employee, or contractor, thereof, shall not knowingly disclose or otherwise make available to any person or entity personal information about any individual obtained by the department in connection with a motor vehicle record.

(b) Permissible uses.—Personal information referred to in subsection (a) shall be disclosed for use in connection with matters of motor vehicle or driver safety and theft, motor vehicle emissions, motor vehicle product alterations, recalls, or advisories, performance monitoring of motor vehicles and dealers by motor vehicle manufacturers, and removal of non-owner records from the original owner records

331

Reprinted with permission from Thomson Reuters/West, *United States Code Annotated*, Title 18 (2000), p. 331. © 2000 Thomson Reuters/West.

initial search revealed, your research would not be accurate. Because electronic sources often retrieve individual code sections as separate documents, it is especially easy to lose sight of the need to research multiple sections when you are working online. Whether you use print or electronic sources for statutory research, however, be sure to research the entire statutory scheme to ensure that you consider all potentially applicable code sections.

Once you have located a relevant code section, the easiest way to research a statutory scheme is to use the statutory outline or table of contents to identify related code provisions. In print, you will often find a chapter or subchapter outline of sections. Figure 19.4 shows the outline for a chapter within Title 18 of the federal code. And of course, all you have to do is turn the pages to see preceding and subsequent code sections. Electronic sources often either display or provide links to statutory outlines or tables of contents, and many have functions that allow you to browse preceding and subsequent code sections.

An overview of how to research statutes in print and electronically is provided in the Research Checklist at the end of this chapter.

§19.2 Checklist for Statutory Research

1. **LOCATE A STATUTE**
    ☐ In print:
      - Use an index to search by subject.
      - Use the popular name table to locate a statute from its popular name.
      - For federal statutes, use the conversion tables to locate a statute using its public law number.
    ☐ In Westlaw:
      - In Westlaw.com and WestlawNext, select a database to search for statutes from a specific jurisdiction; search by popular name, browse the statutory index or table of contents, or execute a word search.
      - In WestlawNext, pre-filter by jurisdiction and execute a content-driven search to retrieve statutes and other authorities; filter the results to target appropriate statutes.
    ☐ In Lexis.com, select a database to search for statutes from a specific jurisdiction; browse the table of contents or execute a word search.
    ☐ In Lexis Advance, pre-filter by content type (statutes), jurisdiction, and/or topic and execute a search; filter the results to target appropriate statutes.
    ☐ On the Internet, locate statutes on government or general legal research websites.

2. **READ THE STATUTE AND ACCOMPANYING ANNOTATIONS**
    ☐ Use research references to find cases, secondary sources, and other research materials interpreting the statute.

3. **UPDATE YOUR RESEARCH**
   ☐ With print research, check the pocket part accompanying the main volume and any cumulative or noncumulative supplements accompanying the code.
   - In U.S.C.A., update entries to the popular name and conversion tables with the noncumulative supplements.
   - In state codes, check for additional updating tools.
   ☐ With state or federal statutory research, update your research or find additional research references using a statutory citator such as Shepard's in Lexis or KeyCite in Westlaw.
   ☐ With Internet research, check the date of the statute and update your research accordingly; consider using a statutory citator to update your research and find additional research references.

CHAPTER 20

EFFECTIVE WORD SEARCHING

Most electronic research providers offer multiple ways to locate information. Citation and subject searching are discussed in more detail in the chapters devoted to individual types of authority. This section explains techniques for effective word searching that you can use to search for many kinds of authority.

Effective word searching requires an understanding of the types of word searches you can conduct. Understanding these options will help you select the type of word searching best suited to your research task, modify the default result display to highlight the most relevant information, and filter the results of the search effectively.

§20.1 Types of Word Searches

When you execute a word search, the search engine searches a database of documents and retrieves the documents that meet the criteria you set for the search. To do this, the search engine uses an algorithm, or set of rules, to evaluate the search criteria and the documents in the database. A literal search algorithm searches for documents that contain the specific terms in your word search. A non-literal search algorithm also searches for documents that contain the search terms, but it does not limit the result to those documents. It uses the search terms to search background information or meta-data and includes in the results documents that appear relevant to the search terms even though they do not contain those terms. Legal research services use three types of search algorithms: terms and connectors (also called Boolean), natural language, and descriptive term.

A terms and connectors search is a literal search. It identifies documents containing the precise terms you identify, in the precise relationships you request. For example, you could search for documents that contain both the phrase *"ice cream"* and the term *sundae*. Alternatively, you could search for documents that contain either the phrase *"ice cream"* or the term *sundae*, but not necessarily both. AND and OR are examples of connectors, which are the commands that define the relationships among the search terms. A list of the most commonly used commands appears in Figure 20.1.

Because you use commands to steer the search logic, you can control the search results more precisely than you can with other search algorithms. If you search for *"ice cream"* /s *sundae*, the search will retrieve only documents that

Figure 20.1   Common Terms and connectors Commands

Alternative terms	Term1 **or** Term2
All terms	Term1 **and** Term2
Terms with grammatical proximity	Term1 **/p** Term2 (Term1 appears within the same paragraph as Term2) Term1 **/s** Term2 (Term1 appears within the same sentence as Term2)
Terms with numerical proximity	Term1 **/n** Term2 (Term1 appears within a certain number of words of Term2; **n**= a specific number)
Exclude terms	Term1 **but not** Term2 (Westlaw) Term1 **and not** Term2 (Lexis)
Expand terms	Exclamation point (!) for variable word endings (Term! retrieves Term, Terms, Termed, Terming, Terminal, Terminable, and all other variations of the word) (Westlaw and Lexis) Asterisk (*) for variable letters (Te*m retrieves Term, Team, and Teem) (Westlaw and Lexis)

contain the phrase "ice cream" in the same sentence as sundae; if a document contains "ice cream" and sundae but not within the same sentence, that document will not appear in the search results. The search may retrieve any number of documents, or no documents at all, depending on the number of documents that meet the search criteria. Lexis, Westlaw, and most other legal research providers offer the option of terms and connectors searching. More information on specific terms and connectors commands appears below.

A natural language search is also a literal search. Unlike a terms and connectors search, a natural language search does not require you to specify the relationships among the terms in the documents retrieved. Instead, a natural language search uses embedded rules to evaluate the relationships among the search terms, which it then uses to determine which documents meet the search criteria. A natural language search for *ice cream sundae* will retrieve documents that contain all or some of those terms and will rank the results by relevance. Documents in which the terms appear frequently or close together will be ranked higher than documents that contain only one of the search terms.

A natural language search often (but not always) retrieves a predetermined number of documents. For example, if the search is set up to retrieve 100 documents, the results will include 100 documents as long as each document contains at least one of the search terms. If only 75 documents contain the search terms, the search will retrieve 75 documents. It would be unusual for a natural language search to retrieve no documents, although this can happen when your search consists of terms that do not appear in any documents in the database. Lexis, West-law, and most other legal research providers offer the option of natural language searching, and natural language searching is often the default search option. Lexis.-com also offers a simplified form of natural language searching called Easy Search.

A descriptive term search, as that term is used in this text, refers to a variation of natural language searching that is non-literal. It uses embedded rules to evaluate which documents meet the search criteria, but it searches both the text of the documents in the database and meta-data associated with the documents. In addition to retrieving documents that contain the search terms, therefore, it can also retrieve documents that appear relevant according to the embedded search rules even though they do not contain the search terms. It is extremely rare for a descriptive terms search to retrieve no documents. WestlawNext and Google Scholar have descriptive term search engines. To identify relevant documents, a Westlaw Next descriptive terms search looks for your search terms within document text, but then it also searches West topics and key numbers (described in Chapter 17), KeyCite data (described in Chapter 18), and retrieval data from other users who have executed similar searches.

§20.2 Comparing Word Search Options

Your search results can vary substantially depending on whether you use terms and connectors, natural language, or descriptive terms searching. Understanding the results each type of search produces will help you choose the search method best suited to your research task. The research scenario introduced in Chapter 14 provides an example to illustrate the differences among the search methods:

> Your client recently ended a long-term relationship with her partner. She and her partner never participated in a formal marriage ceremony, but they had always planned to get married "someday." They lived together for five years and referred to each other as husband and wife. Your client and her former partner orally agreed to provide support for each other, and your client's former partner repeatedly made statements like, "What's mine is yours." Your client wants to know if she is entitled to part of the value of the assets her former partner acquired during their relationship or to any support payments.

One legal theory you might want to investigate in connection with this scenario is palimony, which is a claim for support made by an unmarried partner after the dissolution of a romantic relationship. It is similar to alimony granted after a divorce. If you execute a search for the term *palimony* in Florida case law, the results will vary depending on the type of word search you conduct. The results of the searches are summarized in Figure 20.2.[1]

---

[1] The search results described in this section are current as of February 1, 2012. The results you get if you execute these searches may vary somewhat over time as new Florida cases are decided. Additionally, the Lexis Advance search engine is relatively new. Its search capabilities have evolved since it was first introduced, and changes to its functionality after this text is published could affect the search results.

Figure 20.2 *Palimony Search Results Comparison*

Service	Westlaw.com and WestlawNext	Lexis.com and Lexis Advance	WestlawNext	Google Scholar
Search Type	terms and connectors and natural language	terms and connectors and natural language	descriptive term	descriptive term
Results (listed by relevance according to the search service's criteria)	1. *Crossen v. Feldman* 2. *Evans v. Wall* 3. *Lowry v. Lowry* 4. *Gilvary v. Gilvary* 5. *Posik v. Layton*	1. *Crossen v. Feldman* 2. *Evans v. Wall* 3. *Posik v. Layton* 4. *Gilvary v. Gilvary* 5. *Lowry v. Lowry* 6. *Evans v. Wall* (unpublished opinion)	1. *Posik v. Layton* 2. *Crossen v. Feldman* 3. *Evans v. Wall* 4. *Poe v. Levy's Estate** 5. *Dietrich v. Winters** 6. *Bashaway v. Cheney Bros., Inc.** 7. *Collier v. Brooks** 8. *Lowry v. Lowry* 9. *Forrest v. Ron** 10. *Gilvary v. Gilvary* 11. *Harrison v. Pritchett** 12. *McLane v. Musick** 13. *Stevens v. Muse** 14. *Tobin & Tobin Ins. Agency, Inc. v. Zeskind** 15. *Addison v. Brown** 16. *Tyson v. State** 17. *Hoffman v. Kohns** 18. *Campo v. Tafur** 19. *Jarrell v. Jarrell** 20. *Newberger v. Newberger**	1. *Crossen v. Feldman* 2. *Evans v. Wall* 3. *Posik v. Layton* 4. *Stevens v. Muse** 5. *Poe v. Levy's Estate** 6. *Gilvary v. Gilvary* 7. *Lowry v. Lowry* 8. *Eberhardt v. Eberhardt**

Marked cases (*) do not contain the search term *palimony*.

A terms and connectors search for *palimony* in Westlaw retrieves the five cases listed in Figure 20.2. The same search in Lexis retrieves the same five cases, plus an additional unpublished opinion. All of these cases contain the term *palimony*.

You get the same results from a natural language search in Westlaw.com, Lexis Advance, or Lexis.com, as well as from an Easy Search search in Lexis.com (although the relevancy rankings differ slightly). This is because the search consists of only one term, and the literal natural language search retrieves only documents that contain the search term. Adding even one additional term (e.g., *palimony support*) increases the search results in Westlaw.com and Lexis.com to the predetermined number of results, usually 100 cases. All of the additional cases retrieved contain only the term *support*, not the term *palimony*. In Lexis Advance, the revised search — *palimony support* — retrieves almost 70,000 cases because there is no limit on the number of documents in the search result, but again, all of the additional cases contain only the term *support*, not *palimony*.

A descriptive term search for the term *palimony* in WestlawNext retrieves 20 cases: five that contain the term *palimony* (and were in the Westlaw.com search results) plus 15 more that do not contain the term *palimony*. The cases are listed in Figure 20.2. WestlawNext retrieved the additional 15 cases because the meta-data they contain indicated that they met the embedded rules for relevance to the search term. A review of the cases reveals that several of them share a common topic heading on informal or invalid marriage, and several of them cite or are cited by the cases that contain the term *palimony*. WestlawNext used these and other criteria to connect the cases to the search term, and most of the additional 15 cases are, in fact, indirectly related to palimony. Several of them concern parties seeking property or support from a former partner or discuss doctrines that have some overlap with palimony, such as constructive trust. A few simply are not relevant.

When only a few documents contain your search terms, documents that do not contain the search terms but that nevertheless meet certain relevancy criteria appear in the WestlawNext search results. The relevance of documents that do not contain any of your search terms may be low, however, so WestlawNext limits these search results to 20 documents. If more than 20 documents had contained the term *palimony*, WestlawNext would not have limited the results to 20 documents. But WestlawNext does place some limits on the number of documents it retrieves. One limit is based on relevance. This limit is not a set number. Once the relevance of the documents containing the search terms gets too low, WestlawNext eliminates them from the search results. WestlawNext also places an outer limit on the number of documents in the search results. It will not retrieve more than 10,000 documents in any single category of authority (e.g., cases, statutes, secondary sources).

A descriptive term search in Google Scholar retrieves the eight cases listed in Figure 20.2. The results include the same five cases the literal searches retrieved and three additional cases that do not contain the search term but that contain meta-data connecting them to the search term. Google Scholar does not search the same meta-data that WestlawNext does and its coverage of state cases does not go back as far in time. This is why it retrieves fewer cases than WestlawNext even though it uses a non-literal search algorithm. Google Scholar does not appear to limit the search results for cases that meet the relevancy criteria based only on meta-data.

Which results are best? The answer depends on your research task. If you only want to retrieve cases that discuss palimony, the literal search results are better suited to your task because you will not have to sort through cases that do not specifically discuss palimony. If you are interested in learning about any claims the client might bring, the non-literal search results may suit your needs better because they may point you toward other legal theories that you had not considered. In a sense, the non-literal search results mimic the results you might get if you looked up a term in a print index and used cross-references to direct you to related topics.

The results in Figure 20.2 are listed by relevance. You can see that different services ranked the relevance of the documents differently. If the results were listed in reverse date order, they would appear as follows: *Posik v. Layton*; *Crossen v. Feldman*; *Givalry v. Givalry*; *Evans v. Wall*; *Lowry v. Lowry*. These differences do not matter much in a search that retrieves only a few documents, but they can matter a lot in a search that retrieves 50, 100, or 1,000 documents. This simply serves to emphasize the importance of being aware of the way the results are ordered and of treating the relevancy rankings as approximate, rather than definitive.

§20.3 Executing, Narrowing, and Reviewing Word Searches in Lexis and Westlaw

Lexis and Westlaw allow you to execute a word search as your initial search for documents or as a narrowing search within your initial search results. This section discusses specific features of word searches in each of these services.

§20.3.1 *Lexis.com*

In Lexis.com, the options for executing your initial search as a terms and connectors, natural language, or Easy Search search appear on the search screen. In a terms and connectors search, words typed in a sequence with no connector will be treated as a search phrase. Thus, a search for *ice cream* is a search for the exact phrase *ice cream*. The results of a terms and connectors search will be listed in reverse date order for cases, numerical order for statutes, and alphabetical order for many secondary sources. Natural language and Easy Search results are listed according to relevance. You can change these default settings using the **Sort by** options.

Once you execute your initial search, you can narrow the results with the **FOCUS™ Terms** function, which allows you to execute a search within the results. A **FOCUS™ Terms** search will be a terms and connectors search even if your initial search was natural language or Easy Search.

§20.3.2 *Lexis Advance*

Lexis Advance will ordinarily treat a search typed into the search box as a natural language search. Lexis Advance automatically interprets many common legal phrases as phrases, rather than as individual search terms. For words that Lexis Advance does not recognize as a phrase, the search algorithm searches each term separately as an individual word. Thus, it treats a search for *ice cream* as a search for *ice OR cream*, which is why a Lexis Advance search can retreive tens of thousands or even hundreds of thousands of documents. You can create a search phrase by putting the search terms in quotation marks.

Although Lexis Advance treats most searches as natural language searches, terms and connectors searching is also an option. Entering a search that incorporates terms and connectors search commands (such as the /*p*, or /*s* conectors) will cause Lexis Advance to execute the search as a terms and connectors search. The **Search Tips** link in the search box shows the connectors Lexis Advance recognizes. **Search Tips** also contains a template you can use to create a terms and connectors search.

The default display for the search results is by relevance. You can change the default display setting using the **Sort by** options.

Once you execute your initial search, you can re-run it as a terms and connectors search by selecting that choice in the **Options** menu. You can also narrow the search results using the criteria in the **Narrow by** menu. If you use **Search within results**, the search will be a terms and connectors search even if your initial search was a natural language search.

§20.3.3 *Westlaw.com*

In Westlaw.com, the options for executing your initial search as a terms and connectors or natural language search appear in the tabs above the search box. In a terms and connectors search, Westlaw.com inserts the *or* connector between words typed in a sequence. Thus, it treats a search for *ice cream* as a search for *ice OR cream*. To create a search phrase, place the terms in quotation marks. The results of a terms and connectors search will be listed in reverse date order for cases, numerical order for statutes, and alphabetical order for many secondary sources. You can change the default setting on the **Preferences** page under **Search**. Natural language results are listed according to relevance.

Once you execute your initial search, you can narrow the results with the **Locate** function, which allows you to execute a search within the results. A **Locate** search will be a terms and connectors search even if your initial search was a natural language search.

§20.3.4 *WestlawNext*

WestlawNext will ordinarily treat a search typed into the search box as a descriptive term search. Even when you put your search terms in quotation marks, the search algorithm searches each term separately. Thus, it treats the search for both *ice cream* and *"ice cream"* the same way. The search algorithm recognizes many common legal phrases. If you search for a common legal phrase, the results may show only documents containing the phrase (as opposed to documents that contain one or more of the terms separately) because the results displayed are subject to relevancy limitations. In other words, although the search for *"ice cream"* searches each term separately, the search results may only display documents that contain the phrase *ice cream* and omit documents that contain only the term *ice* or only the term *cream* if the algorithm recognizes *ice cream* as a phrase.

Although WestlawNext treats most searches as descriptive terms searches, terms and connectors searching is also an option. Entering a search that incorporates a grammatical, numerical, or exclusion connector or a term expander (see **Figure 20.1**) will automatically cause WestlawNext to execute the search as a terms and connectors search. In a terms and connectors search, placing words in quotation marks creates a search phrase. The **Advanced** link in the search box brings up a template you can use to create a terms and connectors search, or you can type *advanced:* followed by a search to execute it as a terms and connectors search. The search results are ranked by relevance, but you can change the default setting using the **Sort by** options.

Once you execute your initial search, you can narrow the search results using the filtering options in the **View** menu. If you use **Search within results**, the search will be a terms and connectors search even if your initial search was a descriptive term search.

CHAPTER 21

DEVELOPING A RESEARCH PLAN

§21.1 Introduction to Research Planning

When you get a research assignment, you might be tempted to begin the project by jumping directly into your research to see what authority you can find. In fact, searching for authority right away is not the best way to start. Thought and planning before you begin researching will help you in several ways. You will research more efficiently if you have a coherent research plan to follow. You will also research more accurately. Searching haphazardly can cause you to miss important authorities, and nothing is more disconcerting than feeling as though you came across relevant authority by accident. Following an organized plan will help ensure that you check all the appropriate places for authority on your issue and will give you confidence that your research is correct and complete.

§21.2 Creating a Research Plan

Creating a research plan requires three steps: (1) obtaining preliminary information about the problem; (2) planning the steps in your research; and (3) working effectively in the library and online. Each of these steps is discussed in turn.

§21.2.1 Obtaining Preliminary Information

When you first receive a research assignment, you might feel like you do not know enough to ask very many questions about it. While this might be true as far as the substance of the problem is concerned, you need to determine the scope of your project by obtaining some preliminary information from the person making the assignment. Specifically:

■ **HOW MUCH TIME DO I HAVE FOR THIS ASSIGNMENT?**
The amount of time you have affects your overall approach, as well as your time management with other projects you have been assigned.

■ **WHAT FINAL WORK PRODUCT SHOULD I PRODUCE?**

You should determine whether you are expected to produce a memorandum, pleading, brief, or informal report of your research results. To a certain extent, this also will be a function of the amount of time you have for the project.

■ ARE THERE ANY LIMITS ON THE RESEARCH MATERIALS I AM PERMITTED TO USE?

As a matter of academic integrity, you want to make sure you use only authorized research tools in a law school assignment. In practice, some clients might be unable or unwilling to pay for research completed with tools requiring additional fees, such as Lexis or Westlaw.

■ WHICH JURISDICTION'S LAW APPLIES?

This is a question the person giving you the assignment might not be able to answer. There will be times when the controlling jurisdiction will be known. In other cases, it will be up to you to determine whether an issue is controlled by federal or state law, and if it is a question of state law, which state's law applies.

■ SHOULD I RESEARCH PERSUASIVE AUTHORITY?

Again, the person making the assignment might not be able to answer this question. You could be asked to focus exclusively on the law of the controlling jurisdiction to answer your research question, or you could be asked specifically to research multiple jurisdictions. If either of those requirements applies to your research, you certainly want to know that before you begin your research. What is more likely, however, is that you will simply be asked to find the answer to a question. If the law of the controlling jurisdiction answers the question, you might not need to go further. If not, you will need to research persuasive authority. Understanding the scope of the assignment will help you focus your efforts appropriately.

In your research class, there will be many parts of the assignment that your professor will expect you to figure out on your own as part of learning about the process of research. In a practice setting, however, you might also ask the following questions:

■ DO YOU KNOW OF ANY SOURCES THAT ARE PARTICULARLY GOOD FOR RESEARCHING IN THIS AREA OF LAW?

Practitioners who are experienced in a particular field might know of research sources that are especially helpful for the type of research you are doing, including looseleaf or other subject-matter services.

■ WHAT BACKGROUND ON THE LAW OR TERMS OF ART SHOULD I KNOW AS I BEGIN MY RESEARCH?

In a law school assignment, you might be expected to identify terms of art on your own. In practice, however, the person giving you the research assignment might be able to give you some background on the area of law and important terms of art to help you get started on your research.

■ **SHOULD I CONSULT ANY WRITTEN MATERIALS OR INDIVID-
UALS WITHIN THE OFFICE BEFORE BEGINNING MY RESEARCH?**
Again, in law school, it would be inappropriate to use another person's research
instead of completing the assignment on your own. In practice, however, reviewing briefs or memoranda on the same or a similar issue can give you a leg up on
your research. In addition, another person within the office might be considered
the "resident expert" on the subject and might be willing to act as a resource
for you.

§21.2.2 *Planning the Steps in Your Research*

Once you have preliminary information on your research project, you are
ready to start planning the steps in your research process. The plan should have
the following components:

- an initial issue statement
- a list of potential search terms
- an outline of your search strategy

§21.2.2.1 *Developing an Initial Issue Statement and Generating Search Terms*

The starting points for your plan are developing an initial issue statement and
generating possible search terms. The issue statement does not need to be a formal statement like one that would appear at the beginning of a brief or memorandum. Rather, it should be a preliminary assessment of the problem that helps
define the scope of your research. For example, an initial issue statement might
say something like, "Can the plaintiff recover from the defendant for destroying
her garden?" This issue statement would be incomplete in a brief or memorandum because it does not identify a specific legal question and might not contain
enough information about the facts. At this point, however, you do not know
which legal theory or theories might be successful, nor do you know for certain
which facts are most important. What this question tells you is that you will need
to research all possible claims that would support recovery.

Alternatively, you might be asked to research a narrower question such as,
"Can the plaintiff recover from the defendant *in negligence* for destroying her garden?" This issue statement again might be insufficient in a brief or memorandum, but for purposes of your research plan, it gives you valuable information.
Your research should be limited to liability in negligence; intentional torts or contract claims are beyond the scope of this project.

Although this might seem like an exercise in the obvious, the discipline of
writing a preliminary issue statement can help you focus your efforts in the right
direction. If you are unable to write a preliminary issue statement, that is an indication that you are not sure about the scope of the assignment and may need to
ask more questions about what you should be trying to accomplish.

Once you have written your initial issue statement, you are ready to generate a list of possible search terms. Chapter 14 discusses how to do this, and the techniques described in that chapter should be employed to develop search terms in your research plan.

§21.2.2.2 *Outlining Your Search Strategy*

Once you have a preliminary view of the problem, the next step in creating an effective research plan is mapping out your search strategy. Unless you have access to WestlawNext or Lexis Advance, you will need to use a source-driven approach. With a source-driven approach, you need to determine which research sources are likely to have relevant information. Then, you must determine the order in which you want to research those sources. If you have access to Westlaw-Next or Lexis Advance, you must decide whether a source-driven or content-driven approach is best for your project. Considerations affecting this assessment are discussed in Chapter 15.

An overview of planning your research strategy is provided in the Checklist for Developing an Effective Research Plan at the end of this chapter.

§21.2.3 *Working Effectively*

§21.2.3.1 *Keeping Track: Effective Note Taking*

Once you have outlined your path, you are ready to begin executing your search plan. Keeping effective notes as you work is important for several reasons. It will make your research more efficient. You will know where you have already looked, so you can avoid repeating research steps. This is especially critical if you will be working on the project for an extended period of time or if you are working with other people in completing the research. You will also have all of the information you need for proper citations. Moreover, if it happens that your project presents novel or complex issues for which there are no definitive answers, careful note taking will allow you to demonstrate that you undertook comprehensive research to try to resolve those issues.

Note taking is an individualized process, and there is no single right way to do it. Some electronic research services will keep track of your research by collecting a list of searches you run and documents you view. You may be able to name and save a record of your searches. This is useful, but unless you conduct all of your research with a single service, it will not be a complete record of your search process, especially if you do some research in print. You may be able to download your search history so that you can integrate information from multiple services into a single record of your own, which you can then annotate with your own notes about steps that did and did not lead to useful information.

Once you begin locating specific sources, you will need to organize what you find. Electronic providers may allow you to create folders for research projects. You can also create your own folders outside of any research service to collect information on your project. You can create a folder on your computer or use a service such as Dropbox to access documents on multiple devices.

When you save or download information, you may want to add notes to it. Electronic research services may have functions that allow you to add "sticky notes" with notes about the document as a whole. You may also be able to highlight or mark text and append notes at a particular location within a document. You can also do these things without using a research service's tools. Free and inexpensive "sticky note" software is available, and many programs have commenting functions you can use to add notes to documents.

When you find useful information, you must decide how to organize your research, which documents or snippets to save, and what notes to add to what you have saved. You will probably want to begin by making a folder for all material related to the project as a whole. Sub-folders for research material, your notes, and any factual documents related to the project may be useful. With respect to research material, you may want to segregate content by issue if you are researching multiple issues or by type of authority if you are researching a single issue.

When it comes to saving documents, there is a constant tension between reading what you find and saving the material itself. Most people save more than they need, and many students use collecting and saving documents as a procrastination technique, promising themselves that they will read the information later. Excessive downloading or copying will not improve your research. Certainly, having access to key authorities is important for accurate analysis, quotation, and citation. Facing a huge, disorganized collection of information, however, can be demoralizing, especially because most of the information will probably prove to be irrelevant in the end if you have not made thoughtful choices about what to save or copy.

The fact is that you will not know for certain at the beginning of your research which sources should be saved and which should not. Only as you begin to understand the contours of the legal issue will the relevance (or irrelevance) of individual legal authorities become apparent to you. Therefore, you should conduct some research before you begin saving material. As you delve into the research, you may find that you need to go back to materials you bypassed originally. You may also find it helpful to have a "maybe" folder for your research where you can collect sources that you are not sure will be helpful. If you do this, however, it is important to return to that information periodically to assess its usefulness.

When you find information you want to save, you may be able to choose between saving the entire document or just a snippet. The benefit of saving a snippet is that you have the precise content that appears relevant.

Saving snippets also presents several potential pitfalls. The passage that seemed most relevant to you at one time may not turn out to be the best part of the document upon later reflection. You also run the risk of taking a passage out of context and representing it inaccurately in your analysis. If you save only snippets, you may be tempted to use a collection of snippets pasted into a document as a substitute for analysis and synthesis of the authorities. This can also lead to inadvertent plagiarism if each snippet is not properly cited.

There are times when just a snippet will do, such as when only a few pages out of a 50-page law review article are relevant to your research. You should be cautious, however, when choosing to save only snippets of documents. Often the better practice is saving the entire document even if you do not plan to use the entire document to analyze your research issue.

The next step in documenting your research is deciding which notes to add to the item you save. For most items you will want to note the following information:

The database or source for the item	If you use a folder in an electronic service, you may not need to note this. If you generate your own folder or import content from another source into a folder housed in an electronic research service, you should note where you located the item.
Citation	This does not need to be in proper citation form, but enough information for a proper citation should be included here. Some electronic services will include this information automatically when you save information within that service. If you are doing your own cutting and pasting, however, you need to take the extra step of noting the source and the citation information. Note that citations provided by publishers often do not conform to *ALWD Manual* or *Bluebook* format.
Method of locating the source	This could include references to a secondary source that led you to this authority or the search terms you used in an index or database. Noting this information will help you assess which search approaches are most effective. A sticky note or comment at the beginning of the document is a good place to record this information.
Summary of relevant information	This might be a few sentences or a few paragraphs, depending on the source and its relevance. Making a note about why you saved the item may jog your memory about its relevance when you go back to review it later.
Updating information	Note whether the source has been updated and the method of updating. If you are researching in print, you might note the date of any pocket part or supplement. For electronic research, you should note the updating date for a statute or secondary source. If appropriate, you should also note which citator you use to verify the validity of the source.

This might not be the only information you need to note. For example, in case research, you may also want to note separately the topics and key numbers in the most important cases. You also may want to make notes or highlight text within the body of a document to make the relevant portions easy for you to find.

At a minimum, however, you should keep track of the pieces of information listed above.

Although many people keep electronic notes and download most of their research material, some people still do better with hard copy. The physical acts of printing important sources, organizing them under tabs in a binder or stacking them in piles on the floor, and marking key portions with a highlighter and sticky notes can give you a different perspective on what you have found. If you have trouble visualizing the big picture of your project with an electronic filing system, consider working with at least some of your research in hard copy as an alternative.

§21.2.3.2 *Deciding When to Stop*

Deciding when your research is complete can be difficult. The more research you do, the more comfortable you will be with the process, and the more you will develop an internal sense of when a project is complete. In your first few research assignments in law school, however, you will probably feel uncertain about when to stop because you will have little prior experience to draw upon in making that decision.

One issue that affects a person's sense of when to stop is personal work style. Some people are anxious to begin writing and therefore stop researching after they locate a few sources that seem relevant. Others put off writing by continuing to research, thinking that the answer will become apparent if they just keep looking a little bit more. Being aware of your work style will help you determine whether you have stopped too soon or are continuing your research beyond what is necessary for the assignment.

Of course, the amount of time you have and the work product you are expected to produce will affect the ending point for your research. If you are instructed to report back in half an hour with your research results, you know when you will need to stop. In general, however, you will know that you have come full circle in your research when, after following a comprehensive research path through a variety of sources, the authorities you locate start to refer back to each other and the new sources you consult fail to reveal significant new information.

The fact that a few of the sources you have located appear relevant does not mean it is time to stop researching. Until you have explored other potential research avenues, you should continue your work. It might be that the authorities you initially locate will turn out to be the most relevant, but you cannot have confidence in that result until you research additional authorities. On the other hand, you can always keep looking for one more case or one more article to support your analysis, but at some point the benefit of continuing to research will be too small to justify the additional effort. It is unlikely that one magical source exists that is going to resolve your research issue. If the issue were clear, you probably would not have been asked to research it. If you developed a comprehensive research strategy and followed it until you came full circle in your research, it is probably time to stop.

§21.3 Finding Help

Even if you follow all of the steps outlined in this chapter, from time to time, you will not be able to find what you need. The two most common situations that arise are not being able to find any authority on an issue and finding an overwhelming amount of information.

§21.3.1 *What to Do If You are Unable to Find Anything*

If you have researched several different sources and are unable to find anything, it is time to take a different approach. You should not expect the material you need to appear effortlessly, and blind alleys are inevitable if you approach a problem creatively. Nevertheless, if you find that you really cannot locate any information on an issue, consider the following possibilities:

- **MAKE SURE YOU UNDERSTAND THE PROBLEM**

One possibility is that you have misunderstood a critical aspect of the problem. If diligent research truly yields nothing, you might want to go back to the person who gave you the assignment to make sure you correctly noted all of the factual information you need and have understood the assignment correctly.

- **RETHINK YOUR SEARCH TERMS**

Have you expanded the breadth and depth of your search terms? You might be researching the right concepts but not have expressed them in a way that yields information in an index or from a word search. Expanding your search terms will allow you to look not only more widely for information, but also more narrowly. For example, if you have searched unsuccessfully using *moving vehicle* as a search term for authority involving transportation equipment, you might need to move to more concrete terms, such as *automobile* or *car*.

In addition, you might need to rethink search terms directed to applicable legal theories. If you have focused on a theory of recovery for which you have not been able to locate authority, you might need to think about other ways to approach the problem. Try not to become so wedded to a legal theory that you pursue it to the exclusion of other viable claims or defenses.

- **GO BACK TO SECONDARY SOURCES**

If you did not consult secondary sources originally, you might want to take that route to find the information you need. The material on the issue might be scattered through many subject areas or statutory sections so that it is difficult to compile the relevant subset of information without secondary sources that tie disparate threads of authority together. In addition, the search terms that seemed applicable when you started your research might, in fact, not be helpful. Secondary sources can help point you in the right direction.

Another difficulty is that you might be looking for the wrong type of authority. Are you sure this is a question of state law? Although a content-driven search will retrieve multiple types of authority, pre-filtering by the wrong jurisdiction will take you in the wrong direction. If you are using source-driven searching, you may need to look in other sources if, for example, statutes as well as cases apply to the situation. Secondary sources can help you determine what type of primary authority is likely to be relevant to the situation.

Finally, secondary sources can help you determine whether you are facing a question of first impression. If the controlling jurisdiction simply has not faced this question yet, secondary sources should direct you to jurisdictions that have. If no jurisdiction has resolved the issue, legal periodicals might direct you to arguments and analogies that could be made.

§21.3.2 What To Do If You Find an Overwhelming Amount of Material

The same strategies that will help you if you are unable to find any material will also help if you find an overwhelming amount of material. Making sure you understand the problem, of course, is critical. Rethinking your search terms to narrow your approach can also help. If you located information primarily using word searches, you might want to try searching by subject, using either print or electronic research tools, because searching by subject instead of by terms in the document might help you focus on relevant authority. Consulting secondary sources, however, is probably the most useful strategy. Synthesizing large amounts of authority is difficult. Secondary sources can help you identify the key authorities and otherwise limit the scope of the information on the issue.

Another consideration here is the scope of your research. If much of the authority you have located is secondary authority or primary persuasive authority, you might need to refocus on primary mandatory authority from the controlling jurisdiction. If the controlling jurisdiction has a sufficient amount of authority for thorough analysis of the issue, you might not need to cite persuasive authority. You might also need to narrow your scope by limiting the legal theories you are considering. If some are clearly more viable than others and you already have an overwhelming amount of authority, you might want to focus on the theories that seem to provide your client with the best chances of prevailing.

Even when you take these steps, finding an overwhelming amount of material is not uncommon with content-driven searching. Because the results include many types of authority and because of the way the search algorithms work, it is not unusual for a content-driven search to return thousands or tens of thousands of documents. This is obviously too much information to be useful.

With content-driven searching, using the relevancy rankings and filtering the search results are critical. Although you should not assume that the very best authority will be the first item in the search results, you must rely to some extent on the relevancy rankings when a search retrieves 10,000 documents. Those at the bottom of the list are not likely to be very relevant; they may contain only one reference to only one of your search terms. Post-search filtering is also important. Even when you pre-filter by jurisdiction, you may retrieve both state and related federal information or cases from all levels of court within the state. Limiting the results to the controlling tribunal or a specific publication, using a date restriction, and searching for terms within the initial results are all good strategies for focusing on the most relevant information.

§21.4 Research Checklists

§21.4.1 Checklist for Developing an Effective Research Plan

1. **OBTAIN PRELIMINARY INFORMATION ON THE PROBLEM**
   - ☐ Determine the due date, work product expected, limits on research tools to be used, controlling jurisdiction (if known), and whether persuasive authority should be located (if known).
   - ☐ If permitted, find out useful research tools, background on the law or terms of art, and whether other written materials or individuals with special expertise should be consulted.

2. **PLAN THE STEPS IN YOUR RESEARCH**
   - ☐ Develop a preliminary issue statement.
   - ☐ Generate a list of search terms.
   - ☐ Identify the type and sequence of research tasks by identifying what you know, what you do not yet know, and how best to fill in the blanks.
     - Narrow the field of legal information using what you already know about the research issue (e.g., jurisdiction).
     - Use the information you already know to determine whether source- or content-driven searching is most efficient for your task.
     - Use secondary sources to narrow the field further.
     - When you are ready to review primary authority, focus on mandatory authority first.
     - Locate persuasive authority later, if necessary:
       - ☐ to buttress an analysis largely resolved by primary mandatory authority;
       - ☐ to locate factually analogous cases from other jurisdictions;
       - ☐ to make an analogy to another area of law when the applicable rule is unclear;
       - ☐ to locate commentary or applicable rules from other jurisdictions on an issue of first impression.
     - Determine the best mix of print and electronic research tools for your research project.

3. **WORK EFFECTIVELY**
   - ☐ Keep effective notes.
   - ☐ Stop researching when your research has come full circle.
   - ☐ Find help if you need it.
     - If you are unable to find anything or find too much material, make sure you understand the problem, rethink your search terms, consult secondary sources, and reevaluate the legal theories you are pursuing.

CLIENT-CENTERED LAWYERING: INTRODUCTION TO INTERVIEWING AND COUNSELING

CHAPTER 22

LAWYERING FOR AND WITH THE CLIENT

§22.1 Client-Centered Lawyering

One lawyer had this to say about legal representation:

> I represent people, not cases.... [W]hen I did criminal defense work[, c]lients came to me with more than just their criminal case. Their families were on welfare, or they'd lose their job if they couldn't make bail. There are drug problems which affect whole families.... One time, my client came to court with her three-year-old child, and the judge rolled her up into jail on some technicality. We [later] got her out on a writ, but I couldn't leave the child there [in the courtroom], so I took her with me.
>
> You've got to go the whole nine yards for your clients. If you don't, you're really not meeting their needs. I had a poor client with a big products liability case. She had almost no clothes and had never been in a courthouse, so we went out and bought her a whole wardrobe for trial. When we won big, we [counseled her to] put money in trust for the kids, and buy a nice home but pay in cash so you don't have monthly payments. Otherwise, the money could have been gone in a year....
>
> I don't want to take over their lives or force them to do something they don't want, but I never want to abandon my clients at the courthouse door. I guess that means getting emotionally involved in your clients' lives.... [T]hat's a price I'll gladly pay to try to help the *person*, not just the case.[1]

A client is not an item of work. You probably dislike it when a doctor treats you as a case of flu rather than as a human being who has the flu. And the problem is more than unpleasantness: a doctor who treats you as a human being with symptoms of the flu might spend enough time with you to learn that you also have other symptoms, and that you therefore do not have the flu, but instead another disease, which should be treated differently. (You can imagine much of how a client experiences an interview with a lawyer simply by remembering how you have experienced contact with doctors.)

---

[1] An anonymous lawyer quoted at Richard A. Zitrin & Carol M. Langford, *Legal Ethics in the Practice of Law* 230 (1995).

The opposite of treating the client as an item of work is "client-centered law-yering," a phrase that originated in a ground-breaking book by David Binder and Susan Price.[2] It means focusing our efforts around what the client hopes for (rather than what we think the client needs) and treating the client as an effective collaborator (rather than as a helpless person we will rescue). We have no special wisdom about what clients should want, and each client has to live with the results of our work long after the case has faded into the back of our memory. Clients are not helpless, and even if they were, only rarely could we rescue them. A better view is this: the client is a capable person who has hired us to help the client accomplish a particular goal.

The client who is not experienced at hiring lawyers is very different from the client (usually a business person) who hires lawyers routinely. The inexperienced client may have more anxiety and may understand less about how lawyers work. The experienced client may have more sharply defined goals and may think of hiring the lawyer as bringing in a specialist to perform an already defined task.

And the client who wants help with a dispute (suing over an auto accident, for example) can be very different from the client who wants assistance complet-ing a transaction (typically, negotiating a contract). If the transaction is important, the transactional client might be experiencing some stress, which might be replaced with happiness if the transaction is successful. But a dispute client has a greater chance of feeling stress, trauma, and anger.

§22.2 The Client As a Colleague and Collaborator

Consider two scenes in two different lawyers' offices. In the first scene, the lawyer sits behind a large desk, and the client sits in a chair on the opposite side of the desk. When the client speaks, it is to supply facts the lawyer has asked for. When the lawyer speaks, it is to provide professional advice and judgment. This is often called the traditional model of the attorney-client relationship: the passive client protected by the powerful professional.

In the second scene, the lawyer and client sit together, perhaps at a confer-ence table. They brainstorm, go over documents, and talk about which of several possible strategies would best accomplish the client's goals — and in doing so, they are both active. This has been called the participatory model of the attorney-client relationship: the lawyer impliedly concedes that he or she does not have all the answers, and the client is enlisted to supply an added measure of creativity and an often superior knowledge of the facts.

Today, many clients want lawyers who know how to use the participatory model, although a significant minority of clients still prefer the traditional model. (Forty or 50 years ago, the reverse was probably true.) A client's preference largely depends on how the client deals with anxiety and acquires trust.

---

[2] David A. Binder & Susan M. Price, *Legal Interviewing and Counseling: A Client-Centered Approach* (1977). A more recent version is David A. Binder, Paul B. Bergman, Susan M. Price & Paul R. Trembley, *Lawyers as Counselors: A Client-Centered Approach* (2d ed. 2004).

A client who prefers the traditional model might reduce anxiety by turning a problem over to a professional, thinking about it as little as possible while the professional works on it, and following the professional's instructions. That client might trust more easily a professional who resembles an authority figure.

A client who prefers the participatory model might reduce anxiety by becoming actively involved in solving a problem. That client might more easily trust a professional who is openly accessible and has a problem-solving style that the client understands and respects.

In a pioneering study, Douglas Rosenthal studied a number of personal injury cases to determine whether — personal preferences aside — one model produces better solutions than the other.[3] Rosenthal examined a number of personal injury cases, categorized the plaintiff's attorney-client relationship in each case as either traditional or participatory, and compared the result in each case with an independent evaluation of what the plaintiff's claim was worth. On average, the participatory plaintiff's lawyers got better results. The gap between the participatory and the traditional results was not huge, and Rosenthal's sample was relatively small. But since then, the impression has become widespread that participatory relationships with clients produce better and more satisfying results than traditional relationships do.

Why does the participatory model seem to work better and to satisfy more clients and lawyers? First, because lawyers are human, they make mistakes, and an actively involved client will catch at least some of those mistakes before they cause harm. Many clients can understand more of how to solve their problems than some lawyers give them credit for, and most clients know at least as much or even more about their own needs than a lawyer will. (For both of these reasons, the lawyer and client working together will come up with more and better solutions than the lawyer working alone.) Third, "[t]he participatory model promotes the dignity of clients as citizens" because it "makes the client a doer, responsible for his choices."[4] Fourth, it reduces the client's anxiety because the client is not kept in the dark about what is happening. Fifth, it protects "the integrity of professionals by liberating them from . . . the burdens imposed [by a] paternal role" and from client suspicion caused by client ignorance.[5] And sixth, it "invites personal contact in a society becoming increasingly impersonal."[6]

The participatory model also carries some burdens. Some clients may find their anxiety increased if they have to think about their problems; they would rather hire a professional and forget about it.[7] A lawyer with an emotional need to be "paternalistic and dominating" will be frustrated and unhappy in participatory relationships with clients. "Lawyers, and perhaps most professionals, seem to have two human needs in disproportionately great measure: the desire to control their environment and aggressive (and competitive) feelings."[8] On the other hand, a

---

[3] Douglas E. Rosenthal, *Lawyer and Client: Who's in Charge?* (1974).
[4] *Id.* at 168.
[5] *Id.* at 169.
[6] *Id.* at 170.
[7] *Id.*
[8] *Id.* at 172–173.

dominating but subtle lawyer might manipulate a client into thinking the relationship is participatory when in fact it is not. (Over time, many clients in this situation can figure out that they have been manipulated, although that might not happen until some time after the lawyer has finished the work.) Finally, the participatory model is more expensive.[9] It takes more time, and time is money. And it also takes more effort, in the form of "energy, intelligence, and judgment" from the client and, from the lawyer, "patience and tolerance built on recognition of an obligation to earn the client's cooperation."[10]

In today's law practice environment, a lawyer will be more effective at getting the desired results and satisfy more clients if the lawyer *usually* develops participatory relationships but can nevertheless work within a traditional relationship with those clients who would find a participatory relationship stressful. This book assumes that participatory lawyering is now the norm and that traditional lawyering is now the exception.

How can you tell one type of client from another? It usually does no good to ask in the initial interview, "Would you rather have a traditional or a participatory relationship?" Only a rare client would be able to answer that question well, even if you were to explain what the terms mean. A better method is to start on a participatory basis and switch to a traditional relationship if you learn along the way that the client would be happier that way.

Are some types of clients more likely to prefer one type of relationship to the other? It is a commonly held view that, with exceptions, the more educated a client is, the more likely the client will feel comfortable working with a professional.[11] If that is true, a well-educated client might readily acclimate to (or even demand) a participatory relationship, while a less-educated client might prefer a more traditional one. But this question is a minefield in which generalizations can be both true and outrageously false at the same time. Every poverty lawyer can describe wonderful participatory relationships with clients who had little formal education. And Rosenthal found some very well-educated clients who preferred a traditional relationship.[12] A busy and well-educated client might have little time to spare for a participatory relationship. Where the client might want involvement but not full participation in decision-making, the lawyer should differentiate between those situations where the client would want to be consulted (or must by law be consulted) and those where the client would prefer that the lawyer simply exercise her expertise.

§22.3 Who Decides What

Regardless of whether the relationship is traditional or participatory, the law of agency, professional responsibility, malpractice, and constitutional criminal

---

[9] *Id.* at 176.
[10] *Id.* at 15.
[11] *Id.* at 184.
[12] *Id.* at 171.

procedure provide that certain decisions are reserved to the client and may not be made by the lawyer. The law of agency matters because the client is a principal whose agent is the lawyer. If the lawyer makes decisions reserved to the client, the lawyer can be disciplined under the rules of professional responsibility, or held liable in malpractice, or both.

The client defines the goals of the representation. The client decides whether to accept an adversary's offer of a negotiated settlement,[13] although the client can preauthorize acceptance of an offer meeting a particular description ("if they'll pay anything over $60,000, I'll take it, but don't stop negotiating until you've gotten them as high above that figure as you think you can"). In a criminal case, the client decides whether to plead guilty or not guilty, "whether to waive jury trial and whether the client will testify."[14] But the client makes all these decisions — which are momentous ones — only after the lawyer has counseled by explaining the alternatives and their advantages, costs, and risks.

Traditionally, the lawyer has decided "technical, legal, and tactical issues,"[15] such as where to sue, what theory of the case to rely on, what evidence to submit and witnesses to call, and what arguments to make. For a long time, the case law has allowed (and still does allow) the lawyer to make these decisions unilaterally, without consulting the client or even over the client's objections. But if you do such a thing, the case law will not stop the client from firing you and telling every other potential client in North America never to hire you. Moreover, the Model Rules of Professional Conduct require not only that a lawyer "abide by a client's decisions concerning the objectives of representation [but also] *consult with the client as to the means by which they are to be pursued.*"[16] And the Model Rules suggest that the lawyer should defer to the client when technical and tactical decisions raise "such questions as the expense to be incurred and concern for third persons who might be adversely affected."[17]

In the participatory model of lawyer-client relations, some of these decisions are made jointly by the lawyer and client: in a surprisingly large number of instances, the client has valuable insights on technical and tactical questions such as where to sue, what theory of the case to rely on, what evidence to introduce and witnesses to call, and what arguments to make. Depending on the client and the circumstances, some of those decisions are more effectively made jointly by the lawyer and client, working together. Sometimes this involves a full counseling session. Sometimes it involves a phone call in which the lawyer describes a technical or tactical action the lawyer is considering — making a particular motion, for example — and asks the client whether the client sees any problems in doing so.

What kinds of problems might the client see? The three most typical are (1) the client has information that changes things, (2) the proposed action would cause difficulties for the client or for someone the client would like to avoid

---

[13] Rule 1.2(a) of the Model Rules of Professional Conduct.
[14] *Id.*
[15] Comment to Rule 1.2(a).
[16] Rule 1.2(a) (emphasis added).
[17] Comment to Rule 1.2(a).

harming, and (3) the client might be reluctant to pay for the proposed action. Let's take each in turn.

Suppose the motion would seek an order compelling the other side to turn over certain documents. Some lawyers would consider such a thing so hyper-technical that they would never consult a client about it. It is true that if the lawyer were to call the client, the latter would often say, in a tentative voice, something like "Sounds O.K. to me." But clients appreciate the courtesy of being told, and Model Rule 1.4(a) requires that you "keep the client reasonably informed about the status of a matter." And every once in a while the conversation might lead to very different results:

Lawyer: [after describing the motion] I just wanted to mention it to you in case you have any thoughts on it.

Client: Let's back up a minute. Would you describe the documents again?

Lawyer: [does so]

Client: I think I might have seen those documents, and I think they don't say what you're hoping they say.

Lawyer: Since your memory is unclear, maybe the safe thing to do is make the motion anyway and see what they look like when and if we get them.

Client: I think I know somebody who has a copy of them.

Lawyer: A complete copy?

Client: I think so. I'll call him as soon as we get off the phone.

This conversation could change everything in the lawyer's plans.

A lawyer is like an elephant in a china shop. Unlike the proverbial bull in the same place, the elephant might not want to break china, but any inadvertent move on his or her part might shatter something precious. There are plenty of ways in which a lawyer, using routine methods of representation, might accidentally damage the client or someone the client wants to avoid harming. A prudent lawyer behaves like an elephant who wants to be able to leave the china shop without having broken anything unnecessarily. Frequent consultation with the client is one of the ways in which effective lawyers assure that.

Clients worry constantly about the cost of legal work. Some lawyers are oblivious to that. Others try carefully to deal with their clients' concerns. If the client is being billed by the hour, the discovery enforcement motion discussed above would cost the client money in lawyer billing time. When a large corporation hires outside litigation counsel, it might initially impose a budget and later want to know things such as how this motion would affect the budget. Even without a budget, the client is entitled to ask how much the motion will cost, what it will probably accomplish, and whether the probable benefit is worth the cost. A lawyer who can answer those questions intelligently, precisely, and nondefensively can earn the loyalty of clients, so that they become repeat customers. A lawyer who cannot do that well risks losing clients to the first kind of lawyer.

To summarize: The client should, of course, decide questions that the law gives the client the right to decide. And even for questions that by law a lawyer can decide unilaterally, you should consult with the client anyway if there is a possibility that the client might be able to add information or ideas or if the client might have preferences about how the question is handled. If in doubt, err on the side of consulting with the client. Not only does consultation improve the odds of getting good results, but it reduces the chances of friction between lawyer and client. Lawyers who often consult with clients seem to have fewer ethics complaints and malpractice actions brought against them. And if the client has preferences on a technical or tactical question that by law the lawyer can decide unilaterally, follow the client's preferences.

The boss is the one who gets to hire and fire. The client hires and can fire the lawyer, not the other way around.

§22.4 What Clients Dislike in a Lawyer

Charles Dickens' novel *Bleak House*[18] concerns, among other things, a lawsuit to divide up an estate. The suit has "become so complicated that no man alive knows what it means."[19] All the parties to the suit are oppressed by it. One of them complains, "We are always appearing, and disappearing, and swearing, and interrogating, and filing, and cross-filing, and arguing, and sealing, and motioning, and referring, and reporting. . . . Law finds it can't do this, Equity finds it can't do that; neither can so much as say it can't do anything, without this solicitor instructing and this counsel appearing for A, and that solicitor instructing and that counsel appearing for B; and so on through the whole alphabet."[20] The same person exclaims, "The Lawyers have twisted [the lawsuit] into such a state of bedevilment that the original merits of the case have long since disappeared from the face of the earth."[21] Finally, nearly 800 pages later, the lawyers declare that the suit is over because the estate is now empty, everything in it having been spent on lawyers' fees.[22]

This is the subliminal fear of everyone with a problem that might have something to do with the law — that if you hire a lawyer, you will have two problems. The first will be the original problem, and the second will be the lawyer.

Consumer Reports magazine did a survey of its readers to find out how satisfied they were with their lawyers. The results were dismal: "Of all the services we've surveyed over the years, only diet programs have received a worse score" than lawyers.[23] The most common complaints were that the lawyers involved ignored the client by failing to return phone calls promptly, or ask the client's opinion about how to proceed, or find ways to reduce the client's aggravation;

---

[18] Charles Dickens, *Bleak House* (1st ed. 1853) (page numbers in the next few footnotes are to the Penguin 1971 edition edited by Norman Page).

[19] *Id.* at 52.

[20] *Id.* at 145–146.

[21] *Id.* at 145.

[22] *Id.* at 920–924.

[23] *When You Need a Lawyer*, Consumer Reports, Feb. 1996, at 34, 34.

neglected the case itself; inaccurately predicted the outcome or how long it would take to get to an outcome; or charged unnecessarily high fees or failed to disclose in advance fees and other costs. Law is a service industry, and people are losing their tolerance for shoddy service in general.

Clients also despise lawyers who make promises they cannot keep, brag, speak in legal jargon, are condescending, and talk too much and listen too little. Clients hate having to fight to get their lawyers' attention. When you and a client are talking together, an interrupting knock on your office door or telephone call demeans the client. Making a client wait is a form of disrespect. Clients "who are made to drive across town and wait with children in a crowded room while their attorney is an hour late for their brief interview may not know whether their attorney is technically knowledgeable, but they certainly understand how little [the attorney] cares about their needs. . . ."[24]

Studies have shown that lawyers who communicate infrequently or badly with their clients have more fee disputes with clients, are sued more often for malpractice, and are complained about more often to bar disciplinary authorities. A study showed that how doctors talk to patients is the strongest predictor of how frequently the doctors will be sued for malpractice.[25] Those who take the time and effort to deal with the patient's thoughts and feelings get sued less than doctors who don't, regardless of the number and severity of the mistakes the doctors make in diagnosis and treatment. (Rule 1.4(a) of the Model Rules of Professional Conduct provides that "[a] lawyer shall keep the client reasonably informed about the status of the matter [and] promptly comply with reasonable requests for information.") The less clients know about what is happening, the more anxious and unhappy they are. (You know this feeling, too. You probably have it when you turn over your car to a mechanic.)

§22.5 How To Work Better With Clients

In the end, clients are loyal if you

1. get results,
2. do so efficiently, in both time and cost,
3. reduce their anxiety and frustration while they await results, and
4. are considerate, likeably human, and in other ways a pleasure to work with.

To accomplish the third and fourth items on this list, don't do the things that aggravate clients (see §22.4). And do some affirmative things as well.

When answering client questions, do not just give an answer that makes sense to you. Give an answer that makes sense to the client, and make sure that the client understands what you've said. Ineffective lawyers toss out quick answers to client questions and then move on to something else, as though the client's worries

---

[24] Martin J. Solomon, *Client Relations: Ethics and Economics*, 23 Ariz. St. L.J. 155, 175 (1991).
[25] Malcolm Gladwell, *Blink: The Power of Thinking without Thinking* 39–43 (2005).

are marginal to the lawyer's work. Clients notice that, although they might not say anything about it at the time. Clients do not want to fight with their lawyers, but when they reach a point of dissatisfaction, they quietly take their business elsewhere.

When communicating with clients, talk and write in plain English. If you have to use a term of art, explain its meaning in an uncondescending way. Use concrete, precise language and not vague generalities. Behave in ways that encourage clients both to tell you things that you need to know and to ask questions about things that make the client anxious. More than anything else, that means be a good listener.

When a client calls, if you cannot come to the telephone immediately, return the call within hours or, if you are in court or its equivalent, have another lawyer or a paraprofessional do so. A law office should be accessible and responsive, not a bureaucracy.

Introduce the client to the people in your office who will do work on the client's behalf, including secretaries. If it's not obvious, explain to the client the role each person will play.

Unless a client would prefer otherwise or there are special reasons not to, send copies to the client of all court papers and your correspondence with other people concerning the client. And whenever a document would not be self-explanatory to a layperson, tell the client why it exists and what it means.

Get to know the client so that you can understand what the client really needs from you. How risk-averse is the client, for instance? The client will have to live with what you do long after you drop out of the picture. If the client is a business, get to know the business as well as the industry in which it operates. For example, you cannot possibly do good general legal work for a symphony orchestra unless you are familiar with things like how grants are obtained from foundations, where the market for classical music recordings is headed, and perhaps even what second violinists are typically paid.

How can you learn about your client's business and industry without embarrassing yourself? You can go to a library and read books on the industry. You can read the relevant trade magazines; every industry has at least one. And you can read articles in the general press, which you can find through an Internet search. You can also visit the client's place of business to get a feel for it physically and organizationally. And you should read as much as you can on your client's website.

Large corporations hire law firms to solve problems that are usually quantifiable in money terms. From the client's point of view, this might be a pure business transaction without any emotional content whatsoever, and the only concerns are results and efficiency. But individuals and small businesses go to lawyers for two reasons. The first is to solve a problem, which might be quantifiable in money terms. The second is for relief from fear and pain. These clients consider it your responsibility to deal with both, and if you want clients to recommend you to their friends and neighbors, you will need to be able to deal with both.

§22.6 Confidentiality

The duty to keep a client's confidences secret is one of the central obligations of ethics law.

In most states, the obligation is defined by Rule 1.6 of the Model Rules of Professional Conduct: "A lawyer shall not reveal information relating to representation of a client." Rule 1.6 provides several exceptions. Some of them have been controversial, and in your state's version of Rule 1.6 the exceptions might differ from the ones presented here. The most recent ABA version of Rule 1.6 sets out the following exceptions (in the words of Rule 1.6):

- the client gives informed consent
- the disclosure is impliedly authorized in order to carry out the representation
- the lawyer reasonably believes [disclosure] necessary . . .
  - to prevent reasonably certain death or substantial bodily harm;
  - to prevent the client from committing a crime or fraud that is reasonably certain to result in substantial injury to the financial interests or property of another and in furtherance of which the client has used or is using the lawyer's services;
  - to prevent, mitigate or rectify substantial injury to the financial interests or property of another that is reasonably certain to result or has resulted from the client's commission of a crime or fraud in furtherance of which the client has used the lawyer's services;
  - to secure legal advice about the lawyer's compliance with these Rules;
  - to establish a claim or defense on behalf of the lawyer in a controversy between the lawyer and the client, to establish a defense to a criminal charge or civil claim against the lawyer based upon conduct in which the client was involved, or to respond to allegations in any proceeding concerning the lawyer's representation of the client; or
  - to comply with other law or a court order.

Rule 3.3 provides two additional exceptions. First, under Rule 3.3(a)(3), if the client testifies falsely and refuses to confess the falsity to the court, the lawyer must take "reasonable remedial measures, including, if necessary, disclosure to the tribunal." Where the client is a criminal defendant, somewhat different principles might govern because of the client's constitutional right to decide whether to testify. The Comment to Rule 3.3 notes that jurisdictions differ on how they handle this problem. Second, Rule 3.3(b) provides that if the client "intends to engage, is engaging or has engaged in criminal or fraudulent conduct relating to the proceeding" — such as bribing a witness — the lawyer again must take "reasonable remedial measures, including, if necessary, disclosure to the tribunal."

These ethical duties are separate from the evidentiary attorney-client privilege, which prohibits an attorney or an attorney's employee from testifying to communications from a client made for the purpose of obtaining legal advice when the client has treated the communications as confidential and has not waived the privilege.

CHAPTER 23

LAWYERING AS PROBLEM-SOLVING

§23.1 Solving Professional Problems

Some lawyer problem-solving is conflict-resolution (winning a lawsuit, for example), but a large amount is transactional (such as negotiating a contract). Conflict-resolution lawyering is mainly reactive: a client has been injured, for example, and hires a lawyer to attack the party that caused the injury. Transactional lawyering, on the other hand, is proactive: it aims at the future to protect the client from potential injury (through careful contract drafting, for example) or by accomplishing the client's desires (such as through a will that distributes the client's property after death).

§23.1.1 How Diagnosis, Prediction, and Strategy are Intertwined in the Practice of Law

Most of the thinking that lawyers do consists of (1) *diagnosing* what is happening now or what happened in the past, (2) *predicting* what will happen in the future, or (3) creating and implementing *strategies* to control what happens in the future.

A lawyer diagnoses by figuring out why events are happening or have happened. Why is the client more upset over a small problem than a big one? Why exactly is Norcomm, Inc., not making deliveries on time? In a negotiation, why is the other side unable to see why your proposal is good for both sides?

A lawyer predicts by prophesying how other people will react to events. If the client sues, who will win? (You already are gaining experience predicting in this way in your study of legal writing.) How will the other side respond to a negotiation offer you are contemplating making?

A lawyer strategizes by developing a plan for solving a problem. When you counsel a client, you will offer several plans as options from which the client can choose. When you prepare to negotiate, you will develop a strategy for getting the other side to agree, as much as possible, to what your client wants.

Suppose the client is a developer who has signed a contract to buy a farm on which he had intended to build tract homes. Before the transaction could be completed, two things have happened. First, the local government has declared a five-year building moratorium because explosive development has outstripped the government's capacity to provide tap water and to process sewage. Second, the client has begun to suffer health problems; his family has persuaded him to go into semi-retirement; and he is entertaining the thought that, rather than develop the land for housing, he would like to live in the farmhouse and hire neighboring farmers to farm the land. The problem is that the contract includes the fields but not the farmhouse. The client has offered to buy the farmhouse as well, but the owners have refused. They do not want to live in the farmhouse themselves. They believe its value will go up substantially in the future, and they simply want to sell it later rather than now. So the client would like to get out of this contract and maybe buy some other farm.

In a client interview and afterward, you diagnose by learning the facts and figuring out how they affect the client legally, financially, and emotionally. To make your diagnosis concrete, you predict how people and courts will treat the client in the future if you do not intervene on the client's behalf. Based on the law, your prediction might be this: *The contract is enforceable. If we sue for recission of the contract, we will lose. If we simply refuse to complete the purchase as laid out in the contract, they will sue us for breach, and we will lose and have to pay their damages.*

You develop several strategies to protect the client. You and the client choose the best strategy based on your predictions of each strategy's likelihood of success and on the client's preferred style of attacking the problem. In the course of that, you might say to the client:

> An obvious strategy is to fight this through a lawsuit. But you will lose, and your litigation expenses, including attorney's fees, would run in the range of an approximate minimum of $15,000 (if there's light discovery, a summary judgment, and no more) to at least $120,000 (if there's a trial followed by an appeal), plus damages if you breach. But the other side does not seem to realize that this transaction is badly structured from their point of view. If you and they go ahead with the deal as it is now structured, they will pay a lot more tax than they need to. We can offer to renegotiate the whole deal to eliminate their unnecessary tax exposure, on condition that they agree to sell you the farmhouse at a reasonable price. If that works, it would satisfy your preference for solving this problem quickly and with as little conflict as possible.

As you implement the chosen strategy, unexpected things can happen. If the unexpected events are harmful, you will diagnose what is going wrong and restrategize (by modifying the strategy or adopting a new one).

> When I called their lawyer and offered to renegotiate, the sellers blew a gasket and made a lot of threats about suing us. I've been trying to figure out why they would react this way. They seemed to be thinking that we were trying to take advantage of them, which makes no sense if they really understood the tax consequences. The sellers refused to meet with us and sent word back through the lawyer that our choice was to go through with the deal as is or get sued for damages. I asked around, and the sellers do not have a reputation for being suspicious by nature or capricious.

So I wondered just how much they really knew about taxes in this kind of transaction. I sent a letter to their attorney offering to pay for a consultation with any tax advisor they chose. We would not be present, and the only condition would be that the tax advisor be given a copy of the contract before meeting with the sellers. Because this was an offer in negotiation, their attorney was ethically obligated to inform them of it.[1] It turns out that they had been doing their own taxes for years and had no idea what a mess they were about to get into. When a neutral tax advisor explained it to them, they realized that it made good financial sense to sell you the farmhouse.

Your diagnosis of what was going wrong allowed you to restrategize and solve the problem.

§23.1.2 *How Lawyers Diagnose, Predict, and Strategize*

Diagnosis, prediction, and strategizing occur through very similar processes of thought. There are six steps, which — taken together — are really the essence of professional creativity.

Preliminarily, let us dispel two myths about creativity. First, creativity is not an innate and mysterious personality trait possessed only by artists and others like them. Creativity is the process of solving problems through insights that you arrive at on your own. Everyone is creative to some extent, although some are more creative than others. Second, creativity is *not* particularly related to academic success. Some students who have received disappointing grades over the years are easily creative in ways not measured by exams. And some students who earn high grades are less naturally creative and have to work at becoming good at the creative process.

The client's creativity matters, too. In the participatory model of client relations (see §22.2), you are not merely receptive to the client's contribution. You want to encourage it.

Here are the six steps:

1. ***Problem-identification.*** You notice a situation that needs to be diagnosed, predicted, or strategized; define exactly what that situation is; and identify the client's goals. Don't underestimate the importance of this step. Consider what happened when the farmland sellers refused to renegotiate the contract. The developer's lawyer could have given up at that point, accomplishing nothing for her client. But she did not give up. She wondered why her initial strategy was failing, diagnosed the cause for its failure, and developed a modified strategy that succeeded. A lawyer who is good at problem-identification is a lawyer who refuses to guess, does not make unnecessary assumptions, is not satisfied with the way things look at first glance, and hates to be at the mercy of events.

---

[1] See §22.3.

2. *Gathering and evaluating information and raw materials.* You learn about the relevant law and facts in a fairly open-ended manner. An insatiable curiosity is valuable here.

3. *Solution-generation.* In diagnosis, think up the largest reasonable number of potential explanations for the events in question. In prediction, think up the largest reasonable number of potential prophesies of the future. And in strategy, think up the largest reasonable number of potential plans for controlling events. *The more possibilities we can generate here, the larger is our field to choose from later.* Imagination is quite helpful, especially if it is grounded in an existing factual context. In this stage, we are not verifying or judging each explanation, prediction, or plan. That is the next step. Here, we are only listing the possibilities.

4. *Solution-evaluation.* In diagnosis, test each potential explanation to see if it accurately tells you why things are happening. In prediction, test each potential prophesy to see how likely it is to happen. And in strategy, test each plan to see how well it would achieve the client's goals. In all three activities, we look for concrete, clarifying facts, evidence, and law. What would confirm that an explanation is accurate (if diagnosing), that a prophesy is likely to happen (if predicting), or that a plan will control events (if developing a strategy)? And we look for negative proof to reduce the number of hypotheses. What information could eliminate an explanation, prophesy, or strategy from consideration?

5. *Decision.* Choose the most accurate diagnosis, the most likely prediction, or the most effective strategy. But do not rush this. Premature judgment or closure will cut off solution-generation and solution-evaluation before they have done their work. The first good idea you come across is not always the best idea you can find.

6. *Action.* If the decision is a diagnosis or a prediction, report it, and the reasons for it, in an office memorandum, an opinion letter, a conversation with the client, or some combination of these. If the decision is selection of a strategy, implement it.

In practice, the six stages are not as neatly segmented as this. Gathering information and solution-generation often happen at the same time. The same is true of solution-evaluation and decision. "In the daily stream of thought the mind may be unconsciously incubating on one aspect of [a problem], while . . . consciously . . . preparing for or verifying another aspect."[2] That is why solutions often surface into consciousness "unexpectedly, with surprising suddenness."[3] And it is why professional work (like any activity involving creativity) is an uneven mixture of "sudden bursts of insight and tiring efforts at execution."[4]

Solution-generation and solution-evaluation pose the greatest challenges for students, in part because they require contrary skills. To generate the largest

---

[2] Graham Wallas, *The Art of Thought* 81–82 (1926).
[3] Teresa H. Amabile, *The Social Psychology of Creativity* 85 (1983).
[4] V. John-Steiner, *Notebooks of the Mind: Explorations of Thinking* 79 (1985).

number of possible solutions, you must be willing to look below the surface of the facts and law for deeper possibilities and meaning. Solution-generation depends on an uninhibited flow of association, during which judgment is suspended and ideas that later evaluation might show to be sound arrive mixed together with ideas that eventually turn out to be wrong or even silly. The poet Schiller wrote that solution-generation is meager:

> if the intellect examines too closely the ideas already pouring in, as it were, at the gates. Regarded in isolation, an idea may be insignificant, and venturesome in the extreme, but it may acquire importance from an idea which follows it; perhaps, in a certain collation with other ideas, which may seem equally absurd, it may be capable of furnishing a very serviceable link. The intellect cannot judge all these ideas unless it can retain them until [all can be seen together. When many alternatives are being collected,] the intellect has withdrawn its watchers from the gates, and the ideas rush in pell-mell, and only then does it review and inspect the multitude. [People who are bad at solution-generation] reject too soon. . . .[5]

The key is to avoid premature judgment, to defer evaluation until after you have created an array of alternatives. If you or someone else makes snap criticisms of your ideas as soon as they come up, your solution-generation will be paralyzed. It is too easy to dismiss as foolishness a partly worked out explanation, prophecy, or plan from which faults have not yet been expunged. Solution-generation can also be hurt by a desire to conform, or by what Kenney Hegland calls the "fear of making a fool of yourself."[6] Lon Fuller, the great contracts scholar, wrote that solution-generation does not easily happen when you ask yourself "anxiously at every turn that most inhibitive of questions, '*What will other people think?*'"[7]

Many lawyers find that they have their best ideas when traveling to or from the office, when showering, when doing the dishes, or when jogging. What all these have in common is that the lawyer is doing something mechanical, freeing the mind to wander. And some lawyers also find it productive to sit with a pad and pencil and make lists about whatever they are working on. The act of list-making seems to open doors in the mind. After two solutions are written down, a third follows, and then a fourth.

Paradoxically, solution-evaluation requires the very qualities that would cripple solution-generation: a ruthless skepticism, a pragmatic sense of the realistic, a precise ability to calculate risk, and a fear that an idea might truly be foolish. The trick is to turn these qualities off while thinking up solutions and then to turn them back on once you have assembled a full range of solutions and are ready to start evaluating them. During solution-generation, you will do best if you think with intellectual freedom and a tolerance for chaos, but during solution-evaluation you must become a completely different kind of person, viewing things with the cold-blooded realism of one who must take responsibility for success or failure.

---

[5] Quoted at Stein, "Creativity as Intra- and Inter-Personal Process," in *The Creative Encounter* 21–22 (Holsinger, Jordan & Levenson eds. 1971).

[6] Kenney F. Hegland, *Trial and Practice Skills in a Nutshell* 181 (1978).

[7] Lon Fuller, *On Teaching Law*, 3 Stan. L. Rev. 35, 43 (1950) (emphasis in original).

The critical thinking on which solution-evaluation depends is prized throughout the practice of law. It is taught throughout legal education, and lawyers by nature tend to be verbally aggressive. But if you allow your skepticism to intrude into solution-*generation*, it will dismiss useful ideas before you can appreciate their potential, and it will inhibit you from imagining the widest range of possibilities. ("The appellate case method and adversarial legal processes . . . train lawyers to be more adept at criticizing ideas than at creating them."[8])

Solution-evaluation also depends on something not provided by law school classes: a good feel for how courts and other people make decisions and for how judges, juries, lawyers, witnesses, and opposing parties and lawyers will react to things you do. Only experience can provide that. Two things can help. The first is a good ability on your part to learn from experience. The second is the ability to recognize gaps in your experience and the willingness to ask for the opinions of more senior people at appropriate times and in appropriate ways.

When you look back on a professional situation that turned out in a disappointing way, it is possible for you to self-critique your own progress through the stages of the creative process. After an interview, counseling meeting, or negotiation, sit in your office for a few minutes and reflect. Did you fail to recognize places where an important decision could have been made by you — a decision that in the end might have altered the result? Was your preparation too cursory, so that you did not have all the information you needed? (Or, conversely, was it so unnecessarily exhaustive that you did not have time to do other things?) Should your list of solutions have been larger? (Is there a solution that you became aware of too late?) Was your evaluation of each solution accurate? Finally, was your decision a direct result of your solution-evaluation? (When you decided, did you forget or ignore some of your solution-evaluation? Did other factors sneak in and influence the result?)

If you are willing to be self-critical, and if you scrutinize your own planning work with a little regularity, you may notice some patterns. In this way, you can figure out which parts of the creative process come naturally to you and which parts you need to improve. Do you tend not to notice opportunities to transform a situation? If so, you might try to improve your recognition skills by disciplining yourself to look for those opportunities. Does important information seem to enter the picture too late to help you? During preparation, you might become more aggressive about figuring out exactly what you do not yet know and then locating the information to fill those gaps. Do your lists of solutions seem to be so short that they produce few meaningful choices about how to proceed? Perhaps your well-developed critical thinking skills are intruding into solution-generation and inhibiting your imagination. Do you generate a large list of solutions but then tend to choose one with a fatal flaw in it? Perhaps those same critical thinking skills are not helping you at the time when you really need them: during solution-evaluation and decision.

---

[8] Paul Brest & Linda Krieger, *On Teaching Professional Judgment*, 69 Wash. L. Rev. 527, 541 (1994).

CHAPTER 24

OBSERVATION, MEMORY, FACTS, AND EVIDENCE

§24.1 The Differences Between Facts, Inferences, and Evidence

A fact is what actually happened (for example, "at the moment the car left the road, it was traveling at 82.4 miles per hour").

A factual inference is not a fact. It is a conclusion derived from facts ("the car was speeding" or "the car left the road because of its speed").

Evidence is proof of a fact ("the state trooper testified that her radar device measured the car's speed as 82.4 miles per hour"). Put another way, evidence is the source of our knowledge that a fact really is true.

Some evidence is testimonial, and other evidence is tangible. Testimony is what witnesses say in court, on the witness stand, after taking an oath to tell the truth. Tangible evidence is evidence you can put your hand on. Examples are the murder weapon, the contract signed by the parties, and the audiotapes on which people are recorded saying things they later regret.

Another way to divide evidence is into direct evidence and circumstantial evidence. Direct evidence proves a fact without the need for inference. A witness's testimony that she saw the defendant get into a car at a certain time and place is direct evidence that the defendant got into the car at that time and place. Circumstantial evidence proves a fact through inference. If a witness testifies that he saw a car leave the road and hit a tree, that the witness got to the car a minute or two after it hit the tree, and that the witness found the defendant behind the wheel, that is circumstantial evidence that the defendant was driving the car just before it left the road. (It's strong circumstantial evidence, but it's not direct evidence unless the witness saw the defendant driving as the car left the road.)

Some of the most persuasive cases are built mostly on circumstantial evidence. Suppose you buy an over-the-counter medication intended to open up your sinuses, suppress your cough, and in other ways relieve you of the symptoms of a cold. You leave the store carrying a small box wrapped in sealed cellophane bearing the manufacturer's trademark. Inside the box is a bottle, the top of which is wrapped in a plastic band that also bears the manufacturer's trademark and can be removed only with scissors. After you have removed all this packaging, you open the bottle and find, in addition to the medicine, the decayed remains of part of an animal.

If you are inclined to sue, how much can you prove through eyewitnesses? You will testify that you bought the product and removed the packaging. It would be helpful, though not absolutely necessary, if somebody who was with you at the time could testify to corroborate that. The packaging and its contents will be tangible evidence. Beyond that, everything is circumstantial. You will probably never find an eyewitness who saw how the animal part got into the medication you bought. But you might not need that witness because the circumstantial inferences from the other evidence tend to show that it probably got into the package before it left the factory.

When you interview clients and witnesses, you have to think in terms of evidence. Judges and juries make their decisions based on the evidence because they can know about a fact only through its proof. For this reason, lawyers develop an evidentiary instinct: when someone mentions a fact, a lawyer wants to know what the evidence for it is.

Admissible evidence is evidence that a court will consider. If evidence is inadmissible, it might be probative of something, but for one reason or another the law will ignore it. The rules on admissibility are so complex that virtually the entire law school course called Evidence is devoted to teaching them.

Although witness interviewing is in many ways different from interviewing clients, nearly all clients are themselves witnesses to at least some of the facts at issue, and clients often do testify if their cases go to trial. In the chapter you are reading now, when we mention witnesses, we mean anybody, including clients, who observed relevant events and might testify about them at trial.

§24.2 The Myths

> Imagination *and* Memory *are but one thing, which for divers considerations hath divers names.*
>
> Thomas Hobbes
>
> [W]*ithout corroboration, there is absolutely no way to know whether somebody's memory is a real memory or a product of suggestion.*
>
> Elizabeth Loftus

For over a century, professors have been illustrating the frailties of eyewitnesses by staging crimes in the classroom. One of the first of these experiments happened in Berlin in 1901:

> [A] professor of criminal law . . . was lecturing to his class when a student suddenly shouted an objection to his line of argument. Another student countered angrily, and the two exchanged insults. Fists were clenched, threats made. . . . Then the first

student drew a gun, the second rushed at him, and the professor recklessly interposed himself between them. A struggle, a blast — then pandemonium.

Whereupon the two putative antagonists disengaged and returned to their seats. The professor swiftly restored order, explaining to his students that the incident had been staged, and for a purpose. He asked the students, as eyewitnesses, to describe exactly what they had seen. Some were to write down their account on the spot, some a day or a week later; a few even had to depose their observations under cross-examination. The results were dismal. The most accurate witness got twenty-six per cent of the significant details wrong; others up to eighty per cent. Words were put in people's mouths. Actions were described that had never taken place. Events that *had* taken place disappeared from memory.[1]

Much of our trust in the ability of witnesses to observe and remember accurately is based on myth. Because of that, a lawyer's ability to "know" the facts is much more limited than you might suppose. Experienced lawyers sense this intuitively, even if they are unaware of the psychological research described in this chapter. In a moment of candor, such a lawyer might tell you that it is easier to prove something than to know that it is true.

Monroe H. Freedman & Abbe Smith, *Understanding Lawyers' Ethics*

205–209 (3d ed. 2004)

A common misconception about memory is that it is a process of reproducing or retrieving stored information in the manner of a videotape or computer. In fact, memory is much more a process of reconstruction. . . .

. . . A great amount of what is said to be perceived . . . is in fact inferred, a process that has been called "inferential construction" and "refabrication." Experiencing a situation that is partially unclear or ambiguous, a witness typically "fills up gaps of his perception by the aid of what he has experienced before in similar situations, or, though this comes to much the same thing in the end, by describing what he takes to be 'fit,' or suitable to such a situation." Thus, "recall brings greater symmetry or completeness than that which was actually observed." Moreover, the process of unconscious reconstruction continues with the passage of time, probably increasing considerably as the event is left farther behind.

We are not talking about dishonesty. A witness may reconstruct events "without being in the least aware that he is either supplementing or falsifying the data of perception. Yet, in almost all cases, he is certainly doing the first, and in many cases he is demonstrably doing the second." The "vast majority" of testimonial errors are those of the "average, normal honest" person, errors "unknown to the witness and wholly unintentional." Such testimony has been described as . . . " *subjectively* accurate but *objectively* false." . . .

---

[1] Atul Gawande, *Investigations Under Suspicion: The Fugitive Science of Criminal Justice*, The New Yorker, Jan. 8, 2001, at 50.

An interesting illustration of the tendency to eliminate ambiguities by imaginative reconstruction was provided in the Senate Watergate hearings. John Dean, who had been President Nixon's White House Counsel, was testifying about a meeting with Herbert Kalmbach, who had been Nixon's private attorney. Dean had no incentive whatsoever to lie about that particular incident; indeed, it was extremely important to him to state the facts with as much exactness as possible.

Dean testified that he had met Kalmbach in the coffee shop of the Mayflower Hotel in Washington, D.C., and that they had gone directly upstairs to Kalmbach's room in the same hotel. Dean was pressed several times on this point, in a way that implied that his questioners had reason to believe that he was not telling the truth as to whether the meeting had taken place at all. Each time, Dean confidently reaffirmed his clear recollection about the incident. Finally, it was revealed that the Mayflower Hotel's register showed that Kalmbach had not been staying at the hotel at the time in question. Dean nevertheless remained certain of the occurrence, putting forth the unlikely theory that Kalmbach had used a false name in registering.

The difficulty was cleared up when someone realized that there is a Mayflower Doughnut Coffee Shop in the Statler Hilton Hotel in Washington — and Kalmbach had been registered at the Statler, under his own name, on the day in question. Thus, Dean's basic story was corroborated. Without realizing it, however, Dean had inaccurately resolved the ambiguity created by the coincidence of the two names by confidently "remembering" the wrong (but more logical) hotel, and by inventing the use of an alias by Kalmbach. He had done so, moreover, in a way that was "subjectively accurate" even though "objectively false."

John Dean is not unusual in this regard. Indeed, "accurate recall is the exception and not the rule." This is true even when the material to be memorized is short and simple, and when the witness knows that he will be asked to describe it later. Thus, in portions of "ostensibly factual reporting," we can be sure that "a large proportion of the details will be incorrect, even though presented with the utmost certitude and in good faith." Victims of assault are "notoriously unreliable" witnesses regarding the description of their assailants, but then "so are onlookers who watched in safety." . . .

[Similar effects] can result from interest or prejudice. A classic example of prejudice is the study in which subjects were shown an illustration of a scene in a subway car, including an African-American man wearing a jacket and tie and a white man dressed in work clothes and holding a razor in his hand. In an experiment in which people serially described the picture to each other (as in the game "telephone"), the razor "tended to migrate" from the white man's hand to that of the African-American man. . . .

Another factor that affects both perception and memory is what witnesses understand . . . to be their own interest. Again, we are not referring to deliberate dishonesty, but to what is colloquially called "wishful thinking." . . .

Similarly, we tend to exaggerate our answers in a way that enhances our prestige and self-esteem. We are more likely to "(mis)remember" that we did vote and that we did give to charity. "People tend to rewrite history more in line with what they think they ought to have done than with what they actually did." . . .

Another important aspect of remembering is the witness's "readiness to respond and his self-confidence when in fact he ought to be cautious and hedge his statements." In an experiment relating to the ability to remember faces (what lawyers call "eye-witness identification") the person who unconsciously invented more detail than any other person in the test group was "completely confident throughout."

In recent years, DNA tests have been able to tell with absolute certainty from whom something like a hair or a spot of blood came. A surprising number of criminal convictions that occurred before DNA tests were developed have been vacated after DNA testing established that the defendant could not possibly have committed the crime.[2] In one case, a defendant had been convicted based on the testimony of five eyewitnesses. He was on death row awaiting execution when DNA testing showed that it was impossible for him to have committed the crime. These exonerations of innocent but convicted people have been studied exhaustively by social scientists.

One study located 340 prisoners who had been convicted were but were later exonerated for various reasons. Nearly all of them had been sentenced to death or to long terms of imprisonment. In 64% of these cases, "at least one eyewitness misidentified the defendant," and in the overwhelming majority of those instances, the eyewitness appears to have been honestly mistaken (and not lying).[3] A different set of data — maintained by the Innocence Project, affiliated with the Benjamin N. Cardozo School of Law at Yeshiva University — shows that more than three-quarters of 258 prisoners exonerated by DNA evidence had been "convicted on the strength of eyewitness identifications."[4] The studies "have consistently shown that mistaken eyewitness identification is responsible for more of these wrongful convictions than all of causes combined."[5] Although juries instinctively treat eyewitness testimony as the gold standard of proof, "eyewitness identification . . . is among the least reliable forms of evidence."[6]

---

[2] See Elizabeth F. Loftus & James M. Doyle, *Eyewitness Testimony: Civil and Criminal* 1 (3d ed. 1997). The Department of Justice's study has been published as *Convicted by Juries, Exonerated by Science: Case Studies in the Use of DNA Evidence to Establish Innocence After Trial* (1996). See also Brian L. Cutler & Steven D. Penrod, *Mistaken Identification: The Eyewitness, Psychology, and the Law* (1995); Daniel L. Schacter, *The Seven Sins of Memory: How the Mind Forgets and Remembers* (2001); Daniel L. Schecter, *Searching for Memory: The Brain, the Mind, and the Past* (1996).

[3] Samuel R. Gross et al., *Exonerations in the United States 1989 through 2003*, 95 J. Crim. L. & Criminology 523, 542 (2005).

[4] James C. McKinley, Jr., *Cleared, and Pondering the Value of 27 Years*, N.Y. Times, Aug. 13, 2010, at A12.

[5] Gary L. Wells, Mark Small, Steven Penrod, Roy S. Malpass, Solomon M. Fulero & C.A. Brimacombe, *Eyewitness Identification Procedures: Recommendations for Lineups and Photospreads*, 22 L. & Human Behavior 603, 605 (1998).

[6] *Id.*

Experiments by social scientists illustrate the same thing. One experiment included two sets of subjects. Some acted as witnesses and others as jurors. Witnesses to a theft identified the thief from an array of photos. The theft had been staged, at the direction of the researchers, and the witnesses did not know in advance that it would happen. (The researchers, of course, knew who the "thief" was — which is what allows the experiment to reveal what it does.) In simulated trials, the second set of subjects — the jurors — observed cross-examinations of the witnesses and decided whether to believe the witnesses' identifications of the "thief." The jurors were divided into panels, and each panel observed one witness's cross-examination. About 80% of the jurors believed the witness they saw cross-examined, but they "were just as likely to believe a witness who had made an incorrect identification as one who had made a correct identification."[7] In another experiment, researchers

> made a video of two teams of basketball players, one team in white shirts and the other in black, each player in constant motion as two basketballs are passed back and forth. Observers were asked to count the number of passes completed by members of the white team. After about forty-five seconds, a woman in a gorilla suit walks into the middle of the group, stands in front of the camera, beats her chest vigorously, and then walks away. "Fifty per cent of the people missed the gorilla," [said one researcher]. "We'd get the most striking reactions. We'd ask people, 'Did you see anyone walk across the screen?' They'd say no. Anything at all? No. Eventually, we'd ask them, 'Did you notice the gorilla?' And they'd say, 'The *what?*' "[8]

Why are fact-finders eager to believe eyewitnesses? There seem to be two reasons. First, "in most of our life experience truly precise memory is not demanded of us. We often do not catch the mistakes of memory that we make, leading us to believe that our memory is more accurate than it actually is. Since people trust their own memories more than they should, they then trust the memories of others."[9]

Second, people are persuaded by stories. Documents, fingerprints, DNA, murder weapons, and other tangible evidence usually do not tell stories, although they provide ingredients out of which a story can be constructed. Eyewitnesses, on the other hand, tell stories from the beginning to the end, explaining who did what when, and adding enough detail to make the story seem real.[10]

---

[7] Elizabeth F. Loftus & James M. Doyle, *Eyewitness Testimony: Civil and Criminal* 2-3 (3d ed. 1997).

[8] Malcolm Gladwell, *Wrong Turn: How the Fight to Make America's Highways Safer Went Off Course*, The New Yorker, June 11, 2001, at 50, 54.

[9] *Id.* at 6.

[10] *Id.* at 5.

§24.3 What Science Knows About Observation and Memory

Elizabeth Loftus has studied extensively "the extraordinary malleability of memory,"[11] and her book *Eyewitness Testimony*[12] is the leading work in the field. According to her and others' research, the following appear to be the major factors affecting the extent to which an eyewitness accurately observes an event, retains the observation in memory, and later retrieves it.

§24.3.1 What Affects Observation

The length of time the witness was exposed to the event.   If a witness has more time, the witness will observe more. It also takes time to begin observing. If you are preoccupied with something else, it takes at least a short while for you to shift your attention and begin to observe an event that is just starting to unfold. Some events are so short that they are over before you can focus on them.

The extent to which the event in question stood out from (or blended with) its surroundings.   Suppose you are traveling on a municipal bus that stops every four or five blocks so passengers can get on or off. You are on the bus for half an hour, during which you see a continual stream of people dressed in everyday clothing going to or from jobs, schools, shopping, and so on. About halfway through the trip, Batman and Catwoman get on the bus, ride for five minutes, and then leave. At the end of the ride, you are asked to describe, in as much detail as possible, everybody you saw. About whom would you have noticed more: Batman and Catwoman or the elderly couple who sat across from you near the end of the trip?

Whether conditions or simultaneous events helped or interfered with observation.   How far was the witness from the event? Was the lighting good or bad? Did anything make it hard or easy for the witness to hear the event? Are the witness's hearing and eyesight good or bad? Did anything happen that would have distracted the witness?

What the witness was doing at the time of the event.   Was the witness's purpose to observe the event? Or was the witness engrossed in some other activity that was interrupted by the event? Did the event cause the witness to do something (such as run away) that would have interfered with observation?

Whether the witness is by nature a careful observer in general or a careful observer of the type of event that is at issue.   Some people often notice a lot of what goes on around them, and others tend to be oblivious. Sometimes, training or experience can heighten an ability to observe because the witness knows what to look for. A structural engineer who sees a bridge collapse might notice things that other witnesses miss. And sometimes much larger factors can make someone

---

[11] *Id.* at 54.
[12] First published in 1979. Citations in this chapter are to the third edition (1997), expanded with a coauthor.

a good or a bad observer of a particular kind of event. During the Second World War, Eric Newby escaped from a prisoner-of-war camp in Italy and tried for many months to disguise himself as an Italian to blend into his surroundings. Although he was at times stopped by German soldiers, they did not recognize him as an Englishman. After carefully studying his identity documents, which had been skillfully forged, the Germans would let him go each time. Their observational skills were bureaucratic — limited to official documents — and they did not seem to observe anything else about him. But Italians could tell just by looking at Newby that he was not whoever he was pretending to be at any given time: invariably, something about whatever clothing he was wearing would turn out to be inappropriate to the role he was trying to play.[13]

Whether the witness was under stress at the time of the event.   A moderate amount of stress has been found to make you more observant, but a greater amount of stress has the opposite effect, making you much *less* observant.

The event itself might stress the witness (violence being an example). It is commonly believed that dramatic events increase a witness's ability to observe. The opposite is true. Dramatic events are often quick and unexpected, which means that witnesses are unprepared to observe. And any event that seriously stresses a witness sharply diminishes the ability to observe carefully. During a robbery, for example, victims and bystanders are usually not taking note of everything about which the police will later be curious; they are just trying to survive. The same thing happens during auto crashes. But later, when lawyers, police, insurance companies, judges, and juries expect reliable information from those present during a stressful event, the witnesses feel compelled to become more reliable than they really can be, which means that at least some of what they say is creative reconstruction.

A witness can, of course, be stressed by things completely unrelated to the event. A witness who is worried about career, family, or health might be a poor observer of things done by strangers in plain view.

The witness's own self-interest, expectations, and preconceptions.   Often, people see what they want or expect to see.

A witness's observations might be colored by the witness's own self-interest. Experiments have shown that if witnesses are given an incentive, even a small one, to see or not see a particular thing, they honestly see and remember that which they have an incentive to see and remember. Sometimes, the incentive can be extraneous (people the witness cares about will be better off if the witness saw and remembers X rather than Y). Sometimes, especially when the witness is a party to the dispute, it is self-contained (the witness will personally profit from a favorable memory). And very often it is simple self-flattery:

> People . . . tend to see themselves as more honest or more creative than the average person. When they work on a joint task, they tend to overestimate their own contribution to the task. . . . People remember themselves as having . . . received higher

---

[13] See Eric Newby, *When the Snow Comes, They Will Take You Away* (1984).

pay for work [than they actually did], purchased fewer alcoholic beverages, contributed more to charity, taken more airplane trips, and raised smarter than average children.[14]

Usually, little or none of this is conscious lying to get a reward or avoid a penalty. The witness honestly remembers observing whatever was in the witness's own self-interest to remember.

Or a witness might "see" something because it conforms to the way the witness assumes the world works. Suppose an airliner develops mechanical problems moments before take-off, and the flight is canceled. A line of anxious passengers forms at the check-in counter, each passenger hoping to make other travel arrangements that will not spoil a vacation or ruin a business meeting. A shouting match begins between one of the passengers and the airline employee working behind the counter, and airport police forcibly take the passenger away. Witnesses who believe that airline employees have difficult jobs will tend to see, hear, and remember details that suggest that the passenger started the argument and abused the airline employee and perhaps the police as well. Witnesses who have the opposite assumptions (perhaps having been treated badly by airlines in the past) will tend to see, hear, and remember details that suggest that the airline employee started the argument and abused the passenger, who was then mistreated by police. (These preconceptions are referred to as *schemas.*) Even when a video recording of such a scene is shown to jurors (converting the jurors into witnesses), the same thing can happen. Photographs, film, or video recordings cannot prevent this because our preconceptions shade not only our memory of what we have seen; they also shade what we see from the moment we first see it.

§24.3.2 What Affects Retention in Memory

The amount of time that has passed since the event.   Memory fades fast after observation. Can you remember where you were and what you did exactly one year ago today? If you are like most people, your memory about the day started fading before the day was over, and, unless something especially memorable happened, those memories were completely gone within a few weeks afterward.

The extent to which the witness has had past experience with aspects of the event.   This is particularly important when the witness identifies a defendant in a criminal case. From the research, Loftus concludes that an eyewitness identification of a criminal defendant not already well known to the witness is — scientifically — virtually worthless. We can remember a face that we have seen many times before because we are remembering not just a face but also a person about whom we know other things as well. But it is extremely difficult to remember accurately a face we have seen only once.

---

[14] Loftus & Doyle, *supra* note 7, at 61–62.

Whether the memory has blended with other memories so that an aspect of one event becomes part of the memory of another.   This is called "unconscious transference." It is particularly dangerous in identification testimony. Eyewitnesses have been known to identify as criminals people they saw shortly before or after the crime or even at the same place on a different day.

Contamination of the memory caused by the conduct of other people. Suppose you witness a crime. The police give you a dozen photos to look at and say, "We think the perpetrator might be one of these people." They do not say the perpetrator *is* one of these people, but you are trying to be a good witness. If you say that none of the photos looks familiar to you, you are not helping to identify the criminal. There is a pronounced risk here that unconsciously you will try too hard to see similarities that do not naturally stand out to you. And if you do not do that at first, the police might inadvertently encourage you to. Suppose you look up and say, "I'm not seeing anyone familiar here," and the police say, "Take another look." Will you feel like a failure if you cannot "find" the perpetrator? Suppose you do identify someone and the police look pleased. Will you take that to mean that you are "right"? Two kinds of contamination are going on here. The police are giving you, by implication, new information (that they have reasons of their own to believe that one of the photos represents the true criminal). And their reaction confirms your guess, which encourages you to transmute it into a *confident* memory. The police might not have meant to do any of that, but this scene illustrates how other people — including lawyers asking questions in an interview — can contaminate memory.

Contamination of the memory caused by the witness's own conduct.   You do not need the police to contaminate your memory. You can do it yourself, unassisted. Suppose you are asked what you saw. You give lots of details, trying to be a good witness. Some of the details are not entirely accurate, but once you say them, they become frozen in your memory. Saying them locks them in, even if they are wrong. You will probably not say to yourself afterward that you are afraid you might be mistaken about some of the details. Instead, you will become more confident about all of the details, and the fact that you have lots of details helps you become more confident.

§24.3.3 What Affects Retrieval from Memory

How questions are asked can alter memory:

[E]ven "straightforward questions of fact" may significantly affect what a witness remembers, and leading or loaded questions can be particularly powerful in inducing good faith errors in memory. Illustrative is a study that showed that witnesses' estimates of the speed of an automobile involved in an accident varied in accordance with the verb used by the interviewer in asking the question. For example, when the question was phrased in terms of one car "contacting" the other, the speed averaged 31.8 miles per hour. The speed of the car increased in the witnesses' memory, however, as the verb was modified: "hit" (34.0 mph), "bumped" (38.1 mph), "collided" (39.3 mph), and "smashed" (40.8 mph).[15]

Here is another example:

[S]killed trial lawyers know that once a witness accepts a version of the story, that version can "harden" and become the reality so far as that witness is concerned. An English barrister of long experience used the following hypothetical piece of witness interview to illustrate the point:

Q: When Bloggs came into the pub, did he have a knife in his hand?
A: I don't remember.
Q: Did you see him clearly?
A: Yes.
Q: Do people in that neighborhood often walk into pubs with knives in their hands?
A: No, certainly not.
Q: If you had seen Bloggs with a knife in his hand, would you remember that?
A: Yes, of course.
Q: And you don't remember any knife.
A: No, I don't remember any knife.

During the days or months between the interview and the trial, the story can harden, and what started as "I don't remember" may come out like this at trial:

Q: When Bloggs came into the pub, did he have a knife in his hand?
A: No, he did not.[16]

§24.4 How Courts Treat Observation and Memory

When you interview in preparation for litigation, you need to understand what will happen to observations and memory in the courtroom. At trial, a lawyer who calls on a witness to give evidence might try to bolster the testimony by asking questions that would show the witness to be reliable according to some of the factors listed in §24.3. On cross-examination, the opposing lawyer might ask questions that would show the witness to be unreliable according to other factors listed in §24.3. Otherwise, law and science follow different paths when evaluating eyewitness testimony.

First, the lawyers do not have to ask these questions, and many times they do not. "Repeated surveys of defenders, prosecutors and judges indicate that many (as to some respects, most) lawyers are ignorant" of the scientific

---

[15] Monroe H. Freedman & Abbe Smith, *Understanding Lawyers' Ethics* 210 (3d ed. 2004).
[16] Richard C. Wydick, *The Ethics of Witness Coaching*, 17 Cardozo L. Rev. 1, 11–12 (1995).

research on eyewitness testimony.[17] There are some exceptions. In criminal procedure, for example, the law has been aware of the risks that testimony might be contaminated if a witness is asked in a suggestive manner to identify an accused.[18]

Second, even if the lawyers do ask these questions, the fact-finder — the jury or, in a bench trial, the judge — is free to discount the answers. Fact-finders are more likely to discount answers that suggest that the witness is unreliable. Fact-finders are still persuaded by the aura of an eyewitness. To many fact-finders, "there is almost nothing more convincing than a live human being who takes the stand, points a finger at the defendant, and says, 'That's the one!'?"[19]

Third, juries are instructed to use their own common sense and experience in life when evaluating evidence. This encourages them to subscribe to fallacies that science has shown to have no basis in fact. The most common is the fallacy that a confident witness is a reliable witness. The scientific research shows that confident witnesses can be wrong just as easily as tentative witnesses can be.[20] In fact, tentativeness may be a sign that the witness is aware of the limits of her own knowledge, a humility that can be more trustworthy than misplaced confidence. But many fact-finders appear to consider the witness's confidence to be solid proof of the witness's reliability.[21] The next most common fallacy appears to be the one of detail. Fact-finders are impressed by witnesses who can remember many details, whether or not the details are directly relevant to the factual issues. But "a witness's memory for details about peripheral matters may not be related at all to the witness's accuracy about central aspects."[22] In fact, a witness who can remember an endless supply of details about everything might be a witness with an active *reconstructive* imagination. Juries are at times even specifically instructed by judges to act on particular assumptions that science has shown to be wrong. For example, in criminal cases juries are often instructed that they may take into account the confidence with which a witness makes an identification. Even the Supreme Court has approved such an instruction.[23]

Finally, only in unusual circumstances do judges allow juries to hear expert testimony to the effect that most of the "common sense" about eyewitnesses is in fact myth.[24] In the overwhelming majority of the cases in which a party offers such expert testimony, it is excluded.

---

[17] Loftus & Doyle, *supra* note 7, at 8.
[18] 2 Wayne R. LaFave, Jerold H. Israel & Nancy L. King, *Criminal Procedure* 630–636, 666–689 (1999).
[19] Elizabeth F. Loftus, *Eyewitness Testimony* 19 (1st ed. 1979).
[20] Loftus & Doyle, *supra* note 7, at 66–67.
[21] Loftus & Doyle, *supra* note 7, at 2–4.
[22] Loftus & Doyle, *supra* note 7, at 4.
[23] *Neil v. Biggers*, 409 U.S. 188 (1972). At least one state has decided otherwise. *Commonwealth v. Santoli*, 424 Mass. 837, 680 N.E.2d 1116 (1997).
[24] See *Commonwealth v. Santoli*, 424 Mass. 837, 680 N.E.2d 1116 (1997), and the cases cited there.

§24.5 The Problem of States of Mind

The law's conception of states of mind leads to two problems in trying to learn the facts and prove them.

The first is that it is much harder to remember what you *thought* at any given time in the past than it is to remember what you saw, heard, or did. Your hopes, desires, and fears are so fluid that you have no solid base to start from when trying to remember them later, unless you found a way to make a record of them in something you said or wrote at the time. And because your past thoughts are so fluid, you may, every time you try to remember them, reinvent them to conform to what you would have liked them to have been in retrospect.

The second problem is that the law's state-of-mind formulas — intent, willfulness, maliciousness, voluntariness, and so on — do not fit the patterns in which people normally think. If you doubt this, stop someone who is about to jaywalk and ask whether that person intends to commit comparative negligence or assume the risk of another's carelessness. Even after you explain those terms, the person you have stopped will think you are a nut, even though once she sets foot in the street, the law will probably judge her to have had at least one of those states of mind. Here is another example:

> A young man and a young woman decide to get married. Each has $1,000. They decide to begin a business with those funds, and the young woman gives her money to the young man for that purpose. Was the intention to form a joint venture or a partnership? Did they intend that the young man be an agent or a trustee? Was the transaction a gift or a loan? Most likely, the young couple's state of mind did not conform to any of the modes of "intention" that the law might look for. Thus, if the couple should subsequently visit a tax attorney and discover that it is in their interest that the transaction be viewed as a gift, they might well "remember" that to have been their intention. On the other hand, should their engagement be broken and the young woman consult an attorney for the purpose of recovering her money, she might well "remember," after proper counseling, that it had been her intention to make a loan.[25]

This couple are not lying when they give these answers to their lawyers. People do what they feel like doing, and afterward the law has to put a label on what they thought at the time they acted. As a rule to guide courts' decision-making, the label may work, but it often does not represent precisely what people were really thinking. That is why the jaywalker will think you're peculiar if you ask about an intention to assume risk or commit a form of negligence.

State of mind usually has to be proved through circumstantial evidence. And the law is usually satisfied with whatever the circumstantial evidence shows. Suppose the couple in the example above decide that they want to have the transaction considered a gift. It's honest for their lawyer to figure out what circumstantial evidence might prove a donative intent (an intent to make a gift) and then ask whether that evidence exists. If it does, it's also honest for the lawyer to introduce

---

[25] Monroe H. Freedman, *Lawyers' Ethics in an Adversary System* 70 (1975).

that evidence in court to prove a donative intent, even though the couple have only the vaguest idea of what they had been thinking at the time of the transaction.

But it would be dishonest — a crime, in fact — for the lawyer or the couple to manufacture false evidence, such as a back-dated letter from the woman to the man saying, "Please accept this gift."

§24.6 How to Explore Memory Accurately in an Interview

Traditionally, lawyers have interviewed by asking for a narrative ("please tell me what happened, from beginning to end"), and afterward asking follow-up questions designed to clarify or fill gaps in the narrative ("let's go back to what happened after the accident — how long did it take the ambulance to arrive?").

That is not a bad approach. But it can be improved with modifications that some researchers have called "cognitive interviewing." Cognitive interviewing helps the witness to remember by using any or all of four techniques. The most important is suggesting that the witness reconstruct the scene and relive the event in the witness's own mind before narrating it to the interviewer.

Near the beginning of the discussion, you should ask the witness to include all the details the witness can recall (even those that seem irrelevant); to avoid guessing; and if the witness infers anything, to label it as an inference rather than the witness's direct observation. Most people are not this careful and precise about facts, and most witnesses will need gentle reminders from you about these requests at strategic points during the interview ("Do you remember seeing that event yourself? Or are you inferring that it probably happened because of the other things you did see?").

Richard C. Wydick, *The Ethics of Witness Coaching*

17 Cardozo L. Rev. 1 (1995)

[P]sychologists Edward Geiselman, Ronald Fisher, and their colleagues [have developed] a package of interview techniques that they call the "cognitive interview." . . .

Technique One: Reinstate Context

[A witness remembers best when immersed in an environment substantially similar to the one that surrounded the event to be remembered.] The witness need not return physically to the scene; returning in one's mind is generally enough. Thus, Geiselman and Fisher recommend giving the witness an instruction something like this: "First, try to reinstate in your mind the context surrounding the incident. Think about what the room looked like and where you were sitting in the room. Think about how you were feeling at the time and think about your reactions to the incident."

Technique Two: Tell Everything

. . . Geiselman and Fisher urge witnesses to lower their standards for relevance and to report every scrap they can remember, even if it seems incomplete or irrelevant. The hope is that incomplete or irrelevant scraps of memory might cue other material that could prove useful.

Technique Three: Recall the Event in Different Orders

[T]his technique recognizes that information can be stored in memory according to a variety of patterns, and that one pattern of access may be more effective than others. Geiselman and Fisher recommend instructing the witness in the following manner:

> [I]t is natural to go through the incident from beginning to end, and that is probably what you should do first. However, many people can come up with more information if they also go through the events in reverse order. Or, you might start with the thing that impressed you the most and then go from there, proceeding both forward and backward in time.

Technique Four: Change Perspectives

The fourth technique likewise seeks to open a variety of retrieval paths. After the witness explains what she perceived from her perspective, she should be instructed something like this:

> [Now] try to adopt the perspective of others who were present during the incident. For example, try to place yourself in [X's] role and think about what she must have seen.

[Structuring the Fact-Gathering]

. . . In a cognitive interview . . . , the witness should do most of the talking and hard thinking, while the interviewer should be mostly listening, gently guiding, and probing when necessary. [Getting the facts from the interviewee is a process that can be broken down into three stages.]

Introductory Stage

In the introductory stage, the interviewer should first seek to put the witness at ease. If the witness shows unusual stress, one way to do that is to begin with easy questions to get background information about the witness. Next, the interviewer should seek to build rapport with the witness and should explain the witness's central role in the interview. The witness plays the central role because the witness is the one who knows what the facts are! In a cognitive interview (unlike many ordinary interviews), the witness should do most of the talking and hard thinking, while the interviewer should be mostly listening, gently guiding, and probing when necessary. Finally, the interviewer should explain to the witness the four basic memory enhancing techniques, and encourage their use during the interview.

Open-Ended Narration Stage

In the open-ended narration stage, the interviewer asks the witness one or more broad, open-ended questions that are designed to elicit from the witness a narrative about the entire event. For example, "Tell me in your own words whatever you can remember about the [meeting]. Tell me everything you can in as much detail as you can." Despite the request for details, at this stage the interviewer should be listening, not for details, but for the overall pattern of the witness's memory about the event. This is not an information gathering stage — it is a planning stage, in which the interviewer should be designing the best way to probe the witness's memory.

Probing Stage

The probing stage is the main information gathering stage of a cognitive interview. The interviewer directs the witness's attention back to each significant topic the witness mentioned in the open-ended narration, patiently taking each topic separately and exhausting the witness's memory about that topic before moving on to the next. The interviewer should begin each topic with an open-ended question that asks the witness to give a detailed narrative of everything the witness can remember about it. For example, "You told me earlier that the thin man in the blue suit mentioned something about 'cutthroat bidding.' Tell me everything you remember about that, in as much detail as you can." The interviewer must not interrupt the witness's answer, and must not move to a different topic until the witness's memory about the first topic is exhausted. If the first open-ended question fails to produce the needed detail, the interviewer can follow up with a narrower but still open-ended question, such as, "Tell me what he said about 'cutthroat bidding'." If that does not work, the interviewer can resort to a closed-ended (leading) question, such as, "Did he say that 'cutthroat bidding' is bad for the industry?"

Review Stage

In the review stage, the interviewer should repeat in the witness's presence all of the relevant pieces of information the witness has provided. This has two purposes. First, it gives the witness and interviewer a chance to make sure the interviewer has understood correctly, and second, it gives the witness an additional chance to search for forgotten details. . . .

Practical Suggestions for Cognitive Interviews

... The single most important skill an interviewer can learn is not to interrupt the witness in the middle of a narrative response. When the witness says something worth pursuing, the interviewer should make a note of it and come back to it later. Even if the witness pauses for several moments during the narrative, the interviewer should keep quiet, or perhaps use a gesture, to encourage the witness to continue.

Some interviewers insist on demonstrating dominance during the interview. That can be a big mistake because the witness is the one holding all the memories. . . .

One of the four basic memory enhancing devices urges the witness not to edit out material that seems incomplete or irrelevant. Another urges the witness to consider the event from the perspectives of other people. Some witnesses misinterpret these suggestions as an invitation to guess or fabricate. The interviewer should expressly caution the witness not to guess or fabricate.

The interviewer should avoid skipping from topic to topic during the probing stage of the interview. How many times have we seen some television lawyer interviewing the witness in his office like this:

Q: How tall was he?
A: Oh, average, maybe six feet or so.
Q: What color car did you say he had?
A: Puce. It was a puce Cadillac coupe.
Q: Puce, eh. Any tatoos, scars, or other marks on his face or body?

This interview style makes for fast-paced television, but it wastes the witness's mental effort. It takes effort to summon up the mental image of the car. Instead of skipping to tatoos, scars and marks, a real life interviewer should stay with the car image until the witness cannot summon up any more about it. . . .

In a police department, about half the detectives were trained to interview cognitively. Afterward, researchers studied tape recordings of real witnesses in real cases conducted by these detectives and compared them to similar recordings of interviews conducted in other real cases by the detectives who had not been trained to interview cognitively. "The results were dramatic. The detectives who used the cognitive interview obtained significantly more information."[26]

---

[26] Loftus & Doyle, *supra* note 7, at 73.

CHAPTER 25

INTERVIEWING THE CLIENT

§25.1 Client Interviewing as Problem-Solving

Client interviewing is hard work for two reasons. The first is the intellectual challenge of beginning a diagnosis of the client's problem while, at the same time, carefully discovering the client's goals and the facts known to the client. The second is the emotional challenge of establishing a bond of trust and helping a person who may be under substantial stress.

If you're a very rational person, you might ignore the emotionally charged atmosphere of the interview, much to the frustration of the client. If you are more astute about emotions than about ideas, you might give a client an emotionally satisfying interview while leaving big holes in your development of the facts. (Lawyers more often have the first problem rather than the second, and clients often complain about it; see Chapter 22.) If you are at one or the other of these extremes, you can improve your interviewing by becoming more rounded. Students at one of the extremes often gain a lot of insight about themselves from critiques of their first interviews.

An allied problem is the question of control. The professions in general are attractive careers in part because they offer opportunities to control one's environment. Aggressiveness and competitiveness are useful in performing many of the tasks in a professional's work life (such as trying cases in court). The urge and ability to control can help a lawyer keep an interview focused, but, if not carefully managed, they can also smother a client's communicativeness. Many lawyers find that they must turn their control impulses on themselves, exercising more control over their own behavior than over that of the client. But even this can go too far. Spontaneous warmth and empathy are powerful professional tools.

§25.1.1 Your Purposes in Interviewing Clients

Client representation usually starts with an interview. A person who wants legal advice or advocacy calls to make an appointment. The secretary finds a convenient time and, to help the lawyer prepare, asks what the subject of the interview will be. The person calling says, "I want a new will drawn" or "I've just been sued" or "I signed a contract to buy a house and now the owner won't sell." At the time of the appointment, that person and the lawyer sit down and talk. If the visitor likes the lawyer and is willing to pay for what the lawyer might do, the visitor becomes a client of the lawyer.

During that conversation, the lawyer learns what problem the client wants solved and the client's goals in getting it solved; learns, factually, what the client knows about the problem; and tries to get to know the client as a human being and gives the client a reciprocal opportunity. Then or later, the lawyer and client also negotiate the retainer — the contract through which the client hires the lawyer — but here we focus on other aspects of the interview, especially fact-gathering.

These, then, are the lawyer's purposes in interviewing a client:

1. To form an attorney–client relationship. That happens on three levels. One is personal, in that you and the client come to understand each other as people. To satisfy the client's needs, you have to understand the client as a person and how the problem matters in the client's way of thinking. If you and the client are to work together in the participatory relationship described in Chapter 22, you need to know each other fairly well. And the client cannot trust you without a solid feeling for the person you are. The second level is educational, in that you explain to the client (if the client does not already know) things like attorney-client confidentiality (see §22.6) and the role the client would or could play in solving the problem. The third is contractual, in that the client agrees to hire you and pay your fees and expenses in exchange for your doing the work you promise to do.

2. To learn the client's goals. What does the client want or need to have done? Does the client have any feelings about the various methods of accomplishing those goals ("I don't want to sue unless there is no other way of getting them to stop dumping raw sewage in the river").

3. To learn as much as the client knows about the facts. This usually takes up most of the interview.

4. To reduce the client's anxiety without being unrealistic. On a rational level, clients come to lawyers because they want problems solved. But on an emotional level, they come to get relief from anxiety. Even the client who is not in a dispute with anybody and wants something positive done, such as drafting a will, feels a reduction in anxiety when you are able to say — if you can honestly and prudently say it: — "I think we can structure your estate so that almost nothing would be taken in estate taxes and virtually everything would go to your heirs. It would take some work, but I think we can do it." Most of the time, you cannot offer even this much assurance in an initial interview because there are too many variables and, at the time of the interview, too many unknowns. When first meeting a client, you are almost never in a position to say, "If we sue your former employer, I think we will win." You need to do an exhaustive factual investigation before you can say something like that responsibly.

Most of the time, clients in initial interviews experience a significant degree of relief from anxiety simply from the knowledge that a capable, concerned, and likeable lawyer is committed to doing whatever is possible to solve the problem. When you help a client gain that feeling, you are reducing anxiety without being unrealistic.

§25.1.2 Active Listening and Other Interviewing Dynamics

What is really going on in a client interview? Here are the otherwise hidden dynamics:

Inhibitors.   What might inhibit a client from telling you everything the client thinks and remembers?

The interview itself might be traumatic for the client. It can be embarrassing to confess that a problem is out of control. And the details of the client's problem are often very personal and may make the client look inadequate or reprehensible, even when the client might in the end be legally in the right.

The client might be afraid of telling you things that she thinks might undermine her case. You are part of the legal system, and most inexperienced clients do not realize that you can help only if you know the bad as well as the good.

Traditionally, lawyers are seen as authority figures. A client might feel some of the same inhibitions talking to a lawyer that a student feels when meeting privately with a teacher. And this can lead to etiquette barriers: deference to an authority figure may deter a client from challenging you when the client does not understand what you are saying or when the client believes that you are wrong.

The client might feel inhibited by cultural, social, age, or dialect barriers.

Finally, the client's memory is subject to all of the problems described in Chapter 24.

Facilitators.   What might help a client tell you as much as possible?

You can build a relationship in which the client feels comfortable and trusts easily. And you can show empathy and respect rather than distance. (See §2.2.2.)

You can encourage communication with nonverbal communication and active listening, and you can set up your office in a way that clients find welcoming (see the next few paragraphs).

You can ask clear and well-organized questions (see §25.3.2).

Nonverbal communication.   You are used to "reading" people based on their posture, facial expression, eye contact, and the like. Some of the messages you receive that way are inaccurate, but body language appears to tell us enough about another person's feelings that we take it for granted. A person who looks us firmly in the eye while talking to us seems to be taking us seriously. Someone who leans back in a chair with arms crossed looks bored or impatient, while a person who sits up straight with arms uncrossed appears to want to hear what is being said. When someone nods vertically while we are speaking, we think that means agreement, or at least "I hear you and accept the importance of what you say."

When does body language give us inaccurate messages? Sometimes, it is simple accident. A person might be very interested in what we have to say but lean back lazily because of fatigue. Sometimes, it is because body language means different things in different cultures. For example, in some cultures — including some that can be found in the United States — making eye contact is rude, and looking away from someone while talking to them shows respect.

Sometimes, a client's body language tells you something about the client's feelings. Sometimes, it does not. But you can use your own body language to show your interest in and respect for the client.

Active listening.   The ability to listen well is as important in the practice of law as the ability to talk well (see Chapter 2). Some lawyers just want to get to the heart of the matter and quickly move on to other work, but they are in such a hurry that they leap onto the first important thing they hear, even if it is not in fact the heart of the matter. Instead, relax, let the client tell the story, and listen patiently and carefully.

Passive listening is just sitting there, hearing what is being said, and thinking about it. That is fine as long as the client does a good job of telling the story and is confident that you care.

Active listening, on the other hand, is a way of encouraging talk without asking questions. It also reassures a client that what the client is saying has an effect on you. In active listening, you participate in the conversation by reflecting back what you hear.

Compare these three examples:

1. **Lawyer listens *passively*.**

> *Client:*   I wanted to buy a very reliable car with a manual transmission and a sunroof. The car has to be reliable. I can't spare the time to take it into the shop any more than necessary. You can't get a sunroof and a manual transmission from Toyota. You can at Honda, but the dealer didn't have any cars in stock. I had to special order it. I gave them a $5000 deposit. Two months later, they called to tell me the car had arrived. But it had an automatic transmission and no sunroof. I told them that wasn't the car I ordered. They refused to return the deposit and said I had to accept the car. I don't want it. A sunroof helps cool off the car quickly, and in the winter it lets in light and makes the car feel roomier. And a manual transmission makes the car more fun to drive.

2. **Lawyer listens *actively*.**

Client:	I wanted to buy a very reliable car with a manual transmission and a sunroof. The car has to be reliable. I can't spare the time to take it into the shop any more than necessary. You can't get a sunroof and a manual transmission from Toyota. You can at Honda, but the dealer didn't have any cars in stock. I had to special order it. I gave them a $5000 deposit. Two months later, they called to tell me the car had arrived. But it had an automatic transmission and no sunroof.
Lawyer:	Really?
Client:	I was astounded. I told them that wasn't the car I ordered. They refused to return the deposit and said I had to accept the car!
Lawyer:	You must have been pretty upset.
Client:	Absolutely. I don't want the car. A sunroof helps cool off the car quickly, and in the winter it lets in light and makes the car feel roomier.
Lawyer:	They are nice.
Client:	And a manual transmission makes the car more fun to drive.

3. **Lawyer listens *with a tin ear*.**

Client:	I wanted to buy a very reliable car with a manual transmission and a sunroof. The car has to be reliable. I can't spare the time to take it into the shop any more than necessary. You can't get a sunroof and a manual transmission from Toyota. You can at Honda, but the dealer didn't have any cars in stock. I had to special order it. I gave them a $5000 deposit. Two months later, they called to tell me the car had arrived. But it had an automatic transmission and no sunroof. I told them that wasn't the car I ordered.
Lawyer:	Did you sign a contract with them that specified that the car had to have a sunroof and a manual transmission?
Client:	I didn't sign anything except the $5000 check. They refused to return the deposit and said I had to accept the car.
Lawyer:	Is the car defective in some way, or is it just not the car you want?
Client:	I don't want it. It's not what I ordered, and I shouldn't have to accept it. I want a sunroof and a manual transmission. A sunroof helps cool off the car quickly, and in the winter it lets in light and makes the car feel roomier. A manual transmission makes the car more fun to drive.

In the first example, the client tells the story without any reaction from the lawyer. At some point, most clients would become uncomfortable in such a situation, and eventually the client would stop talking.

In the second example, the lawyer's interjections show understanding and empathy and encourage the client to continue. But notice that the lawyer waits before saying anything. That is because clients "will reveal critical material as soon as they have the opportunity to speak,"[1] and in the first few moments of a client's narrative the lawyer should stay out of the way and let the client talk. Here, the first time the lawyer interjects is the first time that simple courtesy would demand an acknowledgement of the client's predicament. Before that point, it is often better to confine active listening to nonverbal support, such as nods and eye contact.

In the third example, the lawyer asks relevant questions but seems not to have heard any of the emotional content in the client's story, leaving the client with the feeling that the lawyer is unsympathetic. The lawyer asks the questions prematurely. They could have been asked later. When asked here, they get in the way of the client's telling the story. To the client, the lawyer's inability to hear all the client says suggests that the lawyer is not likely to be helpful.

It is the opposite of active listening to say "O.K." in response to a client's description of suffering:

Client: . . . And then the ambulance took me to the hospital. Or I've been told that happened. I wasn't conscious at the time.

Lawyer: O.K. Who did the hospital get to sign the consent-to-treatment form?

From the client's point of view, it is not O.K. O.K. can mean two different things. It can be a throwaway transition word, which is what the lawyer here intended. And it can mean "That's good," which is what many clients would hear. If you find yourself saying "O.K." at times like this, you might be forgetting that the client is a real person who is actually living with the consequences of the facts being described.

An office arrangement comfortable for clients. Consider the furniture arrangement that would help you open up to a lawyer if you were a client. Some people are perfectly willing to talk over a desk to a lawyer. Other people would want something less formal, perhaps two chairs with a small table to the side (all of which can be in the same room as the desk). We believe most clients are more at ease if you are not behind a big desk, which is both a physical barrier and a symbol of your authority. Sitting *with* the client — rather than across from the client — communicates in a subtle way that you are open to the kind of participatory relationship described in Chapter 22.

---

[1] Gay Gellhorn, *Law and Language: An Empirically-Based Model for the Opening Moments of Client Interviews*, 4 Clinical L. Rev. 321, 344 (1998).

Your office should also communicate professionalism. An office that is a mess, with papers piled everywhere, suggests that the lawyer's work is out of control. Some lawyers say that they "know where everything is." Clients instinctively doubt that.

Taking notes.   Clients are not bothered by your note-taking, although the client might appreciate it if you were to ask, "Do you mind if I take notes?" If you become too wrapped up in note-taking, however, it can be hard to listen (and certainly hard to maintain eye contact). The most effective practice is to take minimal notes while the client is telling the story, perhaps writing down only topics you want to go back to later, and then to take a complete set of notes while you are asking questions after the client has told you the story.

The most important dynamic in the room.   "What clients want more than anything is to be understood, both for who they are and what they have suffered."[2]

§25.2 Organizing the Interview

You can do a better interview if you prepare before the interview begins, as described below in §25.2.1. The interview itself can be broken down into five parts.

1. A brief opening part in which the lawyer and client become acquainted and get down to business (see §25.2.2).
2. An information-gathering part (see §25.2.3) — usually the longest part of the interview — in which you learn everything the client knows about the facts; if you are using cognitive interviewing techniques, this part of the interview is subdivided into the stages described in §24.6:
    a. an open-ended narration stage (the client tells the story);
    b. a probing stage (you ask detailed questions);
    c. a review stage (you describe the story as you understand it and the client makes corrections and additions).
3. A goal-identification part, in which you learn exactly what the client wants to accomplish in resolving the problem at hand (see §25.2.4).
4. A preliminary strategy part, in which you might discuss with the client — usually only tentatively — some possible strategies for handling the problem; in a dispute situation, this usually includes some consideration of possible theories in support of the client's position (see §25.2.5).
5. A closing phase in which you and the client agree on what will happen after the interview (see §25.2.6).

---

[2] Anthony I. DeWitt, *Therapeutic Communication as a Tool for Case Theming,* 29 Am. J. Trial Adv. 395, 404 (2005).

In practice, these parts usually overlap. For example, some theory-testing and strategizing (part 4) might happen during information-gathering (part 2). Or the client might volunteer clearly stated goals (part 3) in the first moments of the interview (part 1). Overlap is fine as long as it does not interfere with your own interviewing purposes (see §25.1.1).

§25.2.1 Preparing

You might have spoken with the client briefly over the telephone when the client made the appointment. Otherwise, in a well-run office the secretary will have asked the client the nature of the problem the client is bringing to you. Some clients decline to say, but most of the time, you will have beforehand at least a vague sense of why the client wants to see you.

Unless you know well the field of law that seems to be involved, take a look at the most obviously relevant parts of the law before the client arrives. If the client says she was arrested for burglary, read the burglary statute and browse through the annotations. If the client wants you to negotiate a franchise agreement with McDonald's, look through a practitioner's book that explains how franchising works in the fast-food industry.

The interview is more productive if the client brings the papers that are relevant to the problem. Whoever in your office speaks to the client when making the appointment should ask the client to do that. But clients are not good at judging relevance. Try to be specific. If the client is threatened with mortgage foreclosure, the client should be asked to bring the documents that created the mortgage, all statements sent by the bank that holds the mortgage, records from the checking account used to make mortgage payments in the past, any official-looking notices sent by the bank or a sheriff or a lawyer, and anything else the client has that seems to be related to this mortgage.

§25.2.2 Beginning the Interview

In some parts of the country, "visiting" — comfortable chat for a while on topics other than legal problems — typically precedes getting down to business. In other regions, no more than two or three sentences might be exchanged first, and they might be limited to questions like whether the client would like some coffee.

When it is time to turn to business, the lawyer says something like:

"How can I help?"
"Let's talk about what brings you here today."
"My secretary tells me the bank has threatened to foreclose on your mortgage. You're probably worried. Where shall we begin?"

Soon afterward, the client will probably say something that means a great deal emotionally to her or him. Some examples:

"I've come into some money and would like to set up a trust for my grand-daughter, to help her pay for college and graduate school."

"I've just been served with legal papers. The bank is foreclosing on our mortgage and taking our home away from us."

Too often, when clients say these things lawyers just ask, "Tell me more," and
start taking notes. That may be a sign of the law-trained mind at work, ever quick
to find the legally significant facts. But clients rightfully dislike it. If given a
choice, most clients would rather not hire "a lawyer." They would rather hire a
genuine human being who is good at doing the work lawyers do. If you heard
either of the statements above in a social setting, you would express pleasure at
the first or dismay at the second because empathy and active listening are social
skills that you already knew something about before you came to law school. Do
the same for the client in the office — sincerely.

But do not leap in here with questions. Give the client a full opportunity
to tell you whatever the client wants to talk about before you start structuring
the interview. There are two reasons. First, many clients want to make sure
from the beginning that you hear certain things about which the client feels
deeply. If you obstruct this, you will seem remote, even bureaucratic, to the client. Second, many clients will pour out a torrent of information as soon as you
ask them what has brought them into your office. If you listen to this torrent
carefully, you may learn a lot of facts in a short period of time. You may also
learn a lot about the client as a person and about how the client views the
problem.

If the client is inexperienced at hiring lawyers, you will need to explain attorney-client confidentiality (see §22.6). But the best time to do so is probably not in
the very beginning. It seems awkward and distancing there, and clients are eager
to tell you the purpose of their visit anyway. A better time is in the information-
gathering part of the interview, after the client has told you the story and before
you start asking detailed questions discussed below in §25.2.3. Most clients will
tell you the basic story at the beginning regardless of whether they understand
confidentiality. It is when they begin to answer your questions later that confidentiality encourages clients to be more open with you.

Use the client's name during the interview ("Good morning, Ms. Blount").
Saying the client's name at appropriate points in the conversation shortens the
psychological distance between you and the client because it implies that you recognize the client as a person rather than as an item of work. Which name you
say — the client's first or last name — depends on your personality, your guess
about the client's preference, and local customs. If you live in an area where
immediate informality is expected, it may be acceptable to call the client by first
name unless the client is so much older than you that, out of respect, you should
use the client's last name until the client invites you to switch to first names. But
in most parts of the country, the safest practice for a young lawyer is to start on a
last-name basis with nearly all clients and wait to see whether you and the client
will feel comfortable switching to first names.

§25.2.3 *Information Gathering*

After the client has explained why you are being consulted, the information-gathering part of the interview begins. If it is important for you to learn the details of past events, this is where you use the cognitive interviewing techniques described in §24.6.

Not all clients, however, need cognitive interviews. That is especially true in transactional work. When a client wants you to draft a will or negotiate a contract, you will need to learn many facts, but usually you do not need to worry about the client's memory of past events. Much of the information you need is about current conditions. To draft a will, for example, you need a list of the client's assets, a list of the client's potential heirs, and so on. In situations like this, start by asking the client to tell you everything the client thinks you will need to know. After the client has done that, start asking detailed questions to get the rest of the information you will need.

If, on the other hand, you are using cognitive interviewing techniques, the information-gathering part of the interview is subdivided into three stages:

a. An open-ended narration stage in which the client is asked to describe every-thing the client remembers about the facts at issue.
b. A probing stage in which you go back over the client's story and ask questions to fill in gaps and clarify ambiguities.
c. A review stage in which you reiterate the most important parts of the story as you understand them to give the client an opportunity to correct misunder-standings and to supply additional information.

Before inviting the client to narrate the story, recreate the context and ask the client to describe everything she remembers about the incidents at issue, regardless of relevancy (see §24.6). Say something like this:

Lawyer: I need to learn everything you can remember about what happened inside the store. Let's go back to the point where you got out of your car in the parking lot. Take a few minutes and return in your own mind to that moment. Think about what you were seeing and hearing at the time, as you were walking through the parking lot toward the store. Don't rush this. I can wait until you're ready. And when you are ready, tell me everything you remember — even if it does not seem to be related to the store manager's accusation about shoplifting.

If the client has trouble producing a complete and coherent story, you might ask her to recall the event in a sequence other than chronological, perhaps starting with the thing that impressed the client the most, or you might ask the client to change perspectives and assess what others present might have seen or heard (see §24.6).

While listening to the story, take two kinds of notes. Write down what you are being told, and make a list of topics to go back to later for clarification or to fill in gaps. You can use two pads of paper to do this. Or you can use one pad, drawing a vertical line on each page to separate the two kinds of notes.

After the client has told the story, you can start asking questions. This is the second stage of the cognitive part of the interview. Get a clear chronological view of events from beginning to end, as well as a firm grip on the precise details of the story. For example, exactly when and where did each event happen? See §25.3.1 for what to ask about and §25.3.2 for how to formulate and organize questions.

You can introduce the review stage by saying something like this:

Lawyer: I think I've got a clear picture now. Let me tell you my understanding of what happened. If I've got anything wrong, please correct me. And if you remember anything else as I go along, please interrupt me to point it out.

Then briefly summarize the relevant parts of the story.

Regardless of whether you are using cognitive interviewing techniques, the time to bring up attorney-client confidentiality is when you start asking questions. How should you explain confidentiality? It is not accurate to say, "Everything you tell me is confidential." There are important exceptions to that statement (see §22.6). Most clients, however, do not want to hear a lecture on all the exceptions. A middle course is better:

Lawyer: Before we go further, I should explain that the law requires me to keep confidential what you tell me. There are some exceptions, some situations where I may or must tell someone else something you tell me, but for the most part I am not allowed to tell anybody other than the people who work with me representing you.

You can explain the exceptions if the client asks about them or if one of them is obviously relevant.

Do not label the problem until you have heard all the facts. A client who starts by telling you about a dispute with a landlord might have defamation and assault claims instead of a violation of the lease or of the residential rental statutes.

§25.2.4 Ascertaining the Client's Goals

From the client's point of view, what would be a successful outcome?

If the client wants help in facilitating a transaction, the client will want the transaction to take a certain shape. For example, the client might want to buy a thousand t-shirts with pictures of Radiohead, but only if they can be delivered two days before next month's concert and will cost no more than $6.50 wholesale each, preferably less. And the client will not want the lawyer to kill the deal by overlawyering.

If the client wants help in resolving a dispute, the desired outcome may vary. The client might want compensation for a loss (money damages, for example) or prevention of a loss (not paying the other side damages, not going to jail, not letting the other side do some threatened harm out of court) or vindication (such as a judgment declaring that the client was right and the other side wrong).

Depending on the situation, the client might want or need results very quickly. And most clients also want economy: they want to keep their own expenses (including your fees) to a minimum or at least within a specified budget.

Goals often conflict. A client who wants a large problem solved immediately on a small budget might have to decide which goals are most or least important. If the client has to compromise on something, will the client spend more, wait longer, or accept less than complete justice?

Whether the problem is transactional or a dispute, the client might want comfort and understanding. Some clients are not under stress or would prefer to keep their emotional distance from lawyers. But most stressed clients at least want empathy.

Most clients do not volunteer all of their goals in an interview. Some clients know what their goals are and assume that they should be obvious to the lawyer. The goals might *seem* obvious to the lawyer, but because assumptions are dangerous, it is best to get a clear statement from the client. And some clients have not thought through the situation enough to be sure what their goals are. They need help from the lawyer in figuring that out.

Helping the client identify goals requires patience and careful listening, often for messages that are not literally being expressed in the client's words. "Find[ing] out what the customer wants [is something that l]awyers are famous for [doing badly]. They snap out the questions, scribble on a pad, and start telling you what you're going to do."[3] Here is an example of what might happen when lawyers do not take the time to do this carefully:

> Two law students under the supervision of a law professor represented M. Dujon Johnson on a misdemeanor charge.... The lawyers[4] investigated the case thoroughly, interviewed their client, developed a theory of the case, and represented Mr. Johnson aggressively. When the case came to trial the prosecutor asked the judge to dismiss the case, a victory for the defense. The client was furious....
>
> Johnson ... had been arrested by two state troopers when he pulled into a service station at night [and t]he troopers called out, "Hey, yo," to Johnson, an African

---

[3] Nicholas Carroll, *Dancing with Lawyers: How to Take Charge and Get Results* 5 (1992).

[4] For conciseness, the author of the article from which this excerpt is taken uses the term "the lawyers" to refer to the team made up of the professor and the law students, who were practicing in a law school legal clinic. Because clinic students are not members of the bar, they may not hold themselves out as lawyers, however.

American undergraduate. They ordered him out of the car and asked him to submit to a pat-down search. When Johnson refused, claiming that such a search would violate his constitutional rights, the troopers arrested him for disorderly conduct, searched him, pressed his face on the hood of the car while handcuffing him, and took him to jail.

[When they first interviewed him,] the lawyers did not ask Johnson what his goals were. If they had, they would have learned that he wanted more than simply to be cleared of a misdemeanor charge. As he said later, "I would like to have my reputation restored, and my dignity."

. . . If [the lawyers had inquired more thoroughly], they would have learned that he wanted a public trial. They would have learned that, at . . . arraignment, the prosecutor had offered to dismiss his case if he would pay court costs of fifty dollars, and he had refused. The trial itself was the relief Johnson sought. Without discussing it with their client, the lawyers filed a motion to suppress evidence that, if successful, would have drastically shortened the trial. . . .

. . . [A]fter his case had been dismissed, Johnson said the lawyers had been "patronizing" . . . [that] he was always the "secondary person[," and] that they had treated him like a child.[5]

Here, the client understood what his goals were, but the professionals representing him did not. Another client might have only a vague sense of goals, and one of the lawyer's tasks is to work with the client to clarify them.

For example, after being served with an eviction notice, a client might have come to the lawyer just because that seems like the right thing to do when confronted with confusing and intimidating legal papers. But the problem may be a deeper one. The client might have lost a job, and the client's family might be disintegrating under financial pressures. There are two reasons why you should care. First, there may be legal issues inside the deeper problem (abusive discharge? child custody?). And second, even if there are no legal issues other than the eviction proceeding, the lawyer, as a disinterested observer, is still in a position to offer valuable advice that the client cannot easily find elsewhere (see §22.1).

Here are some questions that help clarify the client's goals:

> *"If you could imagine the best outcome we can reasonably hope for, what would that be?"* You want a list of the things the client wants to accomplish.
>
> *"If we achieve that best outcome, how will it affect you?"* Or *"how will it affect your family?"* Or *"how will it affect your business?"* These tell you why the client has the goals listed in response to the first question. If the goals the client has initially cannot be accomplished, you and the client can try to develop other goals that have as nearly as possible the same effect.
>
> *"What possible bad outcomes are you worried about?"* And *"Are there any other things that you want to make sure do not happen?"* You want to know what the client wants to prevent.

---

[5] Alex J. Hurder, *Negotiating the Lawyer-Client Relationship: A Search for Equality and Collaboration*, 44 Buff. L. Rev. 71, 71–73 (1996) (summarizing Clark D. Cunningham, *The Lawyer as Translator, Representation as Text: Towards an Ethnography of Legal Discourse*, 77 Cornell L. Rev. 1298 (1992)). (Johnson asked that Cunningham use his real name.)

> *"If any of those negative things were to happen, how would each of them affect you?"* (Or *"your family?"* Or *"your business?"*) These tell you why the bad outcomes must be prevented.

§25.2.5 Considering a Strategy During the Interview

During an initial client interview, you will not know enough to start making clear plans for solving the problem. You will probably need to investigate the facts and read the law, and you will certainly need to think over the problem. But you and the client can do some brainstorming, starting the process of generating solutions (see §23.1.2). And you can learn something about the ones that are generated by asking the client for relevant information (including the client's feelings). For example:

Lawyer:	So the Santiagos do not seem to regret signing a contract to buy your house. In fact, they seem eager to move in. I get the sense that the only real problem from their point of view is that they can't get a mortgage because the house has a zoning violation. Am I missing something?
Client:	No. The only complaint I hear from them is about that.
Lawyer:	One way of handling that is to ask the local zoning board to issue a variance. That could take at least two or three months. Do the Santiagos seem to want the house enough to wait that long?
Client:	They like the house a lot. And I think they're worried about having to sue to get their deposit back.
Lawyer:	Do they have a strong need to move into a house — any house — as soon as possible?
Client:	I don't think so. They're living in a rental now, and they haven't given their landlord notice that they're moving out.
Lawyer:	I can't predict at this point whether the zoning board would issue a variance. I'd have to look at exactly what this violation is and then see what your zoning board has done in similar cases in the past. But there is one thing I know right now: if any of your neighbors object, the board might not issue a variance. Do you think we'd have a problem there?
Client:	We're on good terms with our neighbors, and none of them has ever complained about our backyard deck, which seems to be what the violation is all about.
Lawyer:	To get the Santiagos to agree to a delay, we might have to say that you will not return their deposit unless ordered to do so by a court. In other words, we'd be saying that if they won't wait, they'll have to sue to get their money back. Would you be comfortable taking that position?
Client:	I don't mind saying it. But if they actually do sue us, I think I'd rather give them the money and find another buyer. A court fight doesn't seem like the fastest way to get our house sold.
Lawyer:	That's certainly a reasonable way to look at it.

This is a transactional situation on the verge of evolving into a dispute. In addition to some important details, the lawyer learns here that the client prefers to keep the situation transactional and will walk away from the deal to avoid litigation.

In a more typical dispute situation, where litigation is likely, strategizing includes finding the client's persuasive story — finding a way of looking at the facts that will seem most persuasive to a fact-finder. Lawyers call such a way of looking at the facts a factual theory. In an initial client interview, you are not in a position to develop the theory fully. As with strategies generally, you need to do a factual investigation and read the law first. The most you can do in an initial client interview is to come up with some tentative theories and test them against what the client knows of the facts.

In law school you will learn how to develop a theory and what makes one persuasive. For now, however, it is enough to understand two things about effective theories. First, if you will have the burden of proof, your theory must satisfy the elements of the legal tests that make up your burden. If the other side will have the burden of proof, your theory must prevent the other side from satisfying at least some elements of the legal test the other side must prove. Second, a persuasive theory is based on solid evidence and the inferences people will typically draw from that evidence. In court, ambiguous evidence and debatable inferences are usually resolved in whatever way is most consistent with the evidence that cannot be questioned.

§25.2.6 Closing

Assuming that the client wants to hire you and that you want to be hired, two agreements conclude the interview.

One is an agreement that the client is in fact hiring you to do the work discussed in the interview. If the client has not made clear that is happening, you can ask a simple question like this: "Now that we've talked about it, would you like me to defend you in this lawsuit?" Some clients will say yes or no on the spot. Others will want to think about it after the interview. If you are hired, that should be formalized through a written retainer (see §25.4.6).

The other agreement concerns what each party will do — and not do — next. Here is a typical example: the client will provide copy of the lease by the end of today; the lawyer will check the law on constructive eviction and call the client tomorrow; in the meantime, the client will not speak to the landlord and will tell anybody who makes demands to call the lawyer. In agreeing on what to do next, consider the following:

1. The client should not do anything to make the situation worse. Agree specifically on what the client will not do. This could involve restraints that might seem unnatural or abnormal to the client. Most clients do not realize that anything they say to an adverse party might escalate conflict, or that anything

they say to anybody other than you might be later testified to by the other person, perhaps not accurately. In addition, it is part of a lawyer's job to bear some of the pressure that would otherwise be brought to bear on the client. If people have been demanding that the client do something that the client does not want to do, the client should now start telling them to communicate only through you.

2. You should make a realistic and clear commitment of what you will do in the immediate future, together with a schedule for when you will do it. Clients feel much better if you set a schedule for accomplishing certain tasks, keep to the schedule, and report back to the client on what you have accomplished. Otherwise, a client has no idea whether you are working diligently or are ignoring the problem.

3. The client should commit to provide specific things that you need (information, documents) to do your share of the work, and there should be a schedule for this, too. (Paying your retainer is included; see §25.4.6.) Some tasks — for example, writing a letter to the Internal Revenue Service requesting copies of prior tax returns — are things that you and the client are each capable of doing. If the client does some or most of them, the client can avoid paying what it would cost for you to do them.

The end of the interview should provide the client with a sense of closure — a feeling that a problem has been handed over to a professional who will do whatever can be done to solve it. Some clients get closure from the mutual agreements described above. Others may appreciate a comment from you that shows that you understand what this problem means for the client and are concerned about it on a human level.

Explain to the client how best to contact you. That is most easily done by giving the client your business card, which will include your phone number and your e-mail address. Most clients will use the telephone. You might explain your habits in returning phone calls. For example, if you are in court a lot and tend to return most client phone calls late in the day, explain that to the client and add that if the client needs a faster response she should tell whoever takes the message in your office that the client is calling about something urgent.

What if you do not want to be hired to do this particular work? Make absolutely clear that you are not in a position to take it on. If you think another lawyer would do a good job and would want the work, you might make a referral.

If you are not hired — whether by your choice or the prospective client's — it's wise to document that with a follow-up letter to the client in which you thank the client for the interview and reiterate that you have not been hired. Lawyers call this a "nonengagement letter." Some clients do not hear a soft no when a lawyer refuses their case. If such a client were not to seek another lawyer, and some bad thing were to happen (such as the expiration of a statute of limitations), you want it on record that you are not this person's lawyer. A typical nonengagement letter warns the would-be client of a statute of limitations or whatever other deadline might compromise rights if ignored.

§25.3 Questions

Remember that one of the marks of an effective professional is the ability to ask useful questions in a productive way (see §2.2). In a client interview, you need to know what to ask about and how to organize and formulate questions.

§25.3.1 *What to Ask About*

During the information-gathering part of the interview (§25.2.3), be sure to explore the following:

Ask for the raw facts and the client's source of knowledge. Do not ask whether the other driver's car was exceeding the speed limit (a conclusion). Ask how fast it was going and how the client knows that. At trial, the client can testify only to the client's estimate of the car's speed in miles per hour. And that can happen only after the client has laid a foundation by testifying that he has a source of knowledge that the law of evidence recognizes as sufficient. If all you know is that the client thinks the car was speeding, you have no idea what the client will testify to at trial, or even whether the client will be allowed to testify on that point. If the client says he does not know the car's actual speed, but that a friend told him the car had been traveling at about 60 miles per hour, the client will not be allowed to testify to that unless the friend's statement fits within one of the exceptions to the hearsay rule. The friend's name goes on your list of witnesses to interview.

Ask for all the details. If the client says, "Ling told me about that last week," do not go on to the next topic. Ask when this conversation happened — not just the day, but also the time. Where did it happen? Who else was present? What else was discussed? How long did the conversation last? How did it start? How did it end? What words did Ling use, and what did the witness and anybody else present say? You are going to need these details to prepare your case. (Because in nonprofessional life vagueness and approximation are usually enough, young lawyers are too casual about these things. Experienced lawyers know that in representing clients only precision works.)

Ask about everything the client saw, heard, and said. You need to be able to see and hear in your own mind the scene in which the events described by the client occurred. Do not assume anything. If the events happened at the busiest intersection in town, do not assume that cars were whizzing past while the client was standing on the sidewalk. If the cars matter, ask. You might be surprised to learn that the street was torn up for construction and all the traffic routed elsewhere. Ask about *any detail* that might matter.

If a diagram would help you understand what happened, ask the client to draw one. That can be particularly important if the position of people and things in a scene is important.

Make sure you learn all the basic information as well: the client's full name, age, address, all telephone numbers, occupation and job title, employer, job site, and work hours. Get similar information for the client's spouse, as well as the ages of and some details on any children. For each witness or other person with a role in the problem, get as much identifying information as the client can provide.

Ask whatever questions are needed to prevent The Three Disasters. The Three Disasters are (1) accepting a client who creates a conflict of interest, (2) missing a statute of limitations or other deadline that extinguishes or compromises the client's rights, and (3) not taking emergency action to protect a client who is threatened with immediate harm. If you allow any of them to happen, you may commit malpractice and may also be punished for unethical conduct.

A lawyer or a law firm has a conflict of interest where the interests of one client conflict with those of another client, a former client, or the lawyer or law firm.[6] A well-run law office will have a conflicts database so that, if you suspect a conflict, you can quickly find out whether the office represents or has represented a conflicting party. Once a new client has begun to reveal confidential information to you, the damage might be uncontainable, and you or the firm might have to withdraw from representing either client or both. (There are exceptions, which are complicated and explored in the course on Professional Responsibility or Legal Ethics.)

Suppose a client has suffered a wrong and seems to be entitled to a remedy in court. Suppose also that during the interview you don't bother to pin down the date on which the statute of limitations would have begun to run, and after the interview you don't bother to read the statute. And suppose the statutory period expires tomorrow. You have accepted a client and allowed the client's rights to be extinguished. The client still has a remedy, but now it is against you in a malpractice lawsuit. Although the statute of limitations, because of its inflexibility, is the most dramatic example, other deadlines can have similar effects. For example, if the client has been sued by somebody else, when was the client served with the summons and complaint, and when does the time to answer the complaint expire?

Suppose the client has been served with a notice of eviction, and the notice says that the sheriff will evict the client tomorrow. Are there facts on the basis of which a court could grant an emergency order temporarily restraining the sheriff from putting all your client's belongings on the sidewalk? The only way to find out is to ask pertinent questions during the interview so that, if there are grounds, you can start drafting a request for court relief immediately.

Ask about pieces of paper. Ask whether there are any pieces of paper, not already mentioned by the client, that might be related to the problem. (Remember to avoid using lawyer jargon. Do not ask about "documents." Is a memo a document? You might say yes, but many clients would think no.) If relevant pieces of paper exist, ask where they are and who has possession of them. Ask whether the client has *signed* any pieces of paper connected to the problem. In a

---

[6] See Rules 1.7, 1.8, 1.9, 1.10, and 1.11 of the Model Rules of Professional Conduct.

dispute situation, ask whether the client has received any pieces of paper from a court, a lawyer, or a government agency. (Many clients will not understand if you ask whether they have been "served with papers.")

In a dispute situation, ask all the questions needed to find the story in the facts.   In the movie *Amistad*, Africans who have been brought to Connecticut against their will in 1839 sue to gain their freedom. Slave traders claim they own the Africans, who in turn claim they were kidnapped. At a critical point in the movie, one of the Africans' supporters (played by Morgan Freeman) seeks the advice of a former President, John Quincy Adams (played by Anthony Hopkins). The case is going badly for the Africans, and the Morgan Freeman character wants to know how to handle it better. Adams says "Well, when I was an attorney a long time ago . . . , I realized after much trial and error that in a courtroom whoever tells the best story wins. In an unlawyer-like fashion, I give you that scrap of wisdom free of charge."

That is the first of two great insights in the conversation between these two characters. Then, Adams explains how, although the Morgan Freeman character *knows the facts* about the Africans, *he has not yet discovered their story*. The second great insight is that you can know the facts but miss the story. Inside a mass of facts — hundreds of events and circumstances — is a story that touches your heart and makes an audience — the judge and jury — hope that one person gets better treatment in the future and another person gets worse. The story does not leap out of the facts. You have to *find* it. Ask questions that reveal the story you need to represent this client well.

For more on how to do this effectively, go back to §2.2.4 and reread the material on finding and telling stories. We return to this skill in later chapters as well.

In a dispute situation, ask questions that would reveal what arguments the other side might make.   There are two sides to every dispute, and you cannot prepare without knowing what the other side will claim. But you will learn little if you ask in a way that seems threatening to the client. For example, if your client has been charged with a crime, do not ask whether she is guilty. Ask what the police and the complaining witness will say about her. Before doing that, explain in detail why you can be a good advocate only if you know in advance what the other side will claim.

In a dispute situation, explore for other evidence.   For example, ask who else saw or heard any of the things the client describes. Ask who else might know of aspects of the dispute that the client does not know about.

In a dispute situation, evaluate the client's value as a witness in court.   Is this client likely to tell the story in a way that can influence a fact-finder? Is the client credible and likely to earn the fact-finder's respect? Are there any doubts about the client's honesty or ability to observe and remember accurately?

In a dispute situation, ask whether the client has talked with anybody else about the subjects you are asking about.   Those people might help corroborate what your client is telling you. Or they might end up testifying against your client at trial, saying that your client made statements that hurt the client's case.

In a transactional situation, learn the posture of the deal so far.   What is the present state of discussions between the client and the other party? What has already been agreed to? What issues have not yet been resolved? What obstacles does the client see to wrapping up the agreement? How much does the other party want or need this transaction? Is either party in a hurry?

In a transactional situation, learn the parties' interests.   What is the big picture? What about this transaction is most important to the client? To the other party? (In other words, what is each party trying to accomplish?) How will the deal operate financially? Where will the profit be made? How does the client envision, on a practical level, the transaction will operate once agreement is complete? How does the transaction fit into the client's larger plans for the future? Is the transaction part of a long-term relationship — or a hoped-for long-term relationship — between the parties? In agreeing to this deal, is the client relying on factual assumptions about which the other party has or should have superior knowledge? (If so, the client can be protected by drafting the contract so that the other party represents and warrants the truthfulness of those facts.) Is there a risk that the transaction might violate the law? Can the transaction be structured to minimize the client's tax? In drafting the agreement, what potential future difficulties should be provided for in advance? (The most obvious example would be breach: how should the agreement define breach, and what consequences would follow breach?) Are there any other ways that the agreement can be drafted to protect the client? What provisions does the client want in the drafted agreement? In addition, for each type of agreement, there's a laundry list of issues that a prudent lawyer would typically resolve in drafting. (If you rent an apartment, look at your lease; it probably reflects the residential lease version of such a list from the landlord's point of view.) What do you need to know in order to handle the laundry-list issues?

Ask whether the client has talked about this problem with another lawyer. If you are the seventh lawyer the client has consulted about this problem, there is a reason why the other six lawyers have not done what the client wanted. It might be a reason that should not influence you. But most of the time the other lawyers are not presently working for the client because the case is meritless or the client tends to sabotage a lawyer's work.

§25.3.2 Organizing and Formulating Questions

Organizing questions.   When you start exploring various aspects of the problem in detail, try to take up each topic separately. Too much skipping around confuses you and the client.

On each topic, start with broad questions ("tell me what happened the night the reactor melted down") and gradually work your way toward narrow ones ("just before you ran from the control panel, what number on that dial was the needle pointing to?"). Broad questions usually produce the largest amount of information, especially information that you have not anticipated. A versatile broad question is "What happened next?" Narrow questions produce details to fill in gaps left after the broad questions have been asked.

Move gradually from broad questions to narrow ones. If you jump too quickly to the narrow ones, you will miss a lot of information because it is the general questions that show you what to explore. Here's an example of what can go wrong:

Lawyer:	What happened next? [*a broad question*]
Client:	The store manager grabbed me and took me to a back room, where they opened my shopping bag and accused me of shoplifting. They were really abusive and embarrassed me in front of everybody in the store.
Lawyer:	Did they touch you? [*a narrow question, asked before the client has finished answering the broad one*]
Client:	Yeah, the manager grabbed me by the arm and practically dragged me to that back room. And when I tried to leave, a big security guy stood in front of the door, took me by the shoulders and sat me back down.
Lawyer:	How many people heard them call you a shoplifter? [*another narrow question*]
Client:	Maybe a dozen or so. They looked at me as though I was disgusting.
Lawyer:	Do you know any of them by name? [*yet another narrow question*]
Client:	Oh, yeah. A couple of them belong to the PTA at my children's school. Another is the receptionist in my doctor's office.

Here, the lawyer is constructing a case against store personnel for assault, false imprisonment, and defamation. What the lawyer does not know is that the police came and arrested the client, who is scheduled for trial next week. The lawyer missed this by going too fast to narrow questions. If the lawyer had not done that, the following might have occurred:

Client:	The store manager grabbed me and took me to a back room, where they opened my shopping bag and accused me of shoplifting. They were really abusive and embarrassed me in front of everybody in the store.
Lawyer:	Oh, my. That must have been very upsetting. Let's start from the point where the store manager first approached you. Please take a few minutes and remember everything that happened. Then, after you've finished running it through your mind, tell me everything you remember.
[*a period of silence*]	
Client:	O.K. I was standing at the dairy counter. The manager walked up from my left and grabbed me by the arm and said, 'I saw you put something in your bag.' I said, 'What?' or something like that. And he pulled me to that back room, closed the door, and told me to sit down. [*As the*

> *client describes the scene in detail, we learn that the police arrived and arrested the client.*]

Here, the lawyer asked the client to recreate the context, and then let the client tell the whole story before beginning to probe (see §24.6).

Ask broad questions until you are not getting useful information any more. Then go back and ask narrow questions about the facts the client did not cover. While the client is answering the broad questions, you can note on a pad the topics you will explore later by means of narrow questions.

Formulating questions.   Phrase your questions carefully. Remember that how you say something has an enormous effect on how people respond (see §1.2). A good question does not confuse, does not provoke resistance, and does not help distort memory (see Chapter 24).

Ask one question at a time. If you ask two at a time, only one of them will be answered.

Lawyer: How much did Consolidated bid on this project? Were they the low bidder, or was somebody else?

Client: I think somebody else submitted the lowest bid, a company in Milwaukee that later had trouble posting a performance bond.

Did we learn how much Consolidated bid?

A leading question is one that suggests its own answer ("When the store manager took you into the back room, he locked the door, didn't he?"). A leading question puts some pressure on the person answering it to give the answer the question suggests ("Yes, he locked the door"). The question implies one or both of two things. One is that the questioner expects that answer because the questioner already thinks or knows that it is true. The other is that the questioner *wants* that answer (for example, to help prove something, such as false imprisonment).

Because of the malleability of memory (see Chapter 24), leading questions have the potential to cause inaccurate answers. If a leading question — or any type of question — in an interview causes a client to "remember" things more favorably to the client's case, and if the client is later to testify to that "memory" at trial, the leading question creates an ethical problem (see §25.4.1). (At trial, a lawyer is normally not allowed to ask a leading question of the lawyer's own witness on direct examination. But leading questions are permitted when a lawyer cross-examines the other side's witnesses, who can be expected to resist attempts to influence their memories.)

Leading questions, however, can be useful when the client might be fabricating (see §25.4.3) and for the review stage of cognitive interviewing (see §24.6 and §25.2.3).

At times, you can probe for information without using questions at all. For example, active listening or body language indicating that you are particularly interested in what the client is saying can encourage the client to go into the facts in greater detail (see §25.1.2).

§25.4 Special Problems in Client Interviewing

You may face problems of ethics (§25.4.1), information that the client considers private or too unpleasant to discuss (§25.4.2), a possibility that the client is not being honest with you (§25.4.3), pressure from the client to make a prediction before you have had an opportunity to research the law and investigate the facts (§25.4.4), or negotiating a fee agreement with the client (§25.4.5).

§25.4.1 Ethics in Client Interviewing

First and foremost, you and those who work for you are obligated to keep confidential that which the client tells you, with the exceptions noted in §22.6.

In addition, you may not "falsify evidence [or] counsel or assist a witness to testify falsely."[7] If your client will become a party to litigation, your client will probably become a witness. Thus, you may not suggest that your client testify falsely or that your client falsify evidence. Nor may you help your client do either of those things. Falsifying evidence and suborning perjury are also crimes. And "many jurisdictions make[] it an offense to destroy material for purpose of impairing its availability in a pending proceeding or one whose commencement can be foreseen."[8] Even those that do not make it a crime may impose sanctions, including dismissal or claim preclusion on those who fail to preserve evidence crucial to an adversary's case.

Perhaps the best known ethical dilemma in client interviewing is called the *Anatomy of a Murder* problem, after the novel[9] and movie of the same name. There, a lawyer interviews his client, who is accused of murder. Before asking the client for the facts in detail, the lawyer gives the client a lecture explaining all the defenses to a murder charge. After listening to this, the client describes facts that would support a defense of temporary insanity. We are left with the impression that if the client had not heard the lecture, he would have told a different story — that the lawyer essentially told the client what the client would have to say in order to escape conviction.

Lawyers are not allowed to help create false testimony. But clients are entitled to know the law and to get that knowledge from their lawyers. How can you observe both of these principles while interviewing clients? The best approach is to interview for facts first and to explain the law afterward. The reasons are partly ethical and partly practical. In the novel and the film, the client invents a story and wins at trial. That is harder to do in the real world than it is in fiction. There are always other witnesses and evidence and facts, some of them incontrovertible.

---

[7] Rule 3.4(b) of the Model Rules of Professional Conduct.
[8] Comment to Model Rule 3.4.
[9] Robert Traver, *Anatomy of a Murder* (1958).

Not many clients are clever and lucky enough to be able to invent stories that are either consistent with or more believable than everything else the fact-finder will be exposed to at trial. Much of the time, you can do a better job of advocacy if the client does not invent a story.

If the client is an organization, you have some special obligations. You do not represent the organization's officers or employees, even though they are the people you normally deal with. This can be difficult in a situation where the people with whom the lawyer is dealing fear damage to their careers. Rule 1.13(f) of the Model Rules of Professional Conduct requires that, when dealing with officers or employees whose "interests are adverse" to those of a client organization, you make it clear that you represent the organization and not them. The Rule's Comment adds that you "should advise . . . that [you] cannot represent such [a person,] that such person may wish to obtain independent representation[, and] that discussion between the lawyer for the organization and the individual may not be privileged." The evidentiary attorney-client privilege and the ethical duty of confidentiality belong to the client (the organization) and not to the client's officers or employees. In fact, the lawyer is obligated to tell responsible people elsewhere in the organization whatever the officers or employees tell the lawyer.

§25.4.2 Handling Private or Embarrassing Material

If you suspect that the client will be reluctant to talk about some things because they seem embarrassing or especially private, you might wait until the end of the interview to explore them or even wait until a subsequent interview. Give the client time to appreciate that you are a person of discretion who can be entrusted with the kind of information that the client might not even be willing to tell friends about.

When you do raise the topic, begin by saying that you need to ask about something that the client might not find it easy to talk about; that you apologize for having to do so; and that you can do a good job for the client only if you ask these questions. Explain why you need to know, and remind the client of the rules on confidentiality. Then ask, respectfully but precisely.

Sometimes it helps to reverse the normal sequence of beginning with broad questions and moving toward narrow ones. Instead, start with carefully chosen narrow questions that take the client well into the subject. Then ask general questions, such as "Please tell me all about it."

§25.4.3 When The Client is Distraught

Sometimes clients bring an enormous amount of emotional pain with them into a lawyer's office. The situation that has compelled them to seek legal assistance may be one of the most distressing things that has ever happened to them. You have just met this person. What can you do about the pain?

First, do not make superficial comments such as "Everything will be all right" or "I know how you feel." Everything will not be all right. And unless you have suffered something very similar to what the client is suffering, you do not really know how the client feels.

Second, listen, patiently and attentively, to the client's description of the most painful parts of the situation. Listen with care to anything the client says about the emotional aspect. You might be one of the few people to whom the client confides this. Try to understand, and let your tone and body language imply that you consider the emotional aspect important and are trying to understand. The fact that you are trying to understand may be a comfort to the client. Other people might not be trying to understand. You may not be able to understand fully, but your listening in a caring way may mean a great deal to the client.

Third, although you cannot honestly guarantee to solve the problem, your commitment to do the best you can may introduce hope.

§25.4.4 Handling Possible Client Fabrication

When you suspect falsity, the cause might be unconscious reconstruction of memory, semiconscious fudging, or conscious lying. Most clients try to tell you the truth as they understand it, which means that when the client is wrong, there is a good chance that something other than lying is involved.

Unconscious reconstruction of memory. Chapter 24 explains why this can happen, and §24.6 explains what to do about it. We are all capable of unconsciously reconstructing memory. When a client does it, that does not mean the client is a bad person.

Semiconscious fudging. Some people tend to try to bolster their positions by putting a spin on objective facts. If something occurred three times, a person like this might say it happened "many" times (if more is better) or "barely at all" (if less is better). This can become so habitual that the person might not be fully conscious of individual exaggerations. But it is conscious in the sense that the person can stop doing it if she really wants to. When you find someone doing this, it means that even though the person might be wonderful in other ways, she is not always a reliable reporter of facts. The best thing to do is to press hard for precise answers.

Client:	It happened many times.
Lawyer:	How many times — exactly — did it happen?
Client:	I don't know — a lot.
Lawyer:	Let's list each time you can remember. On what date did the first one happen?
Client:	Right after that blizzard we had last February. [*Client gives details.*]
Lawyer:	When was the next time?

You have to ask these precise questions anyway with every person you interview. But with one who is fudging, you have to be firm and determined; do not give in to a fog of vague generalities spoken by the client.

Conscious lying.   Here the client deliberately tells you something that is not true. Some clients do this because they are fundamentally manipulative. But others might be generally honest people who are in desperate or embarrassing situations, are lying reluctantly, and naively do not understand that it is in their own best interests to tell you nothing but the truth.

You probably don't know for sure that the client is lying. If you become annoyed or accusatory, you may damage the attorney-client relationship irretrievably. But you do need to know the truth from the client. The best way to get that is to show the client that it is in the client's own interest to tell you the truth and that other people — a judge and jury, for example — are not going to believe what the client is telling you. (If you say that you do not believe the client, you are accusing the client, and the client will fight back.)

Start by giving the client a motivation to tell you the truth. Explain how you can do a good job only if you know everything — including the unfavorable facts — from the beginning. (You might give one or two illustrations of how disaster can happen if you learn of an unfavorable fact for the first time in the courtroom when there is no longer time to prepare. Choose illustrations that are similar to the situation the client is in.) Say that your first loyalty is to the client, and summarize the rules on attorney-client confidentiality. Do all of this before you turn to the lie you suspect you are being told.

If the client is manipulative, you can use leading questions to box the client into a corner. Think this through very carefully. You do not want to humiliate the client, and you are not absolutely certain the client is lying.

You might explain how opposing counsel will cross-examine at trial and tell the client that you will give a demonstration of what that will be like. Start from what is undeniably true and conduct a determined but polite cross-examination, showing the client how a disinterested fact-finder is not likely to believe what the client is saying, given how inconsistent it is with what is undeniably true. Do this in such a way that the client can begin to tell you the truth without losing dignity.

Alternatively, you can ask questions — some of them leading — based on the assumption that the truth is something other than what the client has said. Do not point out the difference between your assumption and what the client said. If the client answers the questions consistently with your assumption, you have begun to establish the truth without a confrontation.

If the client seems to be a generally honest person who might be lying out of desperation or embarrassment combined with naivete about your role as an advocate, you might use some of the same techniques. But remember that this client does not really want to lie. You can probably be more gentle than you would with a manipulative client.

§25.4.5 *When the Client Wants a Prediction on the Spot*

Clients often want the lawyer to predict immediately whether the client will win or lose. In nearly all instances, you cannot make that prediction. You might have to check the law or investigate the facts, or both. And you need to think about it. Predicting hastily raises the risk of error.

But clients want assurance. What can you give them? Usually, it's enough to explain what work you will do, what issues you need to research, and what facts you need to investigate. You can add that you take the problem very seriously and want to do something about it ("I want to try to find a way to get you compensation for this injury"). Choosing a time by which you will have an answer also helps.

Some lawyers feel comfortable saying something noncommittal about what they are thinking. For example, "I'm hopeful, although I'm also worried about what the harbor master will say about the docking arrangements." Or: "It might be difficult to win unless we can find witnesses who saw the other boat exceeding the speed limit; I want to work on that right away." If these comments accurately summarize the lawyer's reaction, it seems fair to share them with the client. They are explicitly tentative and point to what the lawyer sees are the variables. It would also be prudent to tell the client that the whole situation can change based on other facts that you do not know about yet.

§25.4.6 Negotiating a Fee Agreement

There are four different ways for a client to pay for a lawyer's services.

The client can pay an hourly rate. In a firm, the rate will differ according to the status and experience of the lawyer (senior partner, junior partner, senior associate, junior associate). If two or more lawyers are assigned to the case, the client will be billed at different rates depending on who did what. The advantage of an hourly rate is that the client pays for exactly the amount of effort the lawyer expends. The disadvantage to the client is that the total cost of the work can only be guessed at when the client hires the lawyer. The disadvantage to the lawyer is that she needs to fill out detailed time sheets and have office staff convert them to detailed bills.

Or the client can pay a flat fee for specified work, such as $850 for an uncomplicated will. The client knows from the beginning how much the job will cost, and the lawyer does not need to keep detailed time records. But flat fees are appropriate only for very routine work where the lawyer can predict in advance how much effort the task will take.

Or the client can pay a contingency fee. Typically, the lawyer would be paid a percentage, such as 33%, of any money recovered on behalf of the client. If the client recovers nothing, the lawyer gets nothing. A contingency fee makes justice theoretically available to a client who wants to sue for money damages but cannot afford an hourly fee. In nondamages cases, a contingency fee is impractical, and in criminal and domestic relations cases, it is illegal.[10] Contingency fees are sometimes abused by lawyers, and in many states they are strictly regulated by statute or court rule.

Or the client can pay a percentage of the value of a transaction. To probate an estate, for example, a lawyer might in some situations charge a percentage of the value of the estate.

---

[10] Model Rule 1.5(d).

Usually, the lawyer suggests the type of fee that makes most sense from the lawyer's point of view, and the client either agrees or tries to persuade the lawyer to charge another kind of fee. Whatever the type, a fee is unethical unless "reasonable" according to the rules of ethics.[11] In addition to the fee, the client usually pays certain expenses, such as photocopying, messenger services, court reporter fees, and the like.

The appropriate time to negotiate the fee is usually in the closing part of the interview (see §25.2.6). Earlier, you do not know enough about how much work will be involved, and the client is usually not yet ready to hire you formally. The fee agreement should explicitly define the services you will provide.

Lawyers cost more — often much more — than clients want to pay, and fees generate more conflict between lawyers and clients than almost any other issue. For that reason, in a well-run law office all fee agreements are reduced to writing, usually through an engagement letter, which the lawyer sends or gives to the client. When the client countersigns it, the engagement letter becomes the contract through which the client hires the lawyer and agrees to pay the fee. A thorough engagement letter will describe the work the lawyer is to do, specify the fee and how it will be billed and paid, and so forth.

If the client is ready to hire you on the spot and wants you to start work immediately, you can ask your secretary to word-process an engagement letter quickly so the client can sign it before leaving. Otherwise, the engagement letter can be mailed to the client.

Except when the client will pay a contingency fee, lawyers usually ask for a retainer, which is a payment in advance for the first part of the lawyer's work. The retainer should be large enough to assure the lawyer that the client is serious about paying for the lawyer's work. Retainers of $2,000, $5,000, or $10,000 are common for the typical work that an individual or a family might ask a lawyer to do. Business retainers might be larger.

A careful lawyer usually will not do any work until after the client has signed an engagement letter and paid a retainer.

Many — but not all — lawyers do not charge for the initial client interview.

---

[11] Criteria for "reasonableness" are set out in Model Rule 1.5(a).

CHAPTER 26

COUNSELING A CLIENT

§26.1 Counseling and Advice in Legal Work

It's no accident that when judges talk to lawyers or when lawyers talk to each other, they traditionally use the word "counselor" as a form of address.[1] Some clients hire a lawyer to get advocacy, but *all* clients need and expect advice. For that reason, "[c]ounseling lies at the heart of the professional relationship between lawyer and client."[2] For many lawyers, it also dominates their workday. "Surveys suggest that lawyers spend most of their time in activities that the lawyers themselves describe as 'counseling.'"[3]

What exactly is counseling? Simply put, it is "the process in which lawyers help clients reach decisions."[4] How do lawyers do that? There are two parts to counseling. The first, preparation, includes identifying the client's goals and developing two or more alternative potential solutions that, to varying degrees, might accomplish those goals. The second is a meeting with the client in which the lawyer explains the potential solutions so the client can choose between or among them. A simple example occurs when a defendant makes a pretrial offer to settle. For the plaintiff, one potential solution is to accept the offer. Another is to go to trial in hopes of getting more there.

"Advice" is a broader concept. Counseling is a form of advice, but not all advice is counseling. For example, suppose a judge has just preliminarily enjoined a client; the client asks you whether such an order can be appealed; and you say yes. You have provided advice because you have decoded some of the mystery of the law for a layperson. But you have not counseled because you have not helped the client make a decision (whether to appeal this particular

---

[1] For example: "Good morning, counselor, when will you be ready to proceed?"

[2] Paul Brest, *The Responsibility of Law Schools: Educating Lawyers as Counselors and Problem Solvers* (Issues 3 & 4), 58 Law & Contemp. Probs. 5, 8 (Summer/Autumn 1995).

[3] Thomas L. Shaffer & James R. Elkins, *Legal Interviewing and Counseling in a Nutshell* 7 (4th ed. 2004). "Lawyers spend less time in court or in the library than one would think. . . ." *Id.* at 8.

[4] David A. Binder & Susan C. Price, *Legal Interviewing and Counseling: A Client-Centered Approach* 5 (1977).

preliminary injunction). The decision would require weighing the advantages, costs, risks, and chances of success of one option (in this instance, appealing the injunction) against the advantages, costs, risks, and chances of success of another option (not appealing). Counseling is working out those variables and explaining them to the client in a way that will help the client decide.

Clients want counseling and other advice in two kinds of situations. The first is transactions, such as business contracts, when the client wants to know how to accomplish a given goal at minimum cost and risk (see §26.2). The second is dispute resolution, which is dominated by conflict and where litigation is at least an option and might already be happening (see §26.3).

These two categories can overlap. In part, that is because a transaction-focused client wants to avoid conflict. For example, a client buying land on which to build a shopping center would want to know how to structure the transaction so as to cause the least amount of disagreement with the tax, land use, and environmental authorities. Another reason for overlap is that one method of resolving conflict is to find a way for both parties to improve their situations by collaborating (which often involves a transaction). For example, two home owners feuding over who pays for the care of trees that overhang both plots of land might be able to get a volume discount if they ask tree care companies to bid on working on all the trees on both plots. (This solves conflict and requires two transactions: one between the property owners themselves and the other between them and the tree care company submitting the best bid.)

Counseling and interviewing can overlap, too. Where a deadline or an emergency threatens, you might need to counsel a client on some questions during the initial interview. And if interviewing is for the most part learning facts orally, you will need to do that many times during the representation of a given client, sometimes in preparation for or in the midst of counseling.

Bear in mind three other things if the client is an organization (which usually means a business but might mean a nonprofit organization): First, the more you know the client's business and industry, the better you can perform all of this work. Second, organizations might look monolithic from the outside, but they are not really "cold, impersonal, and rational decision-makers."[5] Instead, organizations "are composed of people, and a merger or acquisition is as likely to occur because someone is empire-building as for any completely rational business reason."[6] Third, organizations speak to their lawyers through managers, executives, and other employees, who may have their own personal worries. But the lawyer represents the organization and not any of the people who work for it. When the interests of employees diverge from those of the organization, the lawyer owes an entire duty of loyalty to it and little, other than some warnings, to the people involved.

Finally, to be a good counselor no matter who your client is, you have to be able to combine empathy and detachment, two things that do not naturally exist side by side. Empathy helps you understand the client's goals and needs.

---

[5] Robert F. Seibel, LAWCLINIC listserv posting dated Nov. 16, 1994.
[6] Id.

Detachment helps you see the problem as it really is, without delusion. "The wise counselor is one who is able to see his client's situation from within and yet, at the same time, from a distance, and thus to give advice that is at once compassionate and objective."[7]

§26.2 Transactional Counseling

When organizational clients want transactional counseling and advice, it is most typically about how to structure deals with other organizations and how to conduct their affairs so as to minimize their taxes and their legal liability (say, in tort). When an individual or a family wants counseling and advice, it might, for example, be about how to plan an estate or buy a home.

Much of what lawyers add to transactions is in the form of advice that might fall short of full counseling. In an organizational setting, the advice might be given in varying degrees of formality:

Answering a point-blank question from the client, often over the telephone. You sit in your office writing or reading. The phone rings, and you pick it up. A client describes a proposed transaction and asks pointedly about several concerns, among them perhaps "whether the transaction is lawful, whether it is consistent with loan or other commitments that the corporation has previously undertaken, whether it will lead to a desired tax treatment,"[8] and so on. Or the client asks a single general question: "Do you see any problems with this?" When you answer, you are not doing full-blown counseling because your role is not to structure the decision. But your answer is advice, and there is a technique to giving it. Take careful written notes of what the other person is telling you. Before answering, make certain that you understand the facts. Summarize them as you think you have heard them and ask the person at the other end of the line whether you have got them right ("Let me make sure I've got the facts right . . ."). Do not answer the other person's questions until you are confident that you know exactly what the law is, and if that involves delay, estimate how long the delay will be ("I want to check a few things, and I'll get back to you later this morning"). Make a written note of the advice you gave over the phone, and keep all of your notes in the client's file in case a misunderstanding later occurs about what you said or why you said it.

Participation in business planning.   This might happen in a meeting in which the lawyer is only one of several people in the room. Depending on the situation, the lawyer might figuratively sit on the sidelines, interjecting advice about legal concerns as they become relevant, or the lawyer might counsel by framing alternatives and estimating their effectiveness.

Counseling about a transaction that is in the formation stage.   The client and another business have talked about how each could earn some money buying

---

[7] Anthony Kronman, *Living in the Law*, 54 U. Chi. L. Rev. 835, 866 (1987).
[8] Robert W. Hamilton, *Fundamentals of Modern Business* 517 (1989).

or selling something to the other. They have already agreed to some of the terms — perhaps price, quantity, delivery dates, and so forth. You have not been part of these discussions because you would not be able to add value to them. At a point when the deal seems to be jelling, the client consults you to "run it past our lawyers" (find out whether the deal would create legal problems) and "reduce it to writing" (ask you to produce a contract, which will govern the transaction). After you and the client talk things over, you write a draft of an agreement. (This is not the final version.) After you and the client review the draft, you rewrite it and send it to the other business's lawyer. (Or if the other business's lawyer has already written a draft, you rewrite that instead.) Negotiations ensue. Afterward, you rewrite the agreement again to reflect the results of the negotiations. At some or a number of points in this story, you and the client have conversations in which you frame alternative ways of solving problems and estimate each alternative's effectiveness.

There are a number of things you should be curious about when a client brings you a business transaction. In addition, ask yourself what *practical* problems you see as a disinterested observer. This does not necessarily have anything to do with law, but it is among the most valuable things a lawyer can provide for a client. A lawyer who confines her-or himself to legal questions is a technician. A lawyer who also goes beyond the legal questions is a problem-solver.

In sum, "The mark of a successful corporation lawyer in giving advice can be simply stated: He or she must consistently give advice that the client believes it can rely on, and that, when followed, usually leads to the desired result (which may simply be that nothing bad happens when the advice is followed)."[9]

§26.3 Dispute Resolution Counseling

If you were asked to imagine dispute resolution counseling, you would probably visualize either or both of two scenes. One would be a prelitigation conversation in which the lawyer helps the client decide whether a lawsuit would be worth the effort, stress, and expense. The other would be a conversation during litigation: the other side has offered to settle, and the question is whether to accept or go to trial. But litigation is not the only way to settle disputes, and, although these scenes are very common, they are not the only ways in which dispute resolution counseling occurs.

When litigation has not yet commenced, it is too simple and too narrow to think of the counseling question as "Should we sue?" The real question is "What method of dispute resolution is best suited to this problem?" These are among the things you might think about:

- Should we negotiate *without* suing? The other side will usually negotiate if you have leverage, and in some circumstances, you might have economic or other leverage even if you do not have a provable cause of action.

---

[9] *Id.* at 517.

- Should we negotiate *before* suing? This might be worthwhile if the other side is confident that you will sue if negotiation fails, and if you are confident that to negotiate you will not need to depose witnesses or pose interrogatories to the other side (which you can do only after suing).
- Should we *arbitrate*? Arbitration is essentially private litigation. The parties can create their own rules of procedure, making them as simple or as complicated as they like. They can choose their own judge (the arbitrator). Or, if they want a panel of three arbitrators, each party names one arbitrator, and those two choose the third. The parties can stipulate that the arbitrator or arbitrators have experience in the subject matter of the dispute. If the dispute involves a collision of ships at sea, for example, the parties can make sure that the arbitrators all have admiralty law experience. Not all arbitrators, however, are lawyers. With very narrow exceptions, the decision of the arbitrators cannot be appealed. Some clients find that frightening; others find it reassuring. Arbitration can be private in another sense as well: the parties can agree that neither they nor the arbitrators will tell anybody else that the arbitration ever happened. Arbitration includes no juries, which makes it unattractive to a client whose case has jury appeal (many tort plaintiffs, for example) but especially attractive to a client (such as a large corporation) distrusted by ordinary people. Arbitrators tend to award less in damages than juries.
- *Can* we arbitrate? By law, some issues cannot be arbitrated. For example, in many states an arbitrator cannot dissolve a marriage or award child custody, but an arbitrator can determine the money and property issues in a divorce.
- *Must* we arbitrate? In some industries, arbitration is difficult to avoid. For example, most stockbrokers and many health maintenance organizations will not do business with you unless you agree in advance to arbitrate any dispute that might subsequently arise. Has the client signed anything that contains an agreement to arbitrate disputes like the one before you? And in some court systems, certain cases are diverted to arbitration rather than to the courtroom.
- Should we *mediate*? Rather than adjudicating a dispute, a mediator tries to help the parties work it out themselves by suggesting possible solutions or helping the parties brainstorm them and by helping the parties to understand each other's point of view. Mediation can be useful where the parties have had and want to continue a relationship important to both of them. It is sometimes attractive where the parties do not anticipate a continuing relationship but for some reason want to resolve their dispute in a way that does not create an obvious "winner" and "loser." Mediation can, however, create hidden winners and losers. If one party is psychologically powerful and the other is psychological vulnerable, the former might intimidate the latter despite the best efforts of the mediator. An example might be where one party has a conciliatory and accommodating temperament and the other is by nature stubborn and unyielding. Another might be a divorce where the money and property issues are being mediated and where one

spouse is bullying and manipulative and the other lacks self-confidence. In both situations, one of these parties needs the advice of somebody who owes a total duty of loyalty to that party — a lawyer who will participate in the mediation on the party's behalf.

Arbitration and mediation are categorized as alternative dispute resolution, or ADR. Businesses are finding them increasingly useful as ways to settle disputes without incurring the expense and delay of litigation. That does not mean that a business client will be eager to mediate or arbitrate. The proportion of business disputes that are arbitrated or mediated is probably still relatively small, although it will likely grow in the future. And although arbitration and mediation are overall cheaper than litigation because they are simpler and faster, they include two expenses that litigation does not. The parties pay arbitrators and mediators for their services, and the parties provide the site at which the arbitration or mediation occurs. (In litigation, the taxpayers provide the judge and courtroom.)

If the client does not have a provable cause of action and has no leverage or other means of getting the adversary into dispute resolution, tell the client that as soon as you know it. Delaying unpleasant news makes it harder on the client to hear it and harder for the lawyer to say it. But do not reject a case just because the means for winning it are not immediately apparent to you when you hear the client's story in the initial interview. Effective theories and strategies take time to develop.

Advice without full counseling can happen inside a dispute resolution situation. Suppose that a corporation has been sued. The complaint alleges that the corporation has dumped lead and mercury in a river, destroying the fishing industry there. The answer denies everything. You represent the corporation, and you receive a phone call from the factory manager, who says, "Environmentalists are in a boat in the river next to our drain pipe. They're sampling the water. Can we have them arrested for doing that?" You read the corporation's deed to the factory land and note that the corporation's property stops at the water's edge. "The answer is no," you say. In this conversation, you are only answering a question about how the law treats certain facts.

§26.4 "Decision Making is an Art"[10]

A well-made decision of any kind is a product of professional creativity operating through the six steps laid out in §23.1.2. In client counseling the steps can be stated as follows:

1. Identify the problem (in counseling, focus on the client's goals);
2. Gather and evaluate information and raw materials that can be used to resolve the problem;

---

[10] Warren Lehman, *The Pursuit of a Client's Interest*, 77 Mich. L. Rev. 1078, 1094 (1979).

3. Generate potential solutions to the problem;
4. Evaluate each potential solution to measure its advantages, costs, risks, and odds of success (in counseling, predict what each potential solution would cause);
5. Choose the best potential solution (in counseling, ask the client to choose);
6. Act on the solution chosen.

You will become better at this as you develop an effective problem-solving style and learn to: identify the few things that really matter; identify the decisive event; and organize strategy around the decisive event. In dispute resolution, plan to prevent the adversary from achieving her or his own decisive event. Treat the entire problem or conflict as an integrated whole. Protect against weaknesses. And resist the temptation to act on motivations that are not strategic, such as your own emotional needs.

§26.5 The Process of Helping Another Person Make a Decision

Counseling falls into two parts.

The first is preparation before meeting with the client. You identify the client's goals; gather and evaluate relevant information about both the law and the facts; generate alternative potential solutions that, to varying degrees, might accomplish those goals; and analyze the advantages, costs, risks, and chances of success of each potential solution. In other words, you go through the first four steps of decision-making listed in §26.4.

In generating and evaluating potential solutions, consider both the legal and the nonlegal aspects and ramifications of the decision. In some settings, business or financial considerations matter. In others, political considerations might matter. And in most settings, interpersonal or emotional factors are important, even if not immediately apparent.

In referring to alternatives available to the client, this book sometimes uses interchangeably the terms "potential solutions," "choices," and "options." But not all options are potential solutions. Where the client has suffered a loss, doing nothing is one of the options, and sometimes it is the only realistic option. But it does not solve the client's problem.

If this were your own decision to make, you would continue through the fifth and sixth steps listed in §26.4 and then be done. But it is not your decision to make. You are designing a decision, but you will not make it. Because someone else will, counseling has a second part, the meeting with the client, in which you give the client your preparation in a way that helps the client make the decision.

During the meeting that is the second part of counseling, go back through the first four steps. Ask questions to make sure that you have understood the client's goals and that they have not recently changed. If any facts or aspects of the law will dominate the decision, describe them to the client (or remind the client of them if she already knows). List the options available to the client and explain what each one is together with its advantages, costs, risks, and chances of success. Then ask the client to choose an option. After the client decides — which might not happen until after the meeting — the counseling job is complete, and you and the client act on that decision.

§26.6 The Four Challenges in Counseling

The four biggest challenges in counseling are:

1. *Creating options:* It is not enough just to identify options that are immediately obvious from comparison of the law to the facts. We have to *create* options that would not be there except for our problem-solving skills. And the options need to go beyond the law: they should be practical solutions that will work in the real world where the client lives, not just in law books.

2. *Working out each option precisely:* Do not stop short of precisely defining the value of an option — especially where the value can be stated in numbers and with certainty. The following does not help the client:

    > If you choose the fourth option, you will be paid $219,000, and you'll have to pay tax on it.

    Here is what the client really needs to know:

    > If you choose the fourth option, you will be paid $219,000 within 30 days, on which you will owe tax of 35% or $76,650, so that you will get to keep $142,350. Therefore, this option is worth $142,350 to you.

    Sometimes defining an option precisely requires predictions that you might not feel confident making. Suppose that another option in the example above is not a certainty but instead a probability or possibility, requiring a prediction concerning odds. Using the concept of expected valuation, you can carry precision to this level:

    > If you choose the second option, I estimate that you stand two chances in three of being paid $400,000, on which you will owe tax of 35%. Because this is a probability and not a certainty, the value of this option — so you can compare it with the other options — is really two-thirds of $400,000, minus tax. [*lawyer then explains why and works out the numbers*]

    It might be hard to work this out, but clients need to know it.

3. *Clarity with the client:* Counseling a client involves teaching the client what the decision is, what the options are, and how to choose among them. You already know a lot about the difference between good teaching and bad teaching. For many beginning lawyers, that is the key to realizing how to explain the decision and the options clearly and in a well-organized way so that the client truly understands them. But counseling is different in one

important way from the teaching you have experienced in school: not only might the client be senior to the lawyer-teacher in age, but the client is in charge because the client has hired the lawyer and, if dissatisfied with the lawyer's work, can fire her.

4. *A helpful professional affect:* Clients need empathy combined with intellectual detachment. When you learn how to do this, you are also learning in general how to relate to somebody else in a professional way.

THE STRUCTURE AND CONTENT OF WRITTEN LEGAL ANALYSIS

CHAPTER 27

FORMS OF LEGAL REASONING

Lawyers and judges use a number of kinds of reasoning to argue and decide cases. They reason by relying on a statement of the law, like a statute or a common law rule articulated in a case (rule-based reasoning). They reason by comparing the facts of earlier cases to the facts of the present case (analogical reasoning). They reason by pointing to a desirable social or economic result, like promoting economic efficiency (policy-based reasoning). They reason by alluding to norms of conduct and customary expectations common in our society, such as how we expect people to act in certain circumstances (custom-based reasoning). They reason by appealing to a moral principle such as honesty or fairness or a political principle such as equality or democracy (principle-based reasoning). They reason by deciding whether a particular factual conclusion would explain the available evidence (inferential reasoning).

In practice, these forms often overlap, but it is helpful to identify them separately in this chapter so that you can learn to recognize them and to use them in your own analyses. Mastering their use is one of the most important goals of a law school education.

This chapter will also cover one more important way lawyers advocate for a result: narrative. Today, we usually use the term "reasoning" to describe only logical processes like those described above, but an earlier understanding of "reasoning" was much broader. It included processes that transcend logical arguments and may even resemble intuition. For lawyers and judges, the most powerful of these nonlogical processes is narrative. No matter what understanding of the term "reasoning" one prefers, lawyers and judges know that narrative functions just as the logical forms do, to justify and persuade. Therefore, this chapter includes narrative along with the logical forms of reasoning. Together, these forms will provide you with a powerful set of tools for analyzing legal issues and for advocating for a particular legal outcome.

§27.1 Rule-Based Reasoning

Rule-based reasoning is the starting point for legal analysis. It justifies a result by establishing and applying a rule of law. It asserts, "X is the answer because *the principle of law* articulated by the governing authorities mandates it."

Rule-Based Reasoning

Harold Collier should not be bound by the contract he signed because he is a minor, and *A v. B* establishes that minors do not have the capacity to execute binding contracts.

Example of Rule-Based Reasoning

"[T]he only lawful means to dispossess a tenant who has not abandoned nor voluntarily surrendered . . . is by resort to judicial process . . . . Applying [this principle of law] to the facts of this case, we conclude, as did the trial court, that because Wiley failed to resort to judicial remedies against Berg . . . , his lockout of Berg was wrongful as a matter of law." *Berg v. Wiley*, 264 N.W.2d 145, 151 (Minn. 1978).

§27.2 Analogical Reasoning (Analogizing and Distinguishing Cases)

Analogical reasoning is another major form of legal reasoning. The most common variety of analogical reasoning justifies a result by making direct factual comparisons between the facts of prior cases and the facts of the client's situation. The comparison can demonstrate factual similarities (leading to a similar result) or factual differences (leading to a different result).[1] A comparison that points out similarities asserts, "X is the answer because the facts of this case are just like the facts of *A v. B*, and X was the result there." Comparing cases to point out similarities is often called "analogizing" cases.

Analogical Reasoning

(Similarities)
Harold Collier should not be bound by the contract he signed because, like the defendant in only sixteen, and in *A v. B* the defendant was not bound by the contract she signed.

A comparison that points out differences asserts, "Even though X was the answer in *A v. B*, that is not the appropriate answer here because the facts in this case are different from the facts in *A v. B*. Comparing cases to point out differences is often called "distinguishing" cases.

---

[1] Comparisons that show differences are often called "disanalogical" or "counterana-logical" reasoning. For simplicity, however, we use "analogical" reasoning to refer both to pointing out similarities and pointing out differences.

Analogical Reasoning

(Differences)

In *C v. D,* the minor was bound by his contract. However, Harold Collier's situation is unlike the situation in *C v. D* because there the defendant had signed a statement asserting that he was nineteen, thus deliberately misrepresenting his age. Harold Collier, however, never made any statement about his age. Therefore, the result in *C v. D* does not control Collier's case.

Example of Analogical Reasoning

"[In *Fahmie,*] property was conveyed to [Fahmie], who had no knowledge of the installation of the culvert [or the violation of state law]. Fahmie made application to the development commission to make additional improvements to the stream and its banks. It was then that the inadequate nine foot culvert was discovered, and the plaintiff was required to replace it.

The case before us raises the same issues as those raised in *Fahmie.* Here, the court found that in 1978 the wetlands area was fi lled without a permit and in violation of state statute. The alleged violation was unknown to the defendant and was discovered only after the plaintiff attempted to get permission to perform additional improvements to the wetlands area. "[The court went on to assert that the result in the pending case should be the same as the result in *Fahmie.*] *Frimberger v. Anzellotti,* 594 A.2d 1029, 1033 (Conn. 1991) (ellipses omitted).

§27.3 Policy-Based Reasoning

Policy-based reasoning justifies a result by analyzing which answer would be the best for society at large. It asserts, "X is the answer because that answer will encourage desirable results for our society and discourage undesirable results."

Policy-Based Reasoning

Harold Collier should not be bound by the contract he signed because he is only sixteen, and people that young should be protected from the harmful consequences of making important decisions before they are mature enough to consider all the options. Further, contract defaults are likely when minors undertake contractual obligations, and contract defaults dampen economic growth and decrease productivity levels.

Example of Policy-Based Reasoning

"To approve this lockout [of a defaulting tenant by a landlord] . . . merely because in Berg's absence no actual violence erupted while the locks were being changed would be to encourage all future tenants, in order to protect their possession, to be vigilant and thereby set the stage for the very kind of public disturbance which it must be our policy to discourage. . . ." *Berg v. Wiley*, 264 N.W.2d 145, 150 (Minn. 1978).

§27.4 Principle-Based Reasoning

Principle-based reasoning justifies a result by appealing to a broad principle or character trait valued by our society, such as a principle of morality, justice, fairness, or democracy. It asserts that "X is the answer because that answer upholds notions of morality, justice, fair-play, equality, democracy, or personal freedom."

Principle-Based Reasoning

Harold Collier should not be bound by the contract he signed because enforcing contracts like his would encourage sales agents to lie and would reward unfair and dishonest sales practices.

Example of Principle-Based Reasoning

"A succession of trespasses . . . should not . . . be allowed to defeat the record title . . . . [T]he squatter should not be able to profit by his trespass." *Howard v. Kunto*, 477 P.2d 210, 214 (1970).

§27.5 Custom-Based Reasoning

Custom-based reasoning justifies a result by reliance on cultural and societal norms of behavior. It asserts, "X is the answer because that result is consistent with what we expect of people in this society." Custom-based arguments often are phrased as statements about what is and is not "reasonable." Some legal rules directly incorporate custom-based reasoning as the operative legal standard, such as the negligence standard ("the reasonable person") or the constitutional standard for judging pornography ("falls outside contemporary community standards") or rules that protect people from "undue" influence.

Custom-Based Reasoning

Harold Collier should not be bound by the contract he signed because it is unreasonable to expect a minor to be able to match wits with an experienced and overreaching sales agent. In our society, people do not make contracts with minors; they deal with the minor's parent or guardian.

Example of Custom-Based Reasoning

"[T]here is no ... reason to deny plaintiff relief for failing to discover a state of affairs which the most prudent purchaser would not be expected to even contemplate." *Stambovsky v. Ackley*, 572 N.Y.S.2d 672, 676 (1991).

§27.6 Inferential Reasoning

Lawyers often use inferential reasoning (abduction) when analyzing a set of facts to decide whether those facts meet the requirements of a rule of law. If a particular factual conclusion would be consistent with the available evidence, that consistency provides some reason to believe that the factual conclusion is true. The possible conclusion would explain the observable facts. For example, assume that a patient had normal blood pressure during all prior phases of treatment and then the doctor changed one of the patient's medications. Immediately after taking the first dose, the patient developed high blood pressure. No other changes in treatment or lifestyle occurred. One could infer from this set of facts that the new medication caused the high blood pressure.

Inferential reasoning is important in analyzing many legal issues. It is especially important when the legal rule calls for a conclusion that cannot be directly observed — questions like causation (as in our prior example), knowledge (whether a person was aware of a certain fact or situation), or motive or intent (whether a person intended to cause a certain result).

Inferential Reasoning

(used to establish whether the sales agent knew or should have known that Collier was a minor)
Collier is a short, smooth-faced boy who looks and acts like the sixteen-year-old he is. He told the agent about his hopes to be selected next year for the high school cheerleading squad. That hope would make no sense if he were already a senior, the year when most students turn eighteen. He said that he should probably call his parents to ask their advice. He said that he had never dreamed that he would have a car sooner than any of his friends, a puzzling comment for an eighteen-year-old to make because many high school students have a car shortly after turning sixteen. Most telling of all, the sales agent asked to see Collier's driver's license to make a copy of it for the dealership's files. Under these circumstances, the sales agent surely either knew or suspected that Harold Collier was a minor.

Example of Factual Inferences

A will is invalid if it was written when the testator was under the undue influence of someone. In *Estate of Lakatosh*, 656 A.2d 1378 (Pa. Super. 1994), the issue was whether Roger exercised undue influence over Rose. The court noted that Roger had met Rose, a woman in her seventies and living alone, and had immediately begun to visit her daily. Within a couple of months, Roger had suggested to Rose that she give him a power of attorney, which she did. A mere eight months after they met, Rose executed the will at issue in the case. The will left all but $1,000 of Rose's $268,000 estate to Roger. The lawyer who drafted the will was Roger's second cousin, to whom Roger had referred Rose.

Identify and explain the inferences implied by this description of the *Lakatosh* facts.

§27.7 Narrative

Narrative justifies a result by telling a story whose theme implicitly calls for that result. Narrative uses the components of a story (characterization, context, description, dialogue, theme, and perspective) to appeal to commonly shared notions of justice, mercy, fairness, reasonableness, and empathy. In this sense, narrative is closely related both to principle-based reasoning and to custom-based reasoning, but narrative is far more contextual, placing these other forms of reasoning in a specific situation. Narrative tells the client's story in a way that encodes but does not directly articulate the commonly held principles and values on which these two logical forms rely.

The governing rule might directly adopt a legal standard easily communicated as a narrative theme. For instance, assume that the applicable rule about the enforcement of contracts made by minors allowed enforcement only if the other party to the contract did not use "undue" influence to convince the minor to enter into the contract. Narrative would use storytelling techniques such as description, dialogue, characterization, perspective, and context to establish that the other party's conduct was or was not "undue."

Narrative

(where the use of undue influence is an issue in the governing rule)
Harold Collier should not be bound by the contract he signed because Jenkins, a car dealer for twenty-two years, discouraged Harold from calling his parents to ask advice and told him that another purchaser was looking at the car at that very moment. Jenkins lowered his voice and said, "Tell you what I'll do. I'll knock off $1,000 just for you—just because this is your first car. But you can't tell anyone how low I went. This will have to be our secret."

Even if the applicable rule does not articulate a legal standard based on a particular narrative theme, however, narrative still persuades. A narrative demonstrating the fairness of a particular result can convince a judge to exercise any available discretion in favor of the client, to create an exception to the general rule of law, or to reinterpret or overturn the rule. The law is not insensitive to justice, mercy, fairness, reasonableness, and empathy, even when those commonly shared values are not directly incorporated in the legal rule. As a matter of fact, those notions underlie much of the more abstract rationales in policy-based or principle-based reasoning. Narrative can serve as a powerful partner with policies or principles, providing a real-life example of the policy or principle that justifies the desired result.

For example, recall that the rule prohibiting enforcement of contracts made by minors is supported by the policy rationale that minors should be protected from the harmful consequences of making important decisions before they are mature enough to consider all the options. Narrative reasoning can bolster that policy point:

Narrative

(consequences to minor not part of rule, but part of policy behind rule)

Harold Collier should not be bound by the contract he signed because he is only sixteen; he has never before shopped for a car; he was pressured by a sophisticated sales agent; he did not have the benefit of advice from any advisor; and the car purchase will exhaust the funds he has saved for college.

Each form of reasoning has persuasive power, and each has particular functions in written legal analysis. As we shall see in Part III of this book, rule-based reasoning establishes the structure of the analysis and organizes the written discussion. Within that structure, a complete analysis includes reasoning based on applicable rules, analogies, policies, principles, norms, factual inferences, and narrative. In addition to its role in the written legal analysis, narrative is paramount in the written fact statement.

Begin to notice the kinds of reasoning you find in the cases you read, the arguments you hear your classmates and your professors make, and your own analysis of hypothetical questions. By next year at this time, your skills in using all of the logical forms of reasoning will have increased dramatically.

CHAPTER 28

THE WRITING PROCESS AND LAW-TRAINED READERS

Now that you understand the legal authorities and the kinds of legal reasoning you will be working with, it is time to turn your attention to the document you will write and to the reader for whom you will write it.

§28.1 The Writing Process

Writing is a process with distinct stages and distinct goals at each stage. Each writing stage serves an important function as you work toward a finished document. This chapter identifies five main stages of a writing task and invites you to use each stage consciously as an opportunity to strengthen your writing.

Stages of the Writing Process

1. Reading and analyzing the materials.
2. Creating an annotated outline.
3. Writing a working draft of the analysis.
4. Converting that analysis into a document designed for a reader.
5. Editing for style and technical correctness.

This section will describe each stage, and writing process hints will be included at appropriate points throughout the rest of the book. For easy identification, this margin symbol will mark those process hints in future chapters. Two caveats about this description of the writing process are in order, however. First, writing processes are as personal as signatures and fingerprints. The stages presented here represent a common way of approaching a writing task, but your own process will be unique to you. What is important is that you find places in your *own* writing process for the *activities* described here.

Second, the writing process is recursive. While you are working on the tasks of one stage, you often will find yourself returning to the tasks of an earlier stage and anticipating those of a later stage. Writing requires you to circle back again and again as you come to understand more about your legal issue, your client's facts and goals, and the available legal strategies. Your willingness to construct, dismantle, and reconstruct your document will be crucial to achieving a good written product.

Stage 1: Reading and Analyzing the Materials. Start by reading carefully all parts of your assignment, paying particular attention to the assignment's articulation of the issue(s). If you have any trouble understanding the issues, try writing them out in your own words and comparing them to the issue statements in the relevant case law. In a law office, you will be encouraged to talk to the assigning lawyer to clarify any confusion over the scope of the issue. In law school writing, to the extent permitted, clarify any questions with your professor.

Then read all of the relevant legal sources, briefing the cases and taking notes on the statutes. Use a separate sheet of paper for each source so you can sort them later. Be sure to keep your legal issue in mind, and look particularly for the ways in which each legal source might tell you something about your legal issue. You are looking generally for answers to the following questions:

Key Information about Legal Authorities

1. What is the governing rule?
2. What do its important terms mean?
3. What are some examples of facts that have satisfied the rule's requirements?
4. What are some examples of facts that have *not* satisfied the rule's requirements?
5. What policies or principles does the rule serve?

Make a note about each thought or question that occurs to you, whether you think it might have merit or not. There will be time later for sorting and discarding. This is the time for wide, creative perception.

Stage 2: Creating an Annotated Outline. At some point, you must arrive at an outline of your analysis. It is ideal if you can create the outline before you begin to compose a draft, even if later you find you must change it. Start by formulating and outlining the governing rule. Then use a version of the rule's outline to create the main categories of your outline. Chapter 29 will explain this process in more detail, but an example here might help. Assume that you have outlined a rule setting out the requirements for revoking a will. The outline of that rule gives you a good starting outline for a written discussion of that issue. Under each element, you would discuss whether your client's facts establish that element.

Outline of will Revocation Issue

To revoke a will, a testator must

1. have the intention to revoke, and
2. take some action that demonstrates that intent.

Once you have the main categories in place, select one of your authorities and ask yourself what it tells you about the first category (the intention to revoke). Does it help you answer any of the five questions we identified in the box labeled "Key Information About Legal Authorities"? If so, write that information on your case brief or other notes for that authority. *Note the page number on which you find the noted information.* You will have to cite to it when you begin to write, and you will save valuable time if you do not have to look for it again. Then move to the second category (an action demonstrating that intent), and go through the same process. Does this legal authority tell you any of the five kinds of information about the second category? Go through this process with each authority, keeping in mind that some authorities will give you information about more than one category.

When you have finished examining each authority, gather all relevant information under the appropriate categories. Use a separate sheet of paper for each category. For each point you have learned, write a complete sentence expressing that information. For instance, under the "intent" category, you might write: "The testator must intend to revoke the will now, not in the future." Under the "action" element, you might write: "The action must not be consistent with any interpretation other than the intent to revoke." These sentences will be the bases for the *thesis sentences* of your paragraphs. And as we shall see, good thesis sentences are crucial.

Now you are ready for the last step in the outlining stage: selecting the authorities you actually will discuss in your analysis. For each piece of information you have listed, select the sources that give you the best support or the most important information for that point. Notice that you do not select the *authorities* you will discuss until you have identified the *points* you plan to make. This writing strategy will help you organize according to the relevant substantive points and not simply list and describe cases.

One more point about outlining your analysis: Outlining comes easily for some people; others find it difficult. If you are in the latter group, there is good news and bad news. The bad news is that a tight, linear structure is essential for a good office memo or brief. The good news is that you do not have to create that structure first. Many people find that they must write a very rough draft before they are ready to create an outline. Writing before you outline usually takes longer, but often the resulting outline is more reliable. The key is finding the method that works best for your own writing process.

Stage 3: Writing a Working Draft of the Analysis. Your first job as a writer is working out your own analysis of the issue. Your primary purpose in writing a working draft is to use the writing process as an analytical tool. Dean and former Judge Donald Burnett put it this way:

> Clear expression . . . is not merely a linguistic art. It is the testing ground for ideas. Through the discipline of putting an argument into words, we find out whether the argument is worth making . . . . The secret . . . is to start verbalizing early — while there is still time to learn from the discipline of forming ideas into words. You must begin by identifying your client's goal and the issues to be resolved. Each issue is defined by a cluster of facts and governing legal principle. If you cannot articulate this nexus of law and fact, you do not yet have a grasp of the case.[1]

Your working draft is where you "grasp the case." It guides, deepens, and tests your analysis, and it forms your ideas into the kind of structured, linear reasoning that lawyers must master. Ultimately, your analysis will take the form of a document designed to communicate with your reader, but do not worry yet about creating that document. First concentrate on working out your own analysis.

Write out your analysis, putting flesh on the outline's bones. Chapters 29-34 will explain how to organize the material. In the working draft stage, focus your attention on the substance and structure of your analysis. Each time you write a statement about what the law is or what an opinion said, note a source and page number. While you are writing your working draft, you need not stop to look up the rules explaining how to cite correctly. The revision stage will give you the chance to correct citation form, spelling, punctuation, and legal usage. In the working draft stage, do the best you can on those matters, but do not let them distract you from your primary task at this stage: creating a solid analysis of your issue.

Try to arrive at the end of Stage 3 with enough time to put down the document for a while. Then return to your draft and revise it, based on what you see when you read with fresh eyes.

Stage 4: Turning the Analysis into a Document Designed for Your Reader. After your analysis is solid, turn your attention toward your reader. The working draft of your analysis will become the Discussion section of your office memo or the Argument section of your brief. In Stage 4 you will check your organization to be sure that it will meet your reader's needs. You will complete the document by writing its statement of facts and its other components.

Stage 5: Editing for Style and Technical Correctness. In this last stage, turn your attention to the fine points of writing. Edit to achieve clarity and correct

---

[1] Donald L. Burnett, Jr., *The Discipline of Clear Expression*, 32 The Advocate 8 (June 1989).

citation form, punctuation, and grammar. These technical matters are the most easily visible criteria for judging writing. Readers will notice these matters first and draw from them conclusions about the skill and care of the writer. A sloppy document causes a reader to doubt the document's substantive accuracy.

Suggestions for Consciously Using the Writing Process. First, be alert for signs that you need to revisit earlier stages. Although the completed document should take the reader on a linear journey toward the document's conclusion, you will find that the process of creating the document is far from linear. Rather, the process returns you again and again to earlier stages to reconsider earlier decisions. The willingness to reconsider earlier writing decisions and to revise existing material is one of the hallmarks of a good writer.

Second, experiment with different writing strategies, and observe your own writing process. What works well for you at each stage? Do you work better if you dictate a draft first? Does free-writing help you? How about charts or colored pens? Each writer's creative and analytical processes are unique. Part of your goal in your first few years of legal writing should be to observe as much as you can about your own process so that you can adopt writing strategies that work for you.

Third, be patient. On your first few writing assignments, take the stages in order without trying to combine or compress them. Your goal on these first assignments is to let each stage of the writing process teach you some critical skills. Soon you will have developed those skills well enough to speed up each stage. You will learn to customize each stage to fit your own skill level, the complexity of the assignment, and your own unique creative processes.

Fourth, master the general principles before you decide to try something new. This introductory course on legal writing teaches the basic principles that operate in most situations. First master the basic substantive and organizational principles covered in this course. Soon you will develop the judgment to know when and how you can depart from them.

Finally, start early. Good writing takes time — almost always more time than the writer first expects.

§28.2 Law-Trained Readers

§28.2.1 *Focus on the Reader*

The goal of an office memo or a brief is to communicate with a reader. As a matter of fact, you can think of a memo or brief as a conversation with your reader. As in any conversation, the better we know our conversational partners, the more effectively we can communicate. The characteristics of your reader will govern many of the choices you make as a writer.

We do not have to be reminded to write to a reader. Whether we realize it or not, we always write to *someone*, but sometimes we find that we are writing to ourselves rather than to the real reader. We are having a conversation with ourselves. Or we might write to the real reader but with inaccurate or incomplete information about that person. We forget to stop before we write and ask, "Who is this person, and what is she likely to be concerned about?"

When you undertake a legal writing task, you might not know your reader well — perhaps not at all. But you can still write with a fairly accurate focus on this unfamiliar reader because law-trained readers share certain characteristics. Even in large cities, lawyers and judges live in a legal community that shares certain values, customs, and forms of expression. Understanding these values, customs, and forms of expression will help you present your message effectively.

The general characteristics of law-trained readers in this chapter introduce you to the study of readers, but do not just accept the principles that follow. Notice your own reactions when you read. Try to be a participant-observer of the reading process. Your observations of your own reactions as a reader will be your best writing teacher. Observe, too, the other law-trained readers you know. This way, as the years of your legal practice go by, your writing will become better and better.

§28.2.2 Attention Levels

Before a speaker can communicate, the audience must be listening. Here is some information about the attention levels of law-trained readers:

1. A reader's attention is finite. Even the most diligent reader will eventually run low or run out.
2. A reader's investment in the nuances of the topic might not be as great as the writer's. Although the law-trained reader will have a particular need to understand the material, these readers are extraordinarily busy. The judge has many other cases and does not have a personal investment in this one. The senior partner has many other obligations and depends on the memo writer to analyze thoroughly but communicate succinctly.
3. A reader's attention is not evenly distributed. It is greatest in the first several pages, and it decreases rapidly from then on.
4. Readers generally save some attention for the conclusion. They are willing to invest attention there, but only if they can locate the conclusion easily and if the conclusion is clear and compelling enough to warrant the investment.
5. Although readers spend more attention on the document's first few pages and on a compelling conclusion, attention levels revive a bit at internal beginnings and endings, like the start of a new issue or the last few paragraphs of a statement of facts. This revival is more likely if the new issue is marked by a heading or subheading.
6. Stories, especially real-life stories, are engrossing. Many readers pay more attention to facts than to abstract legal concepts. This means, for instance, that attention levels are higher in the middle of an effective Statement of Facts than in the middle of the Argument or Discussion section. It also means that, even in the middle of a Discussion or Argument section, a reader's attention level will rise a bit when the material begins to apply law to fact.

Figure 28.1   Attention Levels

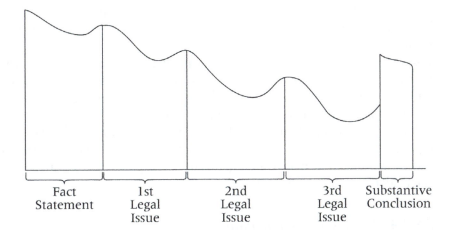

| Fact Statement | 1st Legal Issue | 2nd Legal Issue | 3rd Legal Issue | Substantive Conclusion |

7. A reader's attention level is lowest about three-fourths of the way through the Discussion section of an office memo or the Argument section of a brief.

These observations about readers underlie an important writing principle: Placement of material is one of the important decisions a writer must make. A good writer places the most important parts of the analysis where the reader can find them quickly and give them first priority for her attention.

§28.2.3   Road Maps

Most readers want a road map — some sense of where they are and where they are headed. But law-trained readers have an even greater need for an organizational structure. Here's why:

1. A reader's first priority is to understand the law. A law-trained reader's first step in the process of understanding the law is an outline. This process of learning and applying law set out in outline form is how most lawyers and judges studied law. It is basic to the way law-trained readers think. In the first few semesters of law school, this learning style and thinking process probably came more naturally to some than to others, but by the end of law school virtually all lawyers approach legal analysis by some variation of this method. This process is one of the primary components of "thinking like a lawyer."
2. Lawyers and judges do not read the law out of intellectual curiosity but because they have a problem to solve. They are looking to your memo or brief to help them solve it. This means that your discussion of the law must be

clearly and closely tied to the facts and issues of the case. Your organizational structure serves as the continuing reminder of how your legal discussion relates to the problem to be solved.

3. A law-trained reader constantly assesses the strength and accuracy of the analysis and the credibility of the writer. The most visible part of the analysis, the part the reader first evaluates, is its organization. Here the law-trained reader expects to find the outline of the law. If a reader doubts the organization of the analysis, the reader wonders whether the content of the analysis is reliable.

4. At some point in their legal education or practice, law-trained readers have studied many of the more common rules of law. Such readers will be used to thinking of those rules in a familiar order or structure. Even if a reader is not already familiar with a particular rule of law, a statute or a leading case might set out the rule in a particular structure. A law-trained reader will be expecting to analyze the issue in this familiar order or structure. Many law-trained readers are not comfortable with organizational surprises, and an uncomfortable reader is an unreceptive reader.

§28.2.4 Readers as Commentators

It is easy to assume that writing is a one-way street, with the discourse all flowing in one direction. We tend to think that we, as writers, are the only speakers. We think this because we cannot hear anyone else talking. In reality, the most important party to the conversation, the reader, *is* talking, but we can't hear her. Each of us has a voice in his or her mind — an opinionated, talkative "Commentator." We've already observed this character at work because when a writer mistakenly begins writing to herself, she is writing to her own internal Commentator.

The reader has such a Commentator too, and that little voice will chatter at every opportunity. The Commentator will be saying things like "No, that's not right, because . . ." or "What in the world do you mean by that?" or "But wait, where is the discussion about . . . ?" Think of yourself as a reader. Haven't you been reading this chapter listening to both the written word and to your own Commentator?[2]

The reader's Commentator will not remain completely silent, and there is nothing the writer can do to change that. The Commentator's participation can even be helpful. Yet each time the Commentator speaks, the reader must listen to two voices at once; the writer must compete with the Commentator for the reader's attention.

The writer, then, has two objectives: (1) The writer wants to keep the reader's Commentator relatively quiet, resolving its concerns at the points where they arise, and (2) when the Commentator does speak, the writer wants it to be saying "OK," "right," or "yes," or perhaps even arriving at the writer's conclusions

---

[2] If so, be grateful to your Commentator. The sort of critical reading the Commentator inspires is essential to legal analysis. When you are studying the law and writing about it, your own Commentator is your best friend.

moments before the writer states them. As a writer, you must anticipate the Commentator's chatter before the conversation occurs and try to preempt that chatter. Your goal is to craft your side of the conversation to keep the Commentator as quiet and agreeable as possible.

§28.2.5 *Judges as Readers*

Judges share the characteristics of other law-trained readers. Their attention is finite. They are busy and may become impatient with delay in getting to the bottom line. They generally focus more attention on the beginning and end of a document or a section than on the middle. They find facts engrossing. They want a road map. They value clear organization that sets out the rule of law. But judges tend to have some additional characteristics as well. Here are some other observations about how judges read.

1. Although any law-trained reader tests the analysis at each step, a judge is particularly apt to do so. This skeptical testing is the heart of a judge's job. Girvan Peck explained it by describing judges as "professional buyers of ideas."[3] However, even a skeptical judge will be less skeptical of the analysis of a lawyer known for careful and honest work than of the analysis of a lawyer with a poor reputation for either competence or candor.

2. Because judges are human, a judge who is already convinced of the equities of your position will be more receptive to your legal arguments. This judge will *want* you to be right on the law. This human desire can help to overcome a little of the judge's natural caution.

3. Most of us are more willing to accept the analysis of someone we like and someone who has been considerate of our needs. This is true of judges as well. This does not mean that judges decide cases on the basis of social and political connections. But a lawyer who treats the judge professionally, with respect and consideration, will be a more effective advocate than the lawyer who does not.

4. As public servants with public responsibilities, judges are concerned about the policy implications of their decisions. However, trial judges and judges serving on intermediate appellate courts often see their role as requiring them to apply the law the way the jurisdiction's highest court would. Not only do judges prefer hearing that they were right, but reversals often mean having to deal with the case again. A judge's goal is to resolve cases, not prolong them.

    Therefore, trial judges and judges serving on intermediate appellate courts are most persuaded by authorities that help them predict how the higher court would decide the question. For judges at these levels, policy arguments are less persuasive than clear mandatory authority. Judges serving on the highest appellate court in the jurisdiction are much more amenable to policy arguments than are their colleagues on lower courts.

---

[3] Girvan Peck, *Writing Persuasive Briefs* 77 (Little, Brown Co., 1984).

5. Because most judges plan to spend many years on the bench, they take a long-term view of each legal issue. Judges are concerned about how an individual ruling could constrain or empower them in future cases.

6. Judges as a group tend to be personally conservative (although not necessarily politically so). Because of the public nature of their job and the fact that they are seen as safeguarders of public morality, lawyers who become judges tend to be conservative in their personal lifestyle.

7. People tend to cling more tenaciously to conclusions they think they have reached by themselves than to those asserted by others. Judges are no different. Thus, when a judge notices that the writer is using a particular technique for persuasion, the technique loses its effectiveness. Heavy-handed use of a persuasive technique usually hurts more than it helps. The most effective persuasive techniques are invisible to the reader.

8. A reader who feels pushed will resist. An effective legal argument will not push an unwilling reader down a path. Rather, an effective legal argument will place the reader at a vantage point that allows the *reader* to see and choose the best path. Thus, as a brief writer, you must decide how far you can take the judge without losing the judge's cooperation in the process. The consequences of pushing a judge to accept an unreasonable argument go beyond the judge's rejection of the *un*reasonable parts of the argument. The judge will tend to reject the *reasonable* parts of the argument as well.

9. Judges read briefs to decide between legal positions. When such readers are presented with categories, particularly categories identified with point headings, they tend to keep score. They might not even realize they are doing it, and they often will not observe that the rhetorical effect of keeping score is to weight each category equally. Knowing this tendency can help a writer select an organizational plan and decide how to subdivide the argument.

10. As decision-makers encounter arguments one by one, they tend to label each argument as "weak" or "strong" before going on to the next argument. Decision-makers are more likely to be convinced by one strong argument than by a series of weaker ones. Also, a strong argument will lose some of its force if it follows or is followed by weak arguments on the same point.

11. The reader's perception of the strength of the first argument affects the reader's perception of the strength of the arguments that follow. As law-trained readers, judges expect to find the strongest argument first. Unless the judge knows of a reason the weak argument had to be discussed first, the judge will presume that the strongest argument is first and thus that subsequent arguments are even weaker.

12. Judges often relate to the lawyers who practice in their courts in much the way that parents relate to children. If you are a parent, you know that there is nothing quite as tiresome and irritating as constant fighting and bickering among children. Most judges have little tolerance for bickering and blustering lawyers. Judges prefer to focus on legal issues rather than personalities.

13. One final observation about judges: The judge may skim the briefs and then ask a law clerk to read and summarize them. The impact of a law clerk on the brief-reading process is a bit of a wild card, but there are two general

observations that you should keep in mind. First is the relative inexperience of most law clerks as compared to most judges. Remembering this inexperience will help you to take care not to leave out steps in the analysis on the assumption that your reader is an expert on your issue. Second, although these readers are often inexperienced, they also tend to be bright. Many judicial clerks served on their school's law review and received much of their formative training in that context. Thus, they expect the details of a brief to be right. They tend to draw conclusions about the reliability of the analysis based on the lawyer's attention to these details. They may well scrutinize every aspect of your brief more thoroughly than a busy judge could.

§28.2.6 *Law Professors as Readers*

Your primary readers for law school documents will be law professors. Undoubtedly, these professors already understand a great deal about the relevant area of law and about the particular authorities on which your analysis will be based.

Ordinarily, a writer should tailor the document to the reader's pre-existing knowledge. If the writer is certain that the reader knows some of the relevant information, the writer would refer generally to the information only when necessary to put new information in context. However, law school writing is a different matter. Unlike most readers, your professor is not reading to learn particular information. Instead, your professor is reading to evaluate what information *you* have learned and how well you can communicate it. If the information is not set out in your document, your professor will not know whether and how well you understand it.

Therefore, in law school writing, assume that you are writing to a law-trained reader who has no particular expertise in the area you are discussing. Your goal is to include the information your professor wants to evaluate without explaining more than the assignment asks.

CHAPTER 29

LARGE-SCALE ORGANIZATION: CREATING AN ANNOTATED OUTLINE

An annotated outline is the most reliable method for making your legal analysis complete and coherent. Without it or its equivalent, you are likely to miss issues and to wander off track as you write. Also, it will provide the structure of the discussion section of your memorandum. If you have carefully prepared the annotated outline, writing the memorandum will flow easily. Your topic headings, thesis sentences, and case citations in support of your explanation and application of the law will already be laid out. This chapter first explains how to identify the structure of a legal rule and to write it out in outline form. Then, the chapter explains how to use that structure to create an annotated outline for your particular assignment.

§29.1 Rule Structures

Rules of law adopt particular structures. Familiarity with these structures will help you in several important ways. First, recognizing a rule structure is a method for quickly deepening your understanding of the rule. This study tool will work well for virtually all of your law school classes. If you are preparing a course outline for contracts, for instance, your outline will be more effective if you consciously outline the legal rules you are studying. Second, the rule's structure will become the basis for the large-scale organization (the outline) of your memo or brief, or even the relevant part of your contracts final exam.

Therefore, when you formulate a legal rule from a case opinion, try to express it in an outline format. Use any version of traditional outline form, with roman numerals, large case letters, Arabic numerals, and small case letters, as necessary. If the rule takes the form of a simple list, you can denote the list using Arabic numbers. This outline of the relevant rule will allow you to focus your analysis on each element in an orderly way, not forgetting any element and not confusing your analysis of any one element with that of any other element.

As you gain experience in outlining legal rules you will notice certain common rule structures. Becoming familiar with these common structures early in your legal training will help you to recognize them quickly and to outline the rule and your legal analysis more easily.

A Conjunctive Test. This kind of rule sets out a test with a list of mandatory elements. For example, consider the following rule: To revoke a will, a testator must have the intention to revoke the will and must take some action that demonstrates that intent. The outline for this rule would set out each of the required elements like this:

To revoke a will, a testator must

1. have the intention to revoke and
2. take some action that demonstrates that intent.

A Disjunctive Test. This kind of rule sets out an "either/or" test. It identifies two or more subparts and establishes a certain result if the facts fall within any *one* subpart. For example, consider the following rule: A lawyer shall not collect a contingent fee in a criminal matter or a divorce. You might outline the rule like this:

A lawyer shall not collect a contingent fee in either of the following kinds of cases:

1. a criminal matter or
2. a divorce.

Notice that the difference between the first two rule structures lies in the introductory language specifying whether all subparts are required or whether any single subpart is sufficient.

A Factors (Aggregative) Test. This kind of rule sets out a flexible standard guided by certain criteria or factors.[1] Some rules condition the legal result on a more or less objective standard. A burglary statute, for instance, defines burglary using a number of fairly objective criteria. Was it a dwelling? Did it belong to another? Did the defendant enter it? However, some rules condition the legal result on a much more flexible standard, giving more discretion to the decision-

---

[1] Some scholars use the term "rule" to refer only to fairly objective, concrete legal tests and use the word "standard" to refer to more flexible tests like a factors test or a balancing test. To avoid confusion, however, we use the term "rule" to refer to both kinds of legal tests.

maker. To keep judges from being totally arbitrary and to help them exercise their discretion wisely and uniformly, rules using flexible standards often identify factors or criteria to guide the decision-maker. Here is an example of such a rule:

> Child custody shall be decided in accordance with the best interests of the child. Factors to consider in deciding the best interests of the child are: the fitness of each possible custodian; the appropriateness for parenting of the lifestyle of each possible custodian; the relationship between the child and each possible custodian; the placement of the child's siblings, if any; living accommodations; the district lines of the child's school; the proximity of extended family and friends; religious issues; any other factors relevant to the child's best interests.

Placed in outline form, the rule would look like this:

Child custody shall be decided in accordance with the best interests of the child. Factors to consider in deciding the best interests of the child are:

1. the fitness of each possible custodian
2. the appropriateness for parenting of the lifestyle of each possible custodian
3. the relationship between the child and each possible custodian
4. the placement of the child's siblings, if any
5. living accommodations
6. the district lines of the child's school
7. the proximity of extended family and friends
8. religious issues
9. any other factors relevant to the child's best interests

Notice the critical difference between this rule structure and a conjunctive test (a rule with mandatory elements). In a conjunctive test, all of the subparts must be met, but here the subparts are just factors to consider rather than separate individual requirements. One or more can be absent from a particular case without necessarily changing the result. The decision-maker has the discretion to gauge the relative importance of each factor.

A Balancing Test. This kind of rule balances countervailing considerations against each other. A rule setting out a balancing test is also inherently flexible, so such a rule often includes factors or guidelines to assist the decision-maker in weighing each side of the balance.

For example, consider this dispute over legal procedure. Prior to trial, parties in civil litigation try to obtain information from each other by using interrogatories (written questions directed to another party and calling for answers under oath). Sometimes, the party receiving a set of interrogatories will object to certain interrogatories, arguing that answering would be unduly burdensome. To decide whether the party must answer the interrogatories, the judge applies the following rule:

> A party must respond to properly propounded interrogatories unless the burden of responding substantially outweighs the questioning party's legitimate need for the information.

To measure "burden," the judge might consider a number of factors, such as the time and effort necessary to answer; the cost of compiling the information; any privacy concerns of the objecting party; and any other circumstances particular to the objecting party's situation. To measure "legitimate need," the judge might consider a number of other factors, such as how important the information would be to the issues of the trial, whether the information would be available from some other source or in some other form, and any other circumstances relating to the party's need for the information. Placed in outline form, the rule would look like this:

> A party must respond to properly propounded interrogatories unless the burden of responding substantially outweighs the questioning party's legitimate need for the information.
>
> A. The burden of answering:
>   1. the time and effort necessary to answer
>   2. the cost of compiling the information
>   3. any privacy concerns of the objecting party
>   4. any other circumstances raised by that particular party's situation
> B. The questioning party's need for the information:
>   1. how important the information would be to the issues of the trial
>   2. whether the information would be available from some other source or in some other form
>   3. any other circumstances relating to the party's need for the information

Compare this rule structure with the factors test. In a factors test, the decision-maker gauges a single interest, for example, "the best interest of the child." In a balancing test, the decision-maker balances two competing and different interests, comparing the strength of each interest against the other. In the discovery rule above, these two interests are the burden of answering and the need for the information.

A Defeasible Rule. A defeasible rule is a rule with one or more exceptions. Here is an example of a rule with an exception:

> A lawyer shall not prepare any document giving the lawyer a gift from a client except where the gift is insubstantial or where the client is related to the lawyer.

Placed in outline form, the rule would look like this:

> A lawyer shall not prepare any document giving the lawyer a gift from a client except
>
> A.   where the gift is insubstantial or
> B.   where the client is related to the lawyer.

Again, notice that the critical distinction between this structure and the others lies in the introductory language defining the subparts as exceptions to a general principle. Notice also that you can accurately articulate some rules using different structures. For instance, do you see how you could easily articulate this rule using a disjunctive rule structure?

A Simple Declarative Rule. A simple declarative rule contains no elements, factors, or other subparts. For example, if you are analyzing the validity of an unsigned will, you might be dealing with a rule like this:

> To be valid, a will must be signed.

If you have looked carefully and find no subparts, factors, or other criteria for applying the rule, you can assume that your rule is a simple declarative rule. In such a case, your structure will be a simple one-point structure. However, take care to assure yourself that your rule has no lurking elements or other subparts. Overlooking elements or other subparts is a common mistake for beginning legal writers.

Rules Combining Several Structures. Some rules use more than one rule structure. Such a rule will use a larger structure like one of the examples set out above. However, the rule's subparts might use another rule structure. For instance, consider this rule governing attacks on the credibility of criminal defendants who testify at trial:[2]

---

[2] At a trial, the judge decides what testimony or documents can be admitted into evidence by applying the rules of evidence in effect for that court. If the judge refuses to admit a document into evidence, that information cannot be considered when deciding the case.

> Evidence that the accused previously was convicted of a crime shall be admitted if the crime involved dishonesty or false statement or if the crime was punishable by death or imprisonment in excess of one year and the conviction's probative value outweighs its prejudicial effect.[3]

This rule uses the disjunctive (either/or) structure for its larger structure, like so:

> Evidence of a prior conviction may be admitted if it falls within either of the following categories:
>
> A.   if it involved dishonesty or false statement, or
> B.   if it was punishable by death or imprisonment in excess of one year and its probative value outweighs its prejudicial effect.

Notice, however, that subpart B contains two requirements (the punishment requirement and the comparison of probative value to prejudicial effect). Notice also that the inquiry about probative value and prejudicial effect is a balancing test. What's more, the cases interpreting this rule probably describe the factors to be considered in gauging "probative value" and "prejudicial effect." Thus, a more detailed outline of the rule might look like this:

> Evidence of a prior conviction may be admitted if it falls within either category A or category B:
>
> A.   if the conviction involved dishonesty or false statement; or
> B.   if both of the following are true:
>   1.   the conviction was punishable by death or imprisonment in excess of one year; and
>   2.   its probative value outweighs its prejudicial eff ect
>   a.   probative value is gauged by:
>   [List factors set out in the cases.]
>   b.   prejudicial effect is gauged by:
>   [List factors set out in the cases.]

---

[3] *See* Fed. R. Evid. 609(a) (paraphrased).

§29.2 Creating an Annotated Outline

As you know, outlines divide material into topics and organize them, using levels to show how the topics relate to each other. The first level of distinction is reserved for the broadest categories. The second level represents the largest distinctions within each of the broad categories. Those second-level topics can be subdivided even further. We begin with the first level of distinction for a legal analysis: the legal question(s) you have been asked to address.

§29.2.1 *The First Level: The Legal Questions You Have Been Asked to Address*

Your writing assignment probably identified the legal question or questions you are to address. If you have been asked to analyze whether William Levitt's actions constituted burglary, you have been asked to address only one legal question. But if your assignment also asks you to address whether his statement to Delores Corbitt, his alleged common law wife, will be admissible at trial, you have been asked two legal questions. The first question will be governed by the rule identifying the elements of burglary. The second question will be governed by a different rule — a rule of evidence.

Use your outline's first level of distinction (roman numerals) to identify the separate legal questions you have been asked to address. At the outline stage, you can phrase these issues as questions or, if you are ready, as your answers to the question. In the example above, the outline's first level of distinction would be:

  I.   Do William Levitt's acts constitute burglary?
  II. Will Levitt's statements to Delores Corbitt be admissible at trial?

If you have been asked only one question, use a roman numeral "I" for that question, and do not be concerned that you will not have more than one roman numeral. Let the use of the roman numeral assure you and your reader that this is the issue you were given and, therefore, that this is the point of connection between that question and your own analysis.

§29.2.2 *The Second Level: Governing Rules*

Whether or not your assignment identifies separate legal questions, your research might reveal that the answer will depend on two different legal issues governed by two different legal rules. Your assignment might ask, "Can our client succeed in a claim for negligence against the other driver?" This is one legal question. However, you might discover that its answer will depend on the answers to two separate legal questions governed by two separate legal rules: (1) whether your client can establish the elements of a negligence claim; and (2) whether the applicable statute of limitations has expired.[4] If your answer to the question will require analysis under two different and unrelated legal rules, use the next level of distinction (uppercase letters) to represent the discussions of these two different rules.

For instance, in our prior example, assume that the second question (admissibility of Levitt's statements) will require analysis using two different governing rules: the rule of evidence that prohibits admission of statements made to a common law spouse and that jurisdiction's rule defining a valid common law marriage. Our outline now looks like this:

  I. Do William Levitt's actions constitute burglary?
  II. Will Levitt's statements to Delores Corbitt be admissible at trial?
      A. Are Levitt and Corbitt married according to common law?
      B. Are statements to a common law spouse admissible at trial?

---

§29.2.3 The Third Level and Beyond: The Rule's Structure

Use your outline of the governing rule(s) to form the next levels of your discussion's outline. For instance, in our example, the next levels under the roman numerals might produce the following outline:

  I. Do William Levitt's actions constitute burglary?
      A. breaking
      B. entering
      C. dwelling
      D. of another
      E. in the nighttime
      F. intent to commit felony therein
  II. Will Levitt's statements to Delores Corbitt be admissible at trial?
      A. Are Levitt and Corbitt married according to common law?
          1. intent of both parties to be married, and
          2. actions holding themselves out to the community as husband and wife.
      B. Are statements to a common law spouse admissible at trial?
          [Statements made to a common law spouse are privileged and therefore not admissible unless the privilege is waived.]
      C. Has Levitt waived the privilege?

---
[4] Statutes of limitation prescribe the time limits within which a claim can be brought.

Notice that your research on the admissibility of statements to a common law spouse has yielded a defeasible rule (a rule with an exception). The rule is a simple declarative statement with one exception: "The statements are inadmissible unless the defendant has waived the privilege." Therefore, you have discovered another subissue: whether Levitt waived the privilege. You must return to your research to learn what kinds of acts would constitute a waiver. When you find the rule that governs waiver, you will use it to structure §29.2.3 in the outline.

Thus, the outlines of the relevant rules provide the organization for your working analysis of each issue. Using this outline, your analysis of the burglary question would discuss each element separately, completing the discussion of one element before proceeding to the next. Then you would proceed to the admissibility question and follow the same process there.

§29.2.4 Omitting Issues Not in Dispute

You might already know that some of the categories on your outline will not be issues in your assignment. For instance, in the burglary example, the "nighttime" issue probably would not be disputed if the entry of the building occurred at 2:00 a.m. You can revise your outline now to delete the "nighttime" category, but you cannot forget the issue just yet. You will need to explain to your reader your reasons for not addressing that element. Chapter 34 will describe how and where to give your reader this information.

To be sure you do not forget the element, you can leave it in its place on your working draft outline and simply skip it when you start to write. After you have written out the other parts of your analysis, you will use your working draft to create the document designed for your reader. At that point, you will be doing some rearranging of the sections anyway, so revising the outline then would be convenient. For example, as Chapter 34 will explain, it probably will be appropriate to place the most dispositive element first in your discussion, and you might not know which element will be most dispositive until you have written out your analysis.

Leaving the category in its place temporarily can be a good idea for another reason. Legal conclusions often turn out to be less obvious than they first appeared. Only after you have researched both law and facts will you be ready to predict how the rule will apply to your client. Only then will you know for certain whether you can treat any parts of the rule as undisputed.

§29.2.5 Uncertainty About Which Rule Your Jurisdiction will Adopt

You might find that your jurisdiction has not yet adopted a rule governing your particular issue. Or perhaps your jurisdiction's rule reflects an unwise approach to the issue, and your client's interests would be served best by the adoption of a different rule. If you are writing an office memo, you will have to predict what rule the court probably would adopt. Then you can analyze the disposition of your client's particular issue, assuming that your prediction is correct. You might also need to analyze the result if the decision-maker adopts the other rule. Your working draft outline might look like this:

    A.   If the court adopts rule *A*, what will be the result?
    B.   If the court adopts rule *B*, what will be the result?
    C.   Which rule is the court most likely to adopt?

In section §29.2.3, in an office memo, you will need to compare the two rules to predict which rule the court is likely to adopt. In a persuasive brief to the court, you will be arguing which rule the court should adopt. In either case, you will need to address the relative strength of the authority supporting each rule.

§29.2.6 *Annotating Your Outline*

Your working outline now provides the structure for your discussion of the authorities. The next step is deciding which authorities you will discuss under each point in the outline and for what purpose. Chapter 28, pages 284–286 described this process. If you have not yet read those pages, do so now. Remember that you should write a complete sentence expressing each relevant point you have learned about the rules of law. *Do not select the authorities you will use until you have identified the points you will make. This way you will find yourself organizing according to the relevant substantive points and not simply listing and describing cases without using them to make a relevant point.*

CHAPTER 30

Overview of Small Scale Organization: "Creac"

§30.1 A Paradigm for Structuring Proof

A conclusion of law is a determination of how the law treats certain facts. In predictive writing, it can be expressed as a present statement ("Medwick is contractually bound by ExitRow.com's Terms and Conditions") or as a prediction ("A court will probably hold that Medwick is contractually bound..."). In persuasive writing, it can be expressed as a present statement or as a recommendation to the court.

In both predictive and persuasive writing, you prove a conclusion of law by explaining the law and the facts in ways that convince the reader that your conclusion is the right one. Organizing what you say is essential to convincing the reader.

A supervising lawyer who reads a predictive Discussion in an office memorandum does so in preparation for making a decision. So does a judge who reads persuasive writing in a motion memorandum or appellate brief. They will make different kinds of decisions. The lawyer will decide what to advise the client or how to handle the client's case. The judge will decide how to rule on a motion or appeal. But both look for a tightly structured analysis that makes your conclusion seem inevitable.

What do these readers need from you? The reader making a decision first needs to know what your conclusion is; then the main rule (or rules) on which your conclusion is based; next, proof and explanation that the rule exists and that you have stated it accurately; and then application of that and subsidiary rules to the facts. If all this turns out to be long and complicated, at the end of it you might restate the conclusion as a way of summing up.

Thus, to the reader who must make a decision, analysis is most easily understood if it is organized into the following formula — or into some variation of it.

To prove a conclusion of law:

1. State your conclusion.
2. State the primary rule that supports the conclusion.
3. Prove and explain the rule through citation to authority, description of how the authority stands for the rule, discussion of subsidiary rules, analyses of policy, and counter-analyses.
4. Apply the rule's elements to the facts with the aid of subsidiary rules, supporting authority, policy considerations, and counter-analyses; and
5. If steps 1 through 4 are complicated, sum up by restating your conclusion.

Acronyms have been used to help students remember this kind of formula. For example, CRAC stands for Conclusion, Rule, Application, and Conclusion. A more complete acronym might be *CRuPAC: Conclusion, Rule, Proof of Rule, Application, and Conclusion.*[1]

What do the ingredients in this formula mean?

Your conclusion is the one you are trying to prove. Some examples are in the first paragraph of this section.

The rule is the principal rule on which you rely in reaching your conclusion. Other rules might also be involved, but this is the main one on which your analysis rests. For the conclusions quoted in the first paragraph of this section, the rule will be one that requires contemporaneous knowledge of a restraint.

Rule proof or ***rule proof and explanation*** is a demonstration that the main rule on which you rely really is the law in the jurisdiction involved. The reader needs to know for certain that the rule exists in the jurisdiction, and that you have expressed it accurately. Both can be done through citations to authority, such as statutes and precedent, together with explanations of how that authority stands for the rule as you have stated it, explanations of policy, and counter-analyses. Subsidiary rules sometimes help explain the main rule.

Rule application is a demonstration that the rule + the facts = your conclusion. Explain your logic and use authority to show that your result is what the law has in mind.

Sometimes authority that you use in rule proof might reappear in rule application, but for a different purpose. For example, suppose that *Alger v. Rittenhouse* held that a boat crew that caught a shark became its owner to the exclusion of the fisherman who hooked but lost the shark an hour before. (In your case, ranchers trapped in their corral a wild mustang that immediately jumped over the fence and ran onto your client's land, where it was captured by your client.) In rule proof, you can use *Alger* to prove that your jurisdiction has adopted the rule that wild animals become the property of the first person to reduce them to possession.

---

[1] *CRuPAC* was suggested by Judith Stinson, Terrill Pollman, and Steve Epstein.

In rule application, you can use *Alger* again — this time to show that your client satisfies that rule because her position is analogous to that of the boat crew.

A *subsidiary rule* is one that guides application of the main rule or works together with it in some way necessary to your analysis. In a criminal case, the main rule would set out the elements of the crime. Among the subsidiary rules would be the one that permits conviction of any crime only on evidence that establishes guilt beyond a reasonable doubt.

A rule's *policy* is the rule's reason for being. The law does not create rules for the fun of it. Each rule is designed to accomplish a purpose (such as preventing a particular type of harm). When courts are unsure of what a rule means or how to apply it, they interpret the rule in the way that would be most consistent with the policy behind it. Thus, policy can be used to show what the rule is (in rule proof) and how to apply it (in rule application).

Counter-analysis is a term used by law teachers, but not by many practicing lawyers. A *counter-analysis* evaluates the arguments that could reasonably be made against your conclusion. Do not waste the reader's time by evaluating marginal or far-fetched arguments. In predictive writing, the counter-analysis is an objective evaluation of each reasonable contrary argument, with an honest report of its strengths and weaknesses. You must report whether your conclusion can withstand attack. And you must consider the possibility that other analyses might be better than the one you have selected. Like authority and policy, counter-analyses can appear both in rule proof and in rule application — but for different purposes. (In persuasive writing in a motion memorandum or appellate brief, a counter-analysis is called a *counter-argument*. It does not objectively consider contrary points of view. It argues against them, stressing their weaknesses and showing their strengths to be unconvincing.)

You will find the paradigm formula to be flexible if you think of it as a tool to *help* you organize. It can be varied in many ways, although you should do so only for good reasons. This chapter explains why readers prefer that you organize your analysis this way.

The formula explained here is designed for practical writing in office and motion memoranda and in appellate briefs. Do *not* use it in this form when you take law school examinations.

§30.2 Why Readers Prefer This Type of Organization

Remember that all of your readers will be practical and skeptical people and will be reading your memorandum or brief because they must make a decision.

State your conclusion first because a practical and busy reader needs to know what you are trying to support before you start supporting it. If your conclusion is mentioned for the first time *after* the analysis that supports it (or in the middle of that analysis), some or all your reasoning seems pointless to the reader who does not yet know what your reasoning is supposed to prove. Effective writers usually state their conclusions boldly at the beginning of a Discussion or Argument ("The plaintiff has a cause of action because . . ."). This may take some getting used to. It is contrary to the way writing is often done in college. And most of us have been socialized since childhood to state a conclusion only after a proof — even in the most informal situations — to avoid appearing opinionated, arrogant, or confrontational.

Far from being offended, however, the reader who has to make a decision is grateful not to be kept in suspense. That kind of reader becomes frustrated and annoyed while struggling through sentences the relevance of which cannot be understood because the writer has not yet stated the proposition the sentences are intended to prove.

State the rule next because, after reading a conclusion of law, the skeptical law-trained mind instinctively wants to know what principles of law require that conclusion instead of others. After all, the whole idea of law is that things are to be done according to the rules.

Then prove and explain the rule because the reader will refuse to follow you further until you have established that the rule is really law the way you say it is and until you have educated the reader somewhat on how the rule works. The skeptical law-trained mind will not accept a rule statement as genuine unless it has been proved with authority. And you cannot apply a rule that the reader has not yet accepted and understood.

Apply the rule last because that is the only thing left. When you apply the rule to the facts, you complete the proof of a conclusion of law.

Along the way, counter-analyze opposing arguments because the skeptical law-trained mind will be able to think up many of those arguments and will want them evaluated. Almost *every* train of reasoning can be challenged with reasonable arguments. If you do not account for them, the reader will doubt you because it will look as though you are avoiding problems rather than solving them.

CHAPTER 31

SMALL-SCALE ORGANIZATION: EXPLAINING THE LAW

After you have a large-scale structure for your discussion, the next step is to write out the analysis, putting flesh on the bones of this structure. Chapters 31 and 32 will explain how to discuss a single legal issue. Chapter 34 will explain how to put the discussions of multiple issues together into one cohesive analysis.

What do we mean by a "single issue"? You will find that phrase used differently in many contexts, but for our purposes, we mean the analysis of a single element of a rule. For instance in the burglary example, each of the elements of the crime of burglary would raise a separate issue.

§31.1 An Overview of the Paradigm for Legal Analysis

A legal issue is analyzed by first identifying and understanding the governing rule and then applying that rule to a particular set of facts. First you must *explain* the rule; then you must *apply* that rule to the facts. "The chart below gives you another view of the basic "CREAC" paradigm for organizing proof of a conclusion of law discussed in the preceding chapter; it divides the paradigm into two halves: "Rule Explanation" and "Rule Application:""

Paradigm for a Working Draft

Rule Explanation

1. Conclusion: State your conclusion about the issue.
2. Rule: State the applicable rule of law.
3. Rule Explanation: Explain the rule.

Rule Application

4. Rule Application: Apply the rule to your client's facts.
5. Conclusion: Restate your conclusion.

This chapter describes the rule explanation half of this paradigm. Many new legal writers are not sure what rule explanation covers. They also might think they have explained the rule more thoroughly than they actually have. These difficulties can be eased if, after the introductory paragraph (described below), you do not allow discussion of your client's facts (the second half of the paradigm) to slip into the first half of the paradigm — your explanation of the rule itself. Mixing explanation and application leads to confusion in identifying rule explanation. If you keep application out of the spot reserved for explanation, you will learn what rule explanation is *not*, which is vital to learning what rule explanation *is*.

Separating the halves of the paradigm also will help you accurately evaluate your own writing. Often a writer states the rule and then proceeds to write several pages about the rule and how it applies to the facts. The discussion seems thorough, but how can the writer tell? An accurate self-evaluation requires checking the depth and breadth of both halves of the reasoning process, and that is difficult to do when the two halves are intermixed. As a discipline, you might want to draw a line on your working draft between the rule explanation and the rule application. The line will remind you to keep your discussion of your client's facts below the line.

Keeping the halves distinct does not mean that while you are engaged in the process of writing the paradigm you must complete rule explanation before you attempt to write any rule application. For early versions of the working draft, you can write more freely. Many writers find this unstructured prewriting helpful. Using the paradigm means simply that at the conclusion of your writing process, the document should reflect distinct sections for rule explanation and rule application.

§31.2 Stating the Conclusion

Law-trained readers want to learn your answer, so the first thing your reader will want to see is your conclusion. If you already know what your conclusion will be, put it in a sentence and use that sentence as the section heading. Then write an introductory paragraph (sometimes called a "thesis paragraph") in which you state your conclusion again in two to three sentences. Place this paragraph immediately after the heading. In these sentences, your reader should learn (1) the issue to be decided, (2) your conclusion on that issue, and (3) your basic reason for that conclusion, if you can state it succinctly. Often the governing rule will be implicit in this statement, but you need not state it directly here because you likely will be stating it as the first sentence in the next paragraph.

For example, assume that your firm represents Linda Pyle, who recently bought a tract of land to use as a commercial horse stable. A lawyer from another firm, Howard Gavin, represented Pyle in the land purchase transaction. After buying the land, Pyle discovered that a neighboring quarry owned an easement across her property, and the use of the easement is interfering with the stable's operation. Pyle has come to a partner in your firm, and the partner has asked you to research whether Gavin's failure to check the title for possible easements constituted legal malpractice. Here is an example of the beginning of the written discussion of this issue:

I. Linda Pyle has a strong claim for legal malpractice against Howard Gavin.
Howard Gavin committed legal malpractice in his representation of Linda Pyle because he did not meet the required standard of professional skill and diligence. The representation called for a basic task common to general practitioners, and the problem could have been prevented simply by doing thorough research.

If you are writing a brief to the court, probably you will already know what your conclusion will be. If you are writing an office memo, however, and if the issue is a close one, you might not be sure what your conclusion will be until you have progressed further in the writing process. If you are not yet sure, you can state the issue here rather than the conclusion, and proceed with writing your analysis. Once you have a solid draft, rewrite the heading and the first paragraph to provide your reader with the information above.

§31.3 Stating the Governing Rule

Next, state the governing rule. Follow it with citations to the primary source(s) for the rule. Here is a rule statement added to our example:

I. Linda Pyle has a strong claim for legal malpractice against Howard Gavin.
Howard Gavin committed legal malpractice in his representation of Linda Pyle because he did not meet the required standard of professional skill and diligence. The representation called for a basic task common to general practitioners, and the problem could have been prevented simply by doing thorough research.
A lawyer has a duty to provide a client with representation that meets or exceeds the standard of *professional skill and diligence commonly possessed and exercised by a reasonably prudent lawyer* in this jurisdiction. *Jacobson v. Kamerinsky* [citation].

Usually the rule statement should be the first sentence in the first paragraph after the introductory (thesis) paragraph. Occasionally, however, an issue is complex enough to require a little context or clarification before stating the rule. If so, *briefly* set out the necessary context or clarification, but get to the rule statement as quickly as you can. Not only will your reader be looking for the rule, but the discipline of concisely stating the rule immediately after the conclusion is an important part of your analytical process. It forces you to articulate the focal point of the first half of the analysis, and it focuses your attention on the rule you are about to explain.

After you have typed your statement of the rule, look for the key term or legal standard. The primary task of your rule explanation is to define that term or standard. Just for the working draft, you might want to use italics for these key words so you can easily refocus your attention on them.

§31.4 Explaining the Rule: Five Components

The third step is explaining where the rule comes from and what it means. Rule explanation usually includes five components. Generally, these components are so closely interrelated that you will not be able to break them out and perform them sequentially. While you are explaining one, you will also be explaining another, so do not use this list as an organizing tool. Instead, use it to evaluate your rule explanation for its completeness:

1. Show how the authorities demonstrate that the rule is what you say it is. Often you can do this by setting out the relevant content of the authorities (facts and holdings of cases or key provisions of statutes). Sometimes, if you have had to formulate the rule by synthesizing or reconciling authorities, you might have to explain your synthesis or reconciliation.

2. Explain the rule's purpose or the policies it serves. The way the rule will apply to your client's facts will be influenced by the rule's purpose and the policies it serves, so your reader will need to understand these underlying rationales. Chapter 35 explains this part of rule explanation in greater detail.

3. Explain how the rule has been applied in the past. Interpreting the language of a rule requires attention to how courts have applied it and how they have not applied it. What are some examples of cases in which the rule's requirements have been met? Have not been met?

4. Explain any additional characteristics that will affect how the rule may be applied. Is this rule to be liberally or strictly construed? Are there burdens of proof or presumptions that might affect how the rule will apply to future cases? Does the rule require an elevated level of proof, like clear and convincing evidence? Will expert testimony be required?

5. To the extent necessary, explain any other possible understanding of the rule. If another reasonable interpretation of the rule exists, your reader will want to know it. In persuasive writing you need address only those competing theories that your adversary has or will raise or that you think the judge might wonder about. In predictive writing, you should address any competing interpretation that is reasonably likely to arise. The explanation of another possible interpretation is sometimes called "counter-analysis" or "counter-explanation."

Match the depth of your discussion to your assessment of the strength of this second interpretation. If it is possible but unlikely that a court would adopt it, cover it briefly. However, if the choice between the interpretations is a closer call, discuss the counter-analysis in more detail, and explain why it is not the best or most likely interpretation.

§31.5 Guidelines for Rule Explanation

Here are some guidelines to keep in mind as you write the rule explanation section:

Use all relevant tools of statutory and case law analysis. Review the tools for case law and statutory analysis. Remember that the value of the information they yield is not simply in reporting (restating) it for your reader, but rather in *using it to make a point about the rule.* The form of reasoning most relevant to rule explanation is rule-based, with some help from policy or principle-based reasoning.

Limit your explanation to those topics that will be relevant to the way the rule will apply to your client's facts. When you explain what the rule means, do not include everything one might ever want to know about the rule. Include only the information that might pertain to your client's situation. This focus will save your reader's patience, and it will save you writing and editing time. Because you have not yet written the section *applying* the rule to your client's facts, you will have to anticipate the application you have not yet written. After you write the application section, you might need to return to the rule explanation section to add or delete topics of rule explanation. Your goal is to match the coverage of the explanation section to the coverage of the application section.

Use only very short quotes of key language. If you force yourself to use your own words for the information you find in the sources, you will understand that information better, and you might be able to state it more clearly than the original writer did. Remember that your analysis must do more than simply retype material from the sources. Analysis begins only when you draw theses from the material in the sources and explain the reasoning that supports your theses.

Order your discussion of the authorities according to their importance, placing the most important authorities early in the discussion. Case authorities are important to an analysis primarily by virtue of their precedential value generally or by the similarity of their particular facts to your client's facts.

Articulate factors or guidelines. When you discuss the cases that are similar factually, try to discern and articulate any factors or guidelines that seem to be operating when the courts apply the rule to these kinds of situations. Sometimes such information will be described explicitly by the courts; sometimes you will have to infer it from other comments the courts have made or from the way the courts have applied the rule.

Do not use authorities just to fill up space or to prove that you have read them. Rather, demonstrate that you have the lawyerly skill of identifying the *key* authorities and analyzing them thoroughly.

Include a description of the rule's historical development if (1) the development is important for understanding the rule's current form; or (2) the rule's current form does not decisively answer your question, but the rule's history establishes a trend that can help you predict or persuade. If you choose to describe the rule's development, tell your reader why. Otherwise, a law-trained reader will become impatient with what might seem like an unnecessary history lesson.

Choose an appropriate option for using cases. You have three options for using cases: (1) using only a citation to the case, (2) using a citation with a parenthetical summary, and (3) using a case with an in-text illustration.[1] Choose among them according to your assessment of the importance of the point you are making. Here are examples of each:

Citation only:
One who is a minor at the time of making a contract can disaffirm the contract within a reasonable time after reaching the age of majority. *Woodall v. Grant*, 9 S.E.2d 95 (Ga. Ct. App. 1940).

Citation with a parenthetical summary:
A minor is estopped from disaffirming a contract if the minor knowingly misrepresented his age at the time he made the contract. *Woodall v. Grant*, 9 S.E.2d 95 (Ga. Ct. App. 1940) (minor did not knowingly misrepresent his age when he signed without reading a contract representing that he was an adult).

Citation with an in-text illustration:
A minor is estopped from disaffirming a contract if the minor knowingly misrepresented his age at the time he made the contract. *Woodall v. Grant*, 9 S.E.2d 95 (Ga. Ct. App. 1940). In *Woodall*, the minor had signed a brokerage contract to purchase stock options, and the contract contained a representation that the purchaser had attained the age of majority. However, the minor had signed the contract without reading it. The court reasoned that the law does not require a minor to read a contract and does not enforce the same consequences on a minor as it would on an adult in the same circumstance. The court held that the minor had not knowingly misrepresented his age and, therefore, that he was not estopped from disaffirming the contract.

---

[1] Michael R. Smith, 1991 Course Handouts, "Techniques for Using Authority in a Memo," on file with the author.

§31.6 Organizing a Pure Question of Law

Occasionally your issue will be a pure question of law. You have a pure question of law if the assignment asks you to analyze only *what the law is* in your jurisdiction and does not ask you to apply that law to your client's facts. For example, you might be asked, "In this jurisdiction, can a husband be forced to testify against his wife?" In such a case, your analysis will consist primarily of rule explanation, culminating with your conclusion about the question of law ("A husband cannot be forced to testify against his wife").

Or perhaps the assignment might ask you to apply the law to your client's facts, but there is no real question about the result of that application. For example, you might be asked "Can Mr. Studdard be forced to testify against Mrs. Studdard?" Once you have explained that a husband cannot be forced to testify against his wife, the application of that rule to Mr. Studdard is clear. In that case, your analysis will consist almost entirely of rule explanation. You will spend most of your time explaining the rule. At the end of the rule explanation, you can apply the rule to Mr. Studdard, but you probably will not need to do more than announce that as Mrs. Studdard's husband, Mr. Studdard will not have to testify.

Here is an example of a working draft of a rule explanation for the Pyle/Gavin issue.

A Working Draft of Rule Explanation

I. Linda Pyle has a strong claim for legal malpractice against Howard Gavin.

> Conclusion

Howard Gavin committed legal malpractice in his representation of Linda Pyle because he did not meet the required standard of professional skill and diligence. The subject matter of the representation is common to general practitioners, and the problem could have been prevented with thorough research.

> Conclusion plus facts

A lawyer has a duty to provide a client with representation that meets or exceeds the standard of professional skill and diligence *commonly possessed and exercised by a reasonably prudent lawyer in this jurisdiction. See Jacobson v. Kamerinsky.* [citation]

> Rule and citation

In *Jacobson,* the lawyer failed to file a timely claim before the medical malpractice screening panel. By statute, a medical malpractice claim cannot be pursued unless it has been filed before the screening panel within the applicable time limit. [citation] Therefore the client's claim was barred. Because a reasonably prudent lawyer would research and comply with the statutory requirements for bringing a particular kind of claim, the court held that the lawyer was liable to his client for the losses that resulted from the failure to file the claim. [citation] One gauge of the prudent lawyer standard is whether the task is something general practitioners are familiar with doing.

> Key facts from cited case

> Holding from cited case

Thesis sentence (a
characteristic the
court found
significant)

Key facts

Court's statement
about those facts

How court's
statement supports
thesis

Thesis sentence
(another significant
characteristic)

Disclosure that
thesis is an
inference

Reasoning from the
court's observation
about the facts

Thesis sentence
(how rule applies to
a particular
situation)

Relevant facts

Holding on this
point

Court's two policy
reasons

Thesis sentence
anticipating an issue

Disclosure of lack of
similar facts

Reasoning (policy)

Thesis sentence
(evidence required)

Disclosure of no
express authority

Inferring a point
from the court's
language

In *Jacobson,* the court had pointed out that the enactment of the screening panel requirement had been widely publicized in newspapers, electronic media, and the state bar journal. However, the court explained that even without publicity, a prudent lawyer would comply with filing requirements because filing lawsuits is something general practitioners are familiar with doing. [citation] Therefore if the task is familiar to general practitioners, the court need not ask whether the particular lawyer should have been aware of the particular requirement.

Another gauge of the prudent lawyer standard is whether the error could have been prevented by research. In *Jacobson,* the court observed that an "error in judgment" does not constitute malpractice. [citation] While *Jacobson* did not expressly define the difference between an error in judgment and a breach of the prudent lawyer standard, the court distinguished the *Jacobson* facts from an "error in judgment" by pointing out that in *Jacobson* the correct answer would have been apparent had the lawyer done the necessary research. [citation] Therefore, although a prudent lawyer can make an error in judgment, a prudent lawyer does not make errors preventable by proper research.

The "prudent lawyer" standard is not reduced for lawyers operating outside their area of special knowledge. In *Jacobson,* the lawyer-defendant had been in practice only ten weeks when he accepted the medical malpractice case. The court held that the lawyer's lack of experience did not excuse his failure. [citation] Clients should be entitled to at least the minimum standard of skill and diligence, according to the court. [citation] Also, a contrary rule would offer no incentive to lawyers to gain necessary knowledge or experience. [citation]

The standard probably would not be affected by facts indicating that the lawyer intended to be particularly careful, or that he was otherwise skilled and diligent, or that he was a well-respected partner of a well-respected firm. Although no facts like these were present in *Jacobson,* the court's language and policy statement explained in the previous paragraph would seem to apply to this question as well.

It is unclear whether the court would rely on expert testimony or would make its own judgment about what a prudent lawyer would do in a particular set of circumstances. This question was not at issue in *Jacobson.* However, It is unclear whether the court would rely on expert testimony or would make its own judgment about what a prudent lawyer would do in a particular set of circumstances. This question was not at issue in *Jacobson.* However, the opinion does not mention the testimony of any expert witness, and the court's statements that a prudent lawyer would research the requirements for bringing a claim seemed to be statements of the court's own opinion rather than statements based on someone's testimony. The court's repeated references to the standard as "the minimum" that "any client should be entitled to expect" [citations] seem to indicate that the court considered itself competent to decide the standard.

Thus, whether certain conduct falls short of the "prudent lawyer" standard appears to be determined on a case-by-case basis, by what the judge thinks a prudent lawyer would do. However, two ways to gauge whether the failure falls below the standard are: (1) whether the task is something general practitioners are familiar with doing; and (2) whether the problem could have been prevented by doing proper research.

Summary of points made in rule explanation

§31.7 Checklist for Rule Explanation

State the Conclusion

State your conclusion on the issue and your basic reason, if you can state it succinctly.

State the Applicable Rule of Law

Place the rule statement immediately after the introductory paragraph.

Explain Where the Rule Comes From and What It Means

- Did you show how the authorities demonstrate that the rule is what you say it is?
- Did you explain the rule's purpose or the policies it serves?
- Did you explain how the rule has been applied in the past?
- Did you explain any additional characteristics that may affect how the rule will be applied?
- If necessary, did you explain any other interpretation of the rule?

Tools for Using Case Authority

- Setting out the facts of the case
- Explaining what the court held about the rule
- Explaining any important dicta
- Explaining how the court applied the rule
- Where appropriate, explaining how the court did *not* apply the rule
- Pointing out any facts the court emphasized
- Explaining what legal commentators have said about the case or the rule

Tools for Interpreting Statutes

- Explaining the statute's plain meaning
- Applying any relevant canons of construction
- Explaining the legislature's intent
- Explaining the policies implicated by the possible interpretation(s)
- Explaining the interpretation of any governmental agencies charged with enforcement
- Explaining the interpretations of courts and respected commentators

General Principles

- Cite a source for each statement of a rule, a holding, the court's reasoning, or facts from a case.
- Do not discuss your client's facts in this section.
- Order your discussion of the authorities according to their importance.
- Articulate any factors or guidelines.
- Identify the *key* authorities and analyze them thoroughly. Include historical development if helpful for prediction or persuasion.
- Choose wisely among the options for using cases.

CHAPTER 32

SMALL-SCALE ORGANIZATION: APPLYING THE LAW TO THE FACTS

Now that you have explained the rule, you are ready to apply it to your client's facts. Remember that this half of the paradigm uses the deductive format of syllogistic reasoning — that is, applying a general, often abstract principle to a particular situation and arriving at a conclusion.

General principle (from rule explanation section)	Covenants not to compete are enforceable if the duration, the geographical scope, and the nature of the activity restrained are reasonable.
Application to particular facts	These three terms of the Watson/Carrolton covenant are reasonable.
Conclusion	Therefore, the Watson/Carrolton covenant is enforceable.

Although rule-based reasoning is still important in this second half of the paradigm, factual inferences, narrative, analogical reasoning, policy and principle-based reasoning, and custom-based reasoning are at least as important to rule application.

§32.1 Two Approaches to Writing the Application Section

Because the point of the paradigm is to apply the rule you have just explained, the rule application section should track the rule explanation section. Each aspect of the rule you described in the rule explanation section should now be applied to your client's facts. Thus, some writers use the rule explanation section as their outline as they write the rule application section. If you use this approach, simply work your way through the application section by applying each point you discussed in the explanation section. This way you are sure to apply the rule you just explained instead of allowing your application section to wander.

You might find, however, that a slightly different approach works better for you. Although a written legal analysis ultimately should be framed in tightly reasoned logic, you might find that rigid allegiance to the structure of the rule explanation section stifles your own writing process. If you choose to open your early drafts to a broader writing process, you can begin writing the rule application section by focusing on the narrative (the facts) without looking back to the rule explanation section. You will have the rule in mind, but more impressionistically so. This strategy frees you to think like a storyteller and to focus more on the narrative themes the key facts suggest, and on the policies and principles they implicate. Be sure to compare your client's facts to the facts of precedent cases, pointing out relevant similarities and differences.

When you have a draft of each section, revise them both so the rule explained in the first half matches the rule applied in the second half. Perhaps you will need to add application of a point you discussed in rule explanation but forgot to apply in the application section. However, just as often, you will need to return to the explanation section to add or edit the discussion of a point you had not noticed until you began to write about your client's facts. No matter which way you approach the writing process, the end result should be the same — a logical analysis built on a narrative theme.

§32.2 Content of Rule Application

Although the organization of each rule application section will be unique to the rule and the facts involved, here are some general principles to keep in mind:

1. *Begin with a sentence or two stating your factual conclusion,* for example: "A judge would probably find that a reasonably prudent lawyer in Howard Gavin's situation would have checked the title for easements."
2. Then *apply each point from the rule explanation section,* keeping the most important points early in the discussion.
3. For each point, *write a thesis sentence* stating how that point will apply to your client's case.
4. In one or more paragraphs following each thesis sentence, *use your client's facts to explain why your thesis sentence is accurate.* If your role is predictive, explain the inferences and factual conclusions you think a judge or jury would draw from these facts. If your task is persuasive, use the facts to set out and support the inferences you want the court to draw.

    Use common sense. Imagine the situation your client has described to you. What would it have looked like? Seemed like? What other things might have been true if these are the facts? What additional unconfirmed facts might you be assuming? How might the scenario look to a judge or a jury? What facts would be important to a judge or a jury? Could someone else take the same facts and characterize them differently — that is, paint a different picture using the same facts?

5. Where possible, *support your thesis with direct fact-to-fact comparisons.* Identify the factual similarities between your client's situation and relevant precedent cases, explaining how these similarities demonstrate your points. Also, identify any significant factual *differences*, and explain the point they demonstrate. Chapter 35 explains this important reasoning skill more thoroughly.

6. If helpful, *apply the rule's underlying policies to your client's situation.* Your client's facts might raise the precise concerns the rule was designed to address. If so, a court will be more likely to apply the rule strictly to your client's situation. A court will be less likely to limit the rule or to apply an exception. A court will be more likely to resolve doubts of application in favor of achieving the policy results the rule seeks. Conversely, if your client's facts do not raise the policy concerns the rule was designed to address, the court will be less willing to apply it strictly to your client.

   Reread the sample office memo in Chapter 39, this time noticing particularly the uses of policy to help predict a result. A similar use of policy can persuade as well.

7. In an office memo, *identify any unknown facts that would be important to a resolution of the legal issue.* The assigning attorney will need to know if potentially important facts are missing from the analysis.[1]

8. Where necessary, *refute any alternative rule applications.* In Chapter 31, we saw that you sometimes need to address and refute alternative interpretations of the rule. Just so, in the rule application section, there might be alternative views of how the rule might apply to your client's facts. This process is sometimes called "counter-application" or simply "counter-analysis." In predictive writing, your reader will need to understand these alternative views. In persuasive writing, you will need to address and refute your opponent's position.

   Note the difference between counter-analysis in the two stages: In the rule explanation stage, the theories disagree over what the rule means. Here, the alternative theories disagree over how the rule should apply to the facts. In either case, however, do not let your analysis become lost in your focus on counter-analysis. Good writing and effective advocacy call for keeping your own explanation and application of the rule at the center of the conversation.

9. *Restate your conclusion.* After you have worked through your explanation of how the rule applies to your client's facts, restate the conclusion. If the analysis has been long or complex and your document will not have a separate "Conclusion" section, summarize the key reasons supporting the conclusion.

§32.3 Common Trouble Spots in Rule Application Sections

The three most common weaknesses in rule application sections are (1) failing to apply the rule as the first half of the paradigm explained it, (2) asserting the

---

[1] In a law office setting, if you realize that facts are missing, it is best to inform the assigning attorney immediately in case the facts can be obtained readily and therefore included in the memo's analysis.

predicted outcome without sufficiently explaining the reasoning that supports the prediction, and (3) failing to realize the diverse possible interpretations of the facts. Understanding these three weaknesses will help you avoid falling victim to them in your own analysis.

We have already discussed in some detail the first common weakness: failing to apply the rule as it was explained. Yet this is such a common difficulty that it merits a reminder. Be sure to complete the rule application section by matching its coverage and approach to the explanation section. Equally important, be sure to revise the rule explanation section to reflect the deepened and sharpened rule understanding you gained by writing out the factual analysis. This double-checking of rule-based and narrative reasoning against each other is an example of why both are critical to good legal writing.

The second common weakness may result from a belief that the application of the rule to the client's facts is so obvious that no explanation of the supporting reasoning is necessary. Nearly always this belief is erroneous. Explaining the supporting reasoning is particularly important because sometimes this process shows the writer that the application might not be as obvious as it first appeared. Even in cases where the application is clear, *some* explanation of the supporting reasoning is necessary.

The third common weakness is failing to realize the diverse possible interpretations of the facts. Sometimes this weakness results from forgetting to think independently and realistically about the facts. Many writers new to law study fall into the trap of assuming the infallibility of the inferences that someone else — like the client or the requesting attorney — has drawn from the facts. Yet, rare is the set of facts that does not support diverse inferences and interpretations.

Another and more insidious cause of this weakness is the difficulty of imagining multiple interpretations simultaneously. Perhaps an analogy will demonstrate how hard this can be. Look at Figure Figure 32.1. You might have seen a graphic like this before. Do you see the old woman in this graphic? Do you see a young woman as well? Your brain can organize the black and white shapes of the graphic into a picture of either, but most of us can only see one at a time. More pointed for our purposes, once your brain has organized the sections to display one figure, it is difficult to find the other figure at all. Imagining diverse interpretations of facts is at least as hard as imagining diverse interpretations of these black and white shapes.

Not "seeing" these diverse interpretations of the facts is the most difficult weakness for a writer to diagnose and cure. If your assignment permits, ask others to help you imagine diverse interpretations of the facts. Present a friend or colleague with a simple chronology or other sanitized version of the facts rather than with your written description of them.[2] Your goal is to learn what story someone else might see in the facts, especially someone who has not first seen the story through your or your client's eyes.

If you must work alone, you must think both critically and creatively about the facts. Try to imagine how the various other parties to the situation would describe it. Imagine how you would describe it if you were representing those

---

[2] Take care not to breach client confidentiality. *See* Model R. Prof. Conduct 1.6 (2007).

Figure 32.1   How Old Is This Woman?

parties. Imagine how the facts might appear to someone who disliked your client and was therefore looking for an interpretation different from your client's position. This task will never be easy, and it will be particularly difficult in your early years of law study and practice. However, each year of law practice will improve your ability to see diverse interpretations of a set of facts. Take the opportunity presented by your first few writing assignments to begin practicing this lawyering skill.

Here is an example of rule application for the Pyle/Gavin issue.

Pyle/Gavin Example — Rule Application Added

I. Did Howard Gavin commit legal malpractice in his representation of Linda Pyle?   **Issue**

Howard Gavin committed legal malpractice in his representation of Linda Pyle because he did not meet the required standard of professional skill and diligence. The subject matter of the representation is common to general

Conclusion plus
facts followed by
rule and citation

practitioners, and the problem could have been prevented with thorough research.

A lawyer has a duty to provide a client with representation that meets or exceeds the standard of professional skill and diligence commonly possessed and exercised by a reasonably prudent lawyer in this jurisdiction. *Jacobson v. Kamerinsky.* [citation] [*See* pp. 313 for the rest of the rule explanation.]

Thesis sentence
stating factual
conclusion

A judge would probably find that a reasonably prudent lawyer in Howard Gavin's situation would have checked the title for easements. Receipt of title is, after all, the heart of the transaction, and carefully checking the title would be critical to evaluating the title the purchaser would receive from the seller.

Thesis sentence
applying Gavin's
particular facts

The duty to check the title carefully would be particularly clear in a situation like Gavin's where the client has asked specifically whether there would be any problem with using the land for a particular purpose. A prudent lawyer would know that the use of real property can be limited either by law (such as by a zoning regulation) or by private agreement (such as an easement or a restrictive covenant recorded against the title). The client's specific question should have flagged the issue for Gavin, making Gavin's error even less excusable than the error in *Jacobson.* In *Jacobson,* the client did not ask a question that should have reminded the lawyer of the possible problem; yet the lawyer's error constituted professional malpractice anyway. [citation]

Reasoning from
factual
comparisons

Thesis sentence
applying points
from rule
explanation

Comparing facts

Applying 2nd point
and comparing
facts

Further, both of the *Jacobson* gauges point toward liability. Representing a party to a real estate transaction probably falls within the group of tasks a general practitioner is familiar with doing. Basic real estate transactions are as common in the general practice of law as filing law suits. Nor was Gavin's omission a mere error in the exercise of professional judgment. The need to look for an easement would have been apparent if Gavin had done adequate *legal* research, and the easement itself would have been apparent if he had done adequate *factual* research. Just as in *Jacobson,* Gavin's error could have been prevented by proper research.

Thesis sentences
dealing with other
facts

Since the standard is not reduced by virtue of facts particular to the lawyer's experience, Gavin's relative inexperience and his lack of real estate expertise will not affect the legal result. Nor will his status in the bar or his usual skill and diligence. However, these facts do add to the equities of his case, especially since a judge in this jurisdiction would probably be aware of them. Although those facts should not change the ultimate result, they probably mean that the judge will not be happy about having to rule against Gavin. The evidence at trial will have to establish the cause of action clearly.

Flagging the
human impact

Pointing out a
necessary
qualification

Finally, this evaluation that Gavin's representation fell below the prudent lawyer standard is based on an assumption that the standard can be judged without expert testimony. Additional research would be necessary to check this assumption. If the standard must be evaluated by reference to expert testimony, it will be necessary to consult with an expert.

Conclusion State-
ment Summary of
most important
points

The claim that Gavin breached the applicable standard of care is strong. The subject matter of the representation is common to general practitioners. The problem could have been prevented with proper research. If Pyle is interested in pursuing the matter further, our next step should be the completion of our research on the need for expert testimony.

§32.4 Evaluating Your Draft

Once you have completed a working draft of both halves of the paradigm, evaluate the draft. If possible, put it away for a day to let your mind clear. Then go through this procedure:

1. *Check the paradigm.* Mark off and label each part of the paradigm. Check to be sure that each part is there and in its proper order. Be sure that rule explanation and rule application are not intermixed.
2. *Evaluate the depth of rule explanation.* Ask yourself how well settled the rule is and how much explanation is necessary to clarify the rule's meaning.
3. *Evaluate the depth of rule application.* Have you written out a complete discussion of how the rule would apply to your client's facts and what inferences a judge or jury might draw from them? Watch particularly for rules that include an element pertaining to someone's state of mind or rules that set out a flexible standard (such as "a reasonable person" or "the best interests of the child"). When such a rule governs your client's issue, you probably will need to do significant factual analysis in the application section.
4. *Evaluate the content and internal organization of rule explanation and rule application.* First, confirm that the rule you explained is the rule you applied. Now, examine each section in smaller chunks. Identify the blocks of text devoted to particular substantive points, using labels in the side margin as do the sample drafts in this chapter and in Chapter 31. Is your organization logical? Does it communicate good ideas clearly?
5. *Check your perspective.* Remember the difference between predicting and persuading. If you are writing a predictive document, maintaining an objective perspective can be difficult. Many writers find themselves slipping into advocating their prediction rather than objectively evaluating it. After you have written your working draft, set it aside and then reread it to be sure you have not begun inadvertently to write as an advocate.

CHAPTER 33

USING CITATIONS TO SUPPORT YOUR ANALYSIS

§33.1 When and Why to Use Citations

In legal writing, as in other writing, you must cite to your sources for both words and ideas. Citation to authority has twin purposes: (1) to provide your reader with the authority that supports your assertions about the law, and (2) to attribute the words and ideas of another author to that author.

Providing your reader with authority to support your assertions about the law is essential to legal analysis and persuasive argument. Your citations should prove that the law is what you say it is and that it means what you say it means.

A citation is also your attribution to another author, recognizing that the ideas (and the words, if you are quoting) came from that author. Careful attributing is important. Because a reader will attribute uncited material to you, a citation is your way of disclaiming credit for the words and ideas you did not create. Therefore, you should cite when you quote and when you paraphrase (that is, when you rephrase the authority's words).

Use Citations

1. When you assert a legal principle.

"Intent is a required element of the Plaintiff's claim. *Peterson v. Taylor*, [citation]."

2. When you refer to or describe the content of an authority.

"In an earlier opinion, the court held that intent was irrelevant. *Crenshaw v. Baldwin*, [citation]."

3. When you quote.

"The court reasoned that 'the state of mind of the defendant had no impact on the extent of the damages suffered.' *Crenshaw v. Baldwin*, [citation]."

---

§33.2 Citation Form

A citation is your representation to your reader that the cited material stands for the proposition for which you cited it. It also allows a reader to find the source and provides the reader with some basic information for gauging the precedential weight the authority carries. Several commercially published citation authorities exist, and some courts have adopted their own citation rules. The two most often used sets of citation rules are the *ALWD* (pronounced "ALL-wid") *Citation Manual*[1] and *The Bluebook: A Uniform System of Citation* ("the *Bluebook*").[2]

§33.3 Matching the Citation to the Text

A writer tells the reader which proposition the citation establishes by the *placement* of the citation.[3] If the citation appears outside the textual sentence, standing alone as a citation sentence, the reader knows that the citation supports all of the material in the preceding sentence, like so:

> To prove a claim for sexual harassment without showing an adverse employment action, a plaintiff must show that the harassment created a "hostile or abusive work environment" and that the plaintiff indicated that the harassment was unwelcome. *Meritor Sav. Bank v. Vinson*, 477 U.S. 57, 66 (1986).

This sentence says two things: that the plaintiff must show a hostile environment and that the plaintiff must show that he or she communicated that the conduct was unwelcome. The placement of the citation to *Meritor* outside the textual sentence tells the reader that *Meritor* establishes both of these points.

However, if *Meritor* established only one of these points, the citation to *Meritor* would go inside the textual sentence and immediately after the proposition it supports. The writer would need to cite to another authority for the other proposition, like so:

> To prove a claim for sexual harassment without showing an adverse employment action, a plaintiff must show that the harassment created a "hostile or abusive work environment," *Meritor Sav. Bank v. Vinson*, 477 U.S. 57, 66 (1986), and that the plaintiff indicated that the harassment was unwelcome [cite to the other case].

A similar situation exists when the writer has authority for one part of the sentence but no authority for the other part of the sentence. In that case, the writer should still take care to place the citation immediately after the proposition it supports, simply leaving the other proposition unsupported, like so:

---

[1] Association of Legal Writing Directors & Darby Dickerson, *ALWD Citation Manual, Fourth Edition* (Aspen Publishers 2010).
[2] *The Bluebook: A Uniform System of Citation.* (Columbia Law Review Assn. et al. eds., 19th ed. 2010).
[3] ALWD R. 43.1; Bluebook R. 1.1.

Though a plaintiff can prove a claim by showing that the harassment created a "hostile or abusive work environment," *Meritor Sav. Bank v. Vinson*, 477 U.S. 57, 66 (1986), Willingham has made no such showing in this case.

Sometimes a writer points out an aspect of an authority and then uses that aspect of the authority to reason her way to another point about that authority. The first point came from the authority but the second point did not; the second point came from the writer's own reasoning process. Once again, the writer should place the citation to the authority immediately after the point that came from the authority rather than after the writer's reasoning process, like so:

The court has allowed recovery on an attractive nuisance claim by a child who came into the defendants' yard to hide from her friends and fell into a swimming pool while there. [The citation to *Newcomb v. Roberts* goes here.] Though *Newcomb* made no mention of the issue, the court's allowance of recovery on these facts shows that recovery no longer requires that the child be drawn by the artificial condition. [The citation to *Newcomb* does *not* go here because *Newcomb* does not say that actual attraction is no longer required.]

CHAPTER 34

DISCUSSING MULTIPLE ISSUES: PUTTING IT ALL TOGETHER

Chapter 29 explained how to use the question(s) you have been asked and the relevant governing rules to create the outline for your analysis. Chapters 31 and 32 explained how to write the analysis of each single issue identified on your outline. This chapter explains how to finish writing the analysis, connecting these single-issue discussions and putting them in the order your reader will prefer. With very little revision, this completed analysis will become the "Discussion" section of your office memo or the "Argument" section of your brief to the court. Here is an overview of an analysis of multiple issues:

The Multi-Issue Paradigm

1. Heading stating your overall conclusion on a legal question
    [An "umbrella section" introducing the subsections to follow.]
    A. Heading stating your conclusion on the first issue
        - Conclusion
        - Rule statement and explanation
        - Rule application
        - Conclusion on this issue
    B. Heading stating your conclusion on the second issue
        - Conclusion
        - Rule statement and explanation
        - Rule application
        - Conclusion on this issue
    [Add discussions of any other issues.]
    Overall conclusion

---

§34.1 Ordering for your Reader

§34.1.1 Accounting for Elements Not at Issue

Recall from Chapter 29 that your outline did not have to cull out the elements not at issue. Now that you have completed your study of the authorities and how they apply to your client's facts, you can finalize the selection of elements requiring discussion. Remove from your draft the headings for any elements needing no discussion, but make a note of them. You will need to explain to your reader why you are not discussing them. §34.2 explains where and how to give your reader this information.

§34.1.2 Selecting an Order for the Remaining Issues

Now that your analysis is complete, you have the information you need to select the order your reader will prefer. The three most common choices for the order of single-issue discussions are (1) important issues, (2) threshold issues, and (3) familiar order.

1. Important Issues. The important-issues approach places subheadings in the order of importance to the reader and to the analysis.[1] An issue can be important because it is likely to be dispositive. For instance, any burglary element the state cannot prove would be dispositive as the state must prove all elements to win a conviction. The issues most likely to be dispositive usually should be discussed first.

A subissue can be important even if it would not be dispositive alone. For instance, in a factors test, usually no one factor is dispositive; yet the particular circumstances of a case can make some factors more important to the analysis than others. A child custody dispute is a good example. The court will consider many factors in deciding custody. Rarely will one factor be dispositive alone, but several might be especially important. All other things being equal, discuss these first.

Organizing according to importance is an effective tool to help your reader manage a number of issues or subissues. The most important issues are placed where the reader's attention is greatest. The time a busy reader must invest is minimized. The reader can choose how far into the analysis to read and with what degree of care. It assures the reader that the writer's analysis is complete enough to identify the most important issues.

2. Threshold Issues. A threshold issue is one that determines the direction of the analysis from that point on. For instance, assume that a rule of law tells you that if a business is a lending institution, it may not do certain things. The issue of whether your client is a lending institution within the meaning of that rule determines the direction of the analysis from that point on. If your client is *not* a

---

[1] The importance to the reader and the importance to the analysis should be the same unless the writer and the reader have differing views of the analysis. If the writer suspects a difference, the writer should either (1) use the introductory paragraphs to convert the reader to the writer's view of the analysis or (2) order the subpoints by their importance to the *reader's* analysis.

lending institution, the rule prohibiting certain conduct does not apply to your client, and the analysis can move on to any other rules that might apply to your client. But if your client *is* a lending institution, the rule does apply, and the analysis must continue to determine whether your client's proposed conduct falls within the category of conduct prohibited by the rule. Thus, the issue of whether your client is a lending institution is a threshold issue.

When you are analyzing a legal question that includes a threshold issue, consider placing the threshold issue first. The reader probably will expect the analysis to begin with the threshold issue. Also, if you conclude that the threshold step in the analysis is not met, the reader need not devote as much attention to later steps.

Occasionally, however, you might be working with a rule where the analysis of the threshold issue is complex and your answer to a remaining issue makes the complex analysis of the threshold issue unnecessary. For instance, perhaps the issue of whether your client is a lending institution — and therefore whether the statute would apply to your client at all — is a close and complex question. However, even if the statute applies to your client, the statute rather clearly would not prohibit your client's proposed conduct. If this second conclusion is relatively clear and easily explained, your reader might prefer that you organize by importance. Simply explain your organizational choice in the introductory paragraphs. Your reader will appreciate your organizational choice if she understands your reasons.

3. Familiar Order. Many rules of law are familiar to law-trained readers, and the elements of those rules are often listed in a certain familiar order. Often the familiar order is the order the rule uses. Common law burglary is a good example. The definition of burglary is traditionally stated as "the breaking and entering of the dwelling house of another in the nighttime with the intent to commit a felony therein." On a burglary issue, a law-trained reader will be accustomed to thinking of the elements in the order recited in that sentence.

Even if no rule establishes a familiar order of elements, the custom of ordering issues chronologically might establish a familiar order. If the sub-issues pertain to events occurring in a chronology, a law-trained reader probably will expect to analyze the issues in that order. For instance, contracts issues are often ordered by the chronology of events constituting the formation and performance of the contract: offer, acceptance, modification, and performance. Unless the reader's other needs require a different choice, order your discussion in the way the reader is expecting.

§34.2 Umbrella Sections

All the subsections are in place now, but you need introductions so your reader will understand what will follow and why. We will call these introductions "umbrella sections." Umbrella sections are appropriate wherever the analysis is broken down into subsections. Take a moment to read an example of an umbrella section between "I" and "A" in Chapter 39 (Sample Office Memorandum).

The umbrella section can serve four main functions. First, it provides a place to *state the governing rule(s)* so the reader has a road map of the analysis to follow. If you use it for this purpose, provide a citation to the main authority establishing the rule, and include any other information important to how the rule functions. For instance, one party will carry the burden of proof. The rule might require a higher-than-normal level of proof (for example, clear and convincing).[2] Some rules come with a presumption of one variety or another.[3] Some come with policy "leanings" (for instance, case law stating that doubts are to be resolved in favor of the criminal defendant). The procedural posture of a case, such as a motion for summary judgment, a motion to dismiss, or an appeal from a jury verdict, might impose a particular standard more favorable to one party. A canon of statutory construction might call for a strict reading of a particular kind of statute. If the authorities have mentioned any such information, you can include it here.

Second, an umbrella section can *identify elements not at issue.* For each undisputed element, ask yourself whether your conclusion will be readily apparent to your reader or whether the reader will require some (although perhaps simple) analysis to be satisfied on the point. Make this decision based on your assessment of (1) your reader's existing knowledge of the law, (2) the degree of your reader's faith in you as a legal thinker and writer, and (3) your reader's need for certainty. Make these assessments conservatively. If you are in doubt, err on the side of treating an issue as disputed.

If you conclude that an issue is not genuinely disputed, say so. And if your reasons might not be obvious to your reader, provide a cursory explanation of the basis for your conclusion — just enough to reassure the reader that your reasons for this conclusion are consistent with the reader's understanding.

Third, the umbrella section *identifies the remaining issues and explains the order in which you will address them.* Explaining your choice of structures is particularly important if your structure is different from the one the reader expects.

Finally, if necessary to prevent confusion, *identify any related legal issues not covered by the analysis.* If a reader might assume that your analysis includes all relevant legal issues pertaining to the question but it does not, be sure to say so. For example, the requesting attorney might have asked you to analyze claims under only one statute, but claims might exist under other statutes as well. In such a

---

[2] The most common standard for a burden of proof in a civil case is proof by the preponderance of the evidence. That means that the party bearing the burden need only present stronger evidence than that of the opposing party to win. However, in a criminal trial, the prosecution must meet a higher standard of proof—proof beyond a reasonable doubt. In some circumstances, a party might be required to prove certain facts by a higher standard than a mere preponderance, but not beyond a reasonable doubt. Courts often refer to this intermediate standard as "clear and convincing evidence."

[3] In the determination of most legal and factual issues, the decision-maker starts from a neutral posture. However sometimes, as a matter of policy, the law will impose a "presumption" supporting a certain result. For instance, the law imposes a presumption that service of process in a judicial proceeding has been accomplished lawfully. In such a case, the decision-maker presumes the truth of the presumption until sufficient evidence to the contrary has been offered.

case, clarify that your memo covers only possible claims under the identified statute. Your reader will appreciate this clarity, and you will be protected from later misunderstandings.

Often the umbrella section is fairly simple. For instance, in the burglary example, the umbrella section would state the rule defining burglary and cite to the statute establishing it. One item of rule explanation applies to all elements: the burden of proof. If several of the elements are not disputed, the umbrella section would explain their omission and explain organizational decisions. The umbrella section need contain nothing else. It would look like this:

---

1. Jamison's actions probably do not establish the elements of burglary.

To obtain a burglary conviction, the state must prove that Jamison's conduct constituted a breaking and entering of the dwelling house of another in the nighttime with the intent to commit a felony therein. [citation] The state must prove each of these elements beyond a reasonable doubt. [citation] The only elements in dispute are the nighttime element and the intent element. Since the nighttime element is most likely to be dispository, this memo discusses it first.

A. Jamison probably did not enter the building in the nighttime.
   - Conclusion
   - Rule & rule explanation
   - Rule application
   - Conclusion on nighttime element
B. The state probably can prove that Jamison intended to commit a felony inside the dwelling.
   - Conclusion
   - Rule & rule explanation
   - Rule application
   - Conclusion on intent element

Here is an umbrella section for a discussion governed by several separate rules.

---

1. The Foster car sale probably included a warranty.

In [name of jurisdiction], warranties governing U.C.C. transactions are set out in [citation]. Non-U.C.C. warranties are set out in [citation]. Because these warranty provisions differ in critical ways, the first question this memo will discuss is whether U.C.C. warranties would apply to the Foster transaction.

The first section concludes that U.C.C. warranties probably will govern the Foster transaction, so the second section discusses the application of those provisions to that transaction. However, because the application of U.C.C. warranties is a close question, the final section of the memo

> discusses the possible application of non-U.C.C. warranties to that transaction.

Notice that this umbrella section does not attempt to state the warranty rules. Both rules are complex, and each will be the subject of its own subsection. What the reader needs in this umbrella section is a road map of the organization to follow. With this map, the reader will know exactly where to look for the rule statements.

An effective umbrella section provides the reader with the context for the analysis, and it clears away the underbrush — the issues that the reader need not consider. It provides a road map for the remaining issues and explains the organizational choice to follow. In other words, the introduction meets the reader where she is, deals with her immediate needs, and leads her to the starting point of the analysis.

§34.3 The Conclusion

If the format of your document permits, write a conclusion pulling together the results of each separate analysis and setting out the ultimate conclusion on the question presented. Include a summary of the primary reasons for the overall conclusion. Chapter 36 explains the Conclusion section of an office memo.

§34.4 Editing Subsection Lengths

Now that you have your organization in place, check the length and complexity of each of the subsections. If several subsections are short, you might choose to combine them. Remove the original subheadings, leaving the material under one heading that covers it all. Within that new and larger section, use clear transitional phrases or sentences to mark the beginning and end of your discussions of each subissue. Do not be too hasty to obscure the rule's structure like this, however. Law-trained readers generally are less troubled by short sections than by confusion about rule structure.

If a subsection strikes you as particularly long and complex, consider further subdivisions with headings. These subdivisions can reflect different lines of authority, different tests set out in case law, rule explanation versus rule application, or any other points of division that would be helpful to the reader. For length, use three pages as a rough outside limit. Headings and subheadings will constitute your reader's road map. Most busy readers want to orient themselves in the text at least every three pages or so. Also remember that reader attention wanes between subheadings and can be renewed with a new subheading.

Finally, check your headings and subheadings to be sure they communicate your conclusions. Headings are important to readers because they make the large-scale organization visible at a glance. They mark the reader's progress through the analysis, so the reader always knows where she has been and where she is headed. They mark the spots where the reader might choose to invest a bit more attention. They assist the reader in evaluating the analysis itself, and through it the writer's ability and credibility. They enable the reader to consider preliminary issues with the assurance that anticipated sections are coming. They allow busy readers to jump immediately to the particular sections they want to review.

§34.5 Variations of the Multi-Issue Paradigm

Like the paradigm for a single-issue analysis described in Chapters 31 and 32, the multi-issue paradigm provides a format you can adapt to fit each assignment. The most common adaptation of the paradigm is stating and explaining the rules for *all* elements before applying any of them to the facts. An outline for such a discussion would look like this:

I. Conclusion Statement
        [Umbrella section]
    A. Rule statements and explanations
        1. First element
        2. Second element
    B. Rule applications
        1. First element
        2. Second element
        Conclusion

In some situations, you can explain all elements before applying any of them, as this outline does. The rules and rule explanations for each element may be particularly interrelated in the authorities. The distinctions among them might be minor, and separating the rule explanation sections might require you to repeat material. If the courts seem to take a more unified view of the elements, separating the rule explanation sections could even sacrifice some precision in the analysis. If your careful evaluation of the rule convinces you that these descriptions apply to your assignment, you can opt for this variation of the multi-issue paradigm. Remember, though, that the key virtue of the basic paradigm is that its structure forces you to think precisely about each element. Do not discard the advantages of that structure lightly.

CHAPTER 35

DEEPENING YOUR ANALYSIS

Now that you have an overview of the basic structure and content of rule explanation and application, we will explore some ways to deepen and strengthen your analysis.

§35.1 Using Policies and Principles in Rule Explanation

The main forms of legal reasoning used in rule explanation and their common uses are:

Rule-Based	Clarifying the precise language, structure, and meaning of the rule
Policy-Based	Identifying underlying rationales intended to encourage desirable results for the society at large and affecting either the rule's original purpose or the ways the rule might be interpreted now
Principle-Based	Identifying any principles that the rule is intended to serve or that might constrain the rule's interpretation
Custom-Based	Identifying social norms or business customs that the rule formalizes and enforces

Once you have formulated the rule, supported your formulation with citations to authority, and shown how the courts have applied the rule in the past, you have given the basic explanation of the rule. But you should also explain the purpose of the rule to understand and eventually apply the rule with some degree of confidence. In most cases, policy and principle-based reasoning will be your most valuable tools in explaining the rule's purpose. Does the rule embody a broad principle valued by our society, or might its interpretation and application be constrained by such a principle? What did the creator of the rule, be it a legislature or a court, intend to accomplish? To answer these questions, you need policy and principle-based reasoning.

Policies and principles cover many kinds of concerns. Professor Ellie Margolis has identified four common categories:[1]

Policies affecting judicial administration pertain to the practical administration of the rule by the courts.[2] For example, a court's reasons for choosing a flexible factors test might include the ability to fashion a particularized fair result in each future circumstance. The choice of a more rigid rule, however, might be designed partly to maximize people's ability to predict legal outcomes and to bring their conduct into line with that prediction, thus reducing the need for litigation.[3]

Normative policies promote shared societal values. These policies can include moral considerations such as the promotion of honesty and fair dealing, social considerations such as the promotion of stability within families, and corrective justice considerations such as the placement of liability on the most culpable party.[4]

Institutional competence policies recognize the value of relying on the decision-maker who is most capable of resolving the dispute wisely.[5] Perhaps the rule is designed to encourage an appellate court to defer to the trial court because the trial judge is able to see the witnesses and evaluate their demeanor. Perhaps the rule relies on the expertise of an administrative agency staffed by presumably neutral experts in a complex field. Perhaps the rule defers to the legislature because the legislative process allows for more public input and accountability.

Economic policy rationales seek to maximize efficient resource allocation, keep economic costs in line with resulting benefits, and maintain a free market.[6] Economic rationales include such considerations as placing the liability on the party most able to obtain insurance for such losses. They also can include larger scale economic considerations such as balancing the desire to refrain from government interference against the need for protection against practices that, in the long term, would reduce desirable competition.

As we saw in Chapter 27, these policies and principles can help you predict how a court might apply the rule to a particular set of facts, especially in a close case. Most assuredly, policy and principle-based rationales can help you persuade a court to apply the rule in your client's favor. A court will try to apply the rule in

---

[1] Ellie Margolis, Closing the Floodgates: Making Persuasive Policy Arguments in Appellate Briefs, 62 Montana L. Rev. 59 (2001)

[2] Margolis at p. 72.

[3] See also Carol M. Rose, Crystals and Mud in Property Law, 40 Stanford L. Rev. 577 (1988).

[4] Margolis at p. 74. This category is closely related to principle-based reasoning as described in Chapter 27.

[5] Margolis at p. 77.

[6] Margolis at pp. 78-79.

a way that advances the policies and principles the rule is designed to advance. Conversely, the court will try to avoid applying the rule in a way that impedes those policies and principles.

The first and best place to look for policy and principle-based rationales is in the authorities themselves. Often a statute or its legislative history will contain a statement of the purposes for the legislation. Often courts will articulate the rationales their rulings are designed to address. Secondary sources like treatises and law review articles are instructive as well. And you can use your own common sense. What are the most likely goals the legislature or the courts had in mind when they were developing the rule? What long-term results would follow if courts ruled one way rather than the other on your issue? What advantages would be produced? What dangers? To jumpstart your thinking, here are examples of some common policy rationales:

- As between two parties, the law should place the risk of liability on the party most able to prevent a loss.
- As between two parties, the law should place the risk on the party who already bears similar risks and therefore whose legal and practical situation will be least affected by the risk.
- Where the bargaining positions of certain kinds of parties are grossly disparate, the governing rule should protect the weaker party.
- The law should not impose a liability that might limit the ability of people to engage in a particular business in the future, especially if the business provides a socially desirable service.
- The rule should place the burden of proof on the party with the easiest access to the evidence.
- The governing rule should be workable in light of the practical realities of day-to-day life. It should incorporate a realistic view of human psychology and business custom.
- The governing rule should not create a legal standard that is easily subverted by knowledgeable and crafty individuals and businesses. Stability in the law is desirable. The law should not change unless the need for the change is clear.
- The realities of modern life have changed significantly (explain how). The law must be willing and able to change and adapt to changing circumstances.
- The law should resist the temptation to rush to the rescue when a refusal to intervene will encourage people to be diligent and responsible in handling their economic and legal affairs.
- The rule should not create additional costs for a person or an industry unless the harm to be prevented justifies the imposition of those costs.
- The governing rule should not add impediments to the free transfer of assets and the ease of doing business.
- The governing rule should be flexible enough to allow future courts to achieve a fair result in individual future circumstances.

- The governing rule should be concrete enough to insure that future adjudications will be based on objective criteria rather than on prejudices of the decision-maker.
- It is appropriate for the law to require a higher standard of conduct from a commercial party than from an individual not engaged in a particular business.
- The court should adopt a rule that is as consistent with established custom as possible since customs become established because, over time, people have discovered that they work well.

§35.2 Using Analogical Reasoning in Rule Application

In the rule application section, the focus shifts to your client's facts. Each of the forms of reasoning described in Chapter 27 can be brought into play here. You need not use all forms of reasoning in all cases, but you should not neglect to consider how each of them might serve your purpose. The structure, the specific words, and the form of the rule must be related to the situation at hand (rule-based reasoning). But the law is more than words, so you should look behind the words to consider the principles or social policies the rule serves. Consider how those principles and policies could bear on your client's story (policy and principle-based reasoning). Look for any customs, practices, or normal behavior of people in your client's situation, and consider that most rules of law probably intend to codify normative conduct, not prohibit it (custom-based reasoning). Look also for the narrative themes of your client's story, particularly those that might affect the way the rule should be applied (narrative).

All of these forms of reasoning can be helpful in the rule application section, but analogical reasoning is one of the most important. It can provide the critical connection between your client's facts and the way the rule has been interpreted in prior cases. Chapters 27 and 32 introduced analogical reasoning; now we explore it in greater depth. Analogical reasoning compares two things. A lawyer uses analogical reasoning when she compares the facts of a prior case with her client's facts, pointing out similarities that can help her predict or advocate a similar result. This process is sometimes called *analogizing* cases. A lawyer can also compare two cases to find differences that might call for a different result. This process is called *distinguishing* cases.

§35.2.1 Deciding Which Similarities and Differences are Significant

The first step in mastering the skill of analogizing and distinguishing cases is to understand what kinds of similarities and differences could be legally significant. If you have a sense of how you might use a similarity or difference, you will have a better idea of what you are looking for. A similarity or difference is legally significant if it relates to

- a term in the governing rule of law, or
- a policy or principle implicated by the rule or its application in this case.

Comparisons relating to a key term of the governing rule are the most important. The governing rule is the starting point for all legal analysis. No matter how compelling a party's case, the judge must be able to reconcile the result with the governing rule. If a factual similarity or difference would help a court decide how the rule might apply to that party's situation, the comparison will be important.

For example, in most jurisdictions, a seller of real property who knows or should know of material defects in the property must disclose those defects to a potential buyer. Notice that this rule has two elements:

A seller must disclose if:

1. the seller knows or should know of the defect, and
2. the defect is material.

Therefore, factual similarities or differences will be most important if they help the judge decide either of these two elements — what kind of "knowledge" is enough to raise the duty and how to gauge whether a defect is "material."

Similarities or differences that do not relate directly to an element of the rule but do relate to the purpose or policy behind the rule can be important as well. If applying the governing rule in your client's case would not serve the policies the rule was meant to further, a court might be willing to create an outright exception for situations like that of your client.

§35.2.2 Choosing a Format for your Case Comparison

Now that you have identified the comparisons you want to make, you need only decide how much depth you need. Professor Michael Smith has identified two formats for case comparisons: the short form and the long form.[7] Use the long form for important comparisons, for complicated comparisons, or for multiple points of comparison. In all other circumstances, you can use the short form. In either format, however, be sure to give direct, fact-to-fact comparisons. Notice how the examples below make those direct factual comparisons.

§35.2.2.1 Short-Form Case Comparison

Begin with a thesis sentence stating the point of the comparison, and give a factual overview of the cited case, unless your reader is already familiar with its facts. Next state the specific facts that will form the basis of your factual

---

[7] Michael R. Smith, 1992-1994 Class Handouts, "Techniques for Using Case Authority to Discuss 'Points' in a Memo," on file with the author.

comparison, and state the result reached in the cited case. Then use a thesis sentence to state the nature of the similarities or differences you are pointing out. Identify the specific facts from your client's situation to which you are comparing the cited case, and use that comparison to explain why the result in your client's situation should or should not be the same. Here are two examples of a short-form case comparison, one showing differences and the other showing similarities:

Differences

Buckley's representation that she was old enough to buy a car is significantly different from the representations in *Carney*. There, a minor entered into a contract to purchase a car. The minor affirmatively stated to the sales agent that he was twenty-two, and the agent recorded that information on the loan application, which the minor then signed. The court affirmed the holding that the minor had fraudulently misrepresented his age and was therefore estopped from disaffirming the contract. *Id.* at 807–808.

Buckley, however, never stated her age at all. Further, her answer, taken to mean what she intended it to mean, was not even false. The sales agent had asked her whether she was old enough to buy a car. Buckley misunderstood the question, thinking the agent was asking whether she was old enough to drive. She truthfully answered the question she thought the agent was asking. She said "yes," meaning that she was old enough to have a driver's license. Thus Buckley's facts do not constitute misrepresentations according to the *Carney* standard.

Similarities

Buckley's statement is much closer to the situation in *Woodall*, in which the minor made the representation "unknowingly." In *Woodall*, the minor did not realize that he was making a representation of majority because he did not read the form contract he was signing. *Id.* at 97. Similarly, Buckley did not realize that she might be making a representation of majority because she misunderstood the agent's question. In both cases, the requisite intent to deceive is absent. Therefore, the result in Buckley's situation should be the same as the result in *Woodall* — an order permitting disaffirmance.

§35.2.2.2 Long-Form Case Comparison

The long-form case comparison uses an extensive in-text discussion of the case to give the reader more information about the cited case and about the relevant comparisons. Here is an example of a long-form case comparison[8] that demonstrates many factual similarities and also a factual difference:

Fahmie v. Wulster, 408 A.2d 789 (1979), provides the closest analogy to Frimberger's situation. In *Fahmie*, a corporation that originally owned a parcel of property requested permission from the Bureau of Water to place a nine-foot diameter culvert on the property to enclose a stream. The Bureau required instead that a

---

[8] Adapted from *Frimberger v. Anzellotti*, 594 A.2d 1029 (1991).

sixteen-foot diameter culvert should be installed. The corporation, however, went ahead with its original plan and installed the nine-foot culvert.

The property was later conveyed to Wulster, the CEO of the corporation, who had no knowledge of the installation of the nine-foot culvert. Nine years later, Wulster conveyed the property, by warranty deed, to Fahmie.

In anticipation of the subsequent resale of the property, Fahmie made application to the Economic Development Commission to make additional improvements to the stream and its banks. It was then that the inadequate nine-foot culvert was discovered, and the plaintiff was required to replace it with a sixteen-foot diameter pipe.

Fahmie sued Wulster for the cost to correct the violation, claiming a breach of the deed's warranty against encumbrances. The New Jersey Supreme Court concluded that a claim for breach of a covenant against encumbrances cannot be predicated on the necessity to repair or alter the property to conform with land use regulations.

Similarities

The *Fahmie* case is remarkably similar to Frimberger's situation. Like the plaintiff in *Fahmie*, Frimberger is also alleging a breach of the covenant against encumbrances based on the necessity of bringing the property into compliance with a state environmental land use regulation. Just as in *Fahmie*, neither the current owner nor his immediate predecessor knew of the violation of the regulation. In both cases, the violation was created by a remote owner. In both cases, this remote owner knew or should have known that he was creating a violation of the regulation. In neither case did the current owner's deed contain an exception for violations of land use statutes. In both cases, the current owner discovered the violation upon filing an application with the relevant regulatory agency to make further improvements to the property.

Difference

The only relevant difference between the two situations results in an even weaker case for Frimberger. In *Fahmie*, the state agency actually required the plaintiff to replace the inadequate culvert with the larger culvert, thus causing the plaintiff significant expense. In Frimberger's situation, however, the state agency has taken no action to require abatement of the violation. As a matter of fact, the agency has invited Frimberger to apply for an exception to the relevant requirement, a procedure which Frimberger has thus far declined to pursue. Therefore, it is even less likely that Frimberger's facts establish a breach of the covenant than did the facts in *Fahmie*.

This example has three key characteristics: Notice how specific is the discussion of the facts from each case. Notice how many factual similarities and differences are identified (find them and count them). And notice how the theses sentences provide the structure and explain the points of the comparisons they introduce. (Find the theses sentences and underline them.) Emulate these three characteristics in your own case comparisons.

§35.3 Using Factual Inferences in Rule Application

As we saw in Chapter 27, inferential reasoning (abduction) does not provide irrefutable evidence of a conclusion, but it can show that a particular conclusion is consistent with the provable facts. Better yet, it can show that this conclusion is more likely than any other. In Chapter 27 we used this example: Assume that a patient had normal blood pressure during all prior phases of treatment and then the doctor changed one of the patient's medications. Immediately after taking the first dose, the patient developed high blood pressure. No other changes in treatment or lifestyle occurred. One could infer from this set of facts that the new medication caused the high blood pressure.

Inferential reasoning (drawing factual inferences) is important in analyzing many legal issues. It is especially important when the legal rule calls for a conclusion that cannot be directly observed — questions like causation (as in our prior example), knowledge (whether a person was aware of a certain fact or situation), or motive or intent (whether a person intended to cause a certain result). Many rule application sections deal with such legal questions that cannot be answered definitively. Without an undisputed answer, we must rely on inferences.

For much of this book, we have been studying the meaning of "legal analysis" and we have seen a recurring theme: We cannot simply state a conclusion and expect a reader to be satisfied. Merely "telling" the reader the answer is not enough. We must both "show" and "tell." Nowhere is this more true than in the rule application section, where many new legal writers are tempted to state the rule and then simply assert that it is or is not met by the client's facts. Inferential reasoning can be the vital link between the rule and the conclusion.

You might think that the application is obvious and that there is no need to talk about the facts. Talk about them anyway. Explain to the reader exactly why the test is or is not met. The facts will not be as obvious to the reader as they seem to you. Also, as you write out why the facts lead to a certain result, you will think of other reasons that had not occurred to you before, and you might even notice some other facts that call your conclusion into question.

For inferential reasoning, your primary goal is to bolster your conclusion by showing how a particular cluster of facts is consistent with the conclusion you are asserting. If possible, you want to do even more. You want to challenge other possible conclusions by showing that the facts are not consistent with other conclusions. You might even be able to point out missing facts — facts that one would expect to see if the other conclusion were true.

In our blood pressure example, for instance, we are showing that the new medication was the only change relevant to blood pressure and that the high blood pressure occurred immediately after that change. If the change had been caused by something else, we would expect to see facts consistent with that other cause, such as the gradual development of the problem over time, or a sudden increase in salt, a sudden decrease in exercise, or a sudden new anxiety-producing situation in the client's life. If those facts are *not* present, you can draw inferences from their very absence.

To notice the factual inferences you can draw, your imagination is your best friend. If the medication caused the high blood pressure, what facts would you imagine in that scenario? Do the client's facts match your imagination? Do the same for competing conclusions. If the cause were age, nutrition, lack of exercise, or situational anxiety, what facts would you imagine? Are those facts present? Then write out your thought processes, so your reader can see exactly why you think that the facts do or do not establish a certain factual conclusion.

PREDICTIVE LEGAL WRITING: THE LAW OFFICE MEMO

CHAPTER 36

WRITING AN OFFICE MEMO

§36.1 The Function of an Office Memo

An office memo is an internal working document of a law firm or other office. It is not designed for outside readers, although clients and others might receive a copy if the need arises. The function of an office memo is to answer a legal question, usually for a particular client in a particular situation. Often, it will be the primary basis for making a decision with both legal and nonlegal consequences. Also, the firm might have a "form file" in which it keeps, for future use, office memos dealing with particular legal questions. Therefore, your document could have a long life, impact many clients, and create impressions about you in the minds of many future readers.

When you write an office memo, your role is predictive rather than persuasive. You must try to take an objective view of the question you are asked. The client and the requesting attorney need an accurate understanding of the situation. Learning bad news later could be costly for the client, for the firm, and for you. Making an accurate prediction, then, is the function of an office memo.

§36.2 An Overview of the Memo Format

The format of a memo is designed to fit its function and its reader's needs. Because a memo is an internal document, law firms are likely to have a preferred memo format. The firm's preferred format may use various words for the section titles, it may place the sections in an order different from that described here, or it may include other sections. If your reader (your teacher or law firm) has a particular format preference, use it. If not, you can use the standard memo format this text describes. Variations in format are much less important than the accuracy and thoroughness of the analysis. The components of a standard office memo are

1. Heading
2. Question Presented
3. Brief Answer

4.   Fact Statement
5.   Discussion
6.   Conclusion (when appropriate)

Look at the sample memo in Chapter 39 to locate and review each component.

Heading. The function of the heading is to identify the requesting attorney, the writer, the date, the client, and the particular legal matter.

Question Presented. The Question Presented identifies the question(s) you have been asked to analyze. It allows your reader to confirm that you have understood the question(s). It also might remind a busy reader of the question(s) he or she asked you to analyze.

Brief Answer. The Brief Answer provides your answer quickly and up front. The reader then can decide how much attention to invest in the explanation that follows.

Fact Statement. This section sets out the facts on which your answer is based. You probably obtained the facts from your reader (the requesting attorney) in the first place, but your memo must repeat them. Your reader will want to be sure you have not misunderstood any important facts. Also, your reader, who has been busy working on other cases, might need a review of the facts, and other attorneys working on this case or future cases might need access to your analysis. Finally, reading your fact statement in conjunction with your legal analysis could cause your reader to realize that she has neglected to give you a critical fact.

As the writer, you have an interest in reciting the facts as well. Your legal analysis will be based on the facts as you understand them. If the facts were to change, the result might change. If you memorialize the facts you have been given — the facts on which your answer is based — you insure that your work will be evaluated with reference to those facts. No future reader will think you had access to other, different facts and therefore expect you to have reached a different answer.

Discussion. The Discussion section explains to your reader the analysis that led to your answer. Chapters 29-35 explained how to write this section.

Conclusion. You may choose to end with a Conclusion section, a summary of the main points of your analysis. A Conclusion section can be helpful in two ways. First, if the analysis has been complex, a Conclusion section can tie together and summarize the Discussion section. Sometimes, this summary can add a clarity that the Discussion alone might not be able to achieve. Also, a Conclusion can increase your reader's options for deciding how much attention to invest in understanding the details of your analysis. A Conclusion would be a summary with more detail than the Brief Answer but not as much as the Discussion. Therefore a law-trained reader could read your Brief Answer first, then proceed to your Conclusion for somewhat more depth, and finally read your Discussion for even more depth. After reading each section, your reader can decide how far and how deeply to read on.

§36.3 Drafting the Heading

Draft a heading in the format of standard business interoffice communications:

TO: [Name of requesting attorney]
FROM: [Your name]
DATE: [Date]
RE: [Include client's name, the file number, the particular legal matter, and a phrase identifying the particular issue.]

The date is important to both you and your readers. Your readers need the date because the law is subject to change and because your readers can refer to your memo months or even years later. The memo's date will tell them whether and for what period of time the analysis in your memo must be updated. You need the date because you want your work to be evaluated on the basis of the law to which you had access, not later developments you could not have known.

The "Re" section should identify the client and the file number, both for your current reader and so the memo can be returned in case it is later separated from the file. This section also should identify both the legal matter you are working on and the particular issue you have been asked to analyze. Identify the legal matter because your firm might be handling a number of matters for this particular client and your reader will want to know at a glance which of those matters your memo concerns. Identify the issue because this legal matter might raise many issues that will be the subjects of office memos. Your reader will want to know at a glance which issue your memo analyzes.

Here is an example of a heading:

TO: Ramon Caldez
FROM: Marcia Willingham
DATE: March 17, 2003
RE: Sharon Watson (file #96-24795); covenant-not-to-compete against Carrolton; enforceability of the covenant.

---

§36.4 Drafting the Question Presented

The Question Presented, sometimes called the "Issue," states the question(s) you have been asked to analyze. If you have been asked only to research the state of the governing law on a particular question, without reference to a particular client, the Question Presented simply states the legal question:

> Under what circumstances does Iowa law allow recovery on a claim for the wrongful death of a fetus?

If you have been asked to apply a rule to a set of facts and predict a result — the more common scenario — drafting a readable Question Presented can be more of a challenge. The Question Presented should include both the question and the most important facts, and perhaps the governing rule as well. Here are three format options.

Format Option 1

Organize the content of the Question Presented in two sections: a statement of the *legal* question and a concise statement of the major relevant fact(s).

Can ... [state the legal question] ... when ... [state the major facts]?

This format does not state the rule of law as part of the Question. Here is an example:

> Can Carrolton enforce the Watson covenant-not-to-compete when the covenant prohibits Watson from making sales contacts for three years and applies to the three counties closest to Carrolton's headquarters?

Common verbs for beginning a Question Presented in this format are: "Can ... ?" "Did ... ?" "Was ... ?" "May ... ?" and "Is ... ?" Common transitions into the factual description are: "when ..." and "where ...."

Format Option 2

An even simpler version of a Question Presented is the format beginning with "whether" and constituting a clause rather than a complete sentence. This format still begins with the legal question and ends with the significant facts:

> Whether Carrolton can enforce the Watson covenant-not-to-compete when the covenant prohibits Watson from making sales contacts for three years and applies to the three counties closest to Carrolton's headquarters.

When the Question Presented uses the "whether" format, the clause can be followed by a period and treated as a complete sentence although it is not.

Format Option 3

A third format option is the "under/does/when" format. This format usually results in the longest and most complex Question Presented, although it allows for a shorter Brief Answer (the succeeding section). The Question Presented is longer and the Brief Answer shorter because this format puts the statement of the law in the Question rather than in the Answer. Here is an example:

> Under the Georgia common law rule that allows covenants-not-to-compete only when the area restrained, the activities restrained, and the duration of the restraint are reasonable, can a covenant-not-to-compete be enforced when the covenant prohibits the covenantor from making sales contacts for three years, and applies to the three counties closest to the headquarters of the covenant's beneficiary?

The middle verb can vary, using the same common verbs identified above: "can," "did," "was," "may," or "is."

Format Option 4

The factual descriptions of any of these formats can be expanded to include the key facts on both sides of the question. Because a memo's analysis should be as objective as possible, an explicitly balanced description of the key facts can be helpful both to your reader and to you. It gives the reader a quick overview of the most important facts on both sides of the question, and it can remind you to recognize what is compelling about each side's arguments. This format is particularly appropriate when each side would want to emphasize different facts rather than simply construct legal arguments about the same facts. For instance, assume that the question is whether an airline passenger attempted to intimidate a flight crew member. Here is an example of a Question Presented that identifies key facts on both sides of the question:

> Under ___, did Mitchell Sheffield attempt to intimidate the flight crew when he left his seat, approached the door to the control cabin, and shouted at the co-pilot but never articulated any threat or attempted any violent act?

Notice that the key facts tending to show intimidation are grouped together, followed by the key contrasting facts. This structure provides an immediate overview of the factual situation. It also prompts the writer to recognize the factual arguments on both sides.

Use the format your teacher or requesting attorney prefers. If you can identify no preference, consider using the first format, as it results in a simpler, more understandable sentence and because locating the governing rule is usually part of the question you are asked to answer.

Generic Versus Specific References. No matter which format you choose, you will need to decide whether to use a general or a specific Question Presented. For example, Format Options 1 and 2 above refer specifically to Watson and Carrolton, whereas Format Option 3 does not. Option 3 is phrased as a generic legal question without direct reference to Watson or Carrolton. Here is an example of a generic Question Presented drafted in Format Option 1:

> Can a covenant-not-to-compete be enforced where the covenant prohibits the covenantor from making sales contacts for three years and applies to the three counties closest to the headquarters of the covenant's beneficiary?

You will find proponents of both the generic and the specific Question Presented. The specific Question Presented directly states the question the requesting attorney wants to know. The senior attorney who requested the memo is not asking an academic legal question; rather he wants to know the fate of a particular client — Sharon Watson. Although this memo might someday be placed in the firm's memo file and be examined by a future reader for purposes of another case, the primary function of this memo is to answer a question about the *present* client.

The abstract version of the Question Presented refers to the parties involved by characterizing them rather than by naming them. When the requesting attorney reads this characterization, he probably will have to stop as he reads it to substitute in his mind the names of the parties in place of the characterizations. He also will have to ask himself whether the characterizations accurately refer to the parties in this particular case because if they do not, then the answer set out in the memo might not apply to these parties. But the question of whether the law set out in the memo applies to these parties is part of what the senior attorney wants *you* to analyze *for* her.

Finally, as a practical matter, a Question Presented that uses the parties' names rather than characterizations of the parties generally uses fewer words and is more easily readable. Notice how this is true for the examples above. Because some Questions Presented must include a great deal of information, finding ways to reduce the number of words and simplify the sentence structure can be helpful.

On the other hand, a busy attorney with a heavy caseload might not remember the names of the parties as easily as the characterizations (the landlord, the contractor, the lender). If you suspect that your reader is not familiar enough with the case to remember the names, either use generic references or use names with characterizations in parentheses, like this:

> Can Carrolton (the beneficiary) enforce the Watson covenant-not-to-compete when the covenant prohibits Watson (the former employee) from making sales contacts for three years and applies to the three counties closest to Carrolton's headquarters?

Again, use the phrasing you think your teacher or requesting attorney will prefer. As with most other writing decisions, your assessment of your reader's starting point should be the most important factor.

Degree of Detail. Try to limit the Question Presented to one readable sentence. Packing both the legal issue and the major facts into one readable sentence can be quite a challenge. If your draft of the Question Presented is unwieldy, first use some of the editing techniques described in Part I of this text. If those techniques do not allow you to achieve a readable sentence, consider shortening the facts you include. If all else fails, use two sentences. Two clear sentences are better than one confusing sentence.

Assuming the Answer in the Question Presented. Avoid stating the Question Presented in a way that assumes the answer. For instance, in the Watson/ Carrolton case, the following Question Presented assumes the answer:

> Can Carrolton enforce the Watson covenant-not-to-compete when the covenant prohibits Watson from making sales contacts for an unreasonable length of time and applies to an unreasonable geographic area?

According to the governing rule, a covenant with unreasonable terms is not enforceable. But the requesting attorney did not ask merely what rule governs the issue. The requesting attorney has asked how the rule applies to Watson's facts. She has asked whether the Watson terms are unreasonable, so do not phrase the Question Presented so as to assume the very question you are to answer.

§36.5 Drafting the Brief Answer

The Brief Answer gives your busy reader the answer quickly and right up front. Because Questions Presented come in several formats, their Brief Answers do as well. A Brief Answer responding to a Question that does not articulate the rule of law (those described in Formats 1 and 2 on page 355) should state the answer forthrightly ("yes," "probably yes," "no," or "probably not"). The remainder of the Answer should set out, either directly or indirectly, the rule of law governing the issue and a summary of the reasoning leading to the answer. We will assume that you have concluded that Carrolton will be able to enforce the Watson covenant. Your Brief Answer might be:

Probably yes [forthright statement of the answer]. A covenant-not-to-compete is enforceable under Georgia law if the activity restrained, the geographic area of the restraint, and the duration of the restraint are all reasonable **[statement of the governing rule of law].** Several Georgia courts have held that covenants restraining sales contacts are nearly always reasonable as to the activity restrained. Georgia courts have also held covenants reasonable when the duration of the restraint was up to three years and when the area restrained included up to ten counties **[summary of reasoning].**

Brief Answers that respond to Questions in the third format on page 355 (Questions that have already stated the law) can be shorter. When you are using this format, state the answer in the first few words ("yes," "probably Probably yes [**forthright statement of the answer**]. is enforceable under Georgia law if the activity restrained, the geographic area of the restraint, and the duration of the restraint are all reasonable [**statement of the governing rule of law**].

Probably yes [forthright statement of the answer]. Several Georgia courts have held that covenants restraining sales contacts are nearly always reasonable as to the activity restrained. Georgia courts have also held covenants reasonable when the duration of the restraint was up to three years and when the area restrained included up to ten counties **[summary of reasoning].**

Generic Versus Specific References. Use references that match those in the Question Presented. If you used the parties' names in the Question, use them in the Brief Answer. If you used characterizations in the Question Presented, use those characterizations in the Brief Answer as well.

Degree of Detail. An average length for a Brief Answer is one moderate paragraph (about one-third to one-half of a double-spaced page). The function of the Brief Answer is compromised when the Answer is much longer than that. Occasionally, you will be dealing with a rule that is so complex that even a Brief

Answer will take more space, but usually not. Try to limit this section to a maximum of five sentences, like the example above.

Degree of Certainty. For many memo assignments, deciding your degree of certainty is daunting. Perhaps the answer seems clear and certain. Have you simply received an easy, straightforward assignment? Or have you missed another possible way to construe law or facts? Perhaps you think the answer could go either way, and you cannot decide which is more likely; yet you know that the requesting attorney wants an answer, not a coin toss.

There is no easy solution to this discomfort. You are just beginning the lifelong project of developing the legal judgment to gauge the certainty of a predicted result. With experience, you will get better at making these judgments, and in practice you will be able to discuss the law and the facts with other attorneys. For the time being, you must research and analyze thoroughly and then make the best judgment you can.

When you are struggling with the question of the degree of certainty of your answer, keep in mind the possible spectrum:

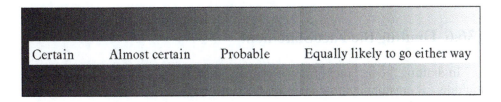

Think carefully before you choose an answer on either end of the spectrum. Some issues actually have certain answers, but before you conclude that yours is one of them, be sure you have done a complete and accurate legal and factual analysis. Some issues actually will be a coin toss, but before you conclude that yours is one of them, ask yourself whether you are simply resisting the discomfort of having to make a prediction in an uncertain area.

Finally, once you decide where your answer fits on the spectrum, communicate that decision clearly in the Brief Answer. Search your draft of the Brief Answer for the words that will tell your reader your degree of certainty, and be sure that you have not sent mixed signals within the Brief Answer itself or between the Brief Answer and the Discussion section.

Here is how the office memo looks so far:

TO: Ramon Caldez
FROM: Marcia Willingham
DATE: August 17, 1996
RE: Sharon Watson (file #96-24795); covenant-not-to-compete
          against Carrolton; enforceability of the covenant.

Question Presented

Can Carrolton enforce the Watson covenant-not-to-compete where the covenant prohibits Watson from making sales contacts for three years and applies to the three counties closest to Carrolton's headquarters?

Brief Answer

Probably yes. Carrolton should be able to enforce the Watson covenant. A covenant-not-to-compete is enforceable under Georgia law if the activity restrained, the geographic area of the restraint, and the duration of the restraint are all reasonable. Several Georgia courts have held that covenants restraining sales contacts are nearly always reasonable as to the activity restrained. Georgia courts have also held covenants reasonable when the duration of the restraint was up to three years and when the area restrained included up to ten counties.

§36.6 Drafting the Fact Statement

In drafting the fact section, your primary tasks are (1) selecting which facts to include, (2) organizing those facts in an effective way, and (3) remembering your predictive role.

§36.6.1 Fact Selection

Often you will know many facts about a particular client's situation. However, your busy reader will want to know only two kinds of facts: (1) facts relevant to the question presented and (2) background facts necessary to provide context for these legally relevant facts. Contextual facts will come to you naturally as you write, so we will focus on identifying the legally relevant facts.

Relevant facts are those that help you decide how the rule of law will apply to your client's situation. For instance, for a covenant-not-to-compete issue, the relevant facts are those that tell you about the kind of activity restrained, the geographic scope, and the duration of the restraint.

Writing your working draft already has given you a good sense of the facts that will be relevant to the issues. Especially as you wrote the "rule application" section of your analysis, you considered how the legal rule would apply to your client's situation. Review your Discussion section to make a list of these relevant facts. Consider each subissue separately so your thinking will be more precise and focused. Your list certainly should include all facts you discussed in your analysis, but do not limit your list to those facts. Let the process of reexamining each part of your legal discussion be an occasion for double-checking your fact application.

You might be surprised at how often you will see a fact in a significant new way when you are working on the fact statement.

Also, include any facts that could have a powerful emotional impact on the decision-maker, even if those facts are not technically relevant to the legal issues. Remember that judges and other decision-makers are human. Few of us can separate completely our objective legal analysis from our reaction to compelling parts of a story. Although legally irrelevant facts theoretically should not affect a result, judges might be more swayed by these inevitable responses than theory contemplates. For instance, in a divorce case, the judge deciding property issues might be influenced by knowing that one spouse has seriously battered the other spouse, even if the applicable law does not make fault relevant to property division. If your case includes an emotionally powerful fact, do not ignore it, especially if the legal rule you are working with gives the decision-maker some discretion.

Finally, include facts only. Save the coverage of legal authorities and arguments until the Discussion section. For cases already in litigation, include the current procedural posture of the case and, if relevant, a summary of the procedural history.

As you compile your list of known relevant facts, ask yourself what other facts you would like to know — what unknown facts might affect your prediction? Once again this will serve both your reader's purposes and your own. First, even if the requesting attorney has not asked you to identify important unknown facts, she almost certainly will appreciate ideas about factual investigation. Second, you will find that legal analysis and fact investigation are inextricably intertwined. Often the process of identifying important unknown facts will yield new insights about rule application, rule explanation, or both. Fact identification is yet another opportunity to deepen your analysis of the question presented.

Use your assessment of the requesting attorney's preference to judge whether and how to pass on a list of unknown facts. One fairly easy way would be to attach the list at the end of the memo as a helpful and practical bonus for your reader, but one that does not interrupt the flow of the material your reader is expecting. If an unknown fact is particularly important, you might even mention it in the Fact Statement. Your goal is to provide your reader with all appropriate information, placed at the most helpful spot.

§36.6.2 Organization

Once you have identified the facts, think about how you want to organize them. Normally your first paragraph should identify your client and briefly describe the client's problem or goal. This paragraph will give your reader a context for the facts that follow. The first or the last paragraph should describe the current status of the situation, including the procedural posture of any litigation. For the material between, the most common format choices are organizing chronologically, or topically, or using a combination of the two.

Chronological Organization. If the legal analysis has not identified complex and distinct factual topics, if the order of events is particularly important, or if there are a number of factual developments in the story, a simple chronology might be best.

Topical. When the facts are complex and cover a number of topics, or when they include more description than plot, a topical organization might work best. For example, consider these facts:

Janet Harbin represented Marcel Myers in a divorce proceeding. Myers made some statements to Harbin that caused Harbin to fear that Myers might physically injure his estranged wife. Harbin disclosed these statements to a police officer. Subsequently Myers filed a disciplinary complaint against Harbin. Assume that under the applicable ethical rule, a lawyer may reveal information if the lawyer reasonably believes that disclosure is necessary to prevent the client from committing a criminal act that is likely to result in imminent death or substantial bodily harm.

Here, chronology might not be important. The facts might simply describe topics: Myers' statement, the circumstances surrounding it, the possible consequences of it, and Harbin's reaction to it. If we had more detailed facts about each of those topics, perhaps each topic might become one or more paragraphs. This would be an example of a topical organization.

Combination of Chronological and Topical. If, as is common, the facts have characteristics of both patterns, using a combination might be the best approach. The overall organization of the fact statement can be topical, devoting a paragraph to each factual topic. However, the topics can appear chronologically, and the facts within the third topic can be presented chronologically.

Identifying format choices will be helpful as you organize your first few fact statements. Many writers find it best to write a preliminary draft, letting the story unfold according to the writer's intuition. Then they can identify the format that emerged, evaluate where it works and where it does not, and edit it in a second draft. Your goal is to use the format that will best meet your reader's needs for clarity and logical presentation.

Remembering Your Role. As you begin to write the Fact Statement, be particularly attentive to your role. Remember that both your legal analysis and your factual description must be as objective as possible. Watch for the tendency to try to prove something by the way you tell the story. Here are three techniques that will help you resist this role confusion:

1. Use neutral language and objective characterizations wherever possible. Rather than writing, "the defendant was speeding through the school zone," write instead "the defendant was traveling 40 MPH through the school zone." Rather than writing, "Wade brutally beat the victim," write instead, "Wade struck Baker on the head several times, resulting in multiple lacerations and a concussion."

2. Include the unfavorable facts. Do not focus primarily on the facts that support your prediction. You may have to remind yourself to identify and include these unfavorable or conflicting facts, but the discipline will help you stay in role.

3. Where appropriate, identify one or two important unknown facts. Pointing out a potentially important but currently unknown fact will help counteract the unconscious tendency to slip into describing the facts with more certainty than a balanced, objective perspective would support.

§36.7 Drafting the Office Memo Conclusion

If your Discussion section is relatively short and clear and if your teacher or requesting attorney does not have a preference, you need not add a separate Conclusion section. A Conclusion section should not simply repeat the Brief Answer. However, if your analysis has been complex or multifaceted, a Conclusion section can tie together and summarize the Discussion. It also can increase your reader's options for deciding how much attention to invest in understanding the details of your analysis. A Conclusion should go into more detail than the Brief Answer but not as much as the Discussion.

§36.8 Checklist for an Office Memo

Heading

- Have you included the name of the requesting attorney, your name, the date, the client's name; the file number; and a phrase identifying the particular legal matter and issue?

Question Presented

- Have you made an appropriate choice of format?
- If you chose the "legal issue/major facts" format, did you state the legal question in the first half of the sentence and the significant facts in the second half?
- If you chose the "whether" format, did you state the legal question first and the significant facts second, all in a clause and ending with a period?
- If you chose the "under/does/when" format, did you state the rule, then the legal question, and then the significant facts?
- Have you made an appropriate choice of generic or specific references?
- Have you edited to achieve one readable sentence?
- Have you maintained an objective perspective?

Brief Answer

- Have you stated the answer in the first several words?
- Have you included a statement of the rule if the Question Presented did not already state it?
- Have you stated a summary of the reasoning leading to the answer?

- Have you chosen either generic or specific references to match the Question Presented?
- Have you kept the Brief Answer to a maximum of one-third to one-half a double-spaced page?
- Have you taken a position, even if you are not sure?
- Have you avoided sending your reader mixed signals about how sure you are of your answer?

Fact Statement

Fact Selection

- Have you included all legally significant facts?
- Have you included sufficient factual context?
- Have you included any major emotional facts?
- Have you avoided including discussion of legal authority?
- Have you avoided drawing legal conclusions?

Organization

- Have you identified the client and the client's situation at the beginning of the Fact Statement?
- Have you selected an appropriate organization (chronological, topical, combination) for the facts?
- Does your last paragraph give the facts closure and lead into the Discussion section by explaining the procedural posture of the legal issue or by some other device?

Role

- Have you maintained neutral language and objective characterizations?
- Have you included both favorable and unfavorable facts?

Discussion

Umbrella Section

- Have you summarized the rule, setting out all subparts and clarifying how they relate to each other?
- Have you included any important information about how the rule functions generally, such as a burden of proof or a relevant presumption?
- Have you identified any genuinely undisputed issues and, if necessary, provided a cursory explanation for why they are not in dispute?
- Have you stated the order in which the remaining issues will be discussed, explaining the reason for this organizational choice?
- If necessary to prevent confusion, have you identified any related legal issues not covered by the memo?

Analysis

- Have you selected an appropriate order for the issues?
- Have you checked section lengths, combining or dividing subsections where appropriate?
- Are your headings complete thesis sentences?
- Have you placed a thesis paragraph at the beginning of the discussion of each issue?
- Have you also used the checklists at the ends of Chapters 31 and 32?

Conclusion

- Have you added a Conclusion section only if your reader prefers or the Discussion has been long and complex?
- Is your Conclusion more detailed than the Brief Answer but significantly less detailed than the Discussion?

§36.8.1 How to Test your Writing for Predictiveness

While rewriting, ask yourself the following questions.

1. Have you refused to hide from bad news? If the client's case is weak, it's better to know that now. Predictive writing is frank diagnosis. Advocacy has another time and place.

2. Have you edited out waffling? Your readers will expect you to take a position and prove it. Mushy waffling with words like "seems," "appears," and their synonyms makes your advice less useful to clients and supervising attorneys. Supervisors and judges are grateful for concreteness, whether or not they agree with you. If somebody disagrees with you, lightning will *not* strike you down on the spot. (It is not waffling to say that "the plaintiff probably will win an appeal" or "is likely to win an appeal." No prediction can be a certainty.)

3. Have you told the reader whether your prediction is qualified in any way? For precision, a prediction should at least imply how confident you are of it. Is the underlying rule a matter of "settled law" and are the facts clear-cut? If your prediction is qualified, you can state precisely the variables on which the prediction is based, such as "The defendant will probably prevail unless. . . ."

4. Have you concentrated on solving a problem, rather than on writing a college essay? A college essay is a vehicle for academic analysis — analysis to satisfy curiosity — rather than practical problem-solving for clients. Legal writing is practical. Solve the problem you were asked to solve. Solve it completely. But don't insert into your writing essays not essential to solving the problem. For example:

Common law courts developed the crime of burglary because in the middle ages, with no police and no electric lights, life was much more dangerous at night. People bolted their doors and windows when the sun went down, but they still felt vulnerable because of the advantage darkness gave to criminals. The courts classified burglary as a felony with the same punishment as murder (execution by hanging) so that people could sleep at night with some sense of security. Modern statutes have reduced the punishment to imprisonment. They often retain something like the common law formulation of burglary as the most serious form of the crime. Lesser statutory forms might omit some of the elements of common law burglary and might be called second- or third-degree burglary or breaking and entering.

This is interesting. It even explains why Goldilocks would not be charged with common law burglary. She got into the bears' house during the daytime, and she didn't have a felonious intent, even if she later ate their porridge and slept in their beds. But it doesn't help predict whether Taylor will be convicted and therefore wouldn't belong in Taylor's memo.

CHAPTER 37

Working with Facts

§37.1 What is a Fact?

Consider the following statements:

1. *The plaintiff's complaint alleges* that, at a certain time and place, the defendant struck the plaintiff from behind with a stick.
2. At trial, *the plaintiff's principal witness testified* that, at the time and place specified in the complaint, the defendant struck the plaintiff from behind with a stick.
3. At the conclusion of the trial, *the jury found* that, at the time and place specified in the complaint, the defendant struck the plaintiff from behind with a stick.
4. At the time and place specified in the complaint, *the defendant struck* the plaintiff from behind with a stick.
5. At the time and place specified in the complaint, the defendant *brutally* struck the plaintiff from behind with a stick.
6. At the time and place specified in the complaint, the defendant *accidentally* struck the plaintiff from behind with a stick.
7. At the time and place specified in the complaint, the defendant *committed a battery* on the plaintiff.

Which of these statements expresses a fact?

Number 7 plainly does not: it states a *conclusion of law* because battery is a concept defined by the law, and you can discover whether a battery occurred only by consulting one or more rules of law. Numbers 5 and 6, however, are a little harder to sort out.

Statement 6 includes the word *accidentally*. The defendant might have wanted to cause violence, or he might have struck the plaintiff only inadvertently and without any desire to do harm. With both possibilities, an observer might see pretty much the same actions: the stick being raised, the stick being lowered, the collision with the back. There might be small but perceptible differences between the two — the defendant's facial expression, for example, or the words spoken immediately before and after the incident. But even those differences might not occur. A cunning defendant intent on harm, for example, can pretend to act inadvertently. The difference between the two possibilities is in what the defendant might have been thinking or feeling when he struck the plaintiff. If we say that the defendant struck the plaintiff "accidentally," we have inferred what the defendant was thinking at the time. That is a factual inference. (It would be a conclusion of law if it were framed in terms that the law defines, such as "intention to cause a contact with another person.") An inference of fact is not a fact: it is a conclusion derived from facts.

Statement 5 contains the word *brutally*, which is a value-based and subjective *characterization*. If one is shocked by the idea of a stick colliding with a human being — regardless of the speed and force involved — even a gentle tap with a stick might be characterized as brutal. (Conversely, an observer who is indifferent to suffering and violence might call repeated lacerations with a stick "playful.") And a friend of the plaintiff or an enemy of the defendant might construe whatever happened as "brutal," while an enemy of the plaintiff or a friend of the defendant might do the reverse. Assuming that we have not seen the incident ourselves, we should wonder whether the word *brutally* accurately summarizes what happened, or whether it instead reflects the value judgments and preferences of the person who has characterized the incident as brutal. A characterization is not a fact; it is only an opinion about a fact.

We are left with statements 1 through 4. Do any of them recite a fact? There are two ways of answering that question. Although the two might at first seem to contradict each other, they are actually consistent, and both answers are accurate, although in different ways.

One answer is that statements 1, 2, and 3 are layers surrounding a fact recited in statement number 4: number 1 is an allegation of a fact; number 2 is evidence offered in proof of the allegation; number 3 is a conclusion that the evidence proves the allegation; and number 4 is the fact itself. This is an answer that might be reached by a perceptive lay person who has noticed what you now know to be a sequence inherent to litigation: the party seeking a remedy first alleges, in a pleading, a collection of facts that, if proven, would merit a remedy, and that party later at trial submits evidence to persuade the finder of fact that the allegations are proven. Notice that this first answer is built on the ideas that a "fact" is part of an objective, discoverable truth and that the purpose of litigation is to find that truth.

The other answer is that numbers 1 through 4 all recite facts, the first three being procedural events inside a lawsuit. This answer is derived from the requirement, inherent to litigation, that the decisions of the finder of fact be based not on an objective "truth" that occurred out of court, but instead on whether *in court* a party has carried her or his burdens to make certain allegations and to submit a certain quantum of evidence in support of those allegations. Because it is not omniscient, a court cannot decide on the basis of what is "true." In a procedural sense, litigation is less a search for truth than it is a test of whether each party has carried burdens of pleading, production, and persuasion that the law assigns to one party or another. Because of the adversary system, the court is not permitted to investigate the controversy: it can do no more than passively weigh what is submitted to it, using as benchmarks the burdens set out in the law. Thus, if a party does not allege and prove a fact essential to that party's case, the court must decide that the fact does not exist. And this is so even if the fact does exist. That is why experienced lawyers tend to be more confident of their abilities to prove and disprove allegations than they are of their abilities to know the "real" truth about what happened between the parties before litigation began.

Both answers are correct, but their value to you will change as time goes on. Right now, the first answer gives you a model of how facts are processed in litigation. But soon the second answer will become increasingly important. That is because, as you learn lawyering, you will have to learn the ways in which the law compels lawyers to focus on whether a party can carry or has carried a burden of pleading, production, or persuasion.

The nonexistence of a fact can itself be a fact. For example, consider the following:

8. At trial, no witness has testified that the defendant struck the plaintiff deliberately or that the plaintiff suffered any physical or psychological injury or even any indignity.

Here, the absence of certain evidence is itself a fact. Consequently, the defendant might be entitled to a directed verdict because some things have not been proved.

Facts have subtleties that can entangle you if you are not careful. Beginners tend to have difficulties with four fact skills: (1) separating facts from other things; (2) separating determinative facts from other kinds of facts; (3) building inferences from facts; and (4) purging analysis of hidden and unsupportable factual assumptions. When you have mastered these skills, you will be able to make reasoned decisions about selecting and using facts. The last few pages have explained the first skill. The remainder of this chapter considers each of the other skills in turn.

§37.2 Identifying Determinative Facts

Facts can be divided into three categories. The first category is made up of facts that are essential to a controversy because they will determine the court's decision: if a change in a fact would have caused the court to come to a different decision, that fact is determinative. The second is a category of explanatory facts that, while not determinative, are nevertheless useful because they help make sense out of a situation that would otherwise seem disjointed. The third category includes coincidental facts that have no relevance or usefulness at all: they merely happened. Part of life's charm is that all three categories of facts — the relevant and the irrelevant — occur mixed up together in a disorderly mess. But lawyers have to separate out the determinative facts and treat them as determinative.

You have already started learning how to do that in this and other courses, mostly through the analysis of precedent. When, for example, you are asked to formulate the rule of a case, you have begun to develop the habit of isolating the facts the court considered determinative and then reformulating those facts into a list of generalities that — when they occur together again in the future — will produce the same result that happened in the reported opinion. But when you look at a given litigation through the lens of an opinion, you are looking at it *after* a court has already decided which facts are determinative: you are explicating the text of the opinion to learn what the court thought about the facts. We are concerned here with another skill: looking at the facts at the *beginning* of the case, before they are even put to a court, and predicting which the court will consider determinative.

Consider the following scenario:

> Welty and Lutz are students who have rented apartments on the same floor of the same building. At midnight, Welty is studying, while Lutz is listening to a Radiohead album with his new four-foot speakers. Welty has put up with this for two or three hours, and finally she pounds on Lutz's door. Lutz opens the door about six inches, and, when he realizes that he cannot hear what Welty is saying, he steps back into the room a few feet to turn the volume down, leaving the door open about six inches. Continuing to express outrage, Welty pushes the door completely open and strides into the room. Lutz turns on Welty and orders her to leave. Welty finds this to be too much and punches Lutz so hard that he suffers substantial injury. In this jurisdiction, the punch is a felonious assault. Is Welty also guilty of common law burglary?

Common law burglary is the breaking and entering of the dwelling of another in the nighttime with intent to commit a felony therein. Whichever way a court rules, the size of the opening between Lutz's door and the door frame is going to be one of the determinative facts because the size of the opening helps to determine whether, at the moment Welty walked in, Lutz's dwelling was surrounded by the kind of enclosure that can be broken. Depending on one's theory, Lutz's activities before Welty knocked on the door could be either explanatory or determinative: they help make sense out of the situation, but they also help explain Welty's actions and intent, which go to other elements of the test for burglary. But you have not been told that Lutz only recently got into hard rock and that previously he had been a devotee of country music; those facts are omitted because they are purely coincidental and do not help you understand the issues.

Of the four fact skills considered in this chapter, isolating the determinative facts is probably the one that seems most obvious from your law school work generally. The first few months of law school are designed to teach two things that are the heart of this skill: rule analysis and a heightened sense of relevance.

§37.3 Building Inferences from Facts

> The main part of intellectual education is . . . learning how to make facts live.
>
> — *Oliver Wendell Holmes*

We will continue a bit further with Welty and Lutz.

One of the elements of burglary is the intent to commit a felony within the dwelling. In the jurisdiction where Welty and Lutz live, that element can be satisfied only if a defendant had that intent at the time that any breaking and entering might have occurred. If the defendant formed the intent for the first time after entering the dwelling, the element is not satisfied. Assuming for the moment that Welty broke and entered Lutz's apartment when she opened the door further and walked in, did she — at the instant she stepped inside — intend to commit a felony there?

Your response may be "Well, let's ask Welty — she's the one who would really know." But things are not so easy. If you are the prosecutor, you may find that the police have already asked her that question and that she has refused to answer or has given an answer that the police consider self- serving. In fact, one rarely has direct evidence of a person's state of mind: people do not carry electronic signboards on their foreheads on which their thoughts can be read at moments the law considers important. Instead, as the prosecutor you would have to prove Welty's state of mind through the surrounding circumstances — for example, through the things she did or did not do, as well as the things she knew other people had or had not done. Although her state of mind would be easier to determine if she had appeared at Lutz's door with an arsenal of weaponry — or, in another situation, with safecracking tools — inferences can be built from circumstances even without such dramatic displays of intent.

Even if you are Welty's defense lawyer and can freely ask her when she formed an intent to hit Lutz, you might not be much better off than the prosecutor. She might tell you something like the following:

> I don't know when I decided to punch him. I had to listen to his loud music on his four-foot speakers for two or three hours while I was trying to study for civil procedure. At least once or twice during that time, I thought that it might be nice to punch his lights out, but I don't know that I had decided then to do it. When I knocked on his door, I thought, "This guy had better be reasonable, or else" — but at that instant I don't know whether I was committed to punching him. When I pushed the door open and stepped inside, I thought, "This joker might learn a little respect for the rest of us if something very emphatic happened to him — something that might help him remember in the future that other people have needs and that he shouldn't be so self-centered." Even then, I wasn't certain that I was going to do anything except try to reason with him. And when he ordered me out, I decked him. Nobody told me that I was supposed to make sure that my thoughts fit into this "state of mind" thing you're telling me about. I have no idea when I "formed an intent" to hit him. I can only tell you what my thoughts were at each step in the story. You're the lawyer. You tell me when I "formed an intent."

Now the problem is something else: a party's thoughts do not mesh nicely with the law's categories of states of mind. Welty's sequence of emotions somehow culminated in an action, but there seems to have been no magical moment at which anger crystallized into a decision that the law might recognize as "intent." A defense lawyer handles this problem in the same way that a prosecutor deals with the absence of direct evidence: each lawyer will build inferences from the circumstances surrounding Welty's actions. As Welty sees the arguments unfold, she might conclude that the law is doing strange and perhaps arbitrary things in categorizing her thoughts. But the law must have a way of judging states of mind, and it relies heavily on circumstances.

Albert Moore has used the term inferential stream to refer to the sequence of circumstantial conclusions that can grow out of a fact or piece of evidence.[1] Circumstantial evidence does not necessarily lead to only one stream of inferences. Consider the evidence in *Smith v. Jones*, where Smith claims that Jones caused an accident by running a red light:

> Jones testifies that his two children, ages five and six, were arguing in the back seat of his car just before the accident occurred. [This] is circumstantial propositional evidence that Jones entered the intersection against the red light because there is a series of valid generalizations that connects this evidence to the factual proposition in question. These generalizations might be stated as follows:

> > *Generalization 1:* People driving with children arguing in the back seat of the car sometimes pay attention to what is happening in the back seat.
> > *Generalization 2:* People who are paying attention to what is happening in the back seat of the car are sometimes momentarily distracted from what is happening on the road in front of them.
> > *Generalization 3:* People who are momentarily distracted from what is happening on the road in front of them sometimes enter an intersection against the red light.
> > *Conclusion:* Jones entered the intersection against the red light.

> Based on the foregoing, one might conclude that this circumstantial evidence tends to prove only that Jones entered the intersection against the red light. One could also, however, conclude that this evidence tends to disprove that Jones entered the intersection against the red light. This conclusion might be based on the following analysis:

> > *Generalization 4:* People driving with children arguing in the back seat are sometimes conscious of the presence of children in the car.
> > *Generalization 5:* People who are conscious of children in their car sometimes drive cautiously.
> > *Generalization 6:* People who drive cautiously sometimes pay close attention to the road.
> > *Generalization 7:* People who pay close attention to the road sometimes do not enter an intersection against the red light.
> > *Conclusion:* Jones did not enter the intersection against the red light.

> In *Smith v. Jones*, therefore, the evidence that Jones' children were arguing in the back of the car just before the accident, by itself, may tend to prove or disprove that Jones entered the intersection against the red light, depending on which set of

---

[1] Albert J. Moore, *Inferential Streams: The Articulation and Illustration of the Advocate's Evidentiary Intuitions*, 34 UCLA L. Rev. 611 (1987).

generalizations is viewed as more reliable and accurate.... Thus, circumstantial propositional evidence may "cut both ways" in two situations: when the same evidence tends to prove or disprove the same factual proposition; or when it tends to prove one factual proposition while also tending to disprove another.[2]

§37.4 Identifying Hidden and Unsupportable Factual Assumptions

As David Binder and Paul Bergman have pointed out, "[i]f in medieval times there was 'trial by combat,' then today we have 'trial by inference.'"[3] Your adversary and the court will mercilessly challenge your inferential streams, looking for weaknesses in the way they were put together. Consequently, you must purge your analysis of hidden assumptions that will not stand up to scrutiny when exposed. Consider the following:

> Detective Fenton Tracem rushes breathlessly into the office of the local prosecutor, Les Gettem, eager to persuade Les to issue an indictment. Fenton describes the evidence he has uncovered:
>
>> Les, we've got a good case for bank robbery against Clyde. The gun the robber used and dropped at the door was originally purchased by Clyde. The owner of A-1 Guns can definitely identify Clyde as the purchaser and the teller can identify the gun. Moreover, the day after the $10,000 was taken, Clyde deposits $7,000 cash in a bank account using the fictitious name of Dillinger. A teller at the bank can definitely identify Clyde. Then later that day, Clyde buys a $1,500 gold watch and pays for it in cash. The owner of A-2 Jewelry can also identify him. Finally, the next day — two days after the robbery — Clyde moves out without giving Ness, his landlord, his two neighbors, Capone and Siegel, or the post office his new address. Ness, Capone, Siegel and the post office clerk are all willing to testify. Les, we're rock-solid on this one.

The detective has disgorged a mass of circumstantial evidence which appears in the aggregate to be quite convincing. The prosecutor cannot, however, be content to rely on this presentation. In order to analyze the probative value of the evidence, Gettem must first expressly articulate the generalization which links each item of evidence to an element.

[E]xpressly articulating generalizations is the key to determining just how strong a piece of evidence is.

Consider, therefore, the generalization the prosecutor might articulate for the first piece of evidence, that the gun used and dropped by the robber was originally purchased by Clyde. The generalization might be something like, "People who have purchased a gun subsequently used in a robbery are more likely to have participated in the robbery than people who have not."[4]

---

[2] *Id.* at 625-27.
[3] David A. Binder & Paul Bergman, *Fact Investigation: From Hypothesis to Proof* 82 (West 1984).
[4] *Id.* at 92-93.

How accurate is this generalization? See what happens when you compare it with *either* of two strings of other generalizations. Here is the first one: "Robbers do not feel morally compelled to pay for what they acquire, and because guns can be stolen, a robber does not have even a practical need to pay for a gun." This is the second string: "Robbers tend to plan their crimes with at least some amount of forethought; some forethought would cause a robber to foresee the possibility of losing control of a gun during the robbery; other forethought would cause a robber to foresee that a gun legally purchased from a merchant might be traced back to the robber; Clyde is bright enough to have come to both of these foresights." Both strings seem more believable than "People who have purchased a gun subsequently used in a robbery are more likely to have participated in the robbery than people who have not" — and *either* string might overcome and negate the generalization on which the detective relies.

> In the beginning years of practice, one must force oneself to articulate explicitly the generalizations on which one relies, for it is not a skill practiced in everyday life. In fact, there is a word for people who state the generalizations underlying all inferences they make: bores. But in the privacy of one's office, one should expressly identify the premises on which one relies [because] by articulating the underlying generalization one can consciously consider the question of how strongly it is supported by common experience.
>
> This point may be seen more clearly if one asked to evaluate another of Det. Tracem's pieces of evidence without the aid of an expressed generalization. "The day after the $10,000 was taken, Clyde deposits $7,000 cash in a bank account using the fictitious name of Dillinger." As D.A. Les Gettem, one is asked how strongly suggestive of Clyde's guilt this piece of evidence is. . . .
>
> . . . If your answer is something like, "The evidence is strongly indicative of guilt" (or "isn't too probative of guilt"), you have had a knee-jerk reaction to the evidence. Undoubtedly some accumulation of common experience was implicit in whatever conclusion you reached. But unless the common experience is crystallized in an explicitly stated generalization, one has no focal point for considering how uniformly common experience supports the gen- eralization.
>
> If your conclusion did include a generalization, it may have been something like, "People who deposit $7,000 in a bank account under a fictitious name are likely to have gotten the money illegally." With this generalization explicitly stated, one has a basis for gauging with some degree of accuracy the probative value of the fictitious bank account evidence. One has an explicit premise which can be tested according to one's own and a factfinder's probable views as to how the world operates. . . .
>
> There are other reasons for articulating generalizations. Their articulation may bring to mind potential exceptions. . . . [O]ne method of testing the degree to which common experience uniformly supports a generalization is to add "except when" to a generalization, and see how many reasonable exceptions one can identify. . . .
>
> [For example, consider] a generalization that one might make in Clyde's case: "People who move without leaving a forwarding address are usually trying to avoid detection." By adding "except when," one sees that this generalization is subject to many exceptions and is therefore less likely to be persuasive. People may be trying to avoid detection, except when they simply forget to leave a forwarding address, or

except when they do not yet know the permanent address to which they will be moving, or except when they will be moving around for a time and will not have a permanent address.[5]

As Binder and Bergman point out, only bores recite for the benefit of others all the generalizations underlying their inferences. Thus, when you build and test your own inferences, you will not commit to paper much of the analysis Binder and Bergman describe. As they suggest, it is thinking reserved for the privacy of your own office.

But things are different when you attack your adversary's inferences. If Clyde becomes your client, you might argue that a directed verdict should be — or, on appeal, should have been — granted because a rational jury would not be able to find guilt beyond a reasonable doubt. In a supporting memorandum or in an appellate brief, you might write, "The evidence that he moved without leaving a forwarding address does not tend to prove guilty flight. It could just as easily prove that he forgot to leave a forwarding address, or that he did not yet know his new permanent address when he moved, or that he would be moving around for a time without a permanent address."

---

[5] *Id.* at 93-96.

CHAPTER 38

WRITING THE FACTS

In the Facts section of the memo, you tell the story. It's probably the easiest section to write — because the facts are often (but not always) the easiest part of the problem to understand. But don't let this lull you into believing you can write the Facts section without much thought or effort. And don't just copy and paste into your memo the facts provided by your professor in the assignment (which may be considered plagiarism). This is a genuine writing task requiring effort and skill.

§38.1 What you Need to Know About an Office Memo's Facts Section

Include every fact you mention in the Discussion section as well as any other fact that's necessary for the story to make sense. Describe the client and what she wants first, and then develop the facts more fully. Some writers like to think of this as the "who, what, where" part of the memo. Include as much detail as necessary either for the analysis or to understand the story. Because including lots of specific dates can clog up your writing and make it harder for the reader to follow, leave out specific dates unless they're relevant to the legal issue (for instance, when the legal issue depends on the timing of particular events, such as in statute of limitation issues, claims regarding default for failure to file an answer, etc.).

Include procedural facts. The Facts section should note what has happened in terms of legal action to date. And as with substantive facts, specific dates aren't necessary unless they're legally significant.

State the facts and just the facts. This section is called the "Facts" for a reason. Don't include the law. That will go in the Discussion section. Similarly, the Facts section is not the place for analysis, characterizations of the facts, or inferences. You'll have plenty of space to do that in the Discussion section. Keep the Facts section clearly factual.

Frame the facts objectively.   The facts should not be told just from your client's perspective (assuming you have been put in the role of an attorney drafting a memo on behalf of your client). The reader needs to understand all sides of the issue. Include facts that hurt your client's case, not just those that help.

Because objective memos are usually used for predictive purposes and strategy, you're not doing the client any favors by making the facts sound more compelling than they actually are. Be accurate, objective, and neutral. This contrasts with a persuasive brief, where you still have to avoid making overt arguments and leaving out relevant facts, but your goal there is for the facts to have a subtly persuasive effect.

Generally write the facts in chronological order.   Stories usually make the most sense when they start at the beginning, then explain what happened in the middle, and then tell what happened at the end. Sometimes, though, another organization makes more logical sense. For instance, if two parallel situations were brewing, explaining the facts in true chronological order would jumble the two scenarios together and likely confuse the reader. As with all writing tasks, use your best judgment, but absent a reason to do otherwise, ordering the facts in chronological order is wise. And because the facts already happened, you'll generally use past tense in the Facts section.

Facts sections are usually written in regular paragraph format.   Unlike complaints and some Statements of Material Facts for motions, which are often drafted using numbered sentences or very short numbered paragraphs, Facts sections in office memos are most often written in regular narrative format. If you have a long Facts section, consider using subheaders to break the facts into logical chunks. This will make the Facts section easier to read and understand.

Be sure to revise the Facts section after you've completed the Discussion section.   Some writers like to begin with the Facts because it's the part of the memo they understand the best. If you do that, be sure to go back and review the Facts section after you've completed the Discussion section, because only then can you appreciate which facts are truly relevant and which aren't.

Every fact that's necessary for the analysis needs to be in the Facts section, so double-check to make sure you've included them all (and correspondingly omit facts irrelevant to the legal analysis unless they're necessary to understand the story). Even though it may seem repetitive to include everything in the Facts section (because all the necessary facts are also in the Discussion section), readers won't always read the memo in order. They may jump around. And Facts sections have a separate purpose. Clients are often told to review the Facts section carefully and make sure that all the facts are correct and none are omitted. In that sense, the Facts section ensures the factual basis for your analysis is accurate and it protects you in the event your analysis is based on a fact that turns out to be inaccurate.

§38.2 How to Write an Office Memo's Facts Section

Now we will walk you through the process of writing the Facts section of an office memo.

PROBLEM

Allison King used her wireless phone, without a hands-free device, while driving in dense fog on a winding road on the edge of an ocean cliff. King placed the call to warn her friends about the dangerous conditions, as they would be meeting later. While she was making the call, she hit and killed a bicyclist. The prosecution will attempt to convict King of vehicular manslaughter by showing that she drove while committing an illegal act (driving while using a wireless phone without a hands-free device) and with gross negligence. King will argue that her actions fit within the emergency exception to the wireless phone prohibition. She will also argue that she did not act with gross negligence.

Step 1: Gather and read all the facts, whether in a case file, a memo from the assigning attorney, or some other source (provided by your professor).   In the cell phone manslaughter problem, the facts are provided in a short summary form. Often, the relevant facts have to be gleaned from other documents. For instance, for a breach of contract claim, you might review the contract and possibly a complaint and answer. Discovery may also be relevant; you may need to review deposition testimony, affidavits, responses to interrogatories, and other evidence. In whatever form you find the facts, your task is to locate and closely review every source that may contain factual information.

Step 2: Determine which facts are relevant.   To determine whether a particular fact is relevant, you need to have some knowledge of the legal issue and the applicable rules. Whether a particular fact is relevant also depends on the surrounding circumstances. For instance, in a negligence suit, the fact that a car involved in an auto accident was white is generally irrelevant. If, however, the accident occurred during a blizzard and the defendant claims he couldn't see the plaintiff's vehicle, the fact that the car was white may very well be relevant.

The following hypothetical, which is based on a new scenario, illustrates how to determine which facts are relevant:

You represent Mark Yokus, who owns R & J Construction Company. Yokus was recently served with a complaint by the Equal Employment Opportunity Commission (EEOC). One of his employees filed a complaint with the EEOC alleging R & J Construction engaged in unlawful employment discrimination in violation of Title VII.

The claimant, Sarah Clark, worked for R & J for five years as a supervising electrician. In that capacity, she regularly earned overtime (working approximately 57 hours per week).

On Friday, May 28, 2010, Yokus learned that Clark was four months pregnant. Yokus became concerned about health and safety risks for Clark and her fetus if she were to continue working as a supervising electrician. The same day, Yokus shared his concerns with Clark and offered to transfer her to an office job for seven months while continuing to pay her at her current hourly rate. But that position is a 40-hour-a-week job that rarely involves overtime, and thus Clark would suffer a reduction in total pay. Clark declined this offer on the spot, but Yokus refused to allow her to continue performing electrician duties.

Clark's next day at work was Tuesday, June 1. (Monday, May 31, was a holiday.) Yokus again refused to allow Clark to perform electrician duties. At noon that day, Clark went home. On the following day, June 2, Yokus told Clark her employment was formally terminated. Clark filed a complaint with the EEOC on November 29, 2010.

If the only issue you're asked to address is whether Title VII's definition of "sex" (in its prohibition of sex discrimination) includes pregnancy, the Facts section might be very short:

> Our client, Mark Yokus, owns R & J Construction Company. One of R & J's employees, Sarah Clark, became pregnant, and Yokus attempted to transfer her position. Clark refused, and Yokus terminated her employment. Clark then filed a complaint with the EEOC alleging sex discrimination in violation of Title VII.

However, if the issue is whether R & J Construction unlawfully engaged in sex discrimination in violation of Title VII, the Facts section would be longer and might look like this:

> Our client, Mark Yokus, owns R & J Construction Company. R & J employed Sarah Clark for five years as a supervising electrician. Yokus learned that Clark was four months pregnant. Concerned for her health and safety as well as the fetus's, Yokus offered to transfer Clark, at her usual hourly rate, to an office position until after the baby was born. Clark refused that offer because the office position did not include regular overtime and as a supervising electrician Clark had averaged seventeen hours of overtime per week.
>
> Clark then filed a complaint alleging sex discrimination in violation of Title VII with the EEOC. The EEOC recently filed a complaint against Yokus on behalf of R & J Construction.

This Facts section doesn't include specific dates. Imagine, though, that Clark has now sued, and the issue is whether Clark has exhausted her administrative remedies in a timely fashion. Some legal research reveals that Title VII requires the employee to file a complaint with the EEOC within 180 days of the adverse employment action. Imagine a case where the definition of "adverse employment action" is an issue. Several events happened and the question is which one of them triggered the start of the 180-day time limit. In that case, additional facts — including dates — would be relevant. That Facts section might look like this:

Our client, Mark Yokus, owns R & J Construction Company. On May 28, 2010, Yokus learned that one of R & J's employees, Sarah Clark, was pregnant. On that day, Yokus told Clark that she could not continue to work as a supervising electrician and could be transferred to an office position at the same rate, although she would lose her customary overtime pay. Clark refused that offer on the spot, and Yokus refused to allow her to perform electrician duties. Her next work day was June 1, 2010, and Yokus again refused to allow her to perform electrician duties. Clark went home at noon. The next day, June 2, Yokus formally terminated Clark's employment.

Clark filed her complaint with the EEOC on November 29, 2010, 185 days after May 28, when Clark was told that she could not continue to work as a supervising electrician and when she refused Yokus' offer to transfer to an office position. November 29, 2010, was 181 days after June 1, when Clark was again prohibited from performing supervising electrician duties and went home at noon. It was 180 days after June 2, when Yokus told Clark that her employment was terminated.

Note how the relevant facts change, depending on the specific legal issue being addressed. The facts themselves don't change, but because the issue changes, their relevancy changes. Some facts are relevant to one issue, and some are relevant to another issue. Some are relevant to all issues. Your Facts section would include the facts relevant to the issue or issues you're addressing. For this reason, don't just copy and paste the facts you were given into your memo.

Step 3: Be especially careful to include the relevant facts that allow you to analogize or distinguish the facts in the precedent cases from the client's facts. For example, in the copyright and fair use problem in Appendix B, the following facts might be helpful in the Facts section — first because they are relevant, and second because they allow you to compare and contrast those facts with the facts in the controlling cases:

Young's song is critical of American politics, and Olds' song reflects pride in American politics.

These facts are relevant and helpful under the Copyright Act's first statutory factor, the "purpose and character of the use." But these facts also create a point of comparison with the *Mattel* case: In *Mattel*, the defendant's works criticized women's traditional role in society, emphasizing that role can put women in ridiculous and even dangerous positions. On the other hand, Mattel's works represented women's traditional role positively, associated with beauty, wealth, and glamour. You'll be able to create stronger analogies and distinctions in the Discussion section if you've included enough facts in the Facts section to draw those explicit comparisons later.

Step 4: Draft a preliminary Facts section. Start at the beginning and work your way through the facts chronologically (unless some other structure works better in your particular case). At this stage, err on the side of over-inclusiveness. You can always delete facts later, but if you've left them out here, you might forget about them when drafting the Discussion section, and that can cause greater problems. Don't worry too much yet about whether each fact will ultimately be relevant. You'll be better able to answer that question after you've completed the legal research and considered how all of the pieces fit together.

Step 5: After you've completed the Discussion section, revise the Facts section. Now you're ready to decide whether each fact in your Facts section is relevant or needed for context. You can tell how much detail the reader needs to understand the analysis in the Discussion section. And now you're ready to revise — not just edit — your Facts section. Recall the first thing you need to know about Facts sections: "Describe the client and what she wants first, and then develop the facts more fully." So start there, explaining, briefly, the client's legal predicament. Then tell the story, making sure that every fact in the Discussion section is indeed in the Facts section. Also make sure the Facts section leaves out irrelevant facts, unless they are necessary for the story to make sense. And make sure it flows, so the reader can follow the story with one quick read.

CHAPTER 39

SAMPLE OFFICE MEMORANDUM

To: Requesting Attorney
From: Summer Clerk
Date: November 9, 2002
Re: Beth Buckley; file # 756385; stolen car; whether Buckley can
         disaffirm purchase of car based on her minority

QUESTION PRESENTED

Can Buckley, a minor, disaffirm the purchase of a car when she misunderstood the sales agent's question and therefore accidentally misrepresented her age as eighteen?

BRIEF ANSWER

Probably yes. A minor can disaffirm a contract unless the minor's fraudulent misrepresentation induced the other party to rely justifiably on the representation. On Buckley's facts, a court would probably rule that an innocent misrepresentation such as Buckley's is not fraudulent and therefore would not prevent a minor from disaffirming a contract. A court might also rule that the seller did not justifiably rely on Buckley's representation.

FACTS

Our client, Beth Buckley, is seventeen and a high school senior. She will turn eighteen on December 15. Two months ago she bought a used car for $3,000 from Willis Chevrolet. She paid cash, using the money she had saved from her summer job. Buckley purchased collision insurance for the car, but she did not insure against theft. Last week the car was stolen, and Buckley has asked what she can do about her loss.

When Buckley first looked at cars on the lot, the sales agent asked if she was old enough to buy a car. Buckley did not realize that she had to be eighteen to enter into a contract, even when paying cash. She thought the sales agent was asking whether she was old enough to drive, so she said "Yes." The agent did not ask to see any identification and did not raise the subject of age again.

The next day Buckley returned to the lot, selected the car she wanted to purchase, and completed the transaction. She recalls "signing a bunch of papers," but she did not read them and does not know what they said. She says that the sales agent did not attempt to explain the documents.

-1-

He simply showed her where to sign, and she signed on those lines. She does not know if she still has copies of the documents, but she will look among her papers and let us know.

DISCUSSION

I. Can Beth Buckley disaffirm the contract?

A minor does not have the capacity to make a binding contract, but a contract made by a minor is not automatically void. *Hood v. Duren,* 125 S.E. 787 (Ga. Ct. App. 1924). Generally, one who is a minor at the time of making a contract can disaffirm the contract within a reasonable time after reaching the age of majority. O.C.G.A. § 13-3-20 (1982); *Merritt v. Jowers,* 193 S.E. 238 (Ga. 1937). The rationale for the rule is the recognition that minors have not yet attained sufficient maturity to be responsible for the decisions they make, so the rule protects them from at least some of the consequences of bad decisions. *See generally White v. Sikes,* 59 S.E. 228 (Ga. 1907).

However, a minor is estopped from disaffirming a contract if (a) the minor made a false and fraudulent representation of his or her age; (b) the contracting party justifiably relied on the minor's representation; and (c) the minor has reached the age of discretion. *Carney v. Southland Loan Co.,* 88 S.E.2d 805 (Ga. 1955). Because the first element is the most problematic in Buckley's case, the memo will discuss it first.

A. Buckley's unintentional misrepresentation of her age probably is insufficient to establish fraudulent misrepresentation.

The first element necessary for estoppel is a false and fraudulent representation. A minor makes a false and fraudulent representation when the minor affirmatively and intentionally states a false age, intending that the seller rely on the information. For instance, in *Carney* the minor told the car sales agent that he was twenty-two, the agent recorded that information on the loan application, and the minor signed the application and purchased the car. The court affirmed the trial court's holding that the minor had fraudulently misrepresented his age and was estopped from disaffirming the contract. *Id.* at 807-808.

Similarly, in *Clemons v. Olshine,* 187 S.E. 711 (Ga. Ct. App. 1936), the minor told the clothing sales agent that he was twenty-one and signed a contract confirming the representation. The court held that his fraudulent misrepresentation estopped him from disaffirming. In *Watters v. Arrington,* 146 S.E. 773 (Ga. Ct. App. 1929), another car purchase case, several agents of the seller testified that the minor had twice affirmatively stated his age to be twenty-one. The court affirmed the jury's verdict for the seller, holding that a minor's fraudulent misrepresentation of age estops the minor from disaffirming the contract.

The courts distinguish this kind of intentional, knowing misrepresentation from unintentional, even negligent misrepresentations of age. For instance, in *Woodall v. Grant & Co.,* 9 S.E.2d 95 (Ga. Ct. App. 1940), the minor had simply signed without reading a form contract that contained a representation that he was of age. There the court held that the representation in the contract did not estop the minor because the minor had not read the contract. The court reasoned that minors are not required to read contracts. *Id.* at 95. The *Carney* decision distinguished *Woodall* by pointing out that in *Woodall* "the minor's only sin, if any, was his failure to read a contract which ... stated that he was of age, while in [*Carney*] the minor falsely gave the information put into the contract." *Carney*, 88 S.E.2d at 808.

The most recent relevant case, *Siegelstein v. Fenner & Beane*, 17 S.E.2d 907 (Ga. Ct. App. 1941), reaffirmed the *Carney/Woodall* distinction. In *Siegelstein*, the jury returned a verdict for the defendant, and the appellate court reversed on other grounds. However, the appellate court affirmed the trial court's jury instruction, stating that a minor's false representation of age "will not affect his power to disaffirm a contract unless [the representation] was made *fraudulently*." *Id.* at 910 (emphasis supplied).

The rule holding minors responsible only for intentional affirmative misrepresentations is consistent with the policy behind allowing minors to disaffirm their contracts. Minors, by definition, are more likely than adults to make errors and other innocent misrepresentations. Given this symmetry of rationale, the courts are likely to continue allowing minors to disaffirm despite innocent, even negligent, misrepresentations.

Here, the sales agent simply asked Buckley whether she was old enough to buy a car. Buckley misunderstood the question, thinking that the agent was asking whether she was old enough to drive. Thus she innocently answered "Yes." She did not affirmatively state an age at all. This kind of misunderstanding is exactly the sort of confusion a minor is likely to experience.

Buckley's representation that she was old enough to buy a car is significantly different from the representations in the cases holding that the minor cannot disaffirm. Unlike the minors in *Carney, Clemons,* and *Watters,* Buckley never stated her age at all. Also unlike the facts in those cases, Buckley's assertion, taken to mean what she intended it to mean (that she was old enough to drive), was not even false. Further, Buckley made only this single, ambiguous statement, in comparison to the several oral and written assertions of a specific age, as in the facts of the earlier cases.

Buckley's statement is much closer to the situation in *Woodall*, in which the minor made the representation unknowingly. In *Woodall*, the minor did not know that he was making the representation because he did not read the form contract he was signing. Buckley did not know that she might be making a representation that she was eighteen because she misunderstood the agent's question. In both cases, the requisite intent to deceive is absent. Because Buckley did not intend to deceive Willis Chevrolet, a court would probably allow her to disaffirm the contract.

However, Buckley must realize that the sales agent's testimony describing their conversation may differ from hers. The agent may remember the conversation differently or may testify falsely. Others may claim to have overheard the conversation. One way or another, Buckley's testimony may be controverted. Further, the documents Buckley signed may have contained representations of age, and other witnesses may testify that Buckley read them. If we decide to proceed with Buckley's case, we will need to learn what testimony Willis Chevrolet will offer and what the documents contain. On the facts we now have, however, a court would probably conclude that Buckley did not fraudulently misrepresent her age.

  B. Willis Chevrolet's reliance on Buckley's representation was probably reasonable.

The next element requires the injured party to have justifiably relied on the representation. *Carney,* 88 S.E.2d at 808. The cases that describe this element allude to the minor's physical appearance, the minor's life circumstances known to the injured party, the lack of any reason to cause the party to suspect the representation, and the lack of a ready means of confirming the representation. *Clemons,* 187 S.E. at 712-713; *Hood,* 125 S.E. at 788; *Carney,* 88 S.E.2d at 808; *Watters,* 146 S.E. at 773-774.

For instance, in *Carney,* the court points out that the minor was married, was a father, and appeared to be of the age of majority. 88 S.E.2d at 808. In *Hood,* the court points to the minor's physical appearance and to the seller's knowledge that the minor had been married and living independently with his wife for about four years. 125 S.E. at 788. While the decisions sometimes articulate the standard as whether the defendant "failed to use all ready means" to ascertain the truth, *see, e.g., Carney,* 88 S.E.2d at 808, none of the reported decisions have found circumstances requiring the defendant to go further than the minor's representation. In fact, *Clemons* specifically held that a contracting party need not undertake an affirmative investigation beyond the representation of age when the contracting party has no reason to doubt the assertion. 187 S.E. at 713-714.

Buckley's facts do not indicate whether the sales agent knew anything about Buckley's life circumstances that would lead the agent to suspect that Buckley might not be eighteen. The facts also do not include a physical description of Buckley, although we can infer that she looks young, as the agent questioned her about her age. Although this issue would be a question of fact at trial, the facts seem similar to the facts in the reported cases. Contrary to the facts in *Hood,* Buckley is close enough to eighteen that an agent probably would not be expected to suspect her minority simply from her appearance. Also unlike the *Hood* facts, we have no reason to believe that the agent knew anything about Buckley's life, nor that he had any reason other than her appearance to suspect that she was a minor. Therefore, the facts may not be sufficient to require the agent to go further than questioning Buckley.

However, one might argue that the agent had at least one "ready means" to verify Buckley's answer, namely asking to see her driver's license. There is no discussion of requiring this simple verification in any of the prior cases, but at least for some of them, that may be because driver's licenses were not required at the time those cases were decided.

Not only would this solution have been simple, but requiring it would facilitate an important policy rationale for the rule. The rule is designed to discourage sellers from being too ready to contract with minors, despite the inherent pressure to make sales. Requiring sellers to verify the ages of buyers who appear young would counteract the possible tendency of sellers to be too easily convinced of a buyer's majority.

The court's ruling on the second element probably would be a close one. However, based on the applicable case law, a court probably would find the agent's reliance reasonable.

C. Buckley had almost certainly reached the age of discretion when she made the representation of her age.

A minor cannot be held responsible for a misrepresentation unless the minor had reached the age of discretion when he or she made the misrepresentation. *Carney,* 88 S.E.2d at 808; *Clemons,* 187 S.E. at 713. A minor reaches the age of discretion when the minor has developed the capacity to conceive a fraudulent intent. *Clemons* points out that most minors have reached the age of discretion for criminal prosecution for fraud at least by the age of fourteen, though probably not by the age of ten. *Clemons* concludes that the eighteen-year-old minor in that case was well within the age of discretion. *Id.* at 713.

Buckley was seventeen when she bought the car, just a few months away from the age of majority. She is three years older than the presumptive age of discretion for criminal prosecution, and criminal prosecution probably requires more assurance of sufficient age than simple estoppel in a contract action. A court almost certainly would conclude that Buckley had reached the age of discretion.

CONCLUSION

Buckley can disaffirm unless (1) she fraudulently misrepresented her age, (2) Willis Chevrolet justifiably relied upon the misrepresentation, and (3) Buckley had reached the age of discretion. On the facts as we presently understand them, a court would probably rule that Buckley did not misrepresent her age. A court might also rule that Willis Chevrolet was not justified in relying on Buckley's representation. Given the probable absence of one required element and the possible absence of another, Buckley can probably disaffirm the contract.

-5-

PART I

MASTERING LEGAL WRITING

CHAPTER 40

GETTING TO KNOW YOURSELF AS A WRITER

§40.1 Product and Process

A writing course focuses on improving both the *product* created through writing and the *process* of creating it. An office memo is an example of product. What should it look like? What should it accomplish? The process of writing is what you do at the keyboard while creating the memo, including what you're thinking while you type.

Process is much harder to teach than product. Product is tangible. It can be held in the hand, and a sample office memo, like the one in Chapter 39, can be discussed in class to learn what makes it effective or ineffective. Process is much harder to observe because it's a series of events that happen mostly in your mind. Imagine a teacher sitting next to you as you write. The teacher would have a difficult time figuring out what you're doing — and you might want the teacher to leave.

There are many different *effective* processes of writing. If you put the 50 best-selling book authors in America into one room and asked them how they write, they would probably give you 50 different answers. But most effective processes of writing share a few basic traits, which we discuss in this and later chapters of this book.

Beyond that, finding the process that works best for you will happen through experimentation in which you simultaneously do *and* think about what you are doing. Notice how you write and reflect on it, by yourself or with your teacher or another student. Reflecting on what you do and how you do it is the most effective way of improving your process of writing.

§40.2 What Do You Do When You Write?

How do you go about writing? What have you done in the past, and how are you doing it in law school? Be completely accurate. If you're asked how you write, it might be tempting to say that you used exactly the process someone recommends — simply because it's human nature to confuse what you set out to do with what you actually did do. (For most people, it takes reflection to separate the two.) If you're open and self-critical about your process, you'll be able to improve it more quickly.

What do you *like* about the way you write? What *frustrates* you? What seems to cause the frustrations? How would you like to be able to write? (What would you like your process to be?) What might it take for you to be able to accomplish that? What methods have you tried out to get there?

When teachers ask individual students questions like these, often the students themselves do most of the brainstorming — because they know themselves better than anybody else can know them and because they really want to find a process that works well for them. That means that you don't need to wait until your next conversation with your teacher to work on your writing process. You can brainstorm with another thoughtful student. Or, while writing, you can have an internal dialog with yourself about what in your process is working and why.

§40.3 Voice

Voice is a personal quality in a person's writing, something that speaks from the page in that writer's own way. Most people have only a slight voice in their writing — and prefer not to write in a way that's unique. There's nothing wrong with that.

Some students enter law school with distinctive written voices of their own. In legal writing courses, they learn that their writing must conform to a number of professional standards. Does that mean that you can no longer write in a voice that is yours? No, but you might need to adapt it to a professional situation. Your voice in professional documents will grow into something different from what it was before law school, but it will still be yours and distinctive — although recognizably professional. Most people who enter law school with distinctive written voices say later, after they have developed a professional voice, that they like the professional version.

§40.4 Confidence

Learning a skill at a higher level of proficiency, with new requirements, can make you feel as though the competency you thought you had before has been taken away from you. Most students feel at least some of that while learning to write at the professional level. The feeling of doubt is sharpest near the beginning. But gradually — very gradually — it is replaced with a feeling of *strength*. By the end of the legal writing course, many students feel much stronger as writers than ever before because they have *become* stronger. For now, please remember this: If in the weeks ahead you fall into doubt about your writing abilities, it will be because you're quickly learning a lot. *It does not necessarily mean you're a bad writer. You might be a good one. Once you absorb what you are learning and start producing professional writing — and that will happen — your prior confidence will return and be stronger than before because you'll now be reaching for mastery.*

Many law students and young lawyers report that while learning legal writing they felt discouraged, but that later they experienced a first moment of validation. That moment might have come late in a semester, when a legal writing professor told them that they had done something really well. Or it might have come in a summer or part-time job, when a supervising lawyer complimented them on a well-written memo. Or it might have come in court when a judge leaned over the bench and said, "It was a pleasure to read your brief, counselor." That first moment of validation was the beginning of the recognition of *mastery*. Mastery was not yet complete; it would take much longer for that to happen. But it had begun.

Many students and young lawyers also say that they wished someone had told them while they were working so hard in legal writing that a moment marking the beginning of mastery would eventually come. That's why we're telling you now that if you're like most students — and even if you feel deeply discouraged along the way — that moment *will* eventually come.

§40.5 Learning Styles and Writing

This section explains three of the most often discussed learning styles. Most people have some of the characteristics of two or all three styles.

Rather than classify yourself in one style or another, you might figure out which style or styles provide your strengths and whether other styles illustrate strengths you want to try to develop. To become effective at learning writing or any other skill, it helps to identify your strengths so you can capitalize on them and identify areas where you need to grow so you can consciously work at causing that growth.

Auditory/sequential learners, or ASLs, absorb information most efficiently by listening. They would rather hear driving directions than look at a map. They tend to think in words rather than pictures. "Sequential" in "auditory/sequential" refers to thinking in a series of ideas that add up in a progression to larger conclusions, like this:

if police violate the Constitution during search or interrogation	→ evidence inadmissible at trial
if police seize stolen property and get a confession	→ both need justification
probable cause for police to stop a car in traffic	→ police had legal authority to do so
no probable cause to search trunk	→ evidence found there should be inadmissible
but driver consented to search	→ evidence found is admissible even though no probable cause

driver in custody after stolen property found in trunk	→ *Miranda* warnings required
driver knowingly and voluntarily waived *Miranda* rights	→ confession admissible
evidence and confession admissible	→ *driver will be convicted of possessing stolen property*

Visual/spatial learners, or VSLs, absorb information most efficiently through seeing — either reading words or looking at pictures, diagrams, or demonstrations. They would rather look at a map than listen to someone give driving directions. More than other people, they think in images, although they also think in words. When reading a story, they often "see" the action in their minds, as though watching a movie, or they create a mental diagram of the relationships among the people involved. "Spatial" in "visual/spatial" refers to several aspects of thinking, among them a tendency to start from an idea and branch out in several directions, sometimes simultaneously, like this:

Tactile/kinesthetic learners, or TKLs, absorb information most efficiently through action. They learn best by doing something rather than by reading or hearing about it or looking at it, especially when doing so involves use of the sense of touch. They also learn well from experience. They would rather explore than look at a map or hear directions. They often think through doing because activity creates insights. While studying, TKLs often feel a desire to move about or do something with their hands because motion is thought.

Imagine that you buy something complicated, perhaps a PC with monitor, keyboard, printer, and speakers. Connecting everything and learning how to use it will be difficult. Inside the boxes are owner's manuals. If you have auditory/sequential strengths, your first instinct might be to read carefully the text in the manuals. If you have visual/spatial strengths, you might look first at the diagrams in a manual and consult the text only if the diagrams don't tell you what you need to know. If you have tactile/kinesthetic strengths, you might toss the manuals aside and start fiddling with the equipment until you've figured out how to install it and how to use it.

This example is somewhat of an oversimplification, but researchers sometimes use it to illustrate differences among the three styles. Manufacturers know about learning styles. They put lots of diagrams in manuals for VSLs, and for TKLs they sometimes include a separate one- or two-page insert with essential information, titled something like "If You Hate Manuals, Use This."

When it comes to writing, people with auditory/sequential strengths tend to focus on the details, and in legal writing, they might intuitively understand how to show the steps of their reasoning in a logical sequence. Regardless of learning style, most students need to improve at explaining their reasoning steps *in depth*. But ASLs and VSLs can be strong at *sequencing* the steps.

People with visual/spatial strengths might more quickly understand an entire situation. They might see the big picture at once. They can seem to sculpt a document rather than writing it from beginning to end. According to a leading researcher in this field,

> For visual-spatials, writing is a lot like painting a picture. They may paint with broad strokes at first, filling in the details as they refine their pictures. In a painting, there's no particular order. You can start in the middle and work toward either end, or you can start at the end and work toward the beginning. I know a VSL who's a superb writer. . . . She cannot show anyone her rough drafts because they are full of holes. These are real gaps in the flow of writing where the picture hasn't formed yet. Being nonsequential in her thinking, she skips around the text, filling in the parts that are clear in her mind, and leaving large, gaping holes. Sometimes these holes are filled in her dreams, as her unconscious supplies the missing words or missing pieces of the picture.[1]

Less is known about TKLs and writing, except that some people with tactile/kinesthetic strengths say that writing helps them think because of the physical activity involved, especially when typing. Some describe this as thinking through their fingers.

In legal writing, *all* of these strengths can be valuable. You can continue to build your skills around the ones you already have. It's *not* necessary to build up the others equally. No one is perfect or equally rounded, and all of us have uneven strengths. Many of the most famous writers can describe in abundant detail where they are weak in the writing process. And everyone can become more effective by identifying areas where they're not strong and by trying to improve there.

Much of education is based on the erroneous assumption that all learners are auditory/sequential. A teacher stands at the front of the room and talks. Students are supposed to sit still for long periods of time. Textbooks are masses of words, and in higher education they have few or no diagrams. In law school, an

---

[1] Linda Kreger Silverman, *Upside-Down Brilliance: The Visual-Spatial Learner* 300 (2002).

exception to all this is in skills courses, where students learn to do things, like write memos or cross-examine witnesses.

Some researchers include learning style categories other than those discussed here, for example *verbal* (learning through reading and writing) and *oral* (learning through talking). These overlap with some of the categories explained earlier in this section. Researchers are still discovering new aspects about learning styles, and much remains to be discovered.

If you want to know more about your learning style or styles, you might look at the books and articles listed in the footnote.[2] And you might do a Web search for the phrase "learning style." The books, articles, and websites explain how people with various learning styles can study more effectively and create more effective learning environments for themselves.

---

[2] Books: Ann L. Iijima, *The Law Student's Pocket Mentor: From Surviving to Thriving* 59-76, 103-106 (2007) and Michael Hunter Schwartz, *Expert Learning for Law Students* (2d ed. 2008). Articles: Robin A. Boyle & Rita Dunn, *Teaching Law Students Through Individual Learning Styles*, 62 Alb. L. Rev. 213 (1998); M.H. Sam Jacobson, *Learning Styles and Lawyering: Using Learning Theory to Organize Thinking and Writing*, 2 J. ALWD 27 (2004); M.H. Sam Jacobson, *How Law Students Absorb Information*, 8 J. of Leg. Writing 175 (2002); and M.H. Sam Jacobson, *A Primer on Learning Styles: Reaching Every Student*, 25 Seattle L. Rev. 139 (2001).

CHAPTER 41

INSIDE THE PROCESS OF WRITING

Learning how to write like a lawyer is the beginning of learning how to make professional decisions. Partly those are analytical decisions, such as determining how a statute affects the client. And partly they're practical decisions, such as how to communicate most effectively to the reader.

§41.1 Five Phases of Writing

Writing happens in five phases:

1. researching authorities and analyzing what you find (*see §41.3*)
2. organizing your raw materials into an outline (*§41.4*)
3. producing a first draft (*§§41.5-41.6*)
4. rewriting it through several more drafts (*§41.7*)
5. polishing it (*§41.9*)

Writing teachers say that writing is recursive and not linear. That means that writers rarely, if ever, start at the beginning, write until they get to the end, and then stop (which would be in a line, or linear). And they do not go through the five phases of writing in strict order, finishing one phase before starting the next one (which also would be linear).

Instead, writers often circle back (recursively) to reopen something already done and redo some aspect of it. You will, for example, continue to analyze while organizing, writing the first draft, and rewriting, although much of the analytical work comes at the beginning. While writing the first draft, you might decide to go back and rewrite something you wrote a few pages ago. While rewriting, you might reorganize.

Still, it helps to think about writing in the five phases listed above. Each phase is a different *kind* of work, requiring somewhat different skills.

§41.2 Managing Time

Suppose your teacher distributes an assignment and sets a deadline three weeks later for submitting your work. On the day you receive the assignment, you have two options.

The first is to toss it aside when you get home so you can try not to think about it for at least two weeks, leaving only the last few days before the deadline to do the entire job. Many students did this in college and turned in their first draft as their final product. When they try it again in law school, the result is usually disappointing because law school writing requires much more preparation and many more drafts. When you're learning professional skills, each new task will usually take longer to accomplish than you might think because the complexities of the task are not immediately apparent. (Later, with experience, you will get much better at predicting how long it will take to get things done.)

The other option is to use the full three weeks to get the job done. Some students have very good internal clocks that pace them through the work without having to set a schedule for themselves. But for most students, time will get out of control unless they schedule. In this sense, planning the work is

1. estimating how long it will take you to do the research, analyze the results, organize your raw materials, produce a first draft, rewrite it through several more drafts, and polish it, and
2. budgeting your time so that you can do each one of these tasks well.

When you first get the assignment, it can seem huge and intimidating. But once you break it down into a group of smaller tasks, it's not as big any more and it seems much more doable. Here is what Amy Stein, a legal writing professor, tells her students:

> When I ask students if they have made a schedule for completing their work, they often look at me as if I have asked them to split the atom. Taking a series of complicated tasks and breaking them into manageable pieces is the best way that I know of to deal with the panic that comes from feeling that I have too much to do in too little time. Preparing a calendar will provide a master plan for all tasks, both work and play.
>
> Students can use a paper calendar or find one on a PDA, calendaring program, or the web. . . .
>
> Building a schedule requires a certain amount of honesty. Students must know their own strengths and weaknesses and be able to answer several questions. . . . Do you work best in short, intense bursts or longer sessions? Where do you work the best? Are you a procrastinator? Are you a morning person or a night person? A morning person should schedule research in the morning and thirty minutes on the elliptical bike at night. . . .
>
> . . . It is marvelously satisfying to cross off what you have accomplished. . . . [1]

---

[1] Amy R. Stein, *Helping Students Understand that Effective Organization Is a Prerequisite to Effective Legal Writing*, 15 Perspectives 36, 37 (2006).

§41.3 Researching and Analyzing

Researching is finding relevant authority, such as statutes and cases. Your teacher has probably assigned a research textbook that explains how to research.

Analysis is deciding which authorities to rely on, figuring out what they mean, and how they govern the client's facts. Students and lawyers usually print out or photocopy the authorities that research suggests might be relevant and mark them up while reading and rereading them, identifying the most significant passages. It helps to outline the statutes and brief the cases.

§41.4 Organizing Your Raw Materials into an Outline

For two reasons, good organization is crucial in legal writing. First, legal writing is a highly structured form of expression because rules of law are by nature structured ideas. The structure of a rule controls the organization of its application to facts — and thus the organization of a written discussion of the rule and its application. Second, legal writing is judged entirely by how well it educates and convinces the reader that your reasoning is correct. Good organization makes your analysis more easily understandable to the reader by leading the reader through the steps of your reasoning.

Many students find that organizing in legal writing is especially challenging. That is why it takes several chapters in this book to explain how to outline and how to organize.

§41.5 Producing a First Draft

Many students treat the first draft as the most important phase of writing. But that is wrong: the first draft is often the *least* important phase. Most of the rest of writing does much more to cause an effective final product. And if you write on a computer, first-draft writing might not be separate from rewriting. That's because of the ease with which you can interrupt your first draft and go back to rewrite something you initially wrote only a few minutes ago.

The only purpose of a first draft is to get things down on the page so that you can start rewriting. The first draft *has no other value*. Despite its many faults, a first draft accomplishes its entire purpose merely by existing.

> All good writers write [awful first drafts]. This is how they end up with good second drafts and terrific third drafts. . . . I know some very great writers, . . . who write beautifully . . . , and not one of them . . . writes elegant first drafts. All right, one of them does, but we do not like her very much. . . .
>
> A friend of mine says that the first draft is the down draft — you just get it down. The second draft is the up draft — you fix it up. . . . And the third draft is the dental draft, where you check every tooth. . . . [2]

---

[2] Anne Lamott, *Bird by Bird*, 21-22, 25-26 (1994).

Do your first draft as early as you possibly can. You can't start rewriting (§41.7) until you have a first draft.

You don't have to write the first draft from beginning to end. You can start with any part of the document that you feel ready to write, no matter where in the document it will be. You can write the middle before you write the beginning, for example. If your mind is mulling over a certain part of the document, start writing that part. You can write the rest later.

§41.6 Overcoming Writer's Block

Suppose you sit down to write your first draft, but nothing happens. You stare at the computer screen, and it seems to stare right back at you. This does *not* mean you're an inadequate writer. Writer's block happens to everybody from time to time, even to the very best writers. What can you do to overcome it? Here are some strategies:

1. Do something unrelated for a while. Prepare for class, do the dishes, or jog. While you're doing something else, your unconscious mind will continue to work on the first draft. After a while, ideas will pop into your conscious mind unexpectedly, and you will need to sit down and start writing again. But be careful: In law, you're usually writing against a deadline, and doing something else cannot go on for too long.

2. If the beginning is blocking you, start somewhere else. The reader starts at the beginning, but you don't have to. A common cause of writer's block is starting to write at the beginning. The beginning of a document is often the hardest part to write. And in each part of the document, the first paragraph is often the hardest to write. One of the reasons is that if you're not sure exactly what you're going to say, you won't know how to introduce it at the beginning.

3. Use writing to reduce your fear. The most effective way to reduce anxiety is to start writing early — long before your deadline — and to keep on working steadily until you're finished. If you start early, you'll lose less sleep and be a happier writer. Many students procrastinate because they worry about writing. But procrastination *increases* anxiety and puts you further and further behind. The only way to break this cycle is to get started on writing so you can bring the task under control.

4. Don't expect perfection in first drafts. If you're chronically blocked when you try to do first drafts, it might be because you expect yourself to produce, in your first draft, a polished final version. That's expecting too much. Even well-known novelists cannot do it. Really bad first drafts are just fine. Keep reminding yourself that the first draft is the *least* important phase of writing. You can afford to write horribly in the first draft because you can fix everything during rewriting.

5. Start writing while researching and analyzing. While you're reading a case, some words of what you would like to say might flash through your mind. Type them or write them down. As you do, sentences might start coming to you. You sat down to research and analyze, but now you're writing. When you run out of steam while writing, go back to researching and analyzing. Experienced writers keep their computer on or a notepad handy while reading statutes, cases, and other authority because reading, thinking, and writing are all part of a single process. To read is to trigger thinking, which can trigger writing. It doesn't matter that you're writing without consulting your outline. You can figure out later where in the document what you are writing goes, or whether it goes in at all.

6. Separate yourself from distractions. If you're distracted by roommates or by the temptation to watch television or play computer games, leave the distractions in one place while you work in another.

§41.7 Rewriting

> There is no such thing as good writing. There is only good rewriting.
> — *Justice Louis Brandeis*

A first draft is for the writer. You write to put your thoughts on the page. But in subsequent drafts, the focus shifts to the reader. How much will *this* reader need to be told? Will she or he understand what you say without having to read twice? Will this reader become convinced that you're right?

To answer these questions while you read your work, pretend to be the reader for whom you're writing. Will this skeptical person see issues that you have not addressed? Will this busy person become impatient at having to wade through material of marginal value that somehow got into your first draft? Will this careful person be satisfied that you have written accurately and precisely?

You'll do a better job of impersonating the reader if, between drafts, you stop writing for a day or two, clear your mind by working on something else, and come back to do the next draft both "cold" and "fresh." Obviously, that cannot happen if you put off starting the project and later have to do the whole thing frantically at the last minute. To make sure that you have time to rewrite, start on an assignment as soon as you get it, and then pace yourself, working at regular intervals within the time allotted.

Actually, with computers, there might not be a clear dividing line between writing a first draft and rewriting it. A writer working on the sixth page of a first draft can interrupt that to rewrite part of page three; return to page six to continue first-draft writing; interrupt that again to make changes in the introduction on page one; then return to page six for more first-drafting; and so on. The writer keeps moving back and forth because while one part of the brain is working on page six, another part is thinking about other pages. This is called *recursive* rather than *linear* writing. You've finished a draft when you feel it's more or less complete, even if you know you'll need to return to it for more rewriting.

Most of the writing you'll do in the practice of law can be made effective in three to five drafts. The paragraphs you're reading now are a fifth draft. (Some parts of this book required 10 or 12 drafts however.)

To experience what the reader will experience, some writers read their drafts out loud, which can alert you to wording problems. Bad phrasing often sounds terrible when you say it. Other writers can get the same effect without speaking because they've developed the ability to "hear" in their minds a voice saying the words they read.

While rewriting, you can test your writing for effectiveness by using the checklists in many chapters of this book. Look for section titles that include the words "Ways to Test."

Don't be afraid to cut out material from your first draft. The fact that you've written something does not mean that you have to keep it.

Eventually, you'll notice, after putting the writing through several drafts, that the problems you find are mostly typographical errors and small matters of grammar, style, and citation. When that happens, you've moved from rewriting into polishing (§41.9), and the project is nearly finished.

For many people, rewriting "is the hardest task of all."[3] Set aside a lot of time for it. Sometimes during rewriting, things will seem discouraging because you will discover that problems you thought you had solved earlier really haven't been. At other times, when you piece things together well, you might experience relief, even exhilaration.

Rewriting may be the hardest phase of writing, but parts of it can be turned into a game. Read the preceding sentence again. During rewriting, the second part of that sentence ("parts of it can be turned into a game") went through the following evolution:

1st draft: . . . there are ways of causing parts of rewriting to include the kinds of fun many people enjoy while playing games.

2d draft: . . . parts of rewriting can be turned into something that includes the fun of a game.

3d draft: . . . parts of it can be turned into a game.

How did this keep getting shorter and more clearer? Convoluted language was made simpler. Things that didn't add understanding were taken out. If games are usually fun, what meaning does the word *fun* add to the word *games*? Rewriting tightened the draft by finding ways to say the same thing more vividly in fewer words.

Look again at the first-draft version above. During rewriting, you would notice its weakness in either of two ways. You might reread it and ask, "What's that supposed to mean? What was I trying to say?" Or a game resembling a treasure hunt might have flagged it.

Overuse of the verb *to be* usually weakens writing. Your writing will become stronger and livelier if you try to replace *is, are, was,* and other forms of *to be* with

---

[3] Peter Elbow, *Writing with Power: Techniques for Mastering the Writing Process* 121 (1981).

action verbs. That doesn't always work, but if you look for opportunities to do it, you'll find some ways to make your writing stronger. (The weakness in the first draft example above begins with "there are," which is a variant of the verb *to be*.)

How can you find all the places where you've used variations of the verb *to be*? Use the "find" feature in your wordprocessor to search for *is*, *are*, and *was*. At every instance, think about replacing the word with an action verb. Sometimes that will strengthen your writing, and sometimes it won't. Decide one way or the other. This might not compare with a top-notch video game, but it does lend itself to thoughts like "Ha! Zapped another one!" You can make a list of words that cause you trouble and do this for each of them.

Although rewriting focuses on the sentence level, it should also consider the big picture. Is your organization natural and effective? As you reread and rewrite, do you have doubts about your analysis? Don't limit yourself to "surface-level changes," but instead use rewriting as "an opportunity to re-see [your] work" as a whole.[4]

Don't confuse rewriting with polishing (§41.9). If all you do is fix typographical errors, awkward wording, grammatical errors, and errors in citation form, you're only polishing, and you've skipped rewriting completely. Rewriting is hard because much of it involves reimagining your first draft and reexamining the decisions you made there. Experienced writers report that they can really enjoy rewriting because of what they can achieve there. "The pleasure of revision [another name for rewriting] often arises when you refine what you intend to say and *even* discover that you have more to say, a new solution, a different path, a better presentation."[5] Research on the writing process has shown that experienced writers use rewriting for deep rethinking, and usually they reorganize the earlier draft.[6]

§41.8 Using Writing to Help You Think

> [T]here is no better way to master an idea than to write about it.
> — *Robert H. Frank*

> I write to discover what I think.
> — *Daniel Boorstin*

> Writing is thinking.
> — *Deirdre McCloskey*

> [L]earning to write as a lawyer is another way to learn to think as a lawyer.
> — *Terrill Pollman*

---

[4] Patricia Grande Montana, *Better Revision: Encouraging Students to See Through the Eyes of the Legal Reader*, 14 J. Legal Writing 291, 292 (2008).
[5] Christopher M. Anzidei, *The Revision Process in Legal Writing: Seeing Better to Write Better*, 8 Leg. Wtg. 23, 44 (2002) (italics added).
[6] *Id.* at 40.

Writing and rewriting will help you expand and refine your analysis. The writing process and the thinking process are inseparable. You can't write without rethinking what you're trying to say.

Wherever you are in writing — in the first draft, in rewriting, or even in polishing — don't be afraid to change your mind about your analysis of the law and the facts. Most writers have abandoned ideas that felt valuable when thought about, sounded valuable when spoken, but nevertheless proved faulty when — in the end — they "wouldn't write."

Most writers have experienced the reverse as well: sitting down to write with a single idea and finding that the act of writing draws the idea out, fertilizes it, causes it to sprout limbs and roots, and to spread into a forest of ideas. The amount of thought reflected in a good final draft is many times the amount that was in the first draft because the writing process and the thinking process are inseparable, each stimulating and advancing the other.

§41.9 Polishing

This is the last phase. Allow a day or more to pass before coming back to the writing to polish it. If you're away from it for at least a day, you'll come back fresh and be able to see things you would otherwise miss.

Print the document so you can see it exactly the way the reader will see it. Readers often see problems on the printed page that aren't so obvious on a computer screen. Before returning to the computer to fix problems, you can mark up the printed copy. This is sometimes called "a red-pen proofread," although you could use another color.

Take one last look for wording that does not say clearly and unambiguously what you mean. This is the biggest reason for waiting at least a day. When you wrote the words, they seemed clear because at that moment you knew what you were trying to say. But after some time has passed, you're no longer in that frame of mind. If you're not sure what the words mean or what you intended them to mean, fix them.

And take one last look for wording that can be tightened up. Can you say it equally well in fewer words? If you can, do so.

Look for typographical errors, awkward wording, grammatical errors, and errors in citation form. Does the formatting make the document attractive to read? If not, choose a different font (but one that looks professional), add white space so the document doesn't seem crowded, or find other ways to make it look attractive.[7] Use your word processor's spellcheck function. Make sure the pages are numbered.

Now, you're finished.

---

[7] See Ruth Anne Robbins, *Painting with Print: Incorporating Concepts of Typographic and Layout Design into the Text of Legal Writing Documents*, 2 J. ALWD 108 (2004).

§41.10 Plagiarism

Plagiarism is using other people's words or ideas as though they were your own. You commit plagiarism if you lift words or an idea from *anywhere* else and put them into your own work without quotation marks (for words) and a citation (for words or ideas).

You already know the ethical and moral reasons not to plagiarize. You heard them in college and high school. Here are three more reasons:

First, you'll feel better about yourself if you don't steal words or ideas from someone else. You can have professional self-respect and pride in your own work only if you did the work yourself. And pride in your own work is one of life's pleasures.

Second, it's so easy to catch plagiarism that you should assume you'll be caught. A teacher can take some of your words and search for them in any of the legal research databases to find the case or article from which they were taken. Many teachers routinely do that. Teachers can also electronically search other students' papers for words like yours. A teacher who designed your assignment and grades the other students' papers knows where all the ideas came from. Even if you copy the detailed structure of your paper from another student, that can be plagiarism, and a teacher who grades both papers will notice it.

Third, your writing actually gains value from appropriate citation to the sources of words and ideas. Much of what you write will have credibility *only* if you show exactly where words and ideas come from. Proper attribution of ideas will allow your reader to rely on your work and to give you credit for ideas that are truly yours.

CHAPTER 42

HOW PROFESSIONAL WRITERS PLAN THEIR WRITING

In college, students are sometimes told that they should do *all* the organizational work in an outline before starting the first draft. Professional writers rarely do that. Before starting the first draft, you need an organization to work from, but it can be flexible. During the first draft and during rewriting, experienced writers typically *re*organize as they write.

§42.1 Myths about Outlines

If you dislike outlining, it may be that you were taught an outlining method that seemed unnecessarily rigid. In college and high school, you might have been told that before you can start writing, you must make an outline with roman numerals, capital letters, and arabic numerals, like this (from a paper on the effectiveness of professional schools):

I. Legal Education
  A. The First Year
      1. Large Classes
      2. The Casebook Method of Teaching
            [and so on]
  B. The Second and Third Years
            [and so on]
II. Medical Education

This is a linear outline. It starts in one place and goes straight from I to II and later from III to IV to the end, with lower-level layers for detail along the way. It outlines the kind of paper you might have written in college and might write for a second- or third-year seminar in law school.

Here, the student has chosen and researched an important topic. But the linear outline might not help the student write. For some students, the linear outline might even make writing more difficult. Many professional writers do *not* plan their work by doing a linear outline in advance. Here's why:

Suppose you're sitting at the keyboard thinking about the project you are working on. Valuable thoughts are running through your mind. At that moment, you are in the groove. Ideas are flowing. This mental state — which some social scientists call "flow" — doesn't happen every day, but you're lucky enough to be in it at this moment. You look at your linear outline (like the one above) and try to find a place to put one of the ideas on your mind. While you're trying to find a place for that idea, all the other ideas in your mind recede. They seem to fly away. And it's hard to find a place in the outline for the one idea that's left because when you made the outline that idea had not yet occurred to you. Trying to deal with your outline has obstructed the flow of ideas.

Or the situation is different: You're not in flow. You haven't written anything yet. But you've made a linear outline. You stare at it and ask yourself, "What should I write under roman numeral I and before letter A?" Five minutes later, you haven't been able to answer that question. You're focused on writing what the outline tells you should be first, but your imagination is dry. The outline hurts you. If you weren't trying to satisfy it, your mind might start thinking about some other part of the project, and ideas would start coming. But as long as you're staring at the outline, your mind shuts down. In fact, "one of the only virtues of linear outlining is that it looks neat, and that very virtue is its downfall. By working to make sure the outline is neat, we effectively cut off any additions or inserts, and new ideas. After all, we do not want to mess up our neat outline."[1]

The principal myth about outlining is that a linear outline helps *everyone* write better. Linear outlining helps some writers, but it hurts others. It might help those who naturally think in a linear fashion. If you don't naturally think that way, a linear outline made before writing might inhibit you from starting to write and might obstruct the flow of ideas while you write. (By the way, if the idea of flow interests you, you might look at some of the books in the footnote.[2] Your university or public library probably has some of them.)

Linear outlining can also interfere with what writing teachers call the recursive nature of writing. Writing as a process does not go neatly from one step to the next. It goes back and forth from one aspect of writing to another and in several directions at once (see Chapter 41). The process through which writers create can be messy. A messy process is fine as long as it leads to a neat and orderly final product.

This is why many students resist outlining in college. Outlining can seem like an arbitrary and useless requirement. But you still need to organize what you will

---

[1] Henriette Anne Klauser, *Writing on Both Sides of the Brain* 48 (1987).
[2] See Susan K. Perry, *Writing in Flow* (2001), as well as the following books by Mihaly Csikszentmihalyi: *Finding Flow* (1998), *Flow: The Psychology of Optimal Experience* (1990); *Beyond Boredom and Anxiety* (1975); *Optimal Experience* (edited with Isabella Selega Csikszentmihalyi, 1988); and *Flow in Sports* (with Susan A. Jackson, 1999).

say, and you will need to create an outline — but maybe not the way you were taught to do it in college.

§42.2 A Method Used by Many Professional Writers to Plan Their Writing

Organizing really means two things: For the writer, organizing is structuring the document. This is part of the *process* of writing explained in Chapters 40 and 41. For the reader, however, organization should be *visible in the product* so the reader doesn't get lost. Thus, you'll organize before the first draft, just to get the writing started in a coherent way. You'll also reorganize during the first draft and later during rewriting — so the reader can understand.

Sometimes the original organization works well and doesn't need much reworking. But often you'll need to do a lot of reorganizing while rewriting until you find a structure that works. When you reorganize a lot, that does not necessarily mean you have been making mistakes and are now fixing them. Most of the time, reorganizing happens because the act of writing teaches you the analysis you are trying to write. *Writing is thinking.* You can't rewrite without rethinking what you're trying to say. Reorganizing is a natural part of rewriting.

This makes outlining easier because it doesn't have to be perfect the first time. Before a first draft, you can do a quick-and-dirty *fluid outline*. Then in later drafts, you can reorganize, if necessary, to meet the reader's expectations. With experience, you'll gain foresight. Your first drafts will become more organized, and you'll need to do less and less reorganizing in later drafts. But even the most experienced writers reorganize a lot of what they write.

Before a first draft: Make a fluid outline, which is just a flexible collection of lists on scratch paper or on your computer. Your raw materials (cases, facts, hypotheses, and so on) flow through it and into your first draft. Begin by identifying the issues. For each issue, identify the rule of law that controls the answer. Then make a list (either on paper or on your computer screen) of everything you found through research that proves the rule is accurate and another list of everything that supports your application of the rule to the facts. With practice, you might not even make lists; you might just make piles of your photocopies or printouts. As you write about an issue during your first draft, cross off things on your list (or move things out of your pile). When you've crossed off everything on your list, go on to the next issue. When you've done all the issues, you have completed a first draft of the Discussion if you are writing an office memo, or of the Argument if you are writing a motion memo or appellate brief.

Many professional writers organize this way: making lists or piles, knowing that they'll be finished when everything is crossed out or a pile is empty. This method is only a suggestion. If you develop a different procedure that works better for you, use yours instead.

In later drafts: Linear outlines are *not* inherently bad. Although linear outlines might obstruct producing a first draft, they can help to improve later drafts during rewriting. To do that, you would create *a post-draft linear outline* — a linear outline of what you've *already* written. That might seem strange, but for many writers it works. *A finished product should be organized the way a linear outline is — even if you used a fluid outline to produce your first draft.*

To find out whether this method would work for you, print out a copy of your draft and read it, asking yourself whether you've incorporated a linear outline into your writing without realizing you were doing so. If the answer is yes, that increases the odds that you have organized effectively.

At each point in your draft where you state an important conclusion or start a new topic, write a heading that reflects that. You can handwrite the headings in the margins of your printed draft. The headings will resemble the items that would be listed in a linear outline. For example, if you were writing a seminar paper on the topic partially outlined at the beginning of this chapter, you would write in the margin "The Casebook Method of Teaching" at the point where you finish talking about whether large classes work well and where you are about to start talking about casebooks.

After you've done this to your entire draft, step back and look at your headings. For the moment, look at the headings alone and ignore the rest of your draft. You're trying to see the big picture. Are the headings in a logical order? Do they cover everything? Do they lay out the analysis in a way that would be clear to the reader? If you answer yes to these questions, you might have a good organization — and you've now produced good headings, which you can insert into your draft if they would help guide the reader.

But if any of the answers is no, use the cut-and-paste feature of your word processor to rearrange portions of your draft. Then reread everything to make sure that individual sentences and paragraphs still work well in their new locations. You might need to reword some things.

§42.3 Some Other Methods Used by Professional Writers to Plan Their Writing

Some writers outline by writing on sticky notes and putting them on a wall. The outline can be reshuffled by moving the notes around.

Some outline by making flowcharts in which the things to be written about appear in boxes or ovals with arrows showing their relationship to each other and the order in which they'll be discussed. For some very visual writers, this accurately reflects how they think about what they are writing.

A few outline with mind-mapping software like Inspiration.

And some outline the linear way, with roman numerals, as illustrated at the beginning of this chapter. It has worked well for them, and they're happy with it.

CHAPTER 43

PARAGRAPHING

This chapter explains how to structure paragraphs to help the reader see your reasoning.

§43.1 How Paragraphs Reveal the Details of your Organization

Most readers unconsciously use paragraph divisions to learn how a writer's thoughts fit together. They assume that each paragraph substantiates or explores a separate and distinct idea or subject. They also assume that the first or second sentence in each paragraph states or implies that idea or subject and, if necessary, shows how it is related to matters already discussed. To the extent that you frustrate these assumptions, your writing will be less helpful to the reader and therefore less influential.

An effective paragraph has five characteristics. First, it has *unity*: It proves one proposition or covers one subject. Material more relevant to other propositions or subjects has been removed and placed elsewhere. Second, an effective paragraph has *completeness*: It includes whatever is needed to prove the proposition or cover the subject. Third, an effective paragraph has *internal coherence*: Ideas are expressed in a logical sequence that the reader can follow without having to edit the paragraph mentally while reading. Fourth, an effective paragraph is of *readable length*: It's neither so long that the reader gets lost nor so short that valuable material is underdeveloped or trivialized. Fifth, an effective paragraph announces or implies its purpose at the outset: Its *first or second sentence states or implies its thesis or topic* and, if necessary, makes a transition from the preceding material.

§43.2 Descriptive Paragraphs and Probative Paragraphs

The way you write a paragraph depends on whether you are describing something or proving something. Compare these paragraphs:

Descriptive	*Probative*
In January in Death Valley, the average high temperature is about 65°, and the average low is about 37°. Spring and fall temperatures approximate summer temperatures elsewhere. In April and in October, for example, the average high is about 90°, and the average low about 60°. July is the hottest month, with an average high of about 116° and an average low of about 87°. The highest temperature ever recorded in Death Valley was 134° on July 10, 1913. Average annual rainfall is about 1½ inches.	The climate in Death Valley is brutal. At Furnace Creek Ranch, the highest summer temperature each year reaches at least 120° and in many years at least 125°. The highest temperature recorded in Death Valley — 134° — is also the highest recorded in the Western Hemisphere and the second highest recorded anywhere on earth. (The highest is 136° — in the Sahara.) In the summer sun, a person can lose four gallons of perspiration a day and — in 3% humidity — die of dehydration.

A topic is a category of information, such as "weather in Death Valley." After reading the descriptive paragraph, you know some weather details about Death Valley. Descriptive paragraphs are *about* things.

A proposition, on the other hand, can be proved or disproved — such "the climate of Death Valley is brutal." After reading the probative paragraph, you have a reaction to that proposition. You might agree with it or disagree. A probative paragraph should try to *prove* something.

If a descriptive paragraph confuses a reader, the reader might ask, "What is this paragraph about?" But if a probative paragraph confuses, the reader might instead ask, "What is this paragraph supposed to prove?"

Probative and descriptive writing can occur in the same document. In an office memo, for example, the fact statement is mostly descriptive, and the Discussion is mostly probative.

Even in probative writing, some paragraphs are descriptive. If it takes three pages to prove a particular proposition, at least a few paragraphs in those three pages will have to describe the raw materials involved — statutes, cases, or facts, for example. Proof is explaining *how* the raw materials support the proposition being proved. Sometimes we have to describe the raw materials before we can explain how they prove something.

§43.3 Proposition Sentences, Topic Sentences, and Transition Sentences

A probative paragraph begins by stating a proposition. The first or second sentence in the paragraph states the proposition and is the *proposition sentence*. The rest of the paragraph should prove the proposition.

A descriptive paragraph provides details about a topic. The first or second sentence in the paragraph, the *topic sentence*, can expressly state the topic or imply it. Sometimes the topic sentence can be omitted if the context implies the topic.

Although in descriptive writing a topic can often be implied, in probative writing the proposition should be expressly stated. A practical reader needs to know what you are trying to prove before you start proving it.

With either type of paragraph, a *transition phrase or sentence* can show the reader how the paragraph is connected to the material before it or the material after it. Although a transition is not required, it often helps the reader understand what you are doing. A transition most often appears at the beginning of a paragraph and less often at the end, as a bridge into the next paragraph. Often the first sentence of a paragraph can both state a proposition or topic and make a transition.

§43.4 How to Test your Paragraphs for Effectiveness

In first drafts, paragraphs are seldom put together well. To identify the paragraphs in need of rehabilitation, ask yourself the following questions. They also appear on this book's website as a checklist, which you can print out.

1. Does each paragraph have one purpose? Prove one proposition or describe one subject. Remove and place elsewhere material that is more relevant to other propositions or subjects.

2. Have you told the reader, near the beginning of each paragraph, the paragraph's proposition (for a probative paragraph) or its topic (for a descriptive paragraph)? If the reader does not learn the paragraph proposition or topic at the beginning, the reader often must read the paragraph two or three times to figure out its purpose. A topic sentence is unnecessary when the topic is clearly implied by the context.

3. Have you broken up paragraphs that were so large that a reader would get lost in them? Paragraphs that wander aimlessly or endlessly confuse a reader. When that happens, you have probably tried to develop two or more complex and separable themes in a single paragraph, perhaps without realizing it. Identify the individual themes and then break up the material accordingly into digestible chunks — which become separate paragraphs.

4. Within each paragraph, have you expressed your ideas in a logical and effective sequence? When a paragraph confuses but nothing is wrong with its size or with the wording of individual sentences, the paragraph usually lacks internal coherence. That happens when ideas within the paragraph are presented in a sequence that makes it hard for the reader to understand them or how they fit together to prove the proposition or illuminate the topic.

CHAPTER 44

WRITING AN EFFECTIVE SENTENCE

§44.1 How to Test your Sentences for Effectiveness

Sentences usually don't become effective until later drafts. While rewriting, ask yourself the following questions. They also appear on this book's website as a checklist, which you can print out.

1. Have you gotten the reader to the verb as fast as possible? The verb holds a sentence together. In fact, a sentence is usually incomprehensible until the reader has identified both a subject and a verb. For example:

> The defendant's use of email spam to solicit contributions to a fake charitable organization purportedly engaged in disaster relief and his use of the contributions to buy a vacation home for himself constitutes fraud.

This sentence cannot be understood in a single reading because it's "front-loaded." You don't reach the verb and object ("constitutes fraud") until after you have plowed through a subject 32 words long. Then, you have to read the sentence again because everything you read before finding the verb made no sense the first time you read it.

During first drafts, writers often ask themselves, "What shall I talk about next?" and then write down the answer. That becomes the subject of a sentence, no matter how unreadable the result. We all do this in first drafts, but in rewriting you can recognize the problem and fix it.

You can fix a front-loaded sentence by reshuffling it to bring the reader to the verb quickly:

> The defendant committed fraud by using email spam to solicit contributions for a fake charitable organization purportedly engaged in disaster relief and by using the contributions to buy a vacation home for himself.

Or you can break up the sentence into two or more shorter sentences:

> The defendant committed fraud. He used email spam to solicit contributions for a fake charitable organization purportedly engaged in disaster relief, and he used the contributions to buy a vacation home for himself.

2. Have you put the verb near the subject and the object near the verb? Many readers get lost in a sentence where something has been inserted between a subject and a verb or between a verb and an object:

> The Wabash Garage Orchestra, even though it includes 32 musicians, some with cellos or other large instruments, played the Philip Glass Violin Concerto while sitting in trees in Fabian Smedley's back yard.

Move the problem words to the end or to the beginning of the sentence, leaving the subject and verb (or a verb and an object) relatively close together.

move phrase or clause to the end of the sentence:	The Wabash Garage Orchestra played the Philip Glass Violin Concerto while sitting in trees in Fabian Smedley's back yard, even though the orchestra includes 32 musicians, some with cellos or other large instruments.
move phrase or clause to the beginning of the sentence:	Even though it includes 32 musicians, some with cellos or other large instruments, the Wabash Garage Orchestra played the Philip Glass Violin Concerto while sitting in trees in Fabian Smedley's back yard.

3. Have you put the most complicated part of the sentence at the end? To understand a sentence, a reader has to figure out its structure. Readers do this quickly and unconsciously while they read. When they can't figure out the structure easily, they have to read the sentence again — or they ignore the sentence and keep reading without ever learning what the sentence meant. Compare these:

complicated part at the beginning:	Because the defendant's website is interactive and allows a person in any state to order a catalogue, send a message to the defendant, and purchase beer or wine by typing in credit card and other information, the court held that it has jurisdiction over the defendant.
complicated part in the middle:	The court held that, because the defendant's website is interactive and allows a person in any state to order a catalogue, send a message to the defendant, and purchase beer or wine by typing in

	credit card and other information, the court has jurisdiction over the defendant.
complicated part at the end:	The court held that it has jurisdiction over the defendant because the defendant's website is interactive and allows a person in any state to order a catalogue, send a message to the defendant, and purchase beer or wine by typing in credit card and other information.

Most readers find the third example the easiest to read because the first thing they see is simple ("The court held that it had jurisdiction over the defendant"). Once they understand that, the complicated part makes sense.

4. Have you put what you want to emphasize at the beginning or at the end of the sentence? The beginning or end of a sentence is more obvious than the middle. Sometimes, the end is more obvious just because that is the last thing the reader reads before going on to something else. And sometimes the beginning is more obvious — for example, if the sentence is the first one in a paragraph.

5. If you need to contrast one thing from another, have you used the most effective sentence structure and wording? Some sentence structures and words show contrast better than others do. For example:

> The Supreme Court has held that a defendant waives the objection by not making it at trial, but the Court has also held that, even without an objection, a conviction should be reversed where a prosecutor's conduct was as inflammatory as it was here.

The word *but*, buried in the middle of a long sentence, only weakly alerts the reader that one idea (the rule about waiver) is being knocked down by another (the exception for inflammatory prosecutorial conduct). Everybody writes this kind of thing in rough drafts, but it should be recognized and cured during rewriting:

> Although the Supreme Court has held that a defendant waives the objection by not making it at trial, the Court has also held that, even without an objection, a conviction should be reversed where a prosecutor's conduct was as inflammatory as it was here.

Although tells the reader right away that the sentence's first clause will turn out not to matter. When *but* appears at the beginning of a sentence, it, too, can show contrast well:

> The Supreme Court has held that a defendant waives the objection by not making it at trial. But the Court has also held that, even without an objection, a conviction should be reversed where a prosecutor's conduct was as inflammatory as it was here.

No rule of grammar forbids starting a sentence with *but* or *and*. Doing it constantly, though, can make your writing tedious.

6. Have you made the subject of a sentence or clause someone or something who is, was, or will be doing something? And have you used a verb in the active voice? If the answer to these questions is no, do you have a good reason for using the passive voice? First, figure out who or what is, was, or will be doing something. Make them or it the subject of the sentence or clause. Then choose a verb in the active voice that expresses what they are doing, have done, or will do. But don't do any of this if you have a good reason to use the passive voice.

In the active voice, the subject of the sentence acts ("Maguire sued Schultz"), but in the passive voice the subject of the sentence is acted upon ("Schultz was sued by Maguire"). Here are two more examples:

passive: The deadline was missed by the student.
active: The student missed the deadline.

The passive voice can be vague, weak, and boring. Although most sentences should be in the active voice, sometimes the passive voice works better. The passive may be more effective when you do not know who acted, when the identity of the actor is unimportant, when you want to deemphasize the identity of the actor, or when you want to emphasize something other than the actor. For example, compare these:

passive: Ms. Blitzstein's assistance-to-needy-family benefits have been wrongfully terminated fourteen times in the last six years.
active: The Department of Public Welfare has wrongfully terminated Ms. Blitzstein's assistance-to-needy-family benefits fourteen times in the last six years.

Depending on the context, the passive sentence might not be vague. Here, the reader might know that the Department is the only agency capable of terminating aid-to-dependent-family benefits, or at least that the Department is being accused of doing so in this instance. And, again depending on the context, the passive sentence may be the stronger and more interesting of the two. If the reader is a judge who is being asked to order the Department to stop this nonsense, the passive is the stronger sentence because it emphasizes the more appealing idea. Generally, a judge is more likely to sympathize with a victim of bureaucratic snafus than to condemn a government agency for viciousness or incompetence.

Sometimes, the passive voice is a good way of avoiding sexist pronouns. See §45.4, question 11.

7. Have you found ways to avoid the verb "to be" ("is," "was," etc.)? In law, people do things to other people and to ideas and objects, which you can describe with verbs that let the reader *see* the action. For example:

weak:	The ginger in the soup was the source of the wonderful smell that was in our house.
much better:	The ginger in the soup made our house smell wonderful.
weak:	There is a possibility of action in the near future by the EPA to remove these pesticides from the market.
much better:	The EPA might soon prohibit sale of these pesticides.

In the "weak" examples, you can barely tell who has done what to whom because the lofty tone obscures the action, and because the nouns and verbs do not stand out, take charge, and create action. In the "much better" examples, the reader immediately knows what's happening and does not have to read the same words twice.

The verb *to be* creates problems. *To be* includes *is, are, was, were,* and some other forms that occur less often. They do a good job of describing condition or status ("the defendant is guilty"). But they obscure action. Legal writing creates temptations to use *there is* and its variations (*there are, there were*). Often — though not always — editing them out creates stronger and tighter wording:

weak:	There are four reasons why the plaintiff will not recover. . . .
much better:	For four reasons, the plaintiff will not recover. . . .

Early drafts often include sentences like the "weak" examples above, but rewriting can produce final drafts that more closely resemble the "much better" ones. While rewriting, look for sentences like the "weak" ones, where the verb obscures action. Figure out what's *really* going on (who is doing what?). You can even use your word processor's "find" function to locate instances where you have used one of the four most common forms of the verb *to be* — *is, are, was,* and *were*. You'd have to search separately for each form. When you find one, ask yourself whether it obscures what's really going on. If the answer is yes, redo the sentence with an action verb. If the answer is no, leave the sentence as it is.

8. If a sentence is too long or too complicated to be understood easily the first time it is read, have you either streamlined it or broken it up into two or more sentences? You can express the sentence's ideas in fewer words. Or you can split the sentence into two or more shorter sentences. Or you can do both.

9. Have you violated any of these guidelines *only when you have a good reason for doing so.* Writing is creative work, and guidelines are meant to be violated — when you have a good reason. To test whether your reason is a good one, try to articulate for yourself exactly what it is. Your teacher might ask, too.

§44.2 Citing with Style and Grace

Citations in the text of a document can make the text hard to read. A reader has to jump over all the names, numbers, and parentheticals; find the spot where the text begins again and then pick back up on the message of the text. Granted, law-trained readers become fairly good at these mental and visual gymnastics, but even law-trained readers can use all the help a writer can give them. Here are some suggestions for minimizing the disruption caused by citations:

1. Case names and citations placed in the middle of the sentence make it hard to find the key parts of the sentence and combine them into a coherent thought. For instance, notice how a reader must hop through this sentence:

> A majority of the Court in *General Electric Company v. Gilbert*, 429 U.S. 125, 136 (1976), followed *Geduldig v. Aiello*, 417 U.S. 484 (1974), and held that pregnancy classifications were not gender classifications.

When possible, use the following techniques to clear the reader's path from subject to verb to object:

a. Move the citation outside the sentence and into its own citation sentence.
b. Move the citation to the beginning of the sentence.
c. When the sentence contains two propositions, each requiring its own authority, consider dividing the sentence into two sentences. Then each citation can be moved outside the textual sentences.
d. Consider moving less important material into a parenthetical in the citation.

Notice how techniques b and d have improved the readability of the sentence:

> In *General Electric Company v. Gilbert*, 429 U.S. 125, 136 (1976) (following *Geduldig v. Aiello*, 417 U.S. 484 (1974)), a majority of the Court held that pregnancy classifications were not gender classifications.

If the case name is not important, you could even move the citation outside the textual sentence, like this:

> In 1974, a majority of the Court held that pregnancy classifications were not gender classifications. *General Electric Company v. Gilbert*, 429 U.S. 125, 136 (1976) (following *Geduldig v. Aiello*, 417 U.S. 484 (1974)).

2. Avoid beginning a sentence with a citation when the citation will make the sentence hard to read. Here is an example of a sentence with this impediment and an improved version:

Change   Public Law 95-555, 92 Stat. 2076, October 31, 1978, included
            a new §701(k).
To   Congress added a new version of §701(k) when it enacted
            Public Law 95-555, 92 Stat. 2076, October 31, 1978.

3. As a general rule, avoid long string citations. *String citation* is the term lawyers use for "stringing" a number of citations together to support the same proposition. Lawyers often cite several authorities for an important proposition, but the longer the "string," the more the citations impair readability. Further, as citations are devoid of discussion, the long list seldom adds much to the legal analysis.

Generally, it is better to cite and discuss the several most important authorities and omit the others. However, string cites are appropriate when your reader needs every relevant authority or when you wish to demonstrate, graphically on the page, the overwhelming strength of support for the proposition.[1]

---

[1] If you do cite to multiple authorities, place them in the order set out by ALWD Rule 45 or *Bluebook* Rules 1.3 and 1.4.

CHAPTER 45

EFFECTIVE STYLE: CLARITY, VIVIDNESS, AND CONCISENESS

In first drafts, style is usually pretty awful. Most writers achieve effective style only through rewriting, as they look for opportunities to make the earlier drafts clearer and more vivid and concise.

§45.1 Clarity and Vividness

> If the reader thinks something you wrote is unclear, then it is, by definition.
>
> — *Deirdre N. McCloskey*

Unclear writing can make it hard or impossible for your reader to agree with you. Even if a reader could — with effort — figure out what you mean, readers in the legal profession usually cannot give you that effort. They don't have the time. A disappointed senior lawyer may return your memo to you and ask you to rewrite it, which may damage your credibility. A judge may rule against you because the judge could not understand your arguments.

Vividness goes a step further. Clear writing communicates a message. Adding a vivid image can make the message memorable and convincing. Vividness isn't always necessary. It's usually enough to concentrate on clarity and to add vividness only when you see an opportunity to do so in a professional way.

Unfortunately, many students arrive in law school without a solid instinct for effective style because much of the assigned reading in college lacks clarity and vividness.

Important-sounding words can be less clear and vivid than simple and straightforward ones. You might be able to sound like a lawyer but fail to *communicate* like one — for example by writing *ingested* (an impressive but vague word) instead of something that would tell exactly what happened, such as *ate* or *drank* or *swallowed*. Judges and senior lawyers want to read straightforward English. In one experiment, some appellate judges and their law clerks were asked to appraise contorted writing in "legalese," while others were asked to evaluate the same material rewritten into "plain English." They thought the original legalese "substantively weaker and less persuasive than the plain English versions."[1] And the judges and law clerks assumed that the lawyers who wrote in plain English worked in higher prestige jobs.[2]

§45.2 Conciseness

> The present letter is a very long one simply because I had no time to make it shorter.
>
> — *Pascal*

First drafts are usually too wordy. In later drafts, you can tighten up the writing by finding ways to say the same things in fewer words so your work can more easily be read and understood. Later drafts might grow in length, however, when you add *ideas* that weren't in the first draft because the process of rewriting helps you see what's missing intellectually. Rewriting for conciseness can help make room for these new ideas.

Compare two versions of the same sentence. The facts — though not the words — come from *Sherwood v. Walker*,[3] a classic mutual-mistake-of-fact case discussed in many Contracts casebooks.

verbose: It is important to note that, at the time when the parties entered into the agreement of purchase and sale, neither of them had knowledge of the cow's pregnant condition.

---

[1] Robert W. Benson & Joan B. Kessler, *Legalese v. Plain English: An Empirical Study of Persuasion and Credibility in Appellate Brief Writing*, 20 Loyola L.A. L. Rev. 301, 301 (1987).
[2] *Id.* at 301-02.
[3] 33 N.W. 919 (Mich. 1887).

concise: When the parties agreed to the sale, neither knew the cow was pregnant.

How did the verbose first draft become the tight rewrite?

It is important to note that	*was deleted*	
at the time when	*became*	when
entered into the agreement of purchase and sale	*became*	agreed to the sale
neither of them	*became*	neither
had knowledge of	*became*	knew
had knowledge of the cow's pregnant condition	*became*	knew the cow was pregnant

Be careful, though, not to edit out needed meaning. It would be a mistake to eliminate so much that a reader would not know that the cow was pregnant when sold or that the parties did not know of the pregnancy at the time.

As you write and rewrite, avoid the temptation to imitate whatever you happen to find in judicial opinions that appear in your casebooks. Opinions appear in casebooks for what they tell you about the law — not for what they tell you about how to write. In the last two or three decades, lawyers and judges have changed the way they think about writing. Verbosity, obscurity, arcaneness, and disorganization that were tolerated two generations ago are now considered unacceptable because they make the reader's job harder. Some of the opinions in your casebooks are hard to understand because they discuss difficult concepts. But some are hard to understand because they're badly written. Before you imitate something you've seen in an opinion, ask yourself whether you want to do so because you feel safer doing what a judge has done — which is *not* a good basis for a professional decision — or because it would actually accomplish your purpose.

§45.3 Our Style and Yours

You might notice places in this book where our own writing can be improved. We can't say that our writing styles are perfect. No style is. The best a writer can hope for is an *effective* style — one that generally provides what the reader needs.

If in our writing you notice clarity, vividness, or conciseness, it might be worth emulating whatever we did to achieve that — *if* doing so would work well in the assignment you are working on. (That's a big *if*.) **But please do *not* emulate the *informal* style of this book.** Informality in a textbook can help students learn difficult skills. The writing you submit to senior lawyers and judges should be formal.

Our own memos and briefs contain no contractions (two words merged with an apostrophe). Contractions might be appropriate in an informal letter to a client, but they have no place in formal documents. In our memos and briefs, you would see far fewer dashes and italics than appear in this book. In a formal document, an occasional dash or italicized word or phrase might help make a point, but not often. Here are some guidelines for formal documents:

contractions: *never*
italics: *rarely* (and only when truly helpful)
dashes: *infrequently* (and only when grammatically correct)

§45.4 How to Test your Writing for Effective Style

While rewriting, ask yourself the following questions. They also appear on this book's website as a checklist, which you can print out.

1. Is everything crystal clear for the reader? Sometimes a phrase or a sentence will seem clear in a first draft. But when you read it again while rewriting, you're not so sure. You have an advantage the reader doesn't: *You* know what you're trying to say. Put yourself in the position of someone who doesn't know that. Will it be clear to that person? Try to read your draft like the supervisor who will read your office memo or the judge who will read your motion memo or brief. It's easier to think like that reader if you allow some time to pass before going back to your draft. A day or two doing something else will help you return to the draft refreshed. Try to read quickly like a busy person and skeptically like someone who must make a decision. Is everything clear? If not, fix the problem.

2. Have you used transitional words to show the relationships between ideas? Transitional words can help lead the reader through ideas by specifying their relationships with each another and by identifying the ideas that are most important or compelling.

when introducing new or supplemental material
additionally
and
besides
furthermore
in addition (to)
in fact
moreover

when explaining how thoughts relate to each other
finally
first . . . second . . . third *(when listing reasons)*
in fact
not only . . . , but also
on these facts

specifically
under these circumstances

when pointing out similarities
analogously
similarly

when introducing inferences or explaining how one thing causes another
accordingly
as a result
because
consequently
for that reason
since
therefore
thus

when pointing out differences, inconsistency, or lack of causation
although
but
conversely
despite
even if
even though
however
in contrast
in spite of
instead of
nevertheless
on the contrary
on the other hand

when introducing examples
for example
for instance
such as

when explaining time relationships
after
afterward
at the same time
before
later
previously
then

Transitional words can be placed at the beginning of a paragraph, at the beginning of a sentence, or inside a sentence. Choose the spot that best makes the point without being awkward.

Some words work better than others at showing causation. *Because* and *since* are usually clearer than *as* and *so*. Both *as* and *so* can confuse a reader who sees them more often doing other things, such as joining contemporaneous events ("the muggles gasped as Harry flew past on his Nimbus 2000") or emphasizing abundance ("they were so astonished that . . .").

3. Have you replaced unnecessarily complicated verbs with simple ones? For example:

delete	*replace with*
entered into an agreement	agreed
gave consideration to	considered
had knowledge of	knew
was aware of	knew
is able to	can
is binding on	binds
made a determination	determined
made allegations of	alleged
made a motion for	moved for
made the argument that	argued that
made the assumption that	assumed that
took into consideration	considered

4. Have you streamlined unnecessarily wordy phrases? For example:

delete	*replace with*
because of the fact that	because
for the purpose of	to
for the reason that	because
in the case of	in
in the event that	if
in the situation where	where (or when)
subsequent to	after
with regard to	regarding
with the exception of	except

5. Have you deleted throat-clearing phrases (also known as "long wind-ups")? Phrases like the ones below waste words, divert the reader from your real message, and introduce a shade of doubt and an impression of insecurity. It's acceptable to write them into first drafts to help you get your thoughts onto the page. But in rewriting, delete them.

It is significant that ...
The defendant submits that ...
It is important to note that ...

6. Have you used lists to express coordinated ideas? When you discuss several ideas collectively, you can lead the reader forcefully if you make that clear, perhaps through some sort of textual list introduced by a transition sentence ("The court rejected that position for four reasons ..."), followed by sentences or paragraphs coordinated to the transition sentence ("First ... Second" and so on).

7. When expressing a list, have you used parallel construction and made sure that every item in the list is consistent with the words that introduce the list? For example:

> Martha Stewart was convicted of obstructing justice, making false statements to government investigators, and because she conspired with her broker to commit various crimes.

You can see the problems more easily when the sentence is tabulated

> Martha Stewart was convicted of
>
> 1.   obstructing justice,
> 2.   making false statements to government investigators, and
> 3.   because she conspired with her broker to commit various crimes.

Parallel construction requires that each item in a list be worded in the same grammatical format as the other items. Martha Stewart's list is not parallel. The first and second items are similarly structured phrases ("obstructing justice" and "making false statements ..."). But, unlike the others, the third is a dependent clause, with a subject ("she") and a verb ("conspired"). The third item is also introduced by "because," which is missing from and inconsistent with the way the others are structured. You would not say "because obstructing justice" or "because making false statements."

Consistency with words introducing the list: You can test each item in a list by ignoring temporarily the other items to see whether the sentence works when you leap straight from the introductory words to the item you are testing. Here, it doesn't: "Martha Stewart was convicted of ... because she conspired with her broker to commit various crimes."

A reader unconsciously looks for parallelism and consistency to figure out where one item in a list ends and the next begins, like this:

> Martha Stewart was convicted of obstructing justice, making false statements to government investigators, and conspiring with her broker to commit various crimes.

8. Have you used terms of art where appropriate? When a term of art communicates an idea peculiar to the law, use that term. It conveys the idea precisely, and often it makes long and convoluted explanations unnecessary. Don't write "the court told the defendants to stop building the highway." A precise statement would be, "the court enjoined the defendants from building the highway." But use a term of art *only* to convey its exact meaning. If you use a term of art (perhaps because it sounds lawyer-like) but don't really intend to communicate the idea the term of art stands for, a reader can assume that you don't understand the term or the law. (See the next question.)

9. Have you edited out imitations of lawyer noises? Notwithstanding grievous misconceptions of what is fit and proper, said lawyer noises have, by undisclosed instrumentalities, been entirely expurgated, expunged, and otherwise eliminated from this textbook, both heretofore and hereinafter. (Translation: We kept that stuff out.)

The most influential memos and briefs are written in real English. For example:

just fine:	Elvis has left the building.
bad:	Elvis has departed from the premises.
worse:	It would be accurate to say that Elvis has departed from the premises.
meaningless:	Elvis has clearly and unequivocally left the building.
meaningful:	Uncontroverted evidence shows that Elvis has left the building.

Why is "clearly and unequivocally" meaningless? Elvis could not unclearly or equivocally leave the building. Either he has left, or he hasn't. Writing something like "clearly and unequivocally" pounds the table without adding meaning. But "uncontroverted evidence" says that some evidence shows that Elvis has left and no other evidence shows that he hasn't — which makes it easy for a court to decide that he has gone. We would expect to read in the next sentence about the 27 witnesses who can testify that they saw Elvis go through the stage door, step into a stretch limo, and disappear into the night.

It can take a while to learn how to distinguish between lawyer noises and true terms of art (see question 8, above). When you come across a word or phrase used exclusively by lawyers, ask yourself the following: Is it part of a rule of law you've read in a case or a statute — for example, in an element of a test? Is it the name of a concept that is part of the law, including the policies or the reasoning behind a legal rule? If either answer is yes, you probably have a term of art, although lawyer noises do appear in some statutes and older cases. If both answers are no, you probably have lawyer noise (although it might be a term of art). The answers don't produce 100% accuracy, but they increase the odds of correctly categorizing the word or phrase.

10. Have you placed modifiers so that they communicate exactly what you mean? When people talk, modifiers sometimes wander all over sentences, regardless of what they are intended to modify. But in formal writing, more precision is required. These sentences all mean different things:

> The police are authorized to arrest only the person named in the warrant.
> *[They are not authorized to arrest anyone else.]*
>
> The police are authorized only to arrest the person named in the warrant.
> *[They are not authorized to deport him.]*
>
> Only the police are authorized to arrest the person named in the warrant.
> *[Civilians are not authorized.]*

11. Have you avoided sexist wording? The English language uses the masculine pronouns *he*, *his*, and *him* to refer generally to people of either sex. English lacks a pronoun that would mean "any person," regardless of sex. Here are some solutions:

	To calendar a motion, an attorney must file his moving papers with the clerk.
replace pronoun with "the"	To calendar a motion, an attorney must file the moving papers with the clerk.
make actor plural	To calendar motions, attorneys must file their moving papers with the clerk.
eliminate actor from sentence	A motion is calendared by filing the motion papers with the clerk.

The solution you choose will depend on what you're trying to accomplish. Here, the last solution is the most concise one. But if you want to warn lawyers who carelessly forget to file their moving papers, that point is lost if lawyers are not mentioned.

12. Have you punctuated correctly? Punctuation is really grammar, not style, but we mention it here anyway. Correct punctuation is not decoration. It makes writing clearer and easier to understand — and it can affect your credibility. Many readers will question your analytical abilities if you do not observe the accepted rules of punctuation. (If you have trouble with punctuation, see Chapter 47.)

CHAPTER 46

QUOTING AND PARAPHRASING

§46.1 Quotations

The most common quotation problems are (1) failing to use quotation marks for borrowed language, (2) using too many quotations, (3) insufficiently editing quotations, and (4) making errors in the mechanics of quoting. The remainder of this chapter deals with these common quotation problems.

§46.1.1 When Quotation Marks are Required

Quotation marks are required to designate places where a writer has used the words of another.[1] Requiring quotation marks furthers several important policies.[2] First, the quotation marks ensure that the creator will have the credit (or blame) for the creation. Second, the quotation marks allow the writer to avoid claiming undeserved credit; even if the creator does not desire recognition, you should not take credit for someone else's work. Finally, the quotation marks inform readers of the source of the creation. Irrespective of the interests of the two authors, readers deserve accurate information about who created what.

For these policy reasons, quotation marks are necessary when you quote the words of another but unnecessary when you paraphrase. However, sometimes it is hard to know whether a particular passage is a quotation or a paraphrase. When are the words yours and when are they "the words of another"?

Start with the proposition that you should attempt to rephrase the thoughts of others into your own words and sentence structures. However, even if you are not looking at the source while you write, you might find that your text turns out to be similar to your source's text. This result can occur because the source uses words that are commonly used to express the idea, because the sentence structure the

---

[1] *Ideas* that come from another author must always be attributed to the other author. This section assumes that you are attributing the *ideas* to their source, according to proper citation form. Here we deal only with deciding when to attribute the *words* as well.

[2] Copyright law can create legal requirements in addition to the policies described here.

source used is commonplace, because without realizing it, you have been thinking of the topic in the source's words, or some combination of all three.

If the original text used the word "table" and you use it, too, no one would
argue that you should put quotation marks around "table" in your document.
However, if your draft shares a whole paragraph in common with the original text,
everyone understands that the paragraph must be designated by quotation marks
or by blocking the material. Somewhere between these two extremes lies the
point at which the words are those of another (and quotation marks become necessary), but no bright-line test will tell you precisely where.

The absence of a clear test is particularly unfortunate for legal writers. Legal
writers rely heavily on sources, and most legal writing texts advise writers to paraphrase rather than quote the majority of those sources. If you follow this good
advice, you will be doing a lot of paraphrasing. How can you know whether your
paraphrase is sufficiently different from the original author's text to free you from
the requirement of using quotation marks?

To gauge how similar your text is to another writer's text, consider the *combined effect* of these factors: (1) the length of the common unit of text, (2) the
number of units in common, (3) whether the sentence structure is the same or
similar, and (4) whether the common units include language that the original
author used in particularly effective ways.

Some writers use a seven-word benchmark as a starting point for measuring
the length of a common unit requiring quotation marks; if seven or more words
used together in your text match the text of the source, use quotation marks for
those words. The benchmark recognizes the unlikelihood of a common seven-
word unit appearing inadvertently in text by different authors. It also acknowl-
edges that a passage of at least seven words is sufficiently long to merit recognition
of the original author for assembling the words into a unit of text, even if it is the
only common unit and even if the unit has no distinctive characteristics or particular merits. So be sure to use quotation marks *at least* for any unit of seven or
more words that your text shares in common with another.

However, don't think you can avoid using quotation marks simply by changing every seventh word. The seven-word benchmark is only an approximate measure of when the writing is similar enough to require quotation marks, and it only
applies when no other similarities are present. You also must consider whether
there are other common units of text and whether the sentence structure is similar. Would an objective reader think that this passage is fundamentally someone
else's, with just a few surface changes?

Finally, consider the nature of the common text, for you must use quotation
marks for language an author has used in a particularly vivid, creative, or unusual
way. Attributing the word or phrase to the original author recognizes that author's
use of those words to convey the idea so effectively. For instance, the first sentence
of the prior paragraph uses the words "you must use quotation marks." The words
number only five, so if there are no other similarities, they probably do not constitute a phrase long enough to merit recognition of the author simply for putting
them together as a unit. Nor was the author particularly original or effective in
selecting those words, in combining them, or in applying them to the idea being

discussed. Using these words probably would not require quotation marks attributing the words to the first author.

However, sometimes an author's use of particular words for a particular idea makes the words stand out. For instance, in *Griggs v. Duke Power Company*, Chief Justice Burger condemned employer practices that function as "built-in headwinds" impeding employment for minority groups.[3] In *Watson v. Fort Worth Bank and Trust*, Justice O'Connor described the positions argued by the parties as "stark and uninviting alternatives."[4] In his dissent in *Wards Cove Packing Company v. Atonio*, Justice Stevens described the living and working conditions at the defendant's canneries as "a plantation economy."[5]

These are examples of words and phrases used in distinctive ways. In each case, the author was especially effective in selecting the words to express the idea. In each case, the author's effective use of language merits recognition, and other writers who use these phrases should give credit to the original author by using quotation marks.

Like the "reasonable person" standard or the "best interests of the child" standard, the "using the words of another" standard is open to interpretation. It is far better either to use quotation marks or to paraphrase the passage more thoroughly than to risk questions about whose writing the passage really reflects.

§46.1.2 *Choosing to Use Quotation Marks*

Even if quotation marks are not required, a legal writer may choose to use them anyway — to communicate information important to the reader. The most common occasions for this kind of quoting are when the analysis must apply a particular legal test or when the analysis must construe particular words of a statute. Here are examples of each:

Particular Legal Test

A lawyer must use the degree of skill commonly exercised by a "reasonable, careful and prudent lawyer." *Cook, Flanagan & Berst v. Clausing*, 438 P.2d 865, 867 (Wash. 1968).

Particular Words of Statute

Title VII makes it unlawful for a labor organization "to exclude or expel" an individual because of religion. 42 U.S.C. §2000-2(c)(1) (1994).

---

[3] 401 U.S. 424, 432 (1971).
[4] 487 U.S. 977, 989 (1988).
[5] 490 U.S. 642, 662 n. 4 (1989).

Even though quotation marks would not be required for these words, the writer should use them anyway to let the reader know that these are the words at issue in the analysis.

§46.1.3 Overquoting

In the working draft stage, the problem with using too many quotations is the danger of confusing copying the authorities with analyzing them. The editing stage raises two more reasons to minimize quotes. First, many readers are tempted to skip quoted material entirely. Perhaps they assume that the quoted material simply supports the points already asserted by the current writer. Perhaps they are discouraged by the single-spacing of a block quote. Whatever the reason, busy readers do tend to skim or skip quoted material.

Second, a quotation seldom communicates your point as clearly, directly, and succinctly as you could. After all, the original writer was not writing about *your* case. Your paraphrase can do what quotations cannot, that is, tie the substance of the precedential source directly to the issues of *your* case.

As a general rule, limit yourself to quoting only in the following circumstances:

1. Quote when the issue will turn on the interpretation of particular words of a statute, rule, or key case, as described above. Limit the quotation to *those particular words* so your reader will understand the issue and your analysis of it. Here is an example of part of a discussion using quotation marks for this purpose:

   > A lawyer must use great care in deciding whether to undertake representation of a new client when that representation might be directly adverse to an existing client. The existing client must consent to the lawyer's representation of the new client. ABA Model R. Prof. Conduct 1.7(a)(2) (1998). However, even if the client consents, the lawyer must not undertake the new representation unless the lawyer "reasonably believes" that the new representation will not "adversely affect the relationship" with the existing client. *Id.* at §1.7(a)(1).

2. Quote *key* language from an authority with a great deal of precedential value. This could be mandatory authority or highly respected persuasive authority such as an opinion of the United States Supreme Court, a provision of a Restatement of Law, or an opinion written by a respected judge.

3. Quote *key* language when the author has found a particularly effective way to express the idea you want to convey.

   > Under Rule 60(b) the court possesses "a grand reservoir of equitable power" to accomplish justice. *Thompson v. Kerr-McGee Ref. Corp.*, 660 F.2d 1380, 1385 (10th Cir. 1981).

§46.1.4 *Editing Quotations*

Edit quotations down to the key words so your reader does not have to sift through the quoted material for your point. Editing must not change the meaning, but within that constraint you have great latitude to clear away the underbrush. Often the most effective quotation has been edited down to a short phrase or even a single word, perhaps with the key language italicized or underlined. Moderate use of italics and underlining in quoted material can help overcome the tendency of busy readers to skim quotations. They might still skim the rest of the quotation, but an italicized or underlined word might draw their attention at least to the most important part.

For instance, assume that you represent the defendant in a case in which the plaintiff alleges that she was sexually harassed when her supervisor pressured her into going to dinner with him and kissing him. You are writing a brief to the trial court on the issue of what the plaintiff must prove. Compare the following quotations:

EXAMPLE 1

The Supreme Court has held that "the District Court in this case erroneously focused on the 'voluntariness' of respondent's participation in the claimed sexual episodes. The correct inquiry is whether respondent by her conduct indicated that the alleged sexual advances were unwelcome, not whether her actual participation in sexual intercourse was involuntary." *Meritor Sav. Bank v. Vinson*, 477 U.S. 57, 68 (1986).

EXAMPLE 2

The Supreme Court has held that a plaintiff cannot prove a sexual harassment claim merely by showing that she participated in the sexual conduct involuntarily. She must prove that "by her conduct [she] *indicated* that the alleged sexual advances were unwelcome." *Meritor Sav. Bank v. Vinson*, 477 U.S. 57, 68 (1986) (emphasis added).

Which manner of quoting distills the key distinction and highlights it for your reader? Which states the legal principle as it would apply to the procedural posture of your case? Which states the legal principle in language that would be applicable to the facts of your case? Which is more readable?

Now that your citations and quotations are in proper form, turn your attention to editing the rest of the document.

CHAPTER 47

TROUBLESOME PUNCTUATION

This is not a comprehensive guide to punctuation. It hits only the persistent issues.

§47.1 Apostrophes, Fingernails, and Chalkboards

For many readers, apostrophe mistakes are like hearing fingernails scraping a chalkboard.

Start by distinguishing among plurals (more than one); possessives (which show ownership or something similar); and contractions (two words mushed together). In a formal memo or brief, don't use contractions, although they're fine in an informal client letter.

NOUNS: A plural noun usually ends in an *s* with no apostrophe ("six plaintiffs"). A singular, possessive noun usually ends in an *s* preceded by an apostrophe ("the plaintiff's complaint").

wrong: Both the legislature and the *court's* have refused to modify the rule.

This concerns more than one court. "Court's" should be plural, but the apostrophe makes it possessive instead.

also wrong: The defendant appealed the *courts* decision.

This is the opposite problem. The court owns the decision and should be possessive. But without an apostrophe, it is plural instead.

PRONOUNS: Pronouns follow different rules. That's where the trouble usually starts. Don't confuse a contraction with a possessive. And be careful with *it*, *who*, and *they*.

it —

contraction:	*it's* = *it is* or *it has* ("It's election day tomorrow.")
possessive:	*its* means that *it* possesses whatever follows ("The state reelected its attorney general.")
fingernails on chalkboard:	writing *it's* when you mean that *it* possesses something (write *its* instead)

who —

contraction:	*who's* = *who is* or *who has* ("Who's going to lunch?")
possessive:	*whose* means that *who* possesses whatever follows ("Whose sandwich is this?")
fingernails on chalkboard:	writing *who's* when you mean that *who* possesses something (write *whose* instead)

they —

contraction:	*they're* = *they are* ("They're late.")
possessive:	*their* means that *they* possess whatever follows ("Their papers were time-stamped too late.")
fingernails on chalkboard:	writing *they're* when you mean that *they* possess something (write *their* instead)

What's wrong with these sentences?

The courts have limited this precedent to it's facts.

The courts can impose sanctions on a party who's complaint lacks a basis in law or fact.

The courts have streamlined they're procedures by adopting a new set of rules.

Here's the basic principle: *Because a pronoun's contraction is formed with an apostrophe, its possessive cannot have an apostrophe.* Otherwise, the contraction and the possessive would look exactly the same.

This box might also help you remember:

the contraction	the possessive
it's ("it is")	its
who's ("who is")	whose
they're ("they are")	their

§47.2 Commas and Introductory Words, Phrases, and Clauses

An introductory phrase or clause is usually set off from the sentence by a comma. Without a comma after "computer," the first example is confusing:

wrong: Frustrated with all the spyware and viruses on his computer the
              mouse potato threw it out the window.
correct: Frustrated with all the spyware and viruses on his computer, the
              mouse potato threw it out the window.

If the introductory word or phrase could have been moved elsewhere in the sentence and would not have needed a comma there, a comma is not usually required to set it off at the beginning of the sentence. But you might want to use a comma anyway for stylistic reasons.

correct: Unfortunately he then sat in front of the television and
                        became a couch potato.
placed elsewhere: He then sat in front of the television and unfortunately
                        became a couch potato.
also correct: Unfortunately, he then sat in front of the television and
                        became a couch potato.

To prevent confusion, set off a *long* introductory phrase with a comma, even if it's not required.

§47.3 Commas Both Before and After an Interruption

If a word, phrase, or clause should be set off with commas because of the way it interrupts a sentence, one comma should precede it and a second comma should follow. You need both the "before" comma and the "after" comma. Don't leave one of them out.

wrong: Joe who has been granted parole, will be released.

Where does the interruption begin? The one comma above tells the reader only where it ends.

wrong: Joe, who has been granted parole will be released.

Now we know where the interruption begins. But will the reader be able to tell — without rereading the sentence — where the interruption ends?

correct: Joe, who has been granted parole, will be released.

§47.4 Commas and Independent Clauses

Two independent clauses can be joined together into one sentence with a conjunction (*and, but, or*). When you do that, put a comma before the conjunction.

wrong: The T-Rex in *Jurassic Park* ate a lawyer and audiences cheered.

This sentence has two independent clauses. Each has a subject ("The T-Rex" and "audiences"). And each has a verb ("ate" and "cheered"). Each clause could be a separate sentence. That's why they're independent. The conjunction "and" is not enough to join them together. It needs a comma as well:

correct: The T-Rex in *Jurassic Park* ate a lawyer, and audiences cheered.

If what comes after the conjunction doesn't have a separate subject of its own, don't add a comma:

wrong: The T-Rex in *Jurassic Park* ate a lawyer, and got indigestion.

"The T-Rex in *Jurassic Park*" is the subject for both "ate a lawyer" and "got indigestion." In a list of two (here, two verbs), no comma separates them. The conjunction "and" does the job.

correct: The T-Rex in *Jurassic Park* ate a lawyer and got indigestion.

§47.5 Commas and Breathing

Don't add a comma just because a person reading the sentence aloud would run out of breath. No rule of grammar justifies the comma in this sentence:

wrong: The argument that Napster did not infringe Metallica's copyrights when distributing the band's music over the Internet, is undermined by case law.

If reading the sentence aloud would cause a breathing problem, something is probably wrong with the way the sentence is structured. Try moving the big, complicated part of the sentence to the end:

restructured: Case law undermines the argument that Napster did not infringe Metallica's copyrights when distributing the band's music over the Internet.

§47.6 Commas and Missing Words

Don't add a comma just because you've left out a word. No rule of grammar justifies the comma in this sentence:

wrong: The court held, abduction by aliens does not excuse failure to attend one's own deposition.

Take out the comma and insert the missing word:

correct: The court held that abduction by aliens does not excuse failure to attend one's own deposition.

§47.7 Punctuation at the End of a Quotation

If you need punctuation at the end of a quotation, does it go inside the quotation marks or outside? A comma or a period goes *inside* the quote marks, even if it's your own comma or period and did not appear in the original quotation. But if you add a colon, semicolon, dash, or question mark, put it *outside* the quote marks.

correct: The defendant may have called the plaintiff "the worst Elvis impersonator in the state," but that is hardly defamatory.

Did the defendant use the comma? Or was it added by the writer? It doesn't matter. Either way, it goes inside the quote marks.

also correct: In fact, it would be futile to try to find defamatory meaning in "the worst Elvis impersonator in the state": our state is so richly endowed with excellent Elvis impersonators that our least talented practitioner might be considered brilliant elsewhere.

Here it does matter where the colon came from. If it was added by the writer, it goes outside the quote marks.

§47.8 Simple and Complicated Lists — Commas and Semicolons

Legal writing is full of lists. Lawyers have to be able to express lists in ways that are crystal-clear to the reader. With a simple and easily understood list, separate the items with commas. Use semicolons instead if the list is so complicated that commas won't clearly show where one item ends and the next begins.

| correct: | The plaintiff sued, went to trial, and lost. |
| **also correct:** | The court ordered the corporation dissolved; placed the property under the control of a receiver; and enjoined the defendants from conducting business by interstate telephone, wire, or delivery service. |

The second example has a list within a list:

- ordered the corporation dissolved;
- placed the property under the control of a receiver; and
- enjoined the defendants from conducting business by
  - interstate telephone,
  - wire, or
  - delivery service.

Using semicolons for the big list allows you to use commas for the little list inside the third item in the big list.

§47.9 Parentheses and Enumeration

Enumeration is the numbering of items in a list. When lawyers and judges state a rule of law, they often enumerate the elements. When you do that, enclose each number completely in parentheses.

| **wrong:** | At common law, a person committed burglary by 1) breaking and 2) entering. . . . |
| **correct:** | At common law, a person committed burglary by (1) breaking and (2) entering. . . . |

APPENDIX

EMAIL MEMORANDA

Why and How Lawyers Write Email Memos

An email memo may be appropriate where a supervisor needs analysis faster and more concisely than an office memo could provide. Speed is crucial. The supervisor needs an answer fast. The email memo has to be written quickly, and the supervisor needs to be able to read and understand it within moments of opening it.

As with every other kind of document, more time spent by the writer should result in less time spent by the reader. Compare the writing and reading times for two email memos:

	Email memo A	Email memo B
writing time	40 minutes	60 minutes
reading time	10 minutes	5 minutes

Assuming that both memos contain the same amount of analysis and that the only difference is how long it takes a reader to understand that analysis, supervisors in most situations would prefer memo B. That would be true of office memos, too, but it is dramatically true of email memos. They are written and read under time pressure, and a supervisor's time is more valuable than that of a recently hired lawyer.

Writing the memo inside your email system might actually be slower than writing it elsewhere and transferring it into an email message. Your word processor (Word or WordPerfect) was designed to help you write and rewrite. It might be more efficient to draft the memo in your word-processor and copy and paste it into an email message. But if you do that, save the word processed version in case something goes wrong while transferring it into email.

Email Memo Format

Office memo format developed over decades, and lawyers generally agree on how an office memo should be structured. Email memos, on the other hand, have developed very recently, and there's no consensus about their format. An email memo might be structured somewhat like an office memo, or it might follow an entirely different format.[1]

Email memo format should be flexible. What works in one situation might not work in another. On Monday, a lawyer might send an email memo concerning a proposed jury instruction in case X. On Friday, the same lawyer might send an email memo to the same supervisor explaining the law concerning a discovery demand in case Y. These email memos might be structured in entirely different ways because the problems they address are different. The following is one way in which an email memo might be structured.

The email's subject line: Specify clearly and concisely what this memo is about ("Smith v. Jones, interrog. 6 in plaintiff's 2d set"). In the inbox on your supervisor's screen, it will appear with many other messages, and the subject line should identify the problem your memo addresses.

The memo's first sentence — or its statement of the issue: Say why you're sending the email memo. It will be read today, but it might be read again in a year's time. Both today's reader and next year's reader should be told exactly why you've written this memo. Here's an example:

> You've asked whether we're required to answer interrogatory 6 in the plaintiff's second set of interrogatories.

Worded this way, no heading is needed. But if you word it as an issue, use a heading:

> **Issue:**
> Are we required to answer interrogatory 6 in the plaintiff's second set of interrogatories?

The answer: State your answer, with the essence of why. This can probably be done in one or two sentences. Use a heading like "Answer" or "Brief Answer."

> **Answer**
> No. That interrogatory seeks material protected by the attorney-client privilege.

An alternative way of beginning the memo: Instead of writing the two components above — the first-sentence/Issue and the Answer — you might combine them under a heading like "Summary":

---

[1] *See* Kristen Konrad Robbins Tiscione, *From Snail Mail to E-Mail: The Traditional Legal Memorandum in the Twenty-First Century*, 58 J. Legal Educ. 32-60 (2008).

Summary:

We are not required to answer interrogatory 6 in the plaintiff's second set of interrogatories. That interrogatory seeks material protected by the attorney-client privilege.

If you do this, *omit* the first-sentence/Issue and the Answer.

The facts: Recite only the few facts that are crucial to your analysis. Your supervisor is working on the case right now and knows the facts generally. Don't recite the entire case story. You've been asked for a fast answer to a specific and narrow question. The only facts that matter are the ones that are essential to answering that question.

Your analysis: Explain why your answer is correct. This might take one paragraph or six paragraphs or something in between. You will need to determine what level of explanation will satisfy your supervisor's two needs: for speed and for confidence that you're right. Finding the right balance becomes easier with experience. If you're not sure how to do that now, err on the side of including more explanation. The heading for this part could be "Analysis," "Explanation," or "Discussion."

Typography, Professionalism, and the Dangerous Send Button

Typography: In email, headings do not center well. You can place headings along the left margin, or you can indent them five or ten spaces from the left margin. Indenting makes them a little more obvious. Headings should be in bold print, unless your email system won't support bold. If it won't, the headings should be entirely in capital letters.

In a printed document, the first line of a paragraph is indented. But that is not true in emails, where a paragraph's first line starts at the left margin.

Professionalism: Even though an email memo is less formal than an office memo, it's still a communication between professionals and should be written in a professional tone and in precise language. It might be informal in some ways, but it is an office memo in miniature

The Dangerous Send Button: Email is so easy to send that it's (1) a marvel of convenience and (2) dangerous. If you accidentally put the wrong address into the "To" box, you might send confidential client information to someone who shouldn't have it. And even if you don't make that mistake, whatever you send can be forwarded to people whom you hadn't imagined would read it.

Check *everything* before you hit Send. Don't let the demand for speed trick you into a painful mistake. Take a long moment and be sure that every detail is exactly as it should be.

LAW SCHOOL EXAMS

I. How Exam Answers Differ from Other Forms of Legal Writing

A supervising lawyer or a judge reads your work for the purpose of deciding what to do in the client's case. But a teacher reads your exam answers to decide something else: how much you have learned in the course. Many students assume that teachers want to know how well students have memorized rules of law. But that is only part of it. A teacher is also interested — and often *much more* interested — in your understanding of how to use the rules and what the law is trying to accomplish with them.

To get credit for what you know about these things, you can structure your exam answers in a way that reveals what the teacher needs to know about you.

Compare a law school examination to a computerized cash register in a grocery store. The cashier places each item above an electronic "eye" that "sees" the item's universal product code and rings up the price. If the cashier does not hold an item at exactly the proper angle, the eye sees nothing and registers nothing. The cashier is able to try again and again and, if necessary, can even ring up a purchase manually. Like the electronic eye, the teacher will give you credit for what you show in the proper form, but, unlike the cashier, you get only one chance.

II. Answering Essay Questions

The traditional law school examination question contains a story, which you are asked to analyze in terms of the field of law covered by the course. This is called an essay question, even though a good answer to it could not accurately be called an essay.

You are graded on how well you identify the real issues in the story, identify the governing rules, state those rules accurately, and apply the rules to the facts. The teacher is less interested in your conclusions than in the analytical skills and understanding you display in arriving at and explaining those conclusions. In answering an essay question, the most effective organization is one that clearly shows the things the teacher is grading: issue spotting, knowledge of legal rules, and the ability to analyze and solve a legal problem in depth. (As you will see in a moment, that will differ from the classic CREAC paradigm formula.)

There are many effective methods of producing an answer to an essay question. Here is one:

Start by reading the question once from beginning to end without using a pen for any reason. Just read, so that you see the big picture. Then read the question again, underlining important things or making notes in the margin. Then read it a third time — but while doing so, make a list on scratch paper of all the issues you see in the question. (Leave plenty of blank space between issues.) Whenever you see a fact relevant to a particular issue, make a note of that fact under the issue in your list of issues.

For each fact, ask yourself why it is there. There are only four possible reasons why a particular fact is in the story: (1) it creates or helps to create an issue because it is inconsistent with another fact or appears to be inconsistent with the law; (2) it helps to resolve an issue because it shows whether the elements of a rule have been satisfied; (3) it is there to tempt you into making a mistake; or (4) it has no legal value and just helps to tell the story. Often reasons overlap. A fact might help create an issue and also provide raw material for resolving it. Or it might create an issue and tempt you into answering incorrectly.

How can a fact tempt you? Every teacher knows of analytical mistakes that some students will make from an incomplete understanding of the subject of the course. For example, on a civil procedure exam, suppose that the summons and complaint are served on the defendant in a way that does not satisfy any formula in Rule 4 of the Federal Rules of Civil Procedure, but the defendant gets copies of the summons and complaint anyway, reads them, and thus understands that the plaintiff is suing her. In the sentence before this one, everything after the word "but" was put there to tempt you into making a mistake. Teachers call facts like these "red herrings." Some students will reason that the failure to follow Rule 4 does not matter because the defendant got notice anyway. But that is not the law. If you fall for the red herring, you will answer incorrectly and get a low score on this issue. But if you recognize it to be a red herring, you will answer that the failure to follow Rule 4 is fatal even if the defendant obtained the summons and complaint through other means. When you later write your answer, use "even if" or similar language to show the teacher that you spotted the red herring and did not fall for it. To get full credit, explain why the red herring does not change your conclusion.

If — while *reading* the question — you assign to each fact one or more reasons for being in the story, you will more likely recognize the true issues in the question (reason 1) and use the facts appropriately to resolve issues (reason 2). And you will be less likely to fall into a trap after falling for a temptation to make a mistake (reason 3).

Now focus on your scratch paper list of issues. Look at each issue individually. What rules are necessary to resolve it? Make a note of each rule in the blank space under the issue. What policy considerations would help resolve the issue? Make a note of them as well. If you think of anything else relevant to the issue, make a note of that as well. In what sequence should the issues be discussed in your answer? Write "1" next to the one that should be discussed first, "2" next to the one that should come second, and so on.

You have just made an outline of your answer. Under exam conditions, you do not have time to make an extensive formal outline, but the one that grew out of your list of issues will be good enough.

Most teachers will tell you, in one way or another, approximately how much time you should spend answering each question on the exam. Do not be afraid to spend a third to half that time reading the question and making an outline. If you do that well, you will have everything you need to write a good answer.

Now write. For each issue, use the following permutation of the classic CREAC paradigm formula:

1. Since the teacher is more interested in your issue-spotting ability than in your conclusion, start by stating the *issue*. You could express the issue as a question ("Does the buyer's email message satisfy the statute of frauds?"). Or instead you could express the issue by stating how you resolve it ("The buyer's email message satisfies the statute of frauds"). Either method will do the job.
2. The governing *rule* or *rules* should normally follow. Use some judgment about this. If the rule is very basic — such as the four elements of negligence — it might not be necessary to state it because if you do a good job of applying a rule that the whole class knows, the teacher could reasonably conclude that you know it, too. But usually the teacher is specifically trying to find out whether you know a rule. If on a Civil Procedure exam, you realize that the court plainly lacks subject matter jurisdiction but the defendant has not moved to dismiss on that ground, the teacher is trying to find out whether you know that defects in subject matter jurisdiction can never be waived.
3. Proof of a rule is usually not necessary (because the teacher is in part testing your ability to remember rules that have been more or less proven in class) and often not possible (because the facts on final exams are frequently set in mythical jurisdictions or no jurisdiction at all). However, in some subjects dominated by uniform or federal statutes, the teacher may be willing to give you a little credit if you are able to refer to specific sections of a code, although such a teacher will not give you credit for good citation form.
4. Having stated the rule, *analyze* the issue by *applying* the rule to the facts. Use additional rules as you need them. You can show intellectual depth by explaining how your analysis is consistent with the policy behind these rules. You can also show intellectual depth by including a counter-analysis. With big issues, you usually cannot get full credit without policy discussions and counter-analyses.
5. If you have not already done so, state your *conclusion* before moving on to the next issue.

Students have traditionally tried to remember this formula by calling it "IRAC": Issue, Rule, Analysis/application, Conclusion. Your answer to each essay question will include several IRAC-structured discussions — one for each issue you identify. But limit the IRAC formula to exam-taking: it does not work well in office memoranda, motion memoranda, or appellate briefs.

As you use each fact, rule, or policy consideration, cross it off the checklist on your scratch paper. Do the same for each issue as you finish it. When you have finished the last issue, go on to the next exam question. (If you have time after answering all the questions, go back and proofread what you wrote.)

Your goal is to accumulate the largest number of points when the teacher grades your answer. (Remember the cash register.) Teachers give points for spotting issues and resolving them in a professional way. If you understand that, you will also understand the two biggest causes for losing points. One is failing to spot issues. If you miss an issue entirely, the teacher cannot give you any points at all.

The other big cause for losing points is failure to explain your reasoning fully. If you identify the issue, state your conclusion on that issue, and then move on to something else, many teachers will give you only a fraction of the points available for that issue, even if your conclusion is absolutely correct. That fraction can be very small. If an issue is worth 15 points, a teacher might give you only three to five points for stating a correct answer and doing nothing more. The proportion of points allocated to your reasoning tends to grow if the issue is a big one and tends to shrink if it is a small one. If the issue is worth only three points, you might get one point for spotting it, one point for resolving it, and one point (only a third of the total) for giving a reason. Teachers' practices on things like this differ widely, and some teachers do not assign a specific number of points to each issue. But if you assume that all teachers grade this way, you are less likely to miss points for not giving reasons.

To get the remaining points, you have to explain why you are right. A good explanation of your reasoning lays out the steps in your logic in a lawyerly manner, using the rules and policies covered during the course. (That is not the same as writing down every thought you have on the subject.) Why are you right? How do the law and facts support that conclusion? What other conclusions did you reject? Why are they inferior? Use facts that support your arguments. If facts could be used to challenge your arguments, show why those challenges should not succeed. Support your reasoning with policy, and show why contrary policy would not change your answer.

And decide. In law, it is a cop-out to go back and forth and then stop ("the plaintiff could argue this, and the defendant could argue that"), which some teachers call ping-ponging. Who will or should win? Why?

III.   Other Types of Questions

There is a non-story variant of the essay question. The teacher might describe a proposed statute and ask you to comment on it. There are no characters and no plot. Here, a good answer might in fact resemble an essay. Figure out how the proposal would alter the way the law functions, and decide whether that would be a good idea or a bad one, remembering the policy considerations that were stressed in class and in the casebook. Then write an answer in which you state your conclusion and substantiate it by analyzing the proposal in policy terms.

Some law school exams include short-answer questions. Several of them might be based on a single set of facts. Each question poses a specific and narrowly framed inquiry, such as "Did the defendant waive defects in personal jurisdiction?" You are given a small space — perhaps enough for a paragraph — in which to give your answer and the reasons for it.

Some exams include multiple-choice questions. To answer them effectively, it helps if you know how multiple-choice questions are created. A teacher thinks up a fact pattern, adds a question ("Did the manufacturer breach the contract's anti-delegation clause?"), supplies the correct answer, and then adds three or four wrong answers to produce a list of answers from which you choose.

People who make their living giving multiple-choice exams — like the SAT and the LSAT — call the wrong answers "distractors" because they are meant to distract and fool you. An effective distractor sounds right, often using phrases or concepts you heard and read often during the course. But the distractor will contain a flaw that makes it ultimately wrong. The flaw could be that although the distractor is literally true, it does not really explain what the law will do; the correct answer does that. Or the distractor might be partly right and partly wrong. Or it might be incomplete — right as far as it goes, but it does not solve the problem. Or it might be all wrong but dressed up in lawyer-like language so that it sounds good anyway. To identify a distractor, look for the flaw. And think carefully about it. Do not make a quick, snap decision. Ask yourself, "What could be wrong here?" You have to understand the law to eliminate a distractor.

How do you identify the correct answer? You have to know the law precisely, and you have to know exactly how to apply it to facts. You really have to know the material.

You can use two methods to choose the correct answer to a multiple-choice question. You can identify the correct answer because you really know it to be correct. Or you can identify all the distractors, thus identifying the correct answer by process of elimination. You are much better off if you use both methods. Use one to make a tentative selection of the correct answer. Use the other method to check and confirm your choice.

You can eliminate the distractors by finding the wrong idea in each one. But to be sure that the only alternative left standing really is the correct answer, you need to examine it carefully to make sure that it really is based on an accurate understanding of the law and that the reasoning in it is also right. You know that you have answered correctly when you know both why the answer you have chosen is right and why the other alternatives are really distractors.

IV.   General Suggestions for Taking Exams

Start preparing for exams long before the end of classes. The best preparation is to make your *own* course outline during the semester from your class notes and from the portions of the text covered by the teacher. The act of making the outline is an irreplaceable self-teaching experience. In structuring the course outline, the casebook's table of contents is more helpful than you might suppose. The table of contents collects the casebook's chapter and section headings, and those headings are the beginning of an outline.

Many students make flow charts instead of, or in addition to, an outline. A flow chart poses a series of questions to ask yourself so you can determine where the facts suggest a particular type of issue. For example, if you need to figure out whether a state has personnel jurisdiction over a particular defendant, start by asking these questions:

1. Does the defendant reside in the forum state?
   (If yes, that state has general jurisdiction over her — jurisdiction to adjudicate any claim against her.)

2.(a) Does the forum state's long-arm statute cover both the claim and the defendant?

   (b) Does the defendant have minimum contacts with the foreign state? *(Here, you could add subsidiary questions that would help you figure out whether the defendant has minimum contacts. For example, did the defendant purposefully avail herself of something beneficial involving the forum state?)*

   (c) Does the claim arise out of those contacts?
   (If the answer to questions 2(a), (b), and (c) is yes, the forum state has long-arm jurisdiction over the defendant.)

3. Was the defendant served with the summons and complaint while she was in the forum state?
   (If yes, the forum state has tag jurisdiction over her.)

4. 4. Has the defendant agreed contractually to submit to jurisdiction in the foreign state?
   (If yes, ...)

To help remember these questions, many students make a chart or a diagram, drawing arrows to show the sequences in which the questions should be asked.

Teachers differ from one another on examination philosophy, and most teachers tell their classes something of their own views on examinations and grading. Take seriously what each teacher tells you.

During the examination, budget your time carefully. One of the tragedies of the examination room is the student who spends so much time on one question that the others cannot be handled adequately.

Read the instructions carefully. Before beginning to answer a question, be sure that you understand the role you have been assigned. Are you being asked to analyze objectively the rights and liabilities of various characters in a story? To state the legal advice you would give to one of the characters if that person were your client? To make arguments on behalf of one character and against others? To write a judicial opinion? *Do exactly what you are instructed to do.* Do it completely. And do not do anything else. The teacher will give you credit only for doing what you were instructed to do.

Do not waste time writing about background matters unless they truly help you resolve the issues in the exam. Most teachers will give you credit only for finding issues and analyzing them. Do not start your answer by repeating the facts. (But do *use* the facts later in your answer by applying the rules to them.) And do not give the historical evolution of the rules you are using unless the evolution is needed to substantiate the position you are taking. If you are given the wording of a statute or if you are taking an open-book exam, you will waste time and get no credit if you hand-copy the statute into your exam book. Instead, refer to the statute and explain how it supports your conclusion.

Your goal is not to find the largest number of issues in each question. It is to identify the issues actually in the question — no more and no less. You will, of course, lose credit for missing issues. But many teachers will also reduce your grade if you "find" issues that are not reasonably suggested by the facts. Even if your teacher does not do that, you waste time if you resolve nonexistent issues.

Analyze every genuine issue, even if you believe that your analysis of one issue would make all the others moot. Not only must you do that in law practice anyway, but you cannot get full credit on examinations without doing it.

Some issues are worth more — often *much* more — than other issues. A one-hour, 33-point essay question might include a five-point issue, an 18-point issue, a six-point issue, and a four-point issue. Some students will spend no more time or space on the 18-point issue than on the others. That can be a disastrous mistake. The big issue is worth 18 points because it is hard. It takes more thought and writing to resolve a big and difficult issue than to resolve a small and easier issue. If you treat all these issues as worth the same amount of effort, you will probably lose most of the points available for the big issue. (Some teachers do not assign specific point values to issues, but they will still penalize a student who gives no more effort to a tough issue than to an easy one.) How can you tell which issues are the big ones? Smaller issues are more easily resolved. Big issues are tougher puzzles and often require several steps of logic.

Many — perhaps most — big issues can reasonably be resolved in more than one way. Remember that the teacher is most interested in the quality of your reasoning (and often less interested in the result of that reasoning). It is not unusual for two students to get full credit for a given issue while coming to opposite conclusions about it. They deserve full credit because both conclusions are reasonable and arguable, and because both students supply knowledgeable and perceptive supporting analyses. But that does not mean that you can adopt any conclusion you please. Some conclusions are more reasonable and easier to prove than others. And some issues on an exam have only one correct answer (usually when the teacher wants to know whether you have understood some very basic concept in the course).

It is, however, never enough to state the arguments for each side and then waffle or avoid stating a conclusion. Take a position and support it with analysis. That is what lawyers are paid to do and what your teachers hope you are learning how to do.

If you make an assumption in answering a question, say so. A sloppy student mushes over a gap in the facts without realizing that the gap is there. A precise student recognizes the gap, defines it exactly, and offers a resolution of the issue while taking the gap into account. (But make assumptions only where there truly is a relevant gap in the facts, which does not happen very often on exams. Do not invent far-fetched facts of your own that distort the question the teacher wants you to answer. The teacher will see that as an attempt to avoid facing the hard aspects of the exam.)

Use terms of art properly. Misuse of a term of art implies that the student's knowledge of the subject is superficial.

Teachers justifiably hate gimmicks in exam answers. Simply write down — in a business-like manner — what the teacher must see if you are to get credit.

The teacher will give you credit only for what is plainly written in the examination booklet. You will get no credit for things that you know but do not expressly state. And you will get no credit for things that you expressly state in handwriting that the teacher cannot read.

Finally, learn from your examinations. Most teachers will let you read your examination after final grades are posted. Many are willing to talk with you individually about what you did well or badly. Some provide written post-mortems (sometimes called model answers) that explain the issues on the exam. Take advantage of all of these things. Sometimes, you will learn more about the subject matter of the course (which may be tested again on the bar examination and in any event will help you later as a lawyer). And sometimes you will learn how to write examination answers more effectively.

INDEX